Beyond the Presidency

John Quincy Adams: A Personal History of an Independent Man

Aaron Burr: Portrait of an Ambitious Man (with Herbert S. Parmet)

Never Again: A President Runs for a Third Term (with Herbert S. Parmet)

BEYOND THE PRESIDENCY

The Residues of Power

BY

MARIE B. HECHT

MACMILLAN PUBLISHING CO., INC.

NEW YORK

Macmillan Publishing Co., Inc.
866 Third Avenue, New York, N.Y. 10022
Collier Macmillan Canada, Ltd.

Library of Congress Cataloging in Publication Data

Hecht, Marie B
  Beyond the presidency.

  Bibliography: p.
  Includes index.
  1. Ex-presidents—United States—History. 2. Political parties—United States—History. 3. Power (Social sciences) I. Title.
JK606.H4   353.03′2   76-7379
ISBN 0-02-550190-9

FIRST PRINTING 1976
Printed in the United States of America

67351

TO MARGARET AND ANGUS,
with affection

We have encountered troubles and at times disaster and we cannot expect to escape a certain grayness in the afternoon of life—for it is not often that life ends in the splendor of a golden sunset.

—THEODORE ROOSEVELT

Contents

Preface: The Twilight Years   xiii

Acknowledgments   xv

PART I: POST-PRESIDENTIAL POWER

1. *Warmaking*   3
2. *Peacemaking*   53
3. *Running Again*   69
4. *Partisan Politics*   117
5. *Tools of the Incumbents*   154

PART II: POST-PRESIDENTIAL CITIZENS

6. *Making Ends Meet*   187
7. *Ex-Monarchs Abroad*   226
8. *The Perfect Careers*   270
9. *Literary Lives*   289

Epilogue: The Proper Use of Ex-Presidents   310

Notes   314

Bibliography   329

Index   337

Preface: The Twilight Years

ON THE NIGHT of his inauguration, John Kennedy verbalized the experience of becoming an ex-president. What an adjustment it must have been for Eisenhower to wake up that morning as President and leave that afternoon as a private citizen, he commented. No matter in what way the former chief executive exited from office, admired or rejected, he suffered the same abrupt change. In the early, simpler days of the eighteenth and nineteenth centuries, the deposed president could play at returning to his natural state of private citizen with reasonable grace. By the mid-twentieth century, however, as George Reedy said, "the presidency had taken on all the regalia of monarchy except robes, a scepter and a crown."[1]

"I shall feel a great sense of relief when public affairs have for me only an interest and no responsibility," Benjamin Harrison asserted upon his retirement.[2] This sentiment was echoed by almost all the presidential exiles. The White House was a great white jail, Margaret Truman quoted her father as saying. But to be cast aside, especially at the end of one's life, is not easy. Some had the satisfaction of knowing, again like monarchs, that they had chosen their successors for good or ill. The Virginia dynasty continued from Washington to Jefferson to Madison to Monroe, broken only by John Adams's one term. However, Theodore Roosevelt was appalled by the "betrayal" of his Square Deal by his heir, William Howard Taft.

Bitterness accompanied the transition when the successor was an antagonistic usurper. Herbert Hoover and Franklin Roosevelt were

(xiii)

hardly civil to each other on that March day in 1933 when the office changed hands. Truman and Eisenhower exchanged angry words on their trip to the inauguration platform. And while Andrew Jackson was taking the presidential oath, John Quincy Adams was riding his horse on the outskirts of the capital city to escape the moment.

The many roles that the former presidents played—elder statesman, political outcast, discarded party leader, founder of colleges, eminent congressman, Confederate politician, chief justice, presidential candidate—suggest many questions. They lived in two worlds by virtue of their pasts, the personal one as private citizens and the political one as former heads of state. The American system does not provide them with an official status after leaving office although it does, finally, provide them with the financial means to live in a dignified manner. The enforced seclusion of James Buchanan can be contrasted with the active life of Theodore Roosevelt, explorer and companion of kings. Grant, in serious consultation with the emperors of China and Japan, stirs the imagination, while Calvin Coolidge's insignificant Vermont retirement has little interest.

Most significant, perhaps, in the examination of these later lives is the use that those in power made of their predecessors. Here, too, the score is uneven. The administrations and the political parties at times exploited their prestige, but sometimes used their talents to advantage. The ex-presidents themselves also had ambitions. Several tried for the presidency again, and Taft satisfied his lifelong ambition to become chief justice of the Supreme Court.

The increase in the power of the presidency in modern times has affected former presidents as well. They are of constant interest to the public, and the media have provided them with an opportunity to make lucrative and ego-building appearances.

The post-White House years are, of necessity, ones of declining power. Just a short time after he left the Oval Office, Lyndon Johnson wrote: "I told them the time would come when I would look back on the majesty and splendor of the Presidency and find it hard to believe that I had actually been there."[3] It is of these twilight years that this book treats.

Acknowledgments

THIS BOOK DOES not attempt to be an exhaustive or encyclopedic account of the last years of the American presidents. Instead, it explores some aspects of their post-White House careers, seeking to determine the residues of power left to them and the use and misuse made of them by their political parties and the administration in power, as well as to provide some glimpses of their finances, their personal lives, and their writings. Some ex-presidents appear frequently in the following pages, because they continued to contribute actively as politicians, public servants, or elder statesmen; others are but shadows. This is inevitable, because some retirees were still vigorous and healthy and enjoyed many years of life, while others were feeble and ill. Since this book deals with the great men in the twilight of their lives, it can, implicitly, be regarded as a study of old age.

Beyond the Presidency owes its greatest debt to Harry S. Truman, who influenced the Congress of the United States to finance the microfilming of the Presidential Papers held by the Library of Congress and to make copies available to readers and scholars all over the country. A copy was conveniently available to me at Columbia University. My gratitude to the staffs of the Herbert Hoover, Harry S. Truman, and John F. Kennedy presidential libraries for their courteous and valuable assistance. I would like to thank Mr. Robert Wood, assistant director of Herbert Hoover Library in West Branch, for sharing with me some of his immense knowledge of Hooveriana. Mr. Dave Powers of the Kennedy Library helped me to understand President John F. Kennedy's interest in and respect for the trio of ex-presidents who were alive during his brief administration. The staff of the Great Neck, Long Island, library was, once again, kind and supportive.

As always, Herbert S. Parmet, my former collaborator, contributed valuable advice and criticism throughout the project and read the entire manuscript. My appreciation to Tommie Wurtsbaugh Glick for important suggestions and careful reading of parts of the manuscript, to Wendy Parmet for help with the pictures, and to Andrew Hecht for patient endurance. Finally, I want to thank Ray A. Roberts of the Macmillan Company for urging me to overcome my reluctance to undertake the writing of this book and for his editorial guidance.

MARIE B. HECHT

Great Neck
September 25, 1975

PART I

Post-Presidential Power

Warmaking

IN JUNE 1798, President John Adams hoped to avoid a declaration of war with France by means of diplomacy. However, realistically, he had to ask Congress, in a special message, for power to appoint commissioned officers for an "Additional Army" of ten thousand men. Permission granted, he received, several weeks later, further powers to expand the "Provisional Army" when and if a full-scale war began or national security mandated it. It was assumed by everyone in the government that these measures would mean George Washington's reemergence from his private role and reappearance as commander of the United States forces.[1]

Washington, unaware of these plans for him, was quite content to remain "seated in the shade of my own vine and fig tree"—an image he liked so much that he used it frequently in his correspondence—completely withdrawn from "the scenes of political life." War with France, he wrote to Secretary of State Timothy Pickering in the summer of 1797, was not one of his fears, because he knew that the Adams administration did not want war with any country. However, he recognized the fact that France had overstepped "the line of rectitude," although he blamed it on encouragement from "a party among ourselves," namely, the Republicans.[2]

Washington stuck to his optimistic analysis through most of the following year, denying to Alexander Hamilton that there was the probability of "open war" or "a formidable invasion by France." They would perceive that they had falsely calculated support from "a large part of the *People*," he insisted. The wily New Yorker, however, was already preparing the stage for his own ambitions by sounding out his former chief. "The public Voice will again tell you to command the armies of your Country," Hamilton predicted. Then he suggested that Washington make a tour through Virginia and South Carolina, under the guise of health, to once again "revive enthusiasm for your person that may be turned into the right chance."[3]

Washington refused the advice but did give his secretary of the treasury some cause for hope. He asked Hamilton whether he would "be disposed to take an active part" if war came. Hamilton was prepared with an answer to the question that he had planted. Once again he had succeeded in maneuvering Washington in the direction that he wished him to travel. Things looked hopeful for Hamilton's military ambitions.

By return mail, Hamilton replied. "*If I am invited to a Station in which the Service I may render may be proportioned to the sacrifice I am to make*," he said, he would be ready. Bluntly, he wrote that he would like to be the inspector general.[4] The stage was now set for the battle of the generals. Washington, of course, was completely unsuspecting.

President Adams, plagued more than he fully realized by Cabinet members whose loyalties to him were questionable, delegated the task of securing Washington to Secretary of War James McHenry. Armed with a commission appointing Washington lieutenant general and commander in chief of all the forces raised in the expected war with France, dated July 4, 1798, the secretary arrived at Mount Vernon.

At this time the former President was described as "uncommonly majestic and commanding in his walk, his address, his figure and his countenance." At sixty-six, his face had a mild though reserved expression.[5] The meeting achieved its purpose. McHenry carried Washington's acceptance back to the President, but with some reservations. He must not be called into the field until the army or hostilities so demanded and he must be consulted about the choice of generals directly under him. The latter was very important since whoever was second in command would be in charge until war actually began and, it must be realized, the commander in chief was an old man. Washington wanted to make the choice himself but feared that Adams would act before him.

The chief contenders for the position were Charles Cotesworth Pinckney, Henry Knox, and Alexander Hamilton. At first, for several reasons, Washington favored Pinckney. When France struck, Washington hypothesized, it would be in the area below Maryland, which was weakest, was closest to the French possessions, and had a slave population that could be armed to attack their owners. Pinckney, who was a Southerner from an influential family and had a very fine military and public reputation, would seem to be the one most able to rally Southern resistance.[6] Knox, the New Englander, was the President's favorite. But Hamilton, who never wavered from his belief that he deserved the post, a notion he had drilled into the minds of his many influential friends, prevailed. He insisted to everyone that he was giving up a flourishing law practice at the expense of his large family for only one reason—the public wanted him.

The order of command that Washington proposed, finally, was Hamilton, Pinckney, Knox—the reverse of what the President wanted. Adams felt that the Northeastern states would be disgusted if Hamilton preceded Knox, and, in truth, preferred to give the former secretary no command at all.[7] When Washington got wind of that, he wrote immediately to McHenry of the President's "forgetfulness" and threatened to resign. Adams capitulated.

The two contestants who lost out responded characteristically. Pinckney, gallant and generous, sent Hamilton a letter saying that he would be happy to serve under him. Knox resigned his commission. It was, perhaps, a Pyrrhic victory for Hamilton, who found himself in charge of all the problems because Washington, as promised, stayed home and waited for hostilities to commence.

The whole controversy was an exercise in futility, because the probability of war faded away at the same time that the battle of the generals was resolved. Its importance was that a precedent had been set in using an ex-president to bolster the administration in office. The former President had been called out of retirement and expected to serve. Washington had accepted the obligation even though the personal cost was great. However, he had some doubts as to "the propriety of reemerging in a Public Theatre" after having given his Farewell Address. But Adams had no doubts that he needed Washington. "I have no qualifications for the martial part of it, which is likely to be essential," he wrote to the ex-President. "If the Constitution and your Convenience would admit of my Changing Places

with you, or of my taking my old station as your Lieutenant civil,
I should have no doubt of the Ultimate Prosperity and Glory of
the Country. . . . We must have your Name."[8]

Adams turned to Washington despite the ex-President's connection
with his bitter enemy, Alexander Hamilton, and the pressure to place
him second in command. When Adams wanted Aaron Burr appointed
a brigadier general, a move that would have been politically advan-
tageous to him, Washington said that Burr was brave but an intriguer.
Adams speculated that Washington had forced him to promote
Hamilton, "the most restless, impatient, artful, indefatigable intriguer
in the United States, if not in the world to be second in command
under himself, and now dreaded an intriguer in a poor brigadier."
The price of ex-presidential help came high.

The second and third presidents of the United States were not
military men, so when the second American revolution occurred
in 1812, neither of them was expected by the incumbent, James
Madison, to answer a call to arms. They were in very different
positions than Washington. The party system was now well established and the two former Presidents were of different parties. Furthermore, Thomas Jefferson had been Madison's mentor.

In 1812, old John Adams had been enjoying his querulously
contented retirement for almost a dozen years. He felt somewhat
vindicated by "Mr. Madison's War," for it proved to his satisfaction
that party factionalism existed in America "from its first plantation."
When he had been "exerting every nerve" to demand redress from
France during the quasi-war, "the arm of the nation was palsied
by one party." Now Madison was in the same predicament against
Great Britain and "the arm of the nation [was] palsied by the opposite party." This was a human condition for which he saw no resolution until there was a "national public opinion."[9]

But Adams wholeheartedly supported the war, thrilled at the
naval victories, and castigated the New England Federalists who
formed the Essex Junto, which opposed the war and proposed secession. He called them a ridiculous "conclave of philosophers, divines,
lawyers, physicians, merchants, pedlars and beggars." It was pathetic,
he wrote to William Plumer, to see "an enterprise promoted by intelligent and honest men who had lost touch with reality."[10]

Already in his late seventies, Adams was not active during the war
but followed his son John Quincy's career very closely. At this time,

the younger Adams was the first American minister to Russia, and he and his father carried on a spirited correspondence though a somewhat circumspect one, because, Adams complained, their mail was often opened and read. When John Quincy Adams was appointed a peace commissioner at Ghent, his father bombarded him with letters rehearsing his favorite principles and reliving his own experiences as peace commissioner after the American Revolution. Though he protested to President Madison, "I will not say to my son" that "I would continue this war forever rather than surrender one acre of our territory, one iota of the fisheries. . . . or one sailor impressed from any merchant ship," he deluged John Quincy with letters that said just that. "Of the importance of the Fisheries, my dear Son, I have a volume to write," he offered in a shaky hand. And, shortly after, advised his son to "demand your recall and refuse your signature to any compact which shall directly or by implication surrender any tittle or Iota" of the 1783 treaty relative to the fisheries.[11] John Quincy Adams quite agreed and worked to retain the fisheries for ungrateful New England.

Thomas Jefferson, Madison's close friend and advisor, could not expect to avoid being asked his opinion on the war. While President, ignoring spiteful accusations that he was a coward, though Napoleon was in power and France and Britain were raging on the seas, Jefferson managed to display consistently what Henry Adams called "a genius for peace." Jefferson handled the British frigate *Leopard*'s attack on the American *Chesapeake* with measures short of war even though well aware that the American people would have supported a war enthusiastically. Even after Britain exacerbated the difficulties by her Orders in Council, which mandated that American ships must sail first to England to be licensed or be subject to capture, Jefferson opted for peace. He recommended an embargo which forbade all American ships to leave for foreign ports. Congress passed it, arousing the fury of maritime New England, which resulted in only partial success for the economic sanctions because fraud and smuggling across the Canadian border became commonplace.

Since Madison was his protégé, Jefferson assumed that he, too, would maintain peace. He wrote: "I am so far . . . from believing that our reputation will be tarnished by our not having mixed in the mad contests of the rest of the world that, setting aside the ravings of pepper pot politicians . . . I believe it will place us high in the scale of wisdom, to have preserved our country tranquil and prosperous during a contest which prostrated . . . every country on the other side of the Atlantic."[12]

By 1812 the probability of war stifled all such hopes. Believing that he must support his friend Madison loyally, Jefferson went along with the war tide. In answer to a request about the public sentiment in his part of the country, Jefferson responded, rather sadly, that, though all regretted it, it was now considered necessary and they would disapprove delaying much longer. To an "ancient friend and classmate," Jefferson justified the American position. There were two items "in our catalogue of wrongs" that had to be righted: the impressment of American seamen and exclusion from the ocean. To another old friend, General Thaddeus Kosciusko, Jefferson bragged, "we shall strip her [England] of all her possessions on this continent." "Upon the whole I have known no war entered into under more favorable auspices," he added.[13]

Nonetheless it was ironic that when war was declared on June 18, 1812, neither the President nor Congress knew that two days earlier, in London, Lord Castlereagh had announced suspension of the Orders in Council. Jefferson's experiment in economic pressure finally had succeeded, but too late. The change had been effected by petitions from both capital and labor to relieve the unemployment, inflation, and decline of their exports caused by the regulations. When the news reached the United States, Jefferson commented that had it come earlier war would have been averted, but now more was needed for peace. The motto of the war should be "Indemnification for the past, and security for the future."

Having decided to support "Mr. Madison's War," Jefferson now started to think about how it could be made more popular. The conquest of Canada, which would stop the Indian atrocities and should be easy, was one way. But most important was the protection of the coastal trade, to avoid the problem caused in the last war when the British captured the American pilot boats and used them to destroy the coasting business. To avoid this, the former President advised that the Atlantic coast be lined with pilot boats filled with armed men. For some reason he believed that only Americans knew how to construct these pilot boats.

The protection of the Chesapeake was high on his priority list. While denying to Secretary of State James Monroe that he was meddling in executive councils as the newspapers asserted, he had to admit that he had a plan to use those "humble and economic vessels, the gunboats, to protect and keep open the Chesapeake which covers five of the most productive states containing 3/5 of the population of the United States." Surely, he suggested coyly, Secretary Monroe, being an inhabitant, would be knowledgeable about the area. Jefferson became so insistent about his gunboats on the Chesapeake that Madison was forced to deflate his coastal strategy. The ex-President accepted the rebuke quietly. It showed how erroneous views may be with those who do not have all in view, he said. "I intended no trouble to you, my dear Sir, and were you to suppose I expected it [an answer] I must cease to offer a thought on our public affairs."[14]

The matter did not quite rest after the rebuff. In June 1813, Jefferson again wrote to Madison emphasizing the need for his gunboats to defend the Chesapeake and thus the Middle states. Because the Middle states were "the most zealous supporters of the war," they were therefore "the peculiar objects of the vindictive efforts of the enemy." The states north of the Hudson did not need to worry, because they were treated by the enemy as neutrals. Cajolingly he pointed out that surely only one hundred gunboats, costing less than one frigate, could not be considered "an over-proportioned allotment to the Chesapeake country against the over-proportioned hostilities pointed at it." Madison maintained a dignified silence and Jefferson dropped the subject.[15]

Jefferson's anger against Massachusetts increased as the behavior of her people became "embarrassing" to the conduct of the war. Let Massachusetts separate, Jefferson felt, there would be in it "no evil but the example," and he added, "I believe the effect would be corrected by an early and humiliating return to the Union." For many reasons the state would find herself in hopeless difficulties if she withdrew. She did not produce enough bread, so if she were excluded from American ports, she would have to depend on Europe. New Englanders were a navigating people without timber for a ship or a pound of anything to export. As rivals of England in manufacturing, commerce, navigation, and fishing, they would compete with her, and Massachusetts would in turn be sacrificed for a treaty with the producing states, and, in a war with the Union, would be one against fifteen. Thus Jefferson disposed of Massachusetts.[16]

As the war continued, Jefferson feared that it would be interminable. He informed Madison that England had changed her objective from a settlement of impressment and the Orders in Council to a war of conquest. Since she would not rest until she took the fisheries, Maine, the Lakes, the territories north of the Ohio, and the navigation of the Mississippi, Jefferson warned that this country must be ready with men and money "to indefinite extent." He had two proposals. First, to class the militia and to assign each class the duties for which it was fit. "It is nonsense to talk of regulars," he said, "among a people so easy and happy at home as ours. We might as well rely on calling down an army of angels from heaven." Second, he proposed a complex system of loans and taxes to pay for the war. For this, Jefferson had prepared a series of tables describing how it would work. Still protesting that he had withdrawn from all political concerns, the former President had gone to the trouble of developing a system.[17]

The war was affecting Jefferson as a plantation owner. His land was producing, but the produce had no value because there was no market for it. "Wheat? We can only give it to our horses, as we have been doing since harvest," he wrote. "Tobacco? It is not worth the pipe it is smoked in. Some say whiskey; but all mankind must become drunkards to consume it."[18]

Throughout the war Jefferson tried to keep some sense of historical perspective. It was no disgrace that the British held "transient possession" of Washington, he argued. Nearly every European country had suffered the same experience at one time or another, although the others had not experienced having their public offices and private dwellings burned. His solution was more privateers to strike at the heart of the enemy—their commerce.[19] Jefferson also took the long view about Jackson's victory at the Battle of New Orleans, which occurred after the peace of Christmas Eve was signed but before the news had reached the United States. True, useless blood had been shed, but it proved the fidelity of the people there and the loyalty of the western country.

Hatred and distrust of England, which had influenced Jefferson's every judgment when he had been in office, was reenforced by the War of 1812. He warned John Jacob Astor, who had just established a settlement on the Columbia River, that he must take care lest the English break it up. "Their bigotry to the bastard liberty of their own country, and habitual hostility to every degree of freedom in any other, will induce the attempt; they would not lose the sale of a bale of furs for the freedom of the whole world."[20] He hoped that the northwest country's independence and safety would be assured at the peace conference.

Jefferson never questioned what his role must be in the national crisis of 1812. Though essentially a man of peace, when his country went to war he felt obliged to render support, particularly since his close friend and rightful heir, James Madison, was at the helm. It made it easier, of course, that the foe was his archenemy, England. Even while rejoicing that France was freed from "that monster" Napoleon Bonaparte, he regretted that Europe and Britain were now free to divide up the continent and possibly eventually to devour the United States.[21]

Ex-President John Quincy Adams, then a much-respected congressman, called President Polk's war message declaring that "Mexico . . . has shed American blood on American soil. . . . War exists," a "recommendation of circumlocution." Only one half of the delegates from his state of Massachusetts voted for "this most unrighteous war." Along with Thomas Hart Benton, John Calhoun, and others, Adams deplored Polk's arrogance in overriding the prerogative of Congress to declare war. And when the Whig Convention unanimously nominated him for reelection to the next Congress, "Old Man Eloquent," as he was then called, believed that his position on the Mexican War had been fully endorsed. Enfeebled as he was by a paralytic stroke, struggling daily to get to his desk in the House chamber, Adams maintained his antiwar stand. When Massachusetts Congressman Charles Hudson proposed that American forces be withdrawn from the east bank of the Rio Grande and that peace terms be negotiated with Mexico without demanding any territorial cession, Adams was one of four members supporting the resolution.[22] By the time the war was over, John Quincy Adams was dead, having fallen in his tracks while serving in the House.

It was proper for a New England ex-president to oppose a war that many from his part of the country believed was an expedition to acquire more slave territory. As an elected representative of his constituency, Adams had no obligation to support President Polk, the office of the presidency, or even the decision of Congress. However, ex-President John Tyler was in a very different position.

Tyler was no partisan of his successor. The former President's one historically important act during his presidency had been his role in the annexation of Texas. Now Calhoun and others were trying to take the credit. Tyler's friends, on the other hand, maintained that had his administration lasted six months longer, the controversy with Mexico, the dispute over the Oregon boundary, the acquisition of California, and many other problems would have been resolved. Tyler thought that the settlement of the Oregon line was connected with the Mexican crossing of the Rio Grande in April 1846. The subsequent decline in British-American relations might mean that Mexico had some hope of British assistance in the war against the United States. He also feared that the slavery issue would erupt again over the annexation of land acquired from Mexico. Just before the war started, Tyler said: "I should deprecate a war as next to the greatest of evils."[23]

But once war started, Tyler supported it. He, too, felt that this was the proper role for an ex-president. He declared publicly that this was the "most just war" ever fought by the American people and wrote to his son Robert that if we got into a war every man should do his duty and "God forbid that a son of mine should be recusant." Robert Tyler, after the war commenced, raised a company of volunteers in Philadelphia, but his request to march them to Mexico was refused by the governor of Pennsylvania, so he never saw the enemy. Another son, John Tyler, Jr., abandoned his law studies to enter the army and was provided with a captain's commission which his father obtained from the President. He, too, never saw action.[24]

Tyler proved to be correct in his prediction that the war would revive sectional strife over slavery. Congressman David Wilmot of Pennsylvania, a Free Soil Democrat, introduced his controversial proviso, which stated that slavery should be excluded from any territory acquired from Mexico as a result of the war, in August 1846. Ex-President Martin Van Buren and his political cohorts supported it enthusiastically, but Virgina-born Tyler, forced to take a stand, took the Southern position. In an angry letter published anonymously in the Portsmouth *Pilot*, he asked what made the Northern states so distrust the South that they wanted to "exclude the Southern States from an equal participation in the full benefits of the Union?" The Wilmot Proviso he found "nothing less than a gratuitous insult on the slave states." Its unfairness to his section and its people infuriated Tyler. It paralyzed the fourteen slave states, he charged, by saying to them: "You may toil and bleed and pay and yet your toil and blood and money shall only be expended" to increase the power of the free states. Further, it was dangerous to be stirring up internal factionalism and likely to "render us, in a

foreign war, the weakest nation in the world." The proviso, after
passing the House, was defeated in the Senate, to Tyler's relief. It
proved to him that it was not "the settled policy of the non-slave-
holding states." Therefore, he concluded, "I go for whipping Mexico
until she cries enough."[25]

The Mexican War divided the ex-Presidents as it did the rest
of the country. Their attitudes were influenced by party and section.
Significantly, their positions were forerunners of the divisions of the
coming conflict that would rend the Union.

Much more delicate a problem than any posed by a foreign war
faced Tyler and the other ex-Presidents during the Civil War. Although John Tyler was the only real Southerner in the group of
five, the others had many friends and supporters from that part of
the country and none of them were ardent Lincolnians. The division
of the states into slave and free had blighted the administrations of
all the living ex-Presidents. Keeping the Union together had been
their major task, although the subject was so painful that it was
often omitted from the hustings. Almost despairing of the problem
in 1860, Tyler wrote, "In view of the constant heartburnings which
prevail, I am not prepared to say that harmony can ever be restored
and sometimes I think it would be better for all peaceably to separate." Both sections then would have homogeneous populations
and soon would resume friendly relations and peace between them.[26]

Convinced that if Lincoln were elected South Carolina would
secede from the Union, Tyler was not surprised at the news a friend
brought back from the Deep South. The South Carolina ladies, he
told the ex-President, would rather be "widows of secessionists than
wives of submissionists." When Lincoln was elected, Tyler lamented
that the "day of doom for the great model Republic is at hand."
He decided that he would not try to work out a solution but would
remain "quiescent." However, as soon as he was approached and
asked to take action to preserve the Union, he accepted promptly.

That Lincoln's election was a clear call to secession was apparent
to ex-President Franklin Pierce of New Hampshire also. He agreed
with his Southern friends that now it was just a matter of time before the United States would outlaw slavery. He did have a program,
however, to delay the inevitable. He advocated the immediate repeal
of all personal liberty laws, measures passed by Vermont and other
states restricting Southern slave owners from entering these states

for the purpose of recovering their fugitive slaves. Pierce pleaded for the recognition of coequal rights for both sections of the country. Despite his sympathy for the South, when John A. Campbell asked him to come to Alabama and see what he could do, the ex-President said he was too ill to travel. He did write a letter that was published throughout the South asking the angry Southerners to allow their Northern friends time to right their wrongs peaceably. If this could not be done in half a year, he suggested that there be a sad farewell but no war. Unfortunately, it was too late for promises.

The two ex-Presidents from New York, aged Martin Van Buren and Millard Fillmore, were also involved in a proposed mission south. At a meeting of merchants and prominent Democratic politicians, among whom was Van Buren, held in an office in New York City, it was decided that some action must be taken to assure protection to the South. Their plan was to write to Fillmore and request him to go south with two others to carry reassurances to the slaveholders that their rights would be maintained. Fillmore refused the mission, stating that the address and resolutions passed by the group were reassurance enough. To go there, he said, would be "in my opinion a work of supererogation." Fillmore pointed out that assurances were needed from the Republicans. When the dominant party was willing to repeal all unconstitutional state laws and live up to the compromises of the Constitution, then he would cheerfully go south to restore harmony. In the meantime, the New York Democrats must "put [them]selves right."[27]

Privately, Fillmore considered the action of the seceding South "suicidal and unjustifiable." He thought that President Buchanan should have regarded the secession conference as an assembly that was about to commit treason. Had he been President, thought Fillmore, he would not have hesitated to coerce a state if conciliation failed.

On his way to Washington, on February 16, 1861, Lincoln stopped off at Buffalo. The town watched to see how their leading citizen, ex-President Millard Fillmore, would behave toward the President-elect. It was a Sunday, so they went to church together and in the evening attended a public meeting in behalf of the Indians. No personal antagonism between the two could be detected, but neither was there any evidence that they discussed anything significant. Later Fillmore wrote that if the rebellion could have been delayed six months, Lincoln could have dealt with it. Nevertheless, Fillmore continued to have some sympathy for the Southern predicament. At a Washington's Birthday celebration held in Buffalo, he said that all must show the South that they were their brethren, ready to conciliate them.[28]

In early 1861, a futile but inevitable effort was made to call together a peace conference in Washington to find an alternative to civil war. Tyler, who would have preferred to remain quietly at Sherwood Forest through all the agony of secession, was pressured from all sides for his opinion. He relented, finally, and allowed his views to be published, hoping that the article would "strengthen our friends in the North." He proposed that the Virginia state legislature call for a convention of the six border slave states—Virginia, Delaware, Maryland, Kentucky, Tennessee, and Missouri—and the six border free states—New Jersey, Pennsylvania, Ohio, Indiana, Illinois, and Iowa. Since those states were the most interested in keeping the peace, if they could not come to some understanding, Tyler felt, the Union was gone. "When all else failed, this could be tried," he wrote to Caleb Cushing.[29]

The resolution passed by the Virginia Assembly on January 7, 1861, did not limit its invitation to border states but invited all states to a peace convention whose purpose was to restore the Union. John Tyler was chosen as a delegate from Virginia and also appointed a commissioner to go to President Buchanan and ask him to see that any move that might cause war be postponed until after the convention. Judge Robertson was sent to South Carolina to accomplish an identical mission.

Though he feared that extending the meeting to include all states would keep the seceding ones away, Tyler agreed to go, and as soon as the news of his appointment reached Sherwood Forest, despite ill health, he traveled to Richmond to consult the governor and on the following morning took the train to Washington. Once arrived in the capital, Tyler sought an interview with the President to present the Virginia proposal.

At their meeting, Tyler told Buchanan that what every Virginian wanted was maintenance of the *status quo*. The President answered that he could give no pledges. It was his duty to enforce the laws, but the power rested with Congress. Unable to shake Buchanan into taking action on his own, Tyler had to be satisfied with the presidential promise that a message would be sent to Congress recommending the peace conference and requesting that no hostile act would be passed until it had been given a chance to restore harmony. When Tyler asked to look at a sketch of the message, Buchanan promised to show it to him in the morning. Tyler was satisfied after he read it, and could suggest no change.

That afternoon, a Friday, the secretary of state and the attorney general called on Tyler carrying the President's regrets that Congress had adjourned until Monday and so had not yet received the message. While they were there, a telegram came from Judge Robertson in Charleston asking whether there was any basis to the rumor that the *Brooklyn*, loaded with troops, had sailed south from Norfolk. Tyler quietly handed the message to the Cabinet members. The attorney general said that he knew nothing about it, but the secretary of state was able to confirm the information that the *Brooklyn* had sailed with troops aboard but he did not know the vessel's destination. Tyler, disturbed that this had happened while he was in Washington, addressed a note to Buchanan which the Cabinet members agreed to deliver. At eleven-thirty that night the President's answer arrived. The *Brooklyn* had left Washington before Tyler's arrival and was on an errand of mercy, not on its way to South Carolina. Tyler, much relieved, could now turn his full attention to the peace conference.

The peace conference met on February 4 at Willard's Hotel. There were one hundred and forty-six delegates from twenty-one states; fourteen free and seven slave. It was christened the Old Gentlemen's Convention by Horace Greeley, who commented, most unkindly, that "these venerable old gentlemen are no more fit to be entrusted with . . . guidance than a bull is fitted to keep a china shop." There were, at the conference, twelve men over seventy; sixty who were sixty years old or more; and seventy-four who were over fifty. However, they were a distinguished company that included six former Cabinet officers, nineteen former governors, fourteen ex-senators of the United States, fifty ex-congressmen, a former ambassador, many judges, and one ex-president.[30] Unfortunately, the extremists from both sides were absent. The secessionists refused to come because, they said, the time for talk had passed. The Northern radicals refused to negotiate with "traitors."

John Tyler, who was committed to a strong Southern rights position, was a central figure from the start. His wife, Julia, who saw no hope of saving the Union, observed that everyone looked to her husband to save it, if it could be saved. To his Southern colleagues, the seventy-one-year-old former President looked like a "slim, tall-looking, high-bread [*sic*] Virginia gentleman." His opponents described him as a "tottering ashen ruin" more despised than anyone who had been president. However, he was, as Julia predicted, unanimously elected president of the conference.[31]

Tyler's acceptance speech was conciliatory. Our "god-like fathers created" the government and now "you have a task before you, gentlemen, a task equally grand, equally sublime . . . to snatch from ruin a great and glorious confederation." After referring flatteringly to each of the states represented, Tyler concluded: "The eyes of the whole world are turned to this hall and to this assembly in expectation and hope." The delegates must overcome party loyalty and, with patriotism, triumph over it.[32] The assembly and the press reacted favorably to Tyler's address.

As in the Constitutional Convention of 1787, the rule of secrecy was adopted, and in spite of the objections of the Radicals, reporters were excluded. But the progress of the conference was often delayed by requests for postponement of decisions, a device used by the Radicals to delay long enough for Lincoln to be inaugurated. The business of the meetings was carried on at a high level of emotion. At one point a brawl was prevented only by President Tyler's sharp call to order. "Shame upon the delegates who would dishonor this conference with violence," he scolded. As the days passed, it became apparent that the border states were the most willing to compromise, because they knew that if war came it would be fought on their land. The Radicals, however, continued to introduce amendments guaranteed to anger the Southerners.

Slavery, of course, was the vital question. Other matters such as tariffs and railroads were examined, but the division was clearly between the slave and free states. As the debates went back and forth, each side's extremists talked angrily of war and blamed the other side for making it inevitable. Consequently, as the days passed in a haze of rhetoric, the possibility of any meaningful action receded in a geometric progression.

When Lincoln arrived in Washington on February 23, Tyler, by direction of the conference, called on him to request an interview for the entire membership. Lincoln consented to meet them that very evening. With curiosity and expectation, the delegates gathered in Parlor Six of Willard's Hotel to see the man of the hour. As he shook each man's hand, Lincoln, true to his style, made an amusing comment. Some of the serious statesmen were irritated by his levity. However, bantering came to an end when James A. Seddon started to bait the President-elect with pointed questions and was followed by others who were more polite but equally challenging.

William Dodge, a New York businessman, asked Lincoln if he would go to war on account of slavery. Lincoln replied, bluntly, that he would take an oath to obey, enforce, and defend the Constitution "let the grass grow where it may." At this, several Southern delegates left the room in a rage. Tyler remained. He awaited Lincoln's answer to whether territories that chose slavery could hope to enter the Union as slave states. "It will be time to consider that question when it arises," the President-elect answered. "In a choice of evils war may not always be the worst."[33]

The interview with Lincoln convinced Tyler that there was no hope for Virginia in the Union. Lincoln was not going to be like poor, weak, indecisive Buchanan, so his state must secede and try to carry with her into the Confederacy New Jersey and other border states. Tyler's somewhat obtuse analysis was that the Confederacy must be strong enough to deter Lincoln from using force on the slave states. A military balance was the only way to preserve peace and, perhaps, influence the North to reconstruct the original Union with safeguards for the Southern way of life.[34]

The conference finally decided to offer the nation a Constitutional amendment. The one offered by James A. Seddon did not pass the convention, but it was rumored that Tyler was its author. It proposed that a state be granted the right to secede when it wished and gave the South a veto on appointments made by the President south of 36° 30'. Tyler defended the second proposal on the basis that Lincoln would appoint his friends to Southern positions, thus sacrificing it to "that wild spirit of propagandism."

After much wrangling, a narrow margin of votes carried an amendment that strongly resembled the Crittenden plan. It provided that north of 36° 30' there would be no slavery; below it slavery would be allowed. In addition, slave owners would be permitted to carry their property into all United States territories. With no conviction that it would do any good, Tyler delivered the peace conference's amendment and, as expected, Congress did not pass it.

Though the conference failed to keep the peace, it did keep the border states in the Union long enough for the electoral votes to be counted. For Tyler, it consolidated his thinking. He now was convinced that Virginia must secede at once and was prepared to go to Richmond and say so.[35]

At the Virginia State Convention, Tyler explained what had motivated him to attend the peace conference. Apart from a "deep solicitude for this country's peril," to have been able to restore the Union to its former perfect state "would have been to me the proud crowning act of my life." It could not be. Instead, after Fort Sumter was fired upon, Virginia passed an ordinance of secession. Tyler, who had advocated the move, was appointed one of the commissioners from Virginia to confer with the Confederacy on his state's becoming a member. The former President was credited with being the author of the temporary agreement.[36]

In March 1861, a new ex-President joined the club. Somewhat apologetic about his do-nothing role, Buchanan retired to Wheatland, his home near Lancaster, Pennsylvania, prepared to defend his administration against inevitable assault by "Mr. Lincoln's Administration." He still believed that no policy other than that of peace could "preserve and restore the union."

Franklin Pierce believed just as strongly in peace. Provisioning Fort Sumter, he argued, would be "idle, foolish, ill-advised, if not criminal." And, later on, he refused to budge from his judgment that the Civil War was "a cruel, heartless, aimless, unnecessary war"; he would not succumb to the "madness and imbecility." He did not believe that the Confederate government had any intention of making an assault upon Washington or, for that matter, involving itself in any armed aggression against the North. It acted only in retaliation against the invasion of its land, he said.[37]

However, in April 1861, when Pierce returned to Concord, New Hampshire, to live, he made some concessions to the local patriotic fervor. From the balcony of the *Eagle*, he delivered a speech on the flag and the obligation to defend it against aggression. "Born in the State of New Hampshire, I intend that here shall repose my bones. I would not live in a State the rights and honors of which I was not prepared to defend at all hazards and to the last extremity," he declared.[38]

When the war came, Pierce found it hard to accept. Having spent many years of his life, particularly during his administration, resisting war along with his friends in the North and South, he had to place the blame on some force. He maintained, finally, that the war was the result of the schemes of the Northern abolitionists. It could not be

the fault of Confederate President Jefferson Davis, who had been
his secretary of war, he felt. Most painful to him was the thought
that the aims of his political life should be "consummated by arms
on bloody fields."[39]

Shortly after Lincoln's inauguration, Pierce wrote to Van Buren
suggesting a meeting of ex-Presidents to consult on "the alarming"
condition of public affairs and to work together to formulate a plan
of action. Van Buren, feeling far removed from the political arena,
was evasive. He answered that he had given the subject much thought
but had doubts about "making a volunteer movement of that description on our parts." He conceded, however, that he would
accept the invitation without hesitation if Pierce called the meeting.[40]

A journey to the West that Pierce took in the summer of 1861
resulted in accusations that pursued him for the rest of his life. The
purpose of the trip, Pierce said, was to satisfy "a long cherished
purpose" to see that part of the country in order to get a better idea
of "its boundless resources." He got as far west as Detroit and Saginaw
City in Michigan and Louisville, Kentucky.

Pierce first learned of the suspicion against him when he received
a letter from Secretary of State William H. Seward which had
enclosed in it an anonymous letter accusing him of going west in
order to help the Knights of the Golden Circle, a secret organization
of antiwar Democrats whose headquarters were in the Northwest.
Based on this evidence, Seward demanded that Pierce give an explanation. Pierce was furious. He disliked the war and the administration that started it and he had been critical of their activities,
but he was not a traitor. When he received Pierce's fiercely indignant
letter, Seward, who had been guilty of other acts of overzealousness,
immediately backed down. He explained that the letter had been
written by his chief clerk, whose only motive was to give Pierce an
opportunity to deny the accusation.

Unable to forget the insult, Pierce showed Seward's letter to
some friends. They all advised him to make the correspondence
public through the press. Pierce delayed doing this until March
1862, after the Detroit *Tribune* published the accusation against him
which was then reprinted in other Republican papers such as the
Boston *Journal* and the New York *Evening Post*. Unable to swallow
the insult, Pierce got friends to submit the documents to a Congressional committee and thus forced the exposure of Seward's apology

to the public. It was then revealed that the perpetrator of the hoax was a Dr. Hopkins.[41]

Other suspicions of Pierce's loyalty had reached the White House. Abraham Lincoln wrote to Secretary of War Simon Cameron while Pierce was on the western trip: "I think it well that F. Pierce is away from the N.H. people. He will do less harm anywhere else; and by *when* he has gone, his neighbors will understand him better." This note was in response to a letter about Pierce written by Henry McFarland, editor of the Concord *Statesman*, to M. B. Goodman that had been referred to Cameron. The letter stated that Pierce was in Louisville, Kentucky, and the suspicion was very general there that "his mission there is not one friendly to the government. . . . If the government has any way to observe his motions I hope it will do so."[42]

No retraction was able to mitigate the reactions of the war-mad public. The controversy over Nathaniel Hawthorne's dedication of his book *Our Old Home: Sketches of England* to Pierce illustrates the intensity of the public's anger against the former President.

That Franklin Pierce had appointed Hawthorne consul in Liverpool, England, was only a "side issue," Julian Hawthorne recorded. His father "loved and respected" Pierce. Therefore, when his Boston publisher tried to persuade Hawthorne to omit the dedication, the author refused. "If he is so exceedingly unpopular that his name is enough to sink the volume, there is so much more the need that an old friend should stand by him," Hawthorne told Mr. Fields.[43] In the preface to *Our Old Home*, so that Pierce's enemies could have no doubt about his feelings, Hawthorne wrote: "I need no assurance that you [Pierce] continue faithful forever to that grand idea of an irrevocable Union. . . . For other men there may be a choice of paths—for you, but one; and it rests among my certainties that no man's loyalty is more steadfast, no man's hopes or apprehensions on behalf of our national existence more deeply heartfelt, or more closely intertwined with his possibilities of personal happiness, than those of FRANKLIN PIERCE."[44] Perhaps sales of the book were affected as Fields feared. It is known that Emerson tore out the dedication pages from his copy.

Bitterness at his treatment by the vindictive public and utter despair over Lincoln's handling of the war appear constantly in Pierce's private correspondence. His friends were informed of Lincoln's error in declaring martial law and depriving American citizens of their personal liberties. As the war continued, Pierce became ever more critical of the President. The Emancipation Proclamation, he complained, was a particular outrage, because it interfered with states' rights and the right of private property.

The Pierces spent more time in Andover than Concord, which gave the ex-President's enemies the opportunity to say that he had been driven from his home because his neighbors would have nothing to do with him. One of the most poignant slights that Pierce suffered was at Hawthorne's funeral. The two friends had been on a trip together to the White Mountains for Hawthorne's health when the author died. At the funeral, the New England fellowship of authors was fully represented—Emerson, Lowell, Whittier, Longfellow, Bronson Alcott, Agassiz. Pierce was there too, hovering protectively around the Hawthorne family, but he was not a pallbearer because public feeling was so intense against him.

Although James Buchanan left the presidency somewhat discredited because of his ineffectiveness, the seventy-one-year-old retired chief executive expected a tranquil existence at Wheatland. In the early months of his administration, Lincoln seemed to be following Buchanan's peaceful policy with the Confederacy, particularly in the case of Fort Sumter. Stanton wrote often that Major Anderson would be withdrawn and that a "continuation of your [Buchanan's] policy *to avoid collision* will be the course of the present administration."[45] Sumter would be evacuated, Joseph Holt, Buchanan's postmaster general, assured his former chief. But these predictions were based on Seward's last-minute efforts to avoid war before the Radical Republicans succeeded in persuading Lincoln to take the opposite course and relieve the fort.

Once the war started, Buchanan became the scapegoat. Violent, insulting, and threatening anonymous letters poured in from Philadelphia until the aging ex-President feared for his life. One morning his housekeeper found a note under the back door warning that Wheatland would be set on fire. Most reluctantly, Buchanan accepted the offer of the Lancaster Masonic Lodge to guard his house. For a long time, dedicated Masons took turns standing guard over Wheatland. Suffering from an acute bilious attack, the ex-President was sick and disgusted. Still, his seventy-first birthday, which was planned to be a joyous occasion, became the start of his struggle to exonerate himself. "Upon reexamination of the whole course of my administration from 6th November, 1860, I can find nothing to regret. I shall at all times be prepared to defend it," he wrote to Stanton.[46]

Buchanan believed that the Lincoln administration deliberately tried to make him appear to be the author of the war. As he stated it: "It is one of the great national prosecutions, such as have occurred in this country, necessary to vindicate the character of the government." He would spare no effort to vindicate the "malignant falsehood," and wrote to friends for documents, papers, and statements that he could use. Holt tried to reason with him, saying that there was no haste; the country was too involved in the war to give any attention to an explanation of the events leading up to it. But Buchanan did not want to listen to him.

Lincoln, in his message to a special session of Congress on July 4, 1861, did not mention Buchanan by name but spelled out charges against "the late administration." He said that "a disproportionate share of the Federal muskets and rifles" had found their way into Southern states "and had been seized, to be used against the government. Accumulations of the public revenue" lying within those states had also been seized. The navy had been out of reach "in distant seas."[47]

Newspapers seized on these statements as they did on a resolution presented to the Senate by Garrett Davis of Kentucky which stated that after it became apparent that "an insurrection against the United States was about to break out in several Southern States," President James Buchanan, "from sympathy with the conspirators and their treasonable project," did not do what was necessary to prevent it. Therefore he should be censured by the American people. Buchanan protested that if, two years after a presidential term had expired, the Senate could try, condemn, and execute the former incumbent, none would accept the office.[48] The Senate did not pass the proposal, but the American people, aided by the press, accepted the basic premise.

Accusations both serious and petty plagued the besieged ex-President. The New York *Herald* published an absurd accusation that Buchanan had removed from the White House portraits of Queen Victoria, Prince Albert, and other members of the British royal family and some gifts from Japan. Harriet Lane, Buchanan's niece, who had been the bachelor President's hostess during the White House years, was informed of the charge, as was Lord Lyon, the British ambassador. The charges were withdrawn finally by the press, but their vicious pettiness disturbed Buchanan. He said, with justification: "The charge is mean & contemptible, as well as false, & if it were true, it would make me a mean and contemptible fellow."[49]

Of much more serious substance and much more disturbing to the former President was an article by Thurlow Weed published in the *London Observer*. It claimed to describe a meeting of Buchanan with his Cabinet after Major Anderson removed his garrison from Fort Moultrie to Fort Sumter. The account stated that Secretary of War John B. Floyd threatened to resign unless Anderson were remanded to Fort Moultrie, whereby Attorney General Edwin Stanton attacked Floyd and the President viciously, saying that he would resign if it were done. The other Cabinet members followed suit, thus forcing Floyd's resignation, which the President accepted and then appointed Postmaster General Joseph Holt to succeed him.

Buchanan was outraged because not only was the story untrue but it had implications that were most humiliating. To begin with, Buchanan had asked Floyd to resign several days before Anderson moved to Fort Sumter. But what was most painful was not that Weed, an administration supporter, would publish the story, whose obvious purpose was to enhance Stanton's prestige, but that not one of his former Cabinet members was willing to tell the truth publicly.

"Strange that four members of my Cabinet whom I treated with great kindness & parted from in a most friendly manner, witnessed without contradiction a statement made by an official of the Government in a foreign newspaper, that they had one after another offered me the grossest insult," he commented. They would not have been in office fifteen minutes had this occurred, he added. It was fear of "Lincoln's and Seward's penitentiary," Buchanan's friends assured him. Stanton had bragged to one of the former President's friends that he had seen to it that Dr. Ives of the New York *Herald* had been arrested and sent to Fort McHenry partly because of abusive articles that he had written about Buchanan. Buchanan, however, concluded that his former associates were mute because "they are willing to profit with their new masters by the slander, rather than speak a word of truth in justice to the old President."[50] For the time being he decided to do nothing.

Millard Fillmore's life during the Civil War was less trying than those of his fellow ex-Presidents. Though not in any way close to Lincoln, he appeared to be approving of his actions. Critical of Buchanan's acceptance of Southern secession and refusal to coerce the seceding states, Fillmore called the South's action "suicidal and

wholly unjustifiable." The South replied in kind. A Richmond newspaper called Fillmore a fair-weather friend and, in New Orleans,
a school named after him had its name changed to Jefferson Davis.[51]

As soon as the Civil War began, Fillmore came out of retirement
to preside over a Union rally. "It is no time now to inquire by whose
fault or folly this state of things has been produced," he said. "We
have a common lot and must meet a common fate."[52] By the end of
April, he had organized a company of men too old for active duty
but ready to defend the city if attacked. Outfitted in colorful uni-
forms, drilled as an escort guard, the Union Continentals, most of
them grandfathers, added distinction to many ceremonial wartime
events. The ex-President marched at the head of the column wearing
a sword and plume, "stately and erect and looking like an Emperor."
Throughout the war, the Continentals marched as a funeral escort
and at Fourth of July celebrations.[53]

Fillmore's greatest concern was the safety of his city. He became
alarmed over the Trent Affair, fearing that Buffalo's security might
be threatened by Great Britain. The crisis occurred because an
American warship stopped the *Trent*, a British vessel that was carrying Confederate Commissioners James Mason and John Slidell to
England, and forcibly removed them. There was a wave of public
outcry for war in England, but Secretary of State Seward ordered
the men released and censured Captain Charles Wilkes, commander
of the American ship, thus averting hostilities. In the meantime, however, Fillmore, visualizing a British attack from Canada, demanded
troops and ammunition to protect Buffalo from the governor of New
York, the secretary of war, and the President. "The safety of this
city is absolutely essential to the security of the commerce of the
Northwestern lakes," he said. In the event of an invasion of Canada,
Buffalo must become the base for the operations against the Upper
Provinces as well as any movement against Montreal and the Lower
Provinces. The War Department must assure Buffalo's safety.[54]

However, before the Civil War was over, Fillmore got into difficulties with the superpatriots. At a Great Central Fair sponsored by the
Ladies of the Christian Mission to make money for the wounded
soldiers, Fillmore had been asked to make the keynote speech. His
words shocked a large part of the audience because, instead of the
jingoistic war cry that was expected, he spoke of the horrors of war,
particularly civil war. War "desolated the forest portions of our
land, loaded the country with an enormous debt that the sweat of

millions yet unborn must be taxed to pay; arrayed brother against brother, father against son in mortal combat; deluged our country with fraternal blood, whitened our battlefields with the bones of the slain, and darkened the sky with the pall of mourning," he said. The stigma of Copperhead was immediately attached to Millard Fillmore's name and it stuck from then on. The crowd was not ready yet to hear a call for extending to the conquered armies "our magnanimity and generosity" and "every act of clemency and kindness in our power" as well as restoring to the Confederates "their constitutional rights." The Buffalo *Commercial Advertiser* admitted that they toned down Fillmore's remarks before printing them, and the editors added the comment that they were obliged now to class him among the bitterest opponents of the war "in the infamous circle made up of such men as Vallandigham."[55]

Public hostility to Fillmore was clearly shown in an incident that occurred after Lincoln's assassination. The citizens of Buffalo draped their doors in black but, it was observed, Fillmore's door was bare. The ardent patriot who noticed this terrible omission, unaware that Fillmore was out of town, smeared the house with black ink. When the ex-President returned to the city, he quietly draped his door. He was then appointed to head a citizens' committee delegated to meet Lincoln's funeral train at Batavia and act as an escort to Buffalo. Hostile and unforgiving reporters wrote an untrue and unsubstantiated story saying that a large group of Buffalo citizens had gathered in front of Fillmore's house and insulted him.

John Tyler died a rebel leader. After the failure of the peace conference, he took his seat in the Virginia State Convention as the elected representative from James City, Charles City, and New Kent. There he was one of the majority who advocated secession. "Revolutions never went backward," he warned; "Mr. Lincoln recognized no . . . principles as lying at the base of American institutions as to the right of the people of any of these states to seek their happiness under any other government than that arranged by himself, of a sectional majority." However, it was not until April 17, 1861, that the former President wrote to his wife at Sherwood Forest: "Well, my dearest one, Virginia has severed her connection with the Northern hive of abolitionists, and takes her stand as a sovereign and independent state." Then he added, "Do dearest, live as frugally as possible in the household—trying times are before us."[56]

Tyler was not elected to represent Virginia in the Confederate

Congress at Montgomery, Alabama, because he was too ill and exhausted to tolerate the hot season in the Deep South. However, in May, when the Confederate capital was moved to Richmond, he was elected unanimously to be a member of the permanent congress. He was aggressive and vigorous in his approach to the war, at one time suggesting that the Confederate cavalry go to Washington and seize the capital, but the majority was opposed to taking the offensive.

The Gardiners, Tyler's in-laws, were afraid that Julia and the children would be living on a battlefield. Mrs. Gardiner suggested that the little children be sent north to her. Tyler protested that the youngsters would always be safe. The North, he said, "was just full of blasts and threats." The Confederacy had more troops ready for the field, "panting for conflict," than the North could arm or provision for a campaign. "The whole state is clad in steel," he boasted, and it had General Lee, the son of Henry Lee of the Revolution, to lead the army. Virginia fighting men numbered 120,000. Besides, at this time, he would not trust "anyone bearing [his] name, even little Pearl," in New York if the sentiments reflected in the newspapers were the true feelings in the North. "If I find our situation dangerous on the river, we will go to the mountains, or other retreats in Virginia," he promised his mother-in-law.

Robert Tyler, the ex-President's son by his first marriage, had to go to Richmond from Philadelphia by a circuitous route. He had been active in Pennsylvania Democratic politics, but after Virginia seceded, his well-known pro-Southern position inspired a vigilante attack on him. He fled to the Southern capital, where Jefferson Davis appointed him register of the Confederate states.

When the permanent Confederate Congress was established, Tyler competed with two personal friends for the Charles City seat. His platform—patriotism and more of it until the enemy was defeated—was well supported, but he stayed home and did not stump for himself. On the morning after the election, a mud-spattered horseman sought out Tyler. He seized the frail old man and shouted happily, "Mr. President, you are elected! You are elected!" Tyler piled up almost twice the combined votes of the two other contestants.[57] His perfect record of never having lost a public election was maintained.

But John Tyler never became a member of the first permanent Congress of the Confederate States. He went to Richmond ahead of Julia, who wanted to meet friends en route to the capital and spend a few days with them. A premonition in the form of a dream made Julia forego her visit and rush to Richmond. She reached her husband on Friday evening, January 10, and found him in perfect health. However, two days later he got up in the morning feeling ill. He went down to breakfast, but shortly afterward he fell unconscious of what was diagnosed as a cerebral vascular accident. Less than a week later he died. The Confederacy buried him with great honor, not at Sherwood Forest as he had wished, but at Holywood Cemetery on a hill overlooking the James River, next to the grave of James Monroe. Despite fifty years of service to the United States, his death was ignored in Washington. If the government thought about it at all, it was probably relieved that the problem of burying a rebel ex-president would never have to be faced.

Julia Tyler, now a forty-nine-year-old widow with seven children, had to cope with a plantation of seventy slaves and sixteen hundred acres, a load of debts, and a war. Like the ex-President, his widow also was ignored by Lincoln. She asked for a pass to go north to her family but was informed that she was subject to the rule that first she would have to take an oath of allegiance to the United States, which she refused to do. Her mother wrote to the President asking that the rule be waived for "Mrs. ex-President Tyler," but there was no reply. Eventually Julia made her own way north.

In May 1864, Sherwood Forest was seized by Union troops and the plantation owner and others arrested and abused. The property was turned over to local Negroes, sacked, and, in June, placed in the care of two of Tyler's former slaves. Eventually all the house furnishings disappeared and the entire place was destroyed.[58]

Franklin Pierce survived the war and lived for several additional years, but remained thoroughly discredited. He did not accept the principle of secession but could not accommodate his thinking to Lincoln's excessive war measures. He believed that the President was completely dominated by Charles Sumner and his crew of abolitionists, because Lincoln was a man of "limited ability" and "narrow intelligence."

On July 4, 1863, Pierce was the chief speaker at a Democratic rally held in Concord. Three years of public silence had so bottled up his anger that he could restrain himself no longer. He said of the Lincoln administration: "True it is, that you, that I, may be the next victim of unconstitutional, arbitrary, irresponsible power." The ill-timed speech went on in a melancholy and pessimistic vein. While the meeting was in progress, news of the great victory at Gettysburg circulated through the crowd. As a result, the public rejected Pierce's eloquent gloom with anger.[59]

Shortly afterward, by sheer ill luck, Union soldiers marching through the South found a letter that Pierce had written to Jefferson Davis in 1860. In it the ex-President endorsed Davis as "the coming man," the best candidate for 1860, a sentiment, he added, that was growing in New England. Pamphleteers delighted in the letter, using it particularly in New England. One of them accused Pierce of encouraging secession by predicting that if war came, it would be fought in Northern cities and towns. Friends tried to neutralize the attacks by publishing a pamphlet called *The Record of a Man*, which contained three Pierce letters written in December 1859 proposing the preservation of the Union.[60] Their efforts were ignored.

Pierce had to endure one last unpleasant challenge to his patriotism. Like Buffalo and most of the other Northern cities, Concord ordered that every citizen must show his grief over Lincoln's death by a public display of mourning, a draped flag. The mob ensured compliance by roaming the streets looking for offending front doors. Forewarned by a young man who worked for him, Pierce was ready for the shouting mob when it arrived at his door. Carrying a small flag, he went outside to face his jeering fellow citizens.

The ex-President agreed to the demand that he make a speech. He had hardly begun to speak about the horror of the assassination when a voice in the crowd shouted at him: "Where is your flag?" Pierce answered that he did not have to show his devotion to the Stars and Stripes on demand. He had served his state and his country for thirty-five years, and if there were still a question as to his devotion to the flag, the Constitution, and the Union, "it [was] too late now" to resolve it. His eloquence calmed the mob, but the Civil War veterans of New Hampshire saw to it that Pierce's home state did not honor its only president for fifty years.[61]

James Buchanan, who remained peacefully at Wheatland through the war, refused to be dragged into post-assassination hysteria even by well-meaning political friends. He penned suitable platitudes in personal letters, calling the fallen martyr "a man of kindly and benevolent heart and of plain, sincere and frank manners." Throughout the war, Buchanan stated, he had been certain that Lincoln would crush the rebellion. "Indeed, I felt for him much personal regard," Lincoln's predecessor wrote. But when he was asked to write a few lines on Lincoln's death to "soothe the bitter prejudices of the Lincoln party against you and your friends," he refused. "I weighed your suggestion carefully," he wrote, but he could not comply, for his words would be, most assuredly, misrepresented.[62] He felt more comfortable talking about Andrew Johnson.

Except for Martin Van Buren, who died in 1862 and was too ill during the war to do more than send an occasional message of support for the administration, the Civil War ex-Presidents were not in sympathy with Lincoln or, to any real degree, the war. All of them had spent their administrations attempting to stave off such a conflict and so were not pleased to see the failure of their efforts. Tyler, of course, was in the uncompromising position of joining the rebellion. Fillmore, Pierce, and Buchanan had to suffer abuse that was often unmerited. Since it was a time of inflamed feelings, anything less than unrestrained enthusiasm for the war had to result in disproportionate abuse. Fillmore made an almost absurd effort to display the outward trappings of militarism but failed to match the fustian when he spoke in public. Pierce's bitter disapproval became so apparent that he was forced to be an exile from his home town. Buchanan, whose "crime" was freshest in the public mind, escaped vigorous abuse only by staying at Wheatland and keeping out of the public's way. In a sense, he was under self-imposed house arrest. Lincoln did not even try to use the ex-Presidents for propaganda purposes. With some distaste, probably, he recognized that they were not good aides for the promotion of his war effort.

McKinley had little more luck with his ex-Presidents when he presided over "that splendid little war" with Spain. Benjamin Harrison, who was in Paris dealing with the Venezuela boundary case, defended American intervention on the grounds that the United States had to act because of Spain's cruelty to the Cubans, but in his opinion it was not the duty of his country to police the world. Major Russell Harrison, the ex-President's son, went to Cuba and supported the war loyally.

But Grover Cleveland made it quite clear that he opposed the war. In a statement to the Associated Press in January 1896, he asserted his status as a private citizen and explained that he was making a public statement only because of a misleading statement that had been made by Senator John T. Morgan. While President, he insisted, he had sent messages to Congress in which he had clearly stated that he opposed recognition of the belligerency of Cuba. He had not deviated from that viewpoint, despite threats against him and his children by "frenzied men and women" who believed him the enemy of the Cuban cause.[63]

Only weeks before the declaration of war, Cleveland believed that it would not come. If it did, he predicted, "the time will not be long before there will be an earnest and altogether successful search by our people for a justification." The ex-President was unmoved by American victories at El Caney and San Juan Hill or the destruction of the Spanish fleet. The conflict appeared to him still as sad indeed. "By the time disgust for the rascally Cubans becomes more general and death in battle and disease has made thousands of American households dark, I shall be prepared for a revulsion of feeling that will start a general and ominous inquiry as to the justification and necessity of this war and as to its prosecution," he wrote.[64]

Cleveland was disgusted by the role of the yellow press in the war machinations. When William Randolph Hearst asked the ex-President, in February 1898, to be a member of a committee that included fifteen governors, fifty mayors, Chauncey Depew, Levi Morton, and other prominent figures to put up a monument dedicated to the heroes of the *Maine*, Cleveland responded caustically. "I decline to allow my sorrow for those who died on the *Maine* to be perverted into an advertising scheme for the New York *Journal*," he said.[65]

Except for a discussion about the threatened war with Spain that took place between the outgoing and incoming Presidents at the White House the night before McKinley's inauguration, Cleveland never afterward either met with or corresponded with McKinley. At that meeting, McKinley's parting words were "Mr. President, if I can only go out of office at the end of my term, with the knowledge that I have done what lay in my power to avert this terrible calamity, with the success that has crowned your patience and persistence, I shall be the happiest man in the world."[66] It was obvious that Cleveland would not be a likely ally. He did not feel that it was his obligation to support American imperialist activity in the Philippines either. "The 'round-up' and slaughter of Philipinos [sic] seems to go merrily on—of course it has little of glorious war about it, but perhaps it's good practice for our army," he wrote to Richard Olney.[67] The brief duration of the Spanish-American War eliminated the need for any significant ex-presidential support. From Cleveland, there would never be any, and he was not a good subject for public intimidation.

The Great War, America's first experience in a foreign war, found its two living ex-Presidents vocal and actively involved. They were not in virtual hiding, silenced, or in opposition, but were instead ready to make the White House and the American people fully aware of their presences.

William Howard Taft, early in 1915, said in an address in Morristown, New Jersey: "We must abide by the judgment of those to whom we have intrusted the authority and when the President shall act, we must stand by him to the end." When Wilson saw a clipping of the speech, he called it "fine and generous." Robert Lansing, responding enthusiastically to the words of the Republican leader, declared that now the administration policy was an American policy.[68]

The ex-President's attitude had developed slowly. The onset of World War I after the tragedy at Sarajevo was, in his opinion, "a cataclysm" and "a retrograde step" in world civilization. Only as he watched the development of the war did he come to sympathize with the Allies and to regard the struggle as one against autocracy. However, Taft was not single-mindedly pro-British. He deplored the blockade that doomed Belgium to starvation and believed that England should allow food supplies in to "that ill-fated state." In that, he agreed with Herbert Hoover and not the belligerent leaders of the prowar wing of the Republican party, Theodore Roosevelt and Henry Cabot Lodge. Rather, at this time, Taft looked to Wilson to find a way to peace. Even the sinking of the *Lusitania* did not constitute for him an adequate cause for entering the war. He did not agree with Theodore Roosevelt's dictum that it was "murder on the high seas" for which all German ships in America must be seized and all commerce with Germany banned. Also, Taft had great empathy for Wilson. "I have been President, and I know what an awful responsibility a man has to carry in such a crisis and how trying such blatherskiting [Roosevelt's] is when a man is trying to find the right way," he said.[69]

Taft's enthusiasm for Wilson's program began to wane by the spring of 1916, partly for political reasons. The Democrats were making frequent references to Taft's support of Wilson's program, an embarrassment to the Republican ex-President, who wished to keep his political lines open. So he started to criticize the President's weakness in the area of military preparedness and came out for compulsory universal military training.

As the Wilsonian slogan "He kept us out of war" swept the country,

Taft started to reverse himself on certain issues. He questioned the President's "dilatory" response to the sinking of the *Lusitania*. Writing a note well and appropriately phrased was not enough and had exposed the nation to ridicule, he declared. For three years, he added, "I have squared my conduct to my conviction that . . . we should forget party and support the President," but now it was his duty to expose the administration's shortcomings. Teddy Roosevelt did not accept the sincerity of Taft's change of tone. He believed that part of the reason for his support of Wilson's position had been the hope that he would be appointed to the Supreme Court. Taft wanted it very much and was disappointed when he was bypassed for Louis D. Brandeis.

Theodore Roosevelt's criticism of Wilson during the war period was merciless. He accused the President of cowardice, timidity, unscrupulousness, and selfishness. Many of Wilson's actions he perceived as cold-bloodedly political, undertaken to placate the pacifists, the Germans, and the extreme Irish. However, TR observed, the British, deceived by his apparent sincerity, would look to him as "a great peacemaker and thus he would gain glory."[70]

The management of foreign relations under Wilson-Bryan was to Roosevelt worse than under Taft. Wilson deserved to be ranked with Buchanan, "beneath contempt." Like Jefferson and Madison a century before, Roosevelt thought that Wilson would drift the country into war. "Wilson even more than Jefferson has been the apologist for and given impetus to our very worst tendencies," the ex-President argued. Action should have been taken when the *Lusitania* went down even if it would have meant the possibility of war.[71]

Military preparedness became Roosevelt's major cause and primary tool for combating what he called the "bleating of the peace people." He disliked it that many people thought him truculent, bloodthirsty, and, what was worse, as in George Creel's article "Red Blood" in Harper's *Weekly*, self-seeking. But nonetheless the Colonel continued his crusade, though well aware that he was out of sympathy with most of the people in the United States. The Progressive party did not support him. Its 1916 platform stated that social and industrial preparedness were equally essential.

Any remnant of hope that TR had that he might be a candidate in 1916 was sacrificed, without regret, to the Allied cause. His controversial speech on "hyphenated Americans" lost him the ethnic vote, particularly the German-Americans'. "I do not believe in hyphenated

Americans," he proclaimed. "I do not believe in German-Americans or Irish-Americans and I believe just as little in English-Americans. . . . Most emphatically I myself am not an Englishman once removed! I am straight United States."[72] Roosevelt's enemies, who were legion, made as much mileage as they could out of these startling remarks.

At this time TR started to picture himself at the head of a cavalry division ready to go into action as soon as the war bell sounded. Letters to suitable friends reflected his plans and sometimes asked them to join his future division. Apparently the bad blood between him and his commander in chief did not worry the Colonel.

Realistically, however, Roosevelt knew that his position as Wilson's antagonist almost completely negated his usefulness to the Allies. A trip to France to help reestablish American prestige there was urged by John F. Bass, an American correspondent in Paris. TR answered: "If I went to Europe at the present time, I would wish to go with arms in my hands, or else as a representative of an armed and resolute nation." He told Arthur Hamilton Lee, more explicitly, that he wished to go to the front at the head of an American division of twelve regiments like the Rough Riders. Anyhow, he added, the English do not want me, they accept Wilson. He must stay home, the ex-President concluded, where he was free to assault the United States President. To the French ambassador, Jean Jules Jusserand, Roosevelt confessed that he was sick at heart that the United States did not take the decisive step. But he gravely doubted the propriety of an ex-President attempting to go to war unilaterally.[73]

Measures short of war angered TR as, for example, the bill for armed neutrality. It was nothing but "timid war," he complained, and the senators who had passed it reached a lower depth than the President—only a little lower, because he was so low "there wasn't much room to get lower." In a speech to the Union League Club, March 20, 1917, TR called the device "intolerable to all self-respecting Americans." Germany, he said, was already at war with us. We must now wage war with Germany.[74]

By February 1917, Taft also considered the United States in the war, without escape. At Wilson's earnest pleading, he agreed to be a member of the Red Cross War Council, from which post he urged that Americans realize the dangers and the hardships of the war. He also served as joint chairman of the National War Labor Board with Frank P. Walsh. The board's purpose was to keep labor disputes from stopping war production. It was a broadening experience for the former President, who had never before been aware of the needs and conditions of work that confronted the workingman. Some of his traditional antilabor attitudes changed when he was faced with issues such as collective bargaining, the minimum wage, and the eight-hour day. "How can people live on such wages?" he asked after attending hearings in the South. He ordered salaries doubled and tripled.[75]

Mutual distrust, even hatred, of the President brought together the two estranged former Presidents. After many years of divergent views, Taft and Roosevelt found themselves on the same side again. They both favored a strong Republican Congress that would push Wilson into a firmer support of the war effort. The two met several times to the delight of the press and the public, but their former easy cordiality was never resumed. The much-publicized face-to-face meeting between them was not arranged. When Taft arrived at the Blackstone Hotel in Chicago on May 31, 1919, he learned that Theodore Roosevelt was in the dining room alone. Taft reported later that he decided spontaneously to see him. He entered the dining room, went up to his former friend, and shook his hand. Roosevelt responded with his natural cordiality, and they discussed their mutual enemy, President Wilson, agreeing amiably. After the meeting, there were some exchanges of letters and advice on the political campaign then going on, but no real renewal of personal friendship.

Though the rapprochement was not a success, it consoled Taft when, almost a year later, he attended TR's funeral. He told Oscar Straus that he felt grateful that he had reestablished their longtime friendship before it was too late. And he was able to write to Teddy Roosevelt's sister Bamie how glad he was that he and Theodore had come together after that long, painful interval. "Had he died in a hostile state of mind toward me, I would have mourned the fact all my life," he said.[76]

Taft was touched personally by the war when his youngest child, Charles, sailed for France in January 1918. He wrote, lovingly, "It is hard, darling boy, to let you go. You are the apple of our eye. But we would not have it different. If sacrifice is to be made who are we that we should escape it." Earlier in his farewell letter, Taft told his "knight *sans peur et sans reproche*" that "demoralization exists as never before in France and you will almost be raped unless you brace yourself." Fortunately he had his loving wife, Eleanor, to think of when he was "confronted by sinful love."[77]

Robert Taft, the ex-President's older son, had been turned down by the services because of his bad eyesight. After rejecting his father's offer to get him into the judge advocate general's office and failing once more at a call for officers, he volunteered his free services to Herbert Hoover, newly appointed head of the Food Administration.

Taft's war concluded with speeches against Wilson's Fourteen Points and in favor of a Republican Congress. The President wanted too much power, Taft insisted, and therefore there must be a Republican Congress to supervise reconstruction and offer constructive criticism of the administration's actions. At New York's unofficial Republican State Convention held at Saratoga Springs, Taft made a surprise appearance. He said jokingly, "You see before you a ghost, emerging from the past to view the new inventions of the present and see what a near convention means." The audience was delighted.[78]

Less than a week after the United States declared war on Germany and her allies, Theodore Roosevelt went to Washington to get Wilson's permission to raise his division. Wilson cleverly delayed and vacillated and got what mileage he could out of TR's great popularity, particularly to get support for the draft bill. Alice Roosevelt Longworth quoted her father as having said to Wilson, while promising him support, "Mr. President, all that has gone before is as dust on a windy street." But all the Roosevelt charm could not obtain the division. It did not matter to Wilson that the public and even Congress liked the idea. Or that important foreign dignitaries wanted TR. Clemenceau wrote an open letter to Wilson published in his own paper, *L'Homme Enchaîné*, saying, "in all candor . . . there is in France one name which sums up the beauty of American intervention. It is the name of Roosevelt, your predecessor, even your rival but with whom there can now be no other rivalry than heartening success. . . . Since it is in your power to give them [the soldiers of France] before the supreme decision the promise of reward, believe me—send them Roosevelt." There is no doubt that the Colonel would have been a mighty ambassador to the admiring Allies, but after a lengthy correspondence, the President and Secretary of War Newton D. Baker refused his request.[79]

In his autobiography, Alvin Johnson reported that Baker told him why Roosevelt did not get his division. It was his obligation to see that our soldiers were as well equipped and led as possible, Baker explained. "We could not risk a repetition of the San Juan Hill

Affair, with the commander rushing his men into a situation from which only luck extricated them."[80] It was a glib explanation but not the whole truth.

The real grounds upon which the popular ex-President was rebuffed could only be political. Roosevelt was, most decidedly, Wilson's predecessor and his rival; therefore there was no place for him in the Wilsonian plan. Later on, when Roosevelt's name was suggested as a member of a commission to be sent to revolutionary Russia, Wilson said very clearly that he could not consider the Colonel as a representative of his administration.[81]

Theodore Roosevelt was bitterly hurt when he received Baker's refusal. He published an open letter to the many volunteers who had applied for service in his stillborn division. The rejected leader advised his followers to "consider themselves absolved from all further connection with his movement." But he could not refrain from quoting the Brooklyn *Eagle*'s statement that Wilson's decision to send the Pershing expedition abroad was a compromise between the general staff's original plan to delay an American expeditionary force for quite some time and Roosevelt's call for an immediate expedition. Thus Rooseveltian agitation can be credited with some results. France got her American soldiers but not Theodore Roosevelt.[82]

Part of the romantic charm that his fantasy division held for TR was that it would include his four sons. Instead, the ex-President had to watch them depart one by one while he stayed behind. In preparation for American entrance into the war, which all the Roosevelts believed was inevitable, Theodore, Jr., Archibald, and Quentin had trained at Plattsburg. Kermit was in South America but planned to return to his own country as soon as war was declared.

Roosevelt was anxious that his sons get to the front as soon as possible and for this he enlisted the aid of General Pershing. "If I were physically fit, instead of old and heavy, I should myself ask to go under you in any capacity down to and including a sergeant," Colonel Roosevelt wrote. With Pershing's assistance, by July 1917 Ted and Archie were in France as combat officers. Kermit, not having the training provided by the Plattsburg summers, was sent to serve under General Maude in Mesopotamia. He and his wife and infant son left on the *Carpathia* while TR, Mrs. Roosevelt, and Alice Longworth waved from the wharf. Ted's wife arranged to work for the YWCA in France and left just before the order went out forbidding wives of servicemen to go abroad. Last to go was the Roosevelt baby, Quentin, a nineteen-year-old Harvard sophomore, who had enlisted as a flying officer and soon went to France. "I would not have stopped him if I could," Theodore Roosevelt told Lawrence F. Abbott in the summer of 1917, "and I could not have stopped him if I would. The more American boys from nineteen to twenty-one join the army the better it is for the country. To take them out of our civil life entails the smallest economic loss upon the Nation, and because of their elasticity and powers of recuperation they are its greatest military asset."[83]

While his sons fought abroad, Teddy Roosevelt raged at home for a more active war. He was the Defender of the Faith, a knight paladin with words only as his weapons. He would define Americanism and decide who merited the title and who was un-American. Roosevelt had a jingoistic streak that ill suited his fine intelligence and inherent gentleness. Carried away by his thesis of "The Foes of Our Own House," the title of a book that he issued containing a selection of his wartime speeches and articles, he advocated some repressive measures. Among them was the dismissal of any teacher who refused to sign a loyalty oath and the banning of the teaching of the German language in the public schools. In a kind of nativist frenzy, he suggested that immigrants who did not learn English in the five-year probation period be deported.

The constant butt of Roosevelt was the President of the United States. Wilson was taking too much power, as in the case of the Food Administration and his appointment of Herbert Hoover as its dictator. If the people knew what was going on, "the President would be impeached tomorrow," TR wrote to Henry Cabot Lodge. Either there were the wrong supplies or none at all going to France, he complained. And in February 1919, the Colonel sent two hundred pairs of shoes to Archibald's men in response to a letter from his son saying that his troops needed them. Thanks to his pen, he wrote to Archie, he was making money, and his only object was to relieve the needs of his boys and their comrades.

Theodore Roosevelt realized that his role as a gadfly reflected the fact that he was not in sympathy with most of his fellow Americans. Therefore, he said, "I am no longer fit to lead the public men and politicians." But he would continue to serve "a very limited public usefulness by telling truths which nobody else will tell."[84]

The old Musketeer was ill in the winter of 1918. He suffered abscesses in his ear and thigh that finally required an operation. For a month he lost his equilibrium and was left with permanent damage to his left ear. This made Arthur Hamilton Lee's invitation to go to England an impossibility. It would not be a good idea anyhow, Roosevelt felt, because he could not be in the confidence of the civil and military authorities and therefore whatever he could do would best be done at home. If he did go abroad, he wrote to Lee, "I know that with cold venom, he [Wilson] would see if there was not some way by which he could do me mischief and cause any effort I could make to fail."[85] After further thought, he concluded that Wilson wanted to make the war his own personal and party success and that therefore a Roosevelt trip to England could only cause harm.

Roosevelt continued to criticize through his new medium, the Kansas City *Star*. An article that appeared on May 7, 1918, defended freedom of speech and press against an announcement forbidding criticism of the President. The ruling that "we are to stand by the President, right or wrong, is not only unpatriotic and servile," he wrote, "but is morally treasonable to the American people."[86]

His sons' honors warmed their father's heart. When Archie won the croix de guerre at the cost of a leg full of shrapnel and a broken arm, TR wrote, "Well we know what it feels like to have a hero in the family." Helping the boys at the front was a sacred cause to Roosevelt. He had given his Nobel Peace Prize money for a foundation to establish an industrial peace fund. Now he wanted the money back to help the soldiers and their dependents. Congress quickly returned the money.

The stodgy rules that kept a soldier's sister from going abroad made Roosevelt impatient. He grieved that Flora Whitney, Quentin's fiancée, was not able to go to France to marry Quentin. Then, Roosevelt wrote to Bamie, "if he were killed, she and he would have known their white hour."

A newspaper report that Quentin had shot down a German plane near Château-Thierry moved the Colonel to write prophetically: "Whatever now befalls Quentin, he has now had his crowded hour, and his day of honor and triumph." Less than a week later, on July 17, 1918, the Roosevelts were informed that Quentin had been shot down behind enemy lines. For a brief period there was hope that he was not dead, but by July 20, the German government had confirmed his death and said that he had been buried with full military honors. The Roosevelts decided not to have Quentin's body moved back to his homeland after the war was over, but planned instead to visit the foreign grave to put up a stone for him.

Roosevelt was stricken by his son's death, though he spoke constantly of how much harder it was for his wife and dear Flora. But when he was asked to run for governor of New York, he could only say that his heart was with his boys at the front and he was not thinking about New York State politics. It consoled him somehow to note that no family except the Garibaldis came out of the war with the "reputation that ours does," he told Ted. For the kaiser, he had nothing but scorn. He and his six sons were "saving their own worthless carcasses and leaving their women like their bones behind them," he wrote. "If ever there was a case where on the last day of fighting the leaders should have died, this was the case." TR was cheated out of a *Götterdämmerung*.[87]

Old wounds and perhaps the fresh one caused by Quentin's death were quickly sapping Roosevelt's strength. Though only sixty, he had apparently pushed the strenuous life too far. In the fall of 1918 he was admitted to Roosevelt Hospital with multiple ills. Somewhat improved, he was allowed to go home to Sagamore Hill for the Christmas holidays. Neither the family nor the patient wanted to acknowledge how tired he was or how much he was suffering. James Amos, his former valet, came to take care of him, but the ex-President lived only a few days. He died in his sleep of a pulmonary embolism. The strenuous life was over at sixty-one.

William Allen White, who was in Paris to cover the peace conference, saw the news of Roosevelt's death in the Paris *Herald*. He expressed the feelings of many when he wrote: "Then he [Ray Stannard Baker] and Ida Tarbell and I sat down to talk it all over; and get used to a world without Roosevelt in it."[88]

William Howard Taft went to TR's funeral. At first he was placed with the family servants, but when Archie Roosevelt spotted him, he went up to him and said, "You're a dear personal friend and you must come up further." He then placed him behind the Vice-President, who was representing Wilson, and in front of the Senate and House representatives. The chosen successor of the man being buried felt grief, he said, but that night he went to the theater.

No president left office as thoroughly unpopular as Herbert Hoover. Further, the rift between the incumbent and his predecessor was so great that the promise and then the onset of war made it, if possible, even greater. Hoover, whose food program had made him an international hero during the World War I period, found that anything he tried to say and do about the deteriorating world situation in the late thirties only made things worse.

Secretary of State Hull, in his *Memoirs*, stated that several times during World War II he suggested to Franklin Roosevelt that Hoover be called in conference, particularly on the subject of food, but the President never invited his predecessor to the White House. Hull saw Hoover unofficially several times at the home of Under Secretary of State William Castle, a place suggested by Hoover. The conferences were fully reported to Roosevelt, but he continued the charade of silence as did Hoover, who probably retained his share of bitterness toward FDR.[89]

Raymond Moley, a brain truster who later became a violent anti-Roosevelt man, attributed the President's attitude toward Hoover to fear that the former President might reemerge as his party's leader and that there might be a Hoover renaissance. There were, however, solid differences between the two men. Hoover believed in American isolationism and, later, in an apolitical humanitarianism which meant feeding the hungry regardless of ideological considerations. His connection with the Lindberghs and other America Firsters caused many ardent interventionists to refer to "the Hoover Circle."

In 1938, Hoover went to Europe at the invitation of Belgium to receive honors and decorations for his work in World War I. While in Berlin for a railway stopover, although it was not in his itinerary, Hoover visited Adolf Hitler. It was a forty-minute visit during which the former President was reported to have told Hitler that National Socialism was built on principles of government that could not be tolerated by the people of the United States. It was hinted, however, that he silently agreed with the German dictator's anticommunism.

Hoover refused to be quoted on his interview with Hitler, saying that it was contrary to the rules of international courtesy. However, years later, in a magazine article for *Collier's*, Hoover quoted some notes that he had made at the interview. He described Hitler as "forceful, highly intelligent, possessed of a remarkable and accurate memory, a wide range of information and a capacity for lucid exposition." He was not a dummy, as so often reported, although some subjects, such as communism and democracy, "set him off like a man in a furious anger." Hitler's reaction to Hoover was not as flattering. "*Ach, ein ganz kleiner Mann; Niveau wie ein Kreisleiter bei uns*

['A small piece of work—suitable in our country for a local party hack']," he said.[90]

While in Berlin, Hoover refused the offer of a degree from the University of Berlin but accepted an invitation from Hermann Göring to lunch at Karinhall. The meal was served with great pomp, and as the guests left, twenty-two huntsmen played old German hunting songs on their horns.

The visit with Hitler resurfaced after World War II when O. John Rogge, a special assistant to the attorney general, told a Swarthmore political science class he was teaching that Göring, von Ribbentrop, and other highly placed Nazis tried to bring about Roosevelt's defeat in the elections of 1936, 1940, and 1944. Among those whom the Nazis thought could be organized against United States participation in the war was Herbert Hoover, Rogge said. The indiscreet official lost his job for breaking the Justice Department rule of confidentiality, but whispering about Hoover's unpopular visit with Hitler was renewed.[91]

No satisfactory explanation can be offered for Hoover's brief encounter with the German fuehrer. It could have been curiosity coupled with unwillingness to offend a national leader. Or, the ex-President's motives might have been more complex. Hoover's virulent anticommunism made him see Russia as the greatest threat possible to the United States and to the American way of life. Hitler was Russia's greatest enemy. If Naziism could remove the Red menace, the lesser evil could then be dealt with. This analysis is borne out by private statements that Hoover made to his friends in 1941, before American entrance into World War II. The former President was certain that Hitler would defeat Russia and then make peace with Great Britain. A Hitler-dominated Europe might force America into economic self-containment, thereby eliminating a basic cause of war. Hoover believed that a fast German defeat of the Russians would be the only hope for the United States to escape war. His "inflexible determination" that the United States "keep out of other people's wars and Europe's age-old quarrels" trapped him into underestimating the Nazi evil.[92]

As Hitler's legions conquered the small European countries, after the outbreak of World War II, Hoover received calls for help from these countries' leaders to supply them with food to save them from starvation. First Poland, then Belgium, then Luxembourg, then Norway made their appeals. After being refused cooperation by the

American Red Cross, Hoover reactivated the American Relief Administration that had functioned after the last war, with many of his old experienced staff on hand again.

During the first few months of the war, both Germany and Great Britain were willing to cooperate, and the Polish Relief Commission was established. The Nazis promised not to interfere, and the British allowed relief ships to pass through their blockade. Then, after most of Europe had fallen to Hitler, Churchill became prime minister of Great Britain. He insisted that a strict blockade was essential for the success of the war effort. Allowing food to come in and nourish the Nazis would "prolong the agony of all Europe," he said. Also, he pointed out, foods were used in the manufacture of vital war matériel: fats to make explosives, potatoes to make the alcohol used in motors, milk to make plastic materials. Hoover thought Churchill in error and had the support of General Pershing and Admiral Pratt, who said it was "nonsense." But the British prime minister was adamant.[93]

The former President went to see Cordell Hull several times to enlist his support for the relief of France, Belgium, and the Netherlands. Here again he ran into solid opposition. The secretary of state appreciated Hoover's sincerity and humanitarianism, he wrote, but could not encourage him, because his plans were in conflict with those of the United States and Great Britain for winning the war.

This matter of food for the overrun countries occupied Hoover full-time. Through public addresses and magazine articles, he tried to influence the American people to back his National Committee on Food for the Small Democracies. The committee published a weekly bulletin called *Facing the Facts* and did receive some support from newspapers and religious groups. At no time was the Hoover Committee seeking money—only support, particularly from the government.

Hoover submitted several plans to the secretary of state. In December 1940, he asked for a release of funds blocked in the United States which belonged to the exiled governments of Belgium, Norway, and the Netherlands. The bread grains these countries needed could be purchased with the money in the Baltic States and so would not have to go through the blockade. "This is not a solution of the food problem in these countries," Hoover told Hull, "but it would unquestionably be a contribution towards delaying an enormous loss of life." Hull replied that in order to put this suggestion into effect, the

Treasury Department would have to consider it, and so he suggested that Hoover take it up with Henry Morgenthau, the secretary of the treasury. Hoover did not recognize Hull's attempt to pass the buck. In March he wrote to Hull again, mentioning that there were many reports that the administration opposed relief for the occupied democracies. This must be a misunderstanding of its position, Hoover ventured, but representatives of the small democracies and Britain understood it to be true. And Hoover enclosed a new proposal.[94]

This time it was a modest proposal, an experiment in Belgium that, if workable, could be extended to the rest of the country and then to other countries. A Belgian committee would distribute food for children—one million bushels of breadstuffs and potatoes coming from Germany and twenty thousand tons of other foodstuffs through the blockade. The plan was designed to answer such British criticism as the fear that the food would actually go to Germany. "I feel deeply concerned that America should ever be thought of as opposing the saving of these millions of people," Hoover wrote to Hull.[95]

Hull's reply was formal, comprehensive, and shattering. The Department of State would continue to welcome further facts and views from any organization about the "broad problem of suffering and need for relief" and would give them "sympathetic consideration," he wrote. Refusal of the Hoover plan was implicit in the letter, the clue being in the first paragraph, in which Hull referred to the limited experiment of supplying food to Belgium, "which brings up the question that Great Britain should lift its blockade for this purpose." Apart from reducing the ex-President to plain citizen, the letter reflected the new phase of American-British unity, achieved by the passage of the lend-lease agreement which, it may be significant to note, Hoover opposed.[96]

Hoover continued to believe that the British were "blundering badly in the range of larger vision" by condemning the people in the small democracies to starvation. The cries that these people would send up as the food situation got acute in May, June, and July would "be a constant menace to good will towards Great Britain," Hoover warned.[97]

This view was not shared by the British, who thought Hoover's stand, quite simply, anti-British. Sir Gerald Campbell of the British legation made this clear to Hoover when he called on him at the Waldorf Towers. Hoover's reply was that the suffering of the British people was a daily shock to everyone, but he could see no reason why "the death of British children required also the death of Belgian and Dutch children—their own allies." At first Campbell denied the possibility that the Germans had agreed to provide food, and then said that even if they had, they would not keep their word. Hoover replied that if the Germans backed down, the operation would cease and the responsibility would be theirs. To which response, Campbell merely repeated that the Hoover Committee was anti-British and pro-German and then closed with a veiled threat. "We will need take measures," he said.[98]

The London *Times* carried an attack on Hoover in April 1941, saying that he was meeting secretly in Washington with the most extreme isolationists to plan the defeat of the lend-lease bill. Hoover, angered, cabled the *Times* and was surprised that his message was published. Hoover described his food plan, pointing out that even if the Germans seized the food sent to Belgium, the quantity involved would not feed Germany for a day. In America, Hoover wrote, he did not answer smear articles, but his feelings for the agonies of the British people and the deep roots of personal contact between the two countries and their joint effort in the last war had made him decide to respond.[99] British pressure against Hoover did not stop. He was not only accused of being pro-German, but, it was said, the small democracies had never appealed to him. The committee then published a long list of government leaders and officials of the small democracies who had begged for relief for their people.

When accusation failed, the British and American administrations exerted pressure on the Belgian ambassador in Washington to state that there was no immediate need for relief in Belgium. Camille Gut, Belgian minister of finance, along with Ambassador Thiers, called on Hoover and, very embarrassed, revealed to the ex-President that he was the stumbling block to their receiving aid, and that if he withdrew from the committee, perhaps someone more agreeable to the Roosevelt administration could take his place.

Other efforts to repudiate Hoover followed. Dr. Carl J. Hambro of Norway, formerly enthusiastic about their work, denounced the Hoover Committee as having taken unauthorized initiative and being, at times, pro-German. The Norwegian ambassador stopped visiting Hoover. The Dutch government in exile withdrew from any contact with the committee. On April 18, General Sikorski, the prime minister for the Polish government in exile, told Hoover that the British were urging him to disavow the committee but that London and Washington would be ignored as long as the Polish people were starving.

Secretary Hull tried to explain "the difficult and highly complicated military and other closely allied considerations" involved in Hoover's many alternative proposals for feeding the small democracies. It was the responsibility and duty of the occupying country to feed the people, but the Germans were taking food from the children of those countries and giving it to persons working for the German military effort. Therefore, he explained, the Germans assented to the Hoover plan because it would release labor required to produce food. Since the Germans never claimed a food shortage for their own people and armies, "which [were] striking at the roots of freedom and civilization wherever they [could]," why didn't the Nazis carry out their obligation to feed the starving peoples of the overrun nations?[100]

Hoover was not interested in these explanations or in rhetorical questions. All he wanted to know was why the American government was allowing millions of children to starve.[101] Hull confided to his *Memoirs* that, at this stage, he was sympathetic to the ex-President's intentions but opposed to his ideas. To relieve Hitler of his obligations was to aid him, Hull felt.

Hoover did not want to see beyond the personal suffering that was being endured in Europe. The reports of his organization, culled from the Belgian Health Department records, told the tragic facts about the physical condition of the starving youngsters. Adolescents between fourteen and eighteen years old showed a weight loss of from eleven to thirteen pounds instead of the expected normal weight gain of more than fourteen pounds.

In October 1941, Hoover made a coast-to-coast radio appeal reviewing his committee's proposals for relief. He pointed out that Britain relaxed her blockade for her prisoners of war in Germany, and that she had allowed Turkey to send food shipments to Greece. His appeal was passionate and touching. "We have been engaged in much discussion over the freedom of religion in foreign countries," he said. "I learned at my mother's knee that compassion and responsibility for my neighbors was a part of our American faith. . . . Have we lost our way entirely? I do not believe it. . . . Hitler cannot be defeated with armies of starving children."[102]

It was a futile appeal. Hoover admitted himself that his organization had been repudiated by the governments of the very nations that he wanted to help. And in less than two months, the United States entered World War II, which altered the situation completely. After Pearl Harbor, the Hoover Committee suspended its activities until it might be approached. Now the exiled governments could ask for help from their new ally, the United States. But President Roosevelt sent no relief.

Before Pearl Harbor, Hoover took a very gloomy view of Allied prospects. In November 1941, he predicted to Alfred Landon that there would be peace discussions between Germany and England in about January or February, and assumed the collapse of Russia by that time. He also suspected that within ninety days the United States would send armored divisions to Persia to support the British Indian army so that the military line the British and Russians would build along the Caucasus could be supplied through Persia. This maneuver, Hoover said, would be "sheer waste of American life," because the military personnel and materials that could be accumulated would not be sufficient to overcome Hitler.[103]

Later that month, Hoover continued with his pessimistic predictions. The United States was heading into war with Japan and planning to ship an expeditionary force to Egypt, which was a mistake. He told Landon that our role should be limited to preparedness and aid to the democracies. Any enlargement of this objective was "wicked" for a number of reasons. A military ending of the war by our armies would be futile and a waste of life, because even if we won, lasting peace would be impossible and we would have developed some sort of collective system in the United States. Aid to Russia might be practical for the moment, but the United States and the world would pay dearly for it in the future. Our dangers were less than they were during World War I because, since the Russian campaign, Hitler's armies had been reduced and "the airplane [had] developed into a complete defense for the Western hemisphere from any kind of invasion." The American people were being driven into a shooting war by the President's deception and violation of the Constitution, which says that Congress alone can make war.[104]

When war came, Hoover issued a suitable statement. "We must fight with everything we have," he said. But obviously he had not had an instantaneous change of mind, nor were his fears and premonitions suddenly banished. The future of America was in jeopardy, he believed. The question would be "whether the people will use the ballot or the Man on Horseback to express themselves." If there were staunch opposition, they would use the ballot box, but otherwise "we shall see a Nazi country under new phrases and terms."[105]

In 1962, Hoover wrote to Harry Truman, himself an ex-President for almost ten years, saying that when Pearl Harbor came he supported Roosevelt and offered to serve in any useful capacity. Because of his experience in World War I, he had felt that he could be useful again. "However, there was no response. My activities in the Second World War were limited to frequent requests from Congressional committees."[106]

His willingness to serve did not mean that Hoover accepted the war or approval of American policy toward Japan. He wrote to Robert Taft on the day war was declared that "like the constant sticking of pins in rattlesnakes," administration policy had to produce the results that it did. Had Japan not been so driven, Hoover declared, she would have collapsed "from her own internal exhaustion," without the loss of a single American life. Even after Pearl Harbor, the ex-President hoped that the area of war would be limited. But on December 11, when Germany and Italy declared war on the United States, his hopes were dashed.

Excluded by FDR's continuing distrust and dislike, Hoover had to endure being denied a public role in World War II. Apparently his support was not considered necessary or even desirable, partly, at least, because of his unfortunate connections with isolationist groups and the "imaginary" Hoover circle. However, in 1944 he had a brief correspondence with the secretary of state over Finland.

Hoover's interest in Finland dated back to the post-First World War period, when he represented President Wilson in the talks on Finnish independence. Now, he argued, "brave little Finland" must be extricated from her war with Russia. Unless the freedom of Finland were finally achieved, he warned Hull, it would be a "sad shock" to the American people, who remembered her as the country that paid its war debts, and a boost to the isolationists. Hull replied to Hoover in a detailed and cautious letter that the efforts that the United States had made to mediate between Finland and the Soviet Union had been accepted by the Soviet Union but refused by Finland.[107] There could be no further correspondence on the subject. Other than the Finland matter, Hoover directed his thoughts to the peace that would follow the war he was not permitted a part in.

One American president was destroyed politically as a result of the long, unpopular, controversial, divisive Vietnam War, which might be called the President's War. Lyndon Johnson's retirement was so dominated by that aspect of his presidency that it had to be a quiet one. It was also a short one.

If frustration can kill, and some psychiatrists believe that it can, this unfortunate war probably helped to shorten Johnson's life. He was a sick man, but it is noteworthy that his death occurred just two days after Richard M. Nixon was inaugurated for the second time. Dr. Sylvia Spingarn of the Menninger Foundation said that this occasion "may well have stirred reminders of the power" Johnson once had and "reluctantly abdicated four years earlier."[108]

Johnson, who received weekly briefings from a Cabinet member, may have known that the final cease-fire agreement in Vietnam was about to be announced. It might have been too much for him. President Nixon's announcement of the war's end came the day after Lyndon Johnson died.

Apparently Johnson never changed his mind about the Vietnam War. In May 1970, in his first public address since leaving office, he told the Chicago Democrats at the one-hundred-dollar-a-plate dinner given for the Democratic party that he supported Nixon's position on the war. "I hope our President's voice will not be drowned out by other voices that may not have all the facts and do not have the responsibility for making these difficult and agonizing decisions," he said.[109]

Doris Kearns, a Harvard University professor who was close to Johnson during his retirement years and had worked with him on *The Vantage Point*, his presidential memoirs, quoted him on this point. "It was the worry of World War III that haunted me every night—even though I knew how long and drawn out the Vietnam War would be, even though I knew how unpopular it would be, even though I knew what it would do to my Great Society programs, still all the horror . . . was acceptable if it prevented the far worse horror of World War III," Johnson said. And "no more war" gave him "goosebumps," because he feared that the United States was entering the withdrawal phase. Then, he believed, first Asia and then Europe would be lost and the United States would be "an island all to ourselves." When that happened, he hated to have to depend on "the Galbraiths and the Harvard crowd to protect my property or lead me to the Burnet cave [a large cave near Austin]."[110]

Johnson attended a luncheon at the Washington *Post* in April 1970, during which he reviewed his entire career from the perspective of his place in history. He said that, after some time for reflection, he wondered if he had been right about the Vietnam War. Not for the reason one would think, he added hastily. He wondered if he had been aggressive enough. Perhaps he should have gone in all of the way or got out. Perhaps, most of all, he should have gone in to win and win quickly. He questioned his decision to deescalate. Whether these comments were sincere or a final act of bravado toward the staggeringly unpopular cause that had ruined him, no one can really know.

While Johnson was an ex-President, he was never allowed to forget the bitter hatred of many of his "fellow Americans." Any public appearance was accompanied by shouting, angry demonstrators who blamed him for the war. In May 1971, at the dedication of the massive Johnson Presidential Library at Austin, Texas, on the campus of the University of Texas, the demonstrators were there in great numbers.

Even while President Nixon spoke, accepting the ostentatious travertine marble building for the country, about two thousand demonstrators were being contained about a mile from the cere-monies. And the wind carried the faint but audible cries of "No more war," "Johnson's war," and other antiwar slogans and some obscenities. Neither the President nor his predecessor took public notice of the demonstration. But they were most certainly aware of it.

The leaders of the demonstration were sixty veterans of the Viet-nam War who said that their purpose was to return the medals and decorations that they had received. Blocked by the police, thirty-nine of the young men threw their awards over the double line of police. Twenty-four demonstrators were arrested.[111]

The other ex-Presidents treaded lightly on the subject of the Vietnam War. They made appropriate supportive statements when they were briefed by the President in office but offered nothing very much unasked. Eisenhower, for example, was rather unhappy with President Johnson's oft-repeated assertion that United States in-volvement in South Vietnam stemmed from the Eisenhower com-mitment of October 1954. At a news conference held on August 18, 1965, Ike insisted that "the communists must be stopped in Vietnam" but at the same time denied that he had ever given a commitment to the government of South Vietnam. There was no need for a military program in 1954, he said; foreign aid was all that was needed.

General John Eisenhower, in his memoirs, mentioned the allegation that the Vietnam situation started during his father's presidency. He noted, in response, that in 1961, when his father left office, the United States had 701 military advisors in Vietnam, an increase of ten from the 692 in 1958. The Boss, the younger Eisenhower said, wrote at the end of his own memoirs that he had left his successor a messy Laotian situation but did not even mention South Vietnam.

In November 1966, President Johnson visited Ike at Bethesda Naval Hospital, where he was recovering from surgery on his old ileitis scar. The President suggested that Eisenhower go on a goodwill mission to Asia and other parts of the world, Vietnam included. The following spring was mentioned as a likely time. These courteous presidential visits were, in part, bids for bipartisan support of the Johnson foreign policy. On this visit, Johnson presented the former President with a pair of gold cuff links carrying the presidential seal. "You are the only one along with Harry Truman who can legitimately wear these, but if you look closely, it doesn't say Democrat or Republican on them," Johnson said. Eisenhower answered that in times of crisis like this, "everybody in the United States has to support the President of the United States and that is what I am going to do."[112]

That spring, Eisenhower seriously considered the suggested world trip including Vietnam. We had never had a nastier war, he commented, but he did not feel strong enough to go. "I don't want to get sick in Thailand, for example," he said.[113]

President and Mrs. Johnson flew to Independence in the spring of 1968 to give former President Truman a personal report on the proposed Vietnam peace talks. After spending an hour talking to Truman, the President said, "I leave refreshed. I've asked him for advice and opinions. . . . He has been with me all the way, all the time." Truman was touched. "Lyndon," he said, "this is the nicest thing you could have done for me." If the President's purpose was public acceptance of the war because the elderly Democratic ex-President received him warmly, he was wasting his time.

At the Republican Convention of 1968, over closed-circuit television from his room at Walter Reed Hospital, Eisenhower took a tough stand on Vietnam. "It is one thing to call for a peaceful settlement of this struggle. It is quite another to call for retreat by America. The latter is the best way I know to stockpile tragedy for our children," he said. There was a round of applause on the convention floor, for the Eisenhower position was wide enough to embrace all shades of thought in the party.[114]

There was no consistent pattern in the wartime activities of the ex-presidents. Their responses to war ranged from official participation, such as George Washington's and Taft's, to frank criticism, as exemplified by the Civil War trio of Fillmore, Pierce, and Buchanan, and later by Grover Cleveland. John Tyler joined the country at war with the United States. Jefferson made modest suggestions which were not accepted, while John Adams cheered from the sidelines, but only as a private citizen.

The presidents in office also failed to act consistently. John Adams begged for Washington's help. FDR behaved as if Herbert Hoover did not exist, as Lincoln did in the case of his ex-presidents. Wilson suffered from Theodore Roosevelt's attacks. Though Johnson successfully enlisted the support of Eisenhower and Truman, it was not sufficient to save him.

Party differences were, undoubtedly, a factor in some of the ex-presidential responses. Most important, however, was the ex-president's ever-present prime consideration—his place in history, which rested on his activities in office. The ex-president has nothing to gain from wholehearted support in wartime and, under certain circumstances, might be taking a stand inconsistent with that which he took during his administration. This was particularly true of the Civil War group whose presidencies were spent avoiding civil war.

The ex-president as a gadfly was demonstrated in some instances. Teddy Roosevelt prodded Wilson to get into World War I and then blasted him for not moving fast enough during the war. Hoover criticized Roosevelt for assuming excessive wartime powers and "collectivizing" the country. Franklin Pierce thought Lincoln's usurpation of wartime powers dangerous and wrong. Perhaps the gadfly role is the ex-president's most important and useful one. War increases the power of the presidency, and it could be that only someone who has been in that high seat can know how great the temptation is to take too much.

Peacemaking

THE SUPPORT of former presidents in the difficult task of making peace would seem to be exceedingly useful to the administration in office. Experienced after years of contending with matters of diplomacy and foreign policy during his own term, the ex-president offers skill, some objectivity, and a sense of history. However, as will be seen, these elder statesmen have seldom been encouraged to participate on any level in the peacemaking process.

Even before the end of the War of 1812, Jefferson had clear ideas on what the peace treaty must contain. Essentially, of course, it must solve the problems that caused the war: it must revoke the Orders in Council and abolish impressment. In addition, England must pay reparations for the American ships they had taken and the thousands of American citizens they had impressed. The western frontier must be guaranteed against the English inciting the Indians to tomahawk and scalp the American settlers. In other words, there must be a return to the *status ante bellum*, but this time the terms of the treaty must be carried out, not ignored as after the American Revolution. Jefferson believed that the negotiations, which were dragging at Ghent, would come to a final solution as soon as the British heard "not of the Congress of Vienna but of Hartford."[1]

With his natural grace, Jefferson congratulated Madison on the peace and "more especially on the éclat with which the war was closed." The affair at New Orleans would, he felt, influence future relations with European nations and show them that the United

States would not take part in their wars. The former President did take the opportunity to restate his policy of disentanglement from European affairs. "We cannot too distinctly detach ourselves from the European system, which is essentially belligerent, nor too sedulously cultivate an American system, essentially peaceful," he wrote. President Madison knew very well that those were Jefferson's principles. He admired the ex-President and respected his opinions, in fact agreed with them, but he did not seek them. He had borne all the criticism for "Mr. Madison's War," and now if there was to be any praise for its outcome, he wanted it to accrue to him.

John Adams had kept in constant touch by letter with his son, John Quincy, a peace commissioner at Ghent. He wrote passionately and eloquently on the necessity of preserving the fisheries for New England no matter what the cost in giving up any of the other items. However, his fervor was unnecessary. He had indoctrinated his son so completely long ago that he was as avid as his father ever had been on the subject of the New England fisheries. It was already an Adams tradition, so any influence that ex-President Adams had on the Treaty of Ghent was purely a family affair.

It was not until the United States became involved in foreign wars that there was serious ex-presidential concern with peacemaking. By this time, the idea of the abolition of war went hand in hand with the making of the particular peace treaty. William Howard Taft, for one, was deeply interested in the judicial settlement of international disputes as an alternative to war. During his presidency, he had proposed arbitration treaties that were turned down by the Senate but aroused some public enthusiasm for peace. He probably went further than any president before or since when he said, in October 1911, "If arbitration is worth anything it is an instrumentality for avoiding war. But, it is asked, would you arbitrate a question of national honor? Of course I would."[2]

Less than six months after World War I started in Europe, the League to Enforce Peace was founded in New York. Its plan was closely akin to the Taft arbitration treaties, with a penalty clause attached. At first fearful that their plan for a league of the great powers of Europe and the United States and an international arbitral court might "turn out to be impracticable," Taft, finally, despite his doubts, introduced the project to the American people in a speech given in Philadelphia on June 17, 1915. He explained that he and his associates wanted "to quiet apprehensions expressed in Allied countries" that their purpose was to "halt the raging war." The league believed it was still necessary to use the threat of overwhelming force, Taft said, and the great league that was envisioned would make good the threat in order to frighten obstreperous nations into using rational and peaceful means to settle their disputes. What was proposed was a forced cooling-off period during which a judicial decision or a conciliatory compromise could be achieved. Such a time period would also give the men of peace in each nation "time to still the jingoes."[3] Taft agreed to be the president of the league, which in a year raised $350,000 for the promotion of its cause.

Theodore Roosevelt immediately came out against the League to Enforce Peace, mocking the "grand Peace Conference" that Taft, Nicholas Murray Butler, Andrew Carnegie, and the rest were holding "to insist that everything shall be arbitrated everywhere."[4] Taft, unperturbed, did not think that the attack would hurt the league. "The fact that I am at the head of the league is like a red flag to a bull to Theodore," he wrote.[5]

The two ex-Presidents remained at odds about the league. TR sniped at many of its pronouncements, calling its position on preparedness "a milk and water statement." The Colonel was annoyed, however, by an innuendo made by Henry Sturgis Drinker, president of Lehigh University, that Roosevelt opposed the league because he was not its head. In a long letter to Drinker, the ex-President clarified his position. If he were president, and the Mexicans murdered our troops and outraged our women, or the Germans, or any nation, murdered our people on the high seas, he would not bring the episodes to an outside tribunal "any more than I would appeal to some outside tribunal if, when I were walking with my wife, someone slapped her face."[6]

President Wilson's attitude toward Taft's league was baffling. He vacillated between approval and a desire to shy away from it. Here, certainly, was a case of rivalry. In his Fourteen Points, presented to Congress as the only possible program "for peace," the fourteenth point was the establishment of an association of nations to preserve their mutual political independence and territorial integrity. This plan was so sacred to Wilson that any other constituted a threat. Hence, Taft's many efforts to involve the President in the league never proved conclusive. Even when Wilson addressed the members of the league at a dinner given on May 21, 1916, instead

of presenting his beliefs as he had promised, he stuck to vague gener-
alizations. Taft, who presided at the dinner, was very disappointed.

Taft's further efforts to communicate with the White House on
the league met with polite rebuffs. In July 1916, the league's leaders
wanted Taft to go abroad to present their proposals to the leading
statesmen in Europe. The former President felt that the trip would
have little value unless it were endorsed by Wilson. The President
was not interested.

In January of the following year, Taft got the presidential endorsement he had been seeking, but it proved to be an embarrassment.
In his speech "Peace without Victory," Wilson included an approving statement about the League to Enforce Peace. "I don't
agree with much of what he says in respect to the kind of peace
that ought to be achieved . . . I don't think a just peace can be
attained without the victory of the allies," Taft commented. He did
admit, finally, that the "agitation for the league" was "a good thing."[7]

In 1917, a trip abroad for Taft was again suggested. This time the
purpose would be for the former President to go to England in order
to explain the war aims of the United States to the British people.
In December Taft visited the White House to discuss the proposed
trip. He would go, he told the President, only if he had an official
invitation from the British government and Wilson's approval. Once
again Wilson withheld his support.

British and American policy differed, the President explained;
the secret treaty between England and Italy proved that. The United
States had pure motives in contrast to Britain's self-seeking ones.
Furthermore, a visit by Taft or any other important American would
alienate the Irish and other anti-British factions in the country and
also make France jealous. To Taft's statement that Walter Hines
Page, the American ambassador to Great Britain, favored his visit,
Wilson replied, "Page is really an Englishman," so his opinion
must be discounted. "I think you ought not to go and the same applies
to the other members of the party," Wilson said decisively.

When Wilson heard that the League to Enforce Peace had plans
for a convention to be held in Philadelphia in May 1918, he made
an unannounced visit to Bainbridge Colby, a member of the Shipping
Board who later became his secretary of state. He told Colby how
alarmed he was about the Philadelphia meeting, and Colby arranged
to see Taft about it as soon as possible.

Taft recorded the long interview he had with Colby, during which he tried to reassure him that the convention's object was not to discuss a league, as Wilson feared, but to support the government in its effort to defeat Germany, "on the ground that no League to Enforce Peace could be useful until we had defeated Germany."[8] Both men decided that it would be best for Taft to see Wilson personally.

Accompanied by President A. Lawrence Lowell of Harvard, Taft met with the President on March 28. During the discussion it appeared to the two men that Wilson had backed down again on the use of force to ensure the preservation of a nation's integrity and territory. He also seemed to be against a definite, detailed program for a league, because the smaller nations had to be protected. Taft found the session discouraging. The President suggested that a convention such as they proposed might make later negotiations for peace difficult for him. He really seemed to take back and give up everything he had said about the league in the past. Finally, after much circuitous talk, Wilson allowed that he did not object to the convention since it was really a win-the-war convention.[9]

Somewhat later, there was another meeting at the White House which Taft, Lowell, and Elihu Root attended. Wilson was still in a negative mood about the league. The Senate would never agree to force by direction of a majority of nations, he declared, quite accurately as it later turned out. But Taft put him down as a "weathercock" who would eventually come round to their view when he realized that the American people wanted "an organized force of the nations."[10]

Wilson told an amusing anecdote about this last visit to pressure him into approval of their league that Taft and his associates staged. "I did not care to be caught," he said, "and while they were all talking there was a noise of something falling. It was Taft's portrait."[11]

Once the Armistice was signed, Taft became very active in support of the peace, which to him as to Wilson meant the league. At first he was against the President's "spectacular" decision to go to Paris and negotiate the treaty himself, but later he reassessed his reaction. It might "bring home to him the demand of the common people of England, France and Italy that we have a League of Nations, and perhaps make him more reasonable," he said. He had advised the President to consult the foreign affairs committees of both houses of Congress on the treaty and warned him that if he did not, he must expect the Senate to scrutinize what he presented to them very closely. Wilson, as was to be expected, ignored his advice and dealt only with his partisan advisors.[12]

Taft would have been an excellent choice for Wilson's peace team. Colonel House had recommended him, as had Attorney General Gregory, but Wilson was not interested in the suggestion. He wanted around him only those men who would be completely subservient to his ideas, and surely not an ex-President who had almost as much of an aura of prestige enveloping him as he himself had. Furthermore, Wilson was thin-skinned, an affliction rather uncommon in a political man, and had neither forgotten nor forgiven Taft's attacks on him during the 1912 campaign. Colonel House's serious and practical idea that former President Taft should prepare the covenant of the league, "a task for which he is eminently fit and to which his heart would have responded in joyous enthusiasm," irritated Woodrow Wilson.[13] Consequently, Taft stayed home, which was very helpful to Wilson, for he was a strong, tireless advocate of the league through all its darkest hours.

In December 1918, Taft was given credit for shifting the Republican senators away from their proposed position that the league be separated from the rest of the treaty. Owing to his efforts, Wilson was not embarrassed by total rejection on the home front for his favorite part of the treaty on his first trip to Europe. Taft told his own party members that if they united against the league, they would be playing into the hands of Wilson and the Democratic party in 1920.[14]

Though Taft supported the League of Nations, he deplored Wilson and his methods, particularly his unstatesmanlike attack on the Republican party. Privately, Taft railed against both Wilson and his chief opponent, Henry Cabot Lodge. Their motives, he said, were "to exalt their personal prestige and the saving of their ugly faces above the welfare of the country and the world."[15] As Taft told J. G. Butler, "I don't like Wilson any better than you do, but I think I can rise above my personal attitude . . . in order to help along the world and the country." To prove his words, Taft appeared at the Metropolitan Opera House in March 1919 on the same platform as Wilson and stated defiantly that, despite the senatorial round robin proposed by Lodge and Connecticut's Frank B. Brandegee to oppose further consideration of the league until after the peace settlement, it would not be possible "to dissect the covenant from the treaty without destroying the whole vital structure."[16]

Taft, who saw the Senate position hardening after the President returned to Europe, and sincerely believed in intelligent compromise, wrote to Wilson suggesting certain modifications in the covenant. Among them were: reservation of the Monroe Doctrine; a fixed term for the league; an addition to Article XV which would provide that when the Executive Council or the body of delegates found a difference growing out of an exclusively domestic policy, it would recommend no settlement. Wilson heeded the suggestions, and Taft continued to stump around the country for the cause because he believed the people wanted the league.

Upon Wilson's return from Versailles, the Senate split into three factions. The Democratic supporters were headed by minority leader Gilbert M. Hitchcock of Nebraska. The Moderates were led by Henry Cabot Lodge, chairman of the Foreign Relations Committee, who was willing to accept the league with reservations that would ensure the protection of American sovereignty. The third group, known as "the irreconcilables," had among its members William E. Borah, Robert La Follette, and Hiram Johnson. Their intention was never to cease their opposition until the league was defeated.

Wilson conferred with the Foreign Relations Committee in August and was willing to go along with the reservations based on interpretation but refused to accept any changes that would require returning the covenant to the other members of the peace commission for reconsideration. Disregarding Wilson's feelings on the subject, the irreconcilables, having a majority on the Senate committee, came up with forty-five amendments and four reservations. Disappointed and furious, Wilson decided to carry his mission to the people. On September 4, he started his trip through the West; it covered 9,500 miles, during which the President made thirty-seven speeches in twenty-nine cities.

Wilson's angry tour discouraged and disgusted Taft. He was particularly critical of the President's style of employing "contemptuous phrases" against his opponents and stubbornly declaring undying opposition to all of the proposed reservations. "Schoolmaster that he is," Taft fumed, he was playing straight into the hands of his enemies. And when the exhausted, distraught chief executive collapsed in Pueblo, Colorado, and had to be brought back to Wash-

ington, where he had a stroke, Taft was not surprised. He had
trusted no one, had insisted on hogging all the authority and had
"broken himself down," Taft wrote to a friend.

In her memoir, *Crowded Hours*, Alice Roosevelt Longworth gives
an excellent account of the nervous, irritable, hostile atmosphere that
pervaded Washington during this time. A violent opponent of the
league, she conveys the bitterness and the sense of determination displayed by both sides and, most poignantly, the inevitable friction
between friends and foes of the League of Nations. Taft was not
immune to the edgy ambiance. He was angry at Kellogg for supporting Hiram Johnson and called Root a Machiavelli. His greatest
anger, understandably, was saved for Wilson, who on November 18
wrote a letter to his supporters urging them to turn down the Lodge
resolutions of ratification. It was unfortunate, Taft observed, because
even with the Massachusetts senator's reservations, the league was
still intact. Had the Democrats supported the resolutions, the treaty
and the league with it would have passed, eighty-one votes to thirteen.
Instead, the Treaty of Versailles, including in it the League of Nations,
was defeated by the American Senate thirty-eight to fifty-three.
Taft called Wilson "the greatest obstructionist in Washington. He
desires to destroy all if he cannot get all. "

Upon their return to Washington for the winter session, the Senate
agreed to resubmit the treaty to the Foreign Affairs Committee. Taft,
Herbert Hoover, Bryan, and others begged Wilson to consider the
reservations. "The Anglo-Saxon idea of government is founded on
the principle of compromise. No public official can have his own
way all the time," Taft said. But all efforts were wasted. Wilson
would not budge, and on March 19 the treaty was definitively defeated.[17]

The Democratic platform in 1920 and the candidate, James M. Cox,
unequivocally supported the league. The Republicans were divided.
Taft tried to guide the Republican candidate, Warren G. Harding,
toward the league, but Harding played the game of politics with both
the Taft leaguers and the irreconcilables. However, on August 28
he issued a statement that seemed to favor the league. He said: "Such
an association I favor with all my heart, and I would make no fine
distinction as to whom credit is due. One need not care what it is
called. Let it be an association, a society or a league, or what not.
Our concern is solely with the substance not the form thereof."[18]
This gave impetus to the Taft Committee statement, signed on

October 14, 1920, by thirty-seven leading Republicans, calling for ratification with mild reservations. In addition to former President Taft, four former Cabinet officers and fourteen presidents of colleges and universities signed it. However, Harding vacillated on the subject during the campaign and, once he was President, talked of not wishing to direct the destinies of the world. He sensed that the American people were tired of the war, the peace squabbles, the war debt, the taxes, and European grumblings about the United States' refusal to cancel the war debt. Harding's promise of a "return to normalcy" was much more appealing than reminders of international obligations. Finally, Harding gave the league its death blow in an address to Congress on April 12, 1921. "It is only fair to say to the world in general, and to our associates in war in particular, that the League covenant can have no sanction by us," he said. The recent election, he believed, had proved that this was what the American people wanted. Taft had deceived himself into thinking that Harding would have endorsed, at the least, "a pasteurized League."[19]

Theodore Roosevelt's flirtation with the League of Nations was erratic, his interest in the peace treaty much more keen. As the war drew to a close, he was anxious about the Republican stand on the armistice. In his newspaper articles, he expressed his fear that Wilson was soft on Germany and was not going to demand unconditional surrender. "Let us dictate peace by the hammering of guns not chat about peace to the accompaniment of the clicking of typewriters," he wrote. For this reason he firmly endorsed the election of a Republican Congress in 1918, which would surely demand unconditional surrender, plus Senate participation in the making of the treaty. Germanism and probolshevism had been dealt a blow, he wrote in the *Star*; now it was most important that the United States adopt a universal military training system modeled on the Swiss.[20]

Roosevelt believed that he had been a "substantial factor" in preventing Wilson, during the final month of the war, from achieving a negotiated peace by double-crossing the Allies. He wrote to Arthur Hamilton Lee from Roosevelt Hospital, where he was a patient because all his ills of the previous winter had multiplied, that had Wilson followed his own path untrammeled, "it would have put him on a pinnacle of glory in the sight of every sinister pro-German and every vapid and fatuous doctrinaire sentimentalist throughout the world." Lee noted in the margin of the letter that it was the only time that he had known TR to speak of his own services. However, he had written that letter on a very trying day. The Bull Moose was very ill and it was Quentin's birthday.[21]

The League of Nations, Wilson's *raison d'être*, was a subject that was not entirely congenial to Roosevelt but one that he knew he had to deal with. He thought it "a pompous plan" akin to the Holy Alliance's plan for perpetual peace, with Wilson playing the role of Czar Alexander. Probably, also, Taft's enthusiasm for the project made it even less attractive.

Roosevelt's final article, written on January 3, 1919, the Friday before his death, was on the League of Nations. Since the league was so vital an issue for the peace conference, the *Star* asked him to discuss the possibilities of a League of Nations as a preventive to war. He agreed to write the article but told the *Star*'s editor that he wanted to follow it with an editorial "on what I regard as infinitely more important, namely our business to prepare for our own self-defense." He died before he could write the second piece.

The problem, as TR saw it, was that, for the moment, the people were not getting a clear idea of what was happening at the peace talks; "the point as to which we are foggy is the League of Nations." We all, he said, desire such a league but we want to be sure "that it will help and not hinder the cause of world peace and justice." Mr. Wilson's talk about the league was "in the stage of rhetoric," just like his Fourteen Points, so that all talk of adopting them as a basis for a peace or a league was "nonsense, and if the talker is intelligent, it is insincere nonsense to boot." The Colonel pointed out that the President did not make clear whether he intended to admit Germany or Russia, Turkey, China, or Mexico, and whether he would offer them full equality. Therefore, TR suggested, it might be better to start with the one league already in existence, the League of the Allies. First, he said, real justice should be done at the peace table for those who fought through the great war. After this was accomplished, then the privileges of the league could be extended, as rapidly as the conduct of these other countries warranted it.

The last paragraph of the Roosevelt editorial plays on all the doubts and fears of the league opponents. "We do not intend to take a position of an international Meddlesome Matty," he warns. "We do not wish to undertake the responsibility of sending our gallant young men to die in obscure fights in the Balkans or in

Central Europe, or in a war we do not approve of." Then he invokes the American sacred cow, the Monroe Doctrine. The American people do not want to give up the Monroe Doctrine. "Let civilized Europe and Asia introduce some kind of police system in the weak and disorderly countries at their thresholds," the former President advises.[22] TR's final editorial proves that he was temperamentally opposed to the idea of any world peace organization despite some protestations to the contrary. Had he been the Republican candidate for the presidency in 1920, as many expected, Taft would have found him even more difficult to deal with on the subject of the League of Nations than vacillating, "back to normalcy" Warren G. Harding.

Unable to proceed with his work of providing food for the over-run countries of Europe and spurned by Franklin Roosevelt, Hoover concentrated on the problem of peace. Having seen the Wilsonian promise of the war to end all wars prove, in twenty years, to be a tragic irony, he was convinced that a new plan for a lasting peace was overdue. In 1943, in collaboration with Hugh Gibson, Hoover published *The Problems of a Lasting Peace*. One of its major proposals was to eliminate the armistice period and to substitute "a quick provisional peace" with a cooling-off period during which there could be the settlement of economic reforms and develpment of machinery for an ideal, lasting peace. The cooling-off period would avoid "a rush arrangement by the present regime" which might do irreparable injury, Hoover told Robert Taft. "By agreement, all of the United Nations and as many neutrals as would want to join would *appoint* the leading powers as 'Trustees' to conduct the world during the transition meeting," the former President explained. He had hopes that the plan would be adopted by the Republican party as part of their foreign policy platform in 1944. The press was extraordinarily enthusiastic about it, except for the Communists and fellow travelers, Hoover maintained, and the scheme could be the basis for national unity.[23]

When the war started to draw to a close and victory could be predicted in the foreseeable future, Hoover reflected seriously on his world peace plans. He was not completely certain that the United Nations was the answer, but he did attempt to convince his stubbornly isolationist friend Alfred Landon that it was worth consideration. The Atlantic Charter, Dumbarton Oaks, Yalta—"all reiterate certain ideals and principles which, if carried out in good faith comprise a foundation" for effective machinery to preserve peace. "The odds are they will not be carried out in good faith" and the promise would come to nothing. However, he observed, we would emerge from the war with many nations in bondage. If Dumbarton Oaks served as a court of appeal, they might have a chance. To take the position of withdrawing from the mess would be futile, because it would not have the support of the American people. Therefore, it was necessary to support the broad purposes of Dumbarton Oaks, try to amend its weaknesses, and insist that its ideals be lived up to. "I am for helping design an experiment. If it has the elements of success, to support it; if it is hopeless, then to damn it. And I want to see its success."[24]

About a month after Harry Truman became President of the United States, former President Hoover received a telegram from him. "If you should be in Washington, I would be most happy to talk over the European food situation with you," it said. "Also it would be a pleasure to me to become acquainted with you." Thus began a new role for Herbert Hoover. His popularity curve rose steadily, starting with his first assignment from President Truman and then continuing with succeeding Presidents until the much-reviled depression President became a respected elder statesman.

At the meeting between Truman and Hoover, which took place on May 28, 1945, the President asked the ex-President's advice on several subjects, including the food problem and the Japanese war. In a memo to himself summarizing the fifty-five-minute interview, Hoover expressed cynicism about Truman's motivation in sending for him but nonetheless sent him the answers that he had requested. Hoover expressed his position on food for Europe carefully. The European people had received less than 100,000 tons per month from the army and other American sources since liberation and that was not enough to last until August, the next harvest. Since there was no food administration that had command of American food, Hoover proposed that the army take over the problem in northwestern Europe and Italy. He recommended that a European economic council be set up and added his views on the domestic food situation. As to Japan, Hoover tried to convince Truman that there should be a separate peace with that country. He also favored assuring Japan that the peace settlement would allow them to keep their emperor. His fears of Soviet aggression were also conveyed. At the end of the meeting, Truman had asked that he be sent a memorandum covering the topics discussed during the meeting. Hoover acceded but recorded for himself the following: "My conclusions were that he was simply endeavoring to establish a feeling of good will in the country, that nothing more would come of it so far as I or my views were concerned."[25] He was wrong. Truman acted on the Hoover proposals by asking him to head a food relief program for Western Europe. He and the President were in agreement that the part of Eastern Europe occupied by the Russians would be excluded. And Truman ignored the State Department's proposal that he should call a conference in Washington of all the nations involved.

Hoover, seventy-one years old, accepted the mission, feeling that his World War I service would make him very acceptable to all the countries. He was able to reassemble several of the men who had served with him in the first famine relief program.

In a large C-54, humorously named the "Faithful Cow," with apologies to FDR's "Sacred Cow," the mission visited thirty-eight countries in Europe, Asia, and Latin America, covering a total of 50,711 miles. From Egypt, Hoover broadcasted a survey of the results of the mission in order to give the American people an idea of the world's food needs. He stressed that the saving of human lives is more than an economic necessity, it is the only path to world stability. It "marks the return of the lamp of compassion to the world," he said.[26]

Hoover had a somewhat different message for the President's eyes. "I would like you to know, confidentially, for yourself," he wrote, "that there is active propaganda to place any responsibility for any failure in food supplies on the United States." Before the visit of the mission, there had been no recognition of the effort of the United States. On the contrary, the supplies had been "brazenly represented" as coming from other countries.[27]

In June 1946, when Hoover saw Truman in Washington, he was able to persuade him to release the Argentine surplus and supply 2,762,000 tons of American exportable grain. He explained that there would be millions of people who would be hungry until the next harvest but no mass starvation except in inaccessible parts of China.

Unfortunately, bad harvests made food shortages a continuing problem and Hoover was recalled to continue his work in January 1947. This time he was asked to go to Germany and Austria, where the shortage was particularly serious. He was hesitant about accepting because he did not approve of American economic and political policies in those countries. He would accept, he wrote to Secretary of War Robert Patterson, if the mission's purpose were broadened. President Truman then wrote to Hoover asking that he go for food purposes alone. Hoover replied that he wished to be of service and would go, but he felt it would be a great shock to the American people to find that, for a second year, the taxpayer would be asked to "expend huge sums to provide food for the enemy peoples." He wanted the mission to inquire into immediate steps for increasing Germany's exports and her ability to be self-supporting. "Without some such inclusive report, the Congress and the taxpayer are left without hope," he said. Apparently Truman was convinced. He answered that the ex-President should undertake this economic mission in regard to food and its collateral problems. "It is hoped that methods can be devised which will release some of the burdens on the American taxpayer," the President wrote.[28]

The Hoover mission's DC-4 left for Germany on a bitter cold February day. Conferences were held in public buildings that were unheated because of the coal shortage, and seventy-five-year-old Herbert Hoover sat in freezing offices wearing his heavy winter coat and sometimes wrapped in blankets as well. He suffered a series of severe colds that finally resulted in permanent injury. Forced to fly in unpressurized planes while suffering from head colds, when his plane came down in Newfoundland, descending rapidly, Hoover's eardrum ruptured. Though the ex-President's hearing was permanently impaired, he always referred to it as the decoration he won on the 1947 German mission.

Hoover's report to Truman upon his return from Germany reiterated his earlier recommendations. German industry must be revived to relieve American and British taxpayers from the burden of preventing starvation there. "These problems also involve economic stability and peace in Europe," he warned.[29] A hungry Germany, he implied, might result in a communist Germany.

General Lucius D. Clay, the United States military governor in Germany, wrote to Hoover in April thanking him for his work. The severe winter had destroyed much of the fall planting, so were it not for the Hoover Report to the War Department, there would be disaster in the months ahead. He also credited the former President with improving the American people's attitude toward the German problem. "I believe we shall pull through with an appreciative economic revival and without substantial loss to communist penetration or influence," he wrote. For Hoover, the last line was surely the most gratifying. "No one else could have accomplished for us what you did," Clay wrote.[30]

Consistent with his point of view, Hoover opposed the Morgenthau plan to limit industry in Germany. He called it "a program of vengeance," which would cause suffering, retard European recovery, and cost the American taxpayer money. Germany and Japan must be fed "because of the ideologic front." Japan was the "real ideologic dam" against communism in Asia, Hoover told George Marshall, just as Germany was in Europe. Theirs must be the priority for food shipments, for political reasons and because the food levels in Germany and Japan were lower than anywhere else in the world.[31]

Germany was very grateful to Hoover. When Chancellor Konrad Adenauer came to New York City in 1953, his first act was to visit the ex-President at the Waldorf Towers and invite him to visit Germany at the government's expense. With the approval of President Eisenhower and Secretary of State Dulles, Hoover went, transported in the *Columbine*, the President's plane. For six days, he was fêted and honored, but the gesture that pleased him the most was having a technical school named after him, the Herbert Hoover Schule, located in the working-class section of Berlin.

Hoover was at his best when he was engaged in humanitarian efforts. Otherwise, he continued to be narrowly insular. He was against American globalism and, to his credit, American imperialism, and clung to the hope that the United States would become almost self-sufficient economically and politically independent. Hence defense should be hemispheric rather than a cordon of American bases circling the globe. The dropping of the atomic bomb struck Hoover as unnecessary. If his advice had been taken—to abandon unconditional surrender, preserve the sanctity of the Japanese emperor, and seek a separate peace with Japan—that country would have given up the war six months to a year before V-J Day. "The use of the atomic bomb, with its indiscriminate killing of women and children, revolts me," he wrote to a friend. The Potsdam Agreement was also unnecessary, Hoover told the historian Charles Beard, whom he asked to observe secrecy on these opinions "for obvious reasons" until he was dead or released them himself.[32]

Except for his work in food relief, any influence that Hoover may have had on keeping the peace was through powerful friends.

Not a cold warrior, although a foe of communism, he was out of step once more with the current administrations. Generally speaking, Hoover preferred that we stay at home.

The Vietnam War, undeclared and painfully controversial, was not a likely occasion for ex-presidential peacemaking. Johnson tried briefly to interest Eisenhower in making a trip to the troubled spot, but Ike was too ill to undertake it. By the time Nixon was ready to end the war, as he had promised to do four years earlier during his presidential campaign, he was certainly not interested in sharing any resultant popularity with an ex-president.

The expertise in handling foreign affairs that a former president developed in office, his connections with statesmen abroad, the mystical aura of the American presidency that still hangs over him—all are threatening assets to the incumbent. An ex-president's success as a peacemaker could promote him as a candidate, help his protégés, or, if he is of a different political persuasion than the President, boost his party. Therefore, his use may seem too risky, as Wilson demonstrated in the case of Taft and Roosevelt in the case of Hoover. The exceptional value of a former president in this capacity destroys the probability of his employment.

Running Again

BEFORE HE BECAME INVOLVED in the quest for renomination by the Republican party in 1912, Theodore Roosevelt said: "I have had all the honor that any man can have from holding the office of President. From every personal standpoint there is nothing for me to gain either in running for the office or in holding the office once more, and there is very much to lose." Yet, given the opportunity, he and several other former presidents competed again for the highest office in the land. One achieved it.

Obviously, then, not all the ex-presidents who retired with protestations of relief at being rid of the yoke of office were content to settle into dignified obscurity. One who was not was Martin Van Buren; he chafed under the stigma of having been a one-term president and was disgruntled by his friendless exile at Lindenwald. After all, he reminded himself, was he not still the great Jackson's heir?

The death of Van Buren's successor, William Henry Harrison, shortly after his inauguration and the accession to the presidency of "unreliable John Tyler" inspired a barrage of letters addressed to the former President. "You are *the* man upon whom the *true* Democracy of the country can and will unite," wrote one well-wisher. Another asked that he give his "early consent" so that his friends could start to advance his cause. Consequently, Van Buren put out feelers to the press, and when they were misinterpreted by some adherents as saying that he did not want to be considered in 1844, he hastened to enlighten them. "I shall most assuredly never take a single step with a

view to be made a candidate," he asserted, but he would not decline
"the performance of any public duty." The news that a caucus of
the Democratic members of both houses of the Indiana legislature
along with Democrats from all over the state had decided that he
"*alone* should be the candidate of the democratic party for the first
office in their gift" pleased him exceedingly.[1] Not one to remain
idle when opportunity beckoned, the Red Fox arranged a pilgrimage
to visit his dying mentor at the Hermitage. The itinerary provided
time for much more than a whirlwind visit to the ailing General
Jackson's bedside.

In the manner of hopeful politicians, the ex-President extended a
month-long trip into a half-year campaign. He went from Kinderhook, New York, to Nashville, Tennessee, by way of the East Coast,
the West, and the South. Not an important city or a significant
colleague was missed along the way. The fiction that Van Buren's
lengthy tour was completely apolitical was carefully preserved. From
New Orleans, John Slidell wrote that the former President's friends
wanted to make some public demonstrations but would desist if it
would be "indiscreet to do so." A Natchez, Mississippi, newspaper
commented that Van Buren had no other object but to see the vast
resources of the South and West and visit "the patriot chief" at the
Hermitage. "Thousands look to this reunion with great interest," the
Daily Free Trader said.[2]

The few days that Van Buren spent with ex-President Jackson
proved to be less important than his response to a letter from Henry
Clay inviting him to Ashland. Van Buren went right from the
Hermitage to confer with one of Jackson's pet hates, a decision he
could not have arrived at casually. Jackson had just recently told
Van Buren that he was happy that Clay, "the old coon," was "really
and substantially dead, skinned and buried," for the General had
never forgiven him for his role in assuring the victory of John Quincy
Adams in the election of 1824.[3]

There is no tangible evidence to prove that Clay's hospitality and
Van Buren's acceptance of it was a cover for a bargain. But subsequent events strongly suggest that the two men agreed at that time
to avoid the question of the annexation of Texas in the next presidential contest. It was a controversial issue that both feared because
President Tyler favored it and it was his only claim to popularity.

Van Buren's triumphant tour was a prelude to encouraging developments in the November elections. The pro-Van Buren wing of

the Democratic party succeeded in New York State and in the United States Congress. However, almost immediately there was a setback when the Van Burenites tried to schedule an early convention for the fourth Monday in November 1843, in order to take advantage of their favorite's boom. Calhoun and other Democratic hopefuls united to balk the effort and succeeded in postponing it until May 1844. Undaunted, Van Buren turned his attention to working out his campaign strategy. He designated Benjamin Butler as his floor leader and James K. Polk, "Young Hickory," for his vice-president. The slogan that was chosen had an appropriate ring: "The sober second thought of the people."

As time passed, the Van Buren candidacy gained in strength. Letters from New Jersey, Pennsylvania, and Washington indicated strong backing. In the Virginia legislature, the former President surpassed Calhoun, and the state party was even more enthusiastic about him. Each month another state joined the bandwagon—Alabama in December, Louisiana in January. To make assurance doubly sure, Benjamin Park asked Silas Wright to prepare a biography of Van Buren to compete with the new life of Calhoun that was being published by Harper Brothers.[4]

At the beginning of 1844, there seemed to be little doubt that a Van Buren candidacy would be "the settled *doom* of the party," as Crittenden saw it. But the subject of Texas annexation that Van Buren thought safely buried refused to stay underground even with Clay's cooperation. The two rivals may have agreed to ignore Texas, but the advocates of annexation were prepared to use Old Hickory to aid their cause. Andrew Jackson, a close friend of Texas President Sam Houston and an ardent advocate of Texas annexation, was deliberately brought into the controversy by W. D. Miller, secretary of the Texas commissioners. He wrote to Jackson from Washington that Clay's supporters in the Senate wanted to postpone any definite action on the treaty to annex Texas but that Van Buren's friends were "generally the open and strenuous and liberal advocates of annexation." He did not know what course Van Buren would decide on, because advocating annexation would help him in the South but probably hurt him in the North. Therefore, he concluded accurately, both rivals for the presidency feared approaching the question and would try to postpone it.

Since Miller's purpose was to get the treaty passed, he did not hesitate to utilize any argument he could to ensure Jackson's support.

Knowing the General's fanatic hatred for England, he wrote: "If she [Texas] be spurned from the threshold of the mother, she may look to a better reception from the grandmother." A defensive and offensive alliance with Great Britain might be the final result and would be "readily formed, you need not entertain a doubt," he warned.[5] As Jackson was being lined up against Van Buren by the Texas annexationists, there were other problems.

Even before Van Buren published his fatal Texas letter, there were traitors in the Democratic ranks. Amos Kendall wrote that many who professed to be friends were trying to prevent his nomination at the Baltimore convention, and Van Buren's son, Smith, reported a general alarm among the Van Buren friends over intrigues in Washington. One of the House members from Indiana explained to the ex-President that he could not carry his state. "You are safe enough with men fresh from the people," Amos Kendall concluded; "all you have to fear is from the politicians."[6]

The simultaneous publication of letters by Henry Clay and Van Buren in the *Globe* and the *National Intelligencer*, respectively, stating that the annexation of Texas would result in war with Mexico and, perhaps, also with a European country, destroyed Van Buren's preconvention lead immediately. Consternation reigned among the former President's Western and Southern supporters. Thomas Ritchie, writing from Richmond, told Van Buren frankly, "We cannot carry Virginia for you—we have lost."[7] Van Buren had handed the opposition the weapon with which to defeat him.

No one was more "mortified" by the letter than General Jackson, who was "very feeble" but "excited by the subject." He asserted, "I am for the annexation regardless of all consequences." In many letters he declared his friendship and esteem for Van Buren and insisted that he "was not a deserter from V.B.," but the name of Polk started to creep into his correspondence and so did references to Van Buren's inevitable defeat.[8]

Upset by this challenge to his loyalty, the old general felt impelled to state his position publicly in a letter to the editor of the Nashville *Union*. He suggested that when the Red Fox was preparing his Texas letter, he did not know of the probability of interference by a foreign power if annexation did not occur. To a friend, he wrote, "I have often wished that I had been at my friend Van Buren's elbow when closing his letter."[9] The only hope, he added, was to support Polk for vice-president.

Now the opposition to Van Buren's candidacy gathered momentum fast. Not only was the Texas letter an issue, but there was also some fear that Van Buren's election would start the succession again and James Barbour would be next in line. By May 1844, John Rives reported that four-fifths of Congress was against the former President. Van Buren told Ben Butler that if the convention went against him, he favored Silas Wright for the candidate.[10]

As soon as the Baltimore Convention adopted the rule that the party nominee must have the support of two-thirds of the convention, Van Buren's defeat was inevitable. On the first ballot he got more than the majority but thirty-two votes less than he needed. By the fifth ballot, Lewis Cass was ahead. Finally James Polk, the dark horse, was unanimously elected. As soon as Polk was nominated, Butler withdrew Van Buren's name and made a powerful speech. "The dark sky of yesterday has been succeeded by the brightest day democracy has witnessed since your election," Andrew Donelson wrote to Jackson about the nomination of "Young Hickory."[11]

Van Buren had been the victim of his own maneuvering, because the two-thirds rule had been engineered by him in 1836 to assure his election. However, had he won the nomination, Texas would have posed a critical problem for him. He had opposed annexation while he was President and was well aware that the real issue behind the controversy was that the addition of Texas to the United States meant the expansion of slave territory. In the next election Van Buren's position would become clearer. In the meantime, the Van Burenites had gone down to defeat with him. His cohorts now expected him to resume his "honorable retirement," carrying with him only their "affection." The victorious Polk gave his version of Van Buren's epitaph to George Bancroft: "[His] magnanimous and zealous support of the nomination . . . places me under lasting obligation to him."[12]

Polk was elected, but in two years' time, Van Buren was receiving feelers about the 1848 election. Polk would not be reelected, a Virginian wrote, "too much distrust of him in New York." It would be "a late sense of justice" to recall "the recluse of Lindenwald." Van Buren was not interested. When the New York Democrats met in May 1848, the ex-President refused the use of his name for nomination.[13]

Van Buren's role in the election of 1848 came about through a series of complicated and unexpected developments. Though the

South had led the movement against him in the previous election because of his position on the annexation of Texas, for most of his political life Jackson's successor had been known as a pro-Southern Northerner. Van Buren's record on antislavery was poor. As Vice-President, he had broken a tie on a bill that prohibited the carrying of abolition literature in the mail—by supporting it. He had opposed abolition for the District of Columbia and had supported the "gag rule," which forbade the reading of abolition petitions to Congress. Yet, ironically, Van Buren found his chance for release from Linden-waldian exile via the antislavery route.

The Van Burenite faction of the New York democracy, which favored the Wilmot Proviso, was called the "barnburners" after the fabled Dutchmen who burned down their barns to get rid of the rats. Allegorically speaking, the barn represented the Union and the rats, slavery. The opposing faction, the "hunkers," was called that because it "hunkered" for the federal spoils of office. By a strange turn-about, Martin Van Buren was now the sponsor of the group that spurned the Jacksonian spoils system and Jeffersonian states' rights. When, how, or if the "little magician" became a serious ideological opponent of slavery must be left to conjecture.

The Barnburners accepted the Van Burens, the former President and his son, "Prince John," as their standard-bearers. After the Barn-burners walked out of the Democratic state convention held at Syracuse because their resolution against the extension of slavery was turned down, they held a hasty convention of their own at the Herkimer railroad station. John Van Buren, the erratic, brilliant son of the ex-President, delivered a memorable address and then went home to stir up his father.

By spring, Van Buren was ready to take a position favoring the Free Soil cause. Armed with his statement and some political advice, the Barnburner delegation, consisting of Churchill C. Cambreleng, Samuel J. Tilden, and Preston King, went to the Democratic national convention in Baltimore but was forced to withdraw when the rival Hunker delegation was seated by the convention. Eventually the Democrats nominated Lewis Cass, who was opposed to the Wilmot Proviso.

Enthusiastic public support for the defecting Barnburners encouraged them to plan for a convention in Utica on June 22. There the trio of John Van Buren, Benjamin Butler, and Preston King made splendid speeches and, despite a letter asking that he not be considered for the nomination, led the others to choose ex-President Van Buren by acclamation. Prince John wrote to his father: "I do not see anything in the Constitution which enables you to forbid our voting for you."[14] Actually, Van Buren was completely rejuvenated by the nomination and presided happily over a gala Fourth of July dinner at Lindenwald to which his son had invited everyone.

Charles Francis Adams, a leader of the "Conscience Whigs" who were now alienated from the Whig party because of their antislavery conviction, tried to pin down the Red Fox as to his views on abolition. "You present in your position assumed in 1844 and again in this year, by your able exposition of the free territory question, perhaps the best point of union in this country," Adams wrote. Then he asked Van Buren outright to state his position on the abolition of slavery in the District of Columbia. The reply was a perfect Van Burenism, confused and confusing.[15]

The Massachusetts Free-Soilers would have to be content with Van Buren's style or find another candidate. Several, including Daniel Webster, were considered and rejected before the name of Judge John McLean was proposed and accepted. Van Buren, it was predicted, would do poorly in Massachuetts whereas McLean could be expected to sweep the state.

The Buffalo Free Soil convention, held on August 9, was dominated by New York, Ohio, and Massachusetts but was attended by 465 delegates from eighteen states, including the three slave states of Maryland, Delaware, and Virginia. The candidates were not present, but their managers were actively working for them. The Democrats had Benjamin Butler and Preston King, the Whigs had Joshua Giddings and Charles Francis Adams, while the Liberty party was headed by Salmon P. Chase and Joshua Leavitt. In order to eliminate division over minor matters, the platform committee emphasized the convention's area of agreement—opposition to the extension of slavery. They adopted the slogan Free Trade, Free Labor, Free Soil and Free Men.

To the surprise and disappointment of the Whigs, Chase announced that Judge McLean did not choose to run. Later there was some talk that Chase had maneuvered the statement for his own benefit and that there had been a swap among the Liberty party, Chase, and the Barnburners. In return for supporting Van Buren, the New Yorkers would agree not to meddle with the platform.[16]

With McLean eliminated, Van Buren's most serious opponent was expected to be the Liberty party's John P. Hale. But when the roll call was taken, the ex-President won with 244 votes against 181 for Hale and 41 for others. It was the Whig support that gave the nomination to Van Buren, because almost all the Liberty party members stayed with Hale. In order to present unity to the world, Joshua Leavitt, a member of the Liberty party and a well-known Massachusetts abolitionist, appealed to the convention to make the nomination of Van Buren unanimous. In an emotional speech, he called the convention "the most moving experience of my life." His rhetoric carried the members along with his request. Somewhat later, Charles Francis Adams was nominated as the vice-presidential candidate. He accepted the nomination as a tribute to his father, John Quincy Adams, who had died in January of that year. The nomination was valuable to him, Adams said, because "it places me somewhat nearer to the level of my father."[17]

General Zachary Taylor, the Whig candidate, was a much more formidable rival than Lewis Cass but, as Van Buren knew, a third party, no matter how enthusiastic, well motivated, and endowed with talent, has small chance of succeeding. Nevertheless, Prince John, particularly eloquent, witty, and charismatic, stumped tirelessly for his father. He drew large crowds wherever he went and was in constant demand for speaking engagements. David Wilmot, whose proviso had been the inspiration for the party, also fought hard for the cause. In Massachusetts, however, Adams's home state, despite the strength of the Free Soil party, Van Buren's candidacy kept many Whigs from supporting the party.

President Polk, who was not a candidate in 1848 and, many said, could not have been if he had wanted to be, was very critical of Van Buren's position. The Free Soil platform, he said, "was a most dangerous attempt to organize geographical parties upon the slave question," and was more dangerous to the country than anything since the Hartford Convention in 1814. Van Buren, Polk recorded in his diary, was "selfish, unpatriotic and wholly inexcusable." This movement of the seceding Democrats must be counteracted by extending the Missouri Compromise line to the new territories, the only way to avoid the formation of "geographical parties," and Congress must be influenced to do so.[18]

Polk's panacea was not adopted. The day after he recorded the Van Buren nomination, he learned that the Senate had rejected the Missouri Compromise amendment to the Oregon Territorial bill. On that same day, the President was further displeased to learn that Charles Francis Adams, "an avowed Abolitionist," was the vice-presidential candidate on the Van Buren ticket. "Mr. Van Buren is the most fallen man I have ever known," Jackson's other heir, "Young Hickory," wrote.[19]

The results of the election served to disturb the President even further. General Taylor's election, he said, was "deeply to be re-gretted" because the general was completely without experience in civil life and knew nothing about politics. Therefore, without any judgment of his own on foreign and domestic subjects, he would have to rely upon "the designing men of the Federal party who will cluster around him."[20] With some justification, Polk could blame Van Buren because, in New York, the split between the Barnburners and the Hunkers had caused the disaster for the Democratic party and ensured Cass the loss of the state and, finally, the election. The slavery question and Van Buren had destroyed the Democratic party.

Van Buren ran ahead of Cass in Massachusetts and Vermont and made a good showing in Ohio, Maine, and Wisconsin. Though he won 291,263 votes, about ten percent of the total vote, he failed to win even one electoral vote. The Free Soil party elected nine members to Congress from the North, none from the South. Some votes had been lost, of course, because individual voters feared that to vote for the Free-Soilers was to throw their votes away, so they supported Taylor as the lesser of two evils lest "Cass and Slavery" might win.

Most of the Free-Soilers felt that they had made a strong showing for beginners. For Van Buren, however, it was the end of the political road. He was now to become a political has-been, living in perpetual and lonely exile at Lindenwald, which was out of the way, especially for his elderly peers.

Suspicion that Van Buren's association with the Free Soil party was mostly opportunistic is borne out by his behavior in later elections. In 1852 the party solicited his support, but he gave it to the Democratic candidate, Franklin Pierce. Van Buren rejected the new-born Republican party, direct descendant of the Free Soil party and, instead supported Democratic James Buchanan in 1856. Now no longer a lapsed Democrat, he voted against Abraham Lincoln in 1860.

When Millard Fillmore turned over the presidency to Franklin Pierce in 1851, his supporters agreed that, at age fifty-three, he was much too young to consider his political career closed and urged him to think about the next election. He was not deaf to their advice, as his response to the mayor of Washington, D.C., during a farewell dinner, revealed. "While I shall retire from this exalted station without a single regret," he said, "I cannot leave your delightful city . . . without feeling a pang of regret." He wanted the White House door left open.[21]

Before leaving office, he made plans for a tour of the South in answer to an invitation from the state of Georgia. Though the trip was supposed to be for sightseeing, the Fillmores and the members of the ex-President's Cabinet who were to accompany them had in mind testing the political atmosphere for future plans. Unfortunately, the expedition had to be abandoned because Abigail Fillmore caught a chill at the Pierce inaugural that turned into pneumonia. Fillmore stayed at his wife's bedside at Willard's Hotel, where they had moved after leaving the White House, but in three weeks she was dead.

A year later, the former President started on his delayed southern trip. He left Buffalo for Lexington, Kentucky, where he delivered two speeches, was given a reception, and paid a respectful visit to Henry Clay's home and tomb. All the stops on the tour were marked by enthusiastic receptions of Southern supporters and gracious speeches by Fillmore, always dwelling on the Compromise of 1850, which Fillmore had signed and which was very popular in the South because it strengthened the federal Fugitive Slave Law. At a reception in Montgomery, Alabama, the ex-President said that he was "overpowered" by the demonstrations and the regard that had met him all the way on his southern journey. It was, in truth, more like the triumphal procession of a conquering general than the reception of a private citizen. Newspapers all along the route reported Fillmore's progress and the news was reprinted all over the country.[22]

Any doubt that his trip was undertaken to marshal political support was dispelled when Fillmore followed the southern jaunt with a "sightseeing" tour of the West. He visited Chicago, St. Paul, and Dubuque making complimentary speeches, being gracious and charming, and never failing to mention his status as a private citizen. No one was fooled. Washington Irving, who was supposed to have gone on the trip, described exactly what happened on it without leaving his writing table at home. "I have no inclination to travel with political notorieties to be smothered by the clouds of party dust whirled up by their chariot wheels and beset by the speechmakers and little great men of every community. . . . Heaven preserve me from any tour of this kind. . . . I would as like go campaigning with Hudibras or Don Quixote."[23] Only the recipient of the adulation with ulterior political motives could tolerate such a trip.

Fillmore became a presidential candidate once again but not under the auspices of his former party, the Whigs. The merger of Millard Fillmore and the strange new Know-Nothing party was a marriage of convenience. An outgrowth of the American nativist movement of the forties, which had its roots in distrust of the growing number of immigrants and fear of Roman Catholic influence, it emerged in the mid-fifties as a political party.

Charles B. Allan of New York founded a secret society called the Order of the Star-Spangled Banner, whose members called themselves Sires of '76. When these sires were asked questions about their organization, they would answer, "I know nothing." Horace Greeley christened them "the Know Nothings," and the name stuck even after they formed the political party known officially as the American party.

There were numerous reasons for the surfacing of such an organization at this time. The number of immigrants had quadrupled in a few years during the 1850s, which reactivated the chronic fear of the workingman that he would be replaced by cheap foreign labor. In addition, most of the new immigrants were Catholic, releasing another source of anxiety—the fear that the pope would take over America.

In the summer of 1854, the Know-Nothing party became a popular national phenomenon. Not only did candy, tea, and toothpicks carry the magic name, but a clipper ship, *The Know Nothing*, was launched with great public interest. Politicians watched the November elections carefully and were surprised at the success of the new party. It carried Delaware, Massachusetts, and, with some Whig support, Pennsylvania. In the South, it almost carried Virginia, Alabama, Georgia, Louisiana, and Mississippi. Only the West was untouched by the virus.[24]

Fillmore was in a susceptible condition. In July his daughter, Mary Abigail, who had been keeping house for him, died suddenly at the age of twenty-two. Heartbroken, his thoughts turned to his only profession, politics. He was ready for his friends in the Know-Nothing party to persuade him. Knowledge of the party had reached him through Solomon H. Haven, his former law partner, who lived in Washington and was a member. Haven told Filmore that the

Know-Nothings represented a true national party, in contrast to the older parties, which were becoming increasingly sectional. The new party, Haven hinted, needed only the right leadership to succeed.

Apparently convinced, Fillmore was initiated into the secret rites of the Order of the Star-Spangled Banner in the library of his house. Charles McComber, who conducted the initiation, said: "Mr. Fillmore, you have taken this step which will certainly land you in the presidential chair in Washington." Fillmore answered candidly, "Charles, I trust so." The prospective candidate was then packed off for a year-long trip through Europe and the Near East, while his managers worked for his candidacy at home.

Though he was not without doubts about becoming President again, saying that he had escaped shipwreck once and "prudence says, tempt not the elements again," he seemed to be willing to take another chance. From Paris, on May 21, 1856, Fillmore acknowledged his unanimous designation as the presidential candidate of the American party. In his acceptance, he explained that "the unexpected communication" met him at Venice and its duplicate, the evening before, at the French capital. Since the close of his administration, he had considered his political life at an end, but had felt impelled, at times, to express his opinions on political subjects when asked and to give his vote and support "for those men and measures, I thought best calculated to promote the prosperity, and glory of our common country." Therefore, he could not shrink from this new duty. "Approving as I do," he said, "of the general objects of the party which has honored me with its confidence, I cheerfully accept its nomination without waiting to inquire of its prospects of success or defeat." Further, he wanted "to quiet the alarming sectional agitation which was pleasing to the European monarchists but saddening to friends of the United States." The new party, Fillmore continued, resulted from these sectional divisions and "of all the political agencies now existing" had the power to silence them. He declared that he adopted all the principles stated in the recent declaration of the national council of the American party which he had received.[25]

The Know-Nothing managers, pleased that their scheme had succeeded, had prepared a gala reception for the returning candidate. When Fillmore's ship, the *Atlantic*, passed Sandy Hook on the evening of June 22, a telegraphed message alerted the delegation in the city that the demonstration could begin. The ship fired a gun which was answered by a fifty-gun salute fired by a group of Know-

Nothings at the Battery, followed by a rocket display that illuminated the sky. A delegation of several thousand waited at the pier for the ship to dock. New York City Alderman Briggs and his entourage welcomed Fillmore and presented him with the keys of the city. He must return to his former office, Briggs said, "to remove the vermin that [had] gathered there during . . . [his] unfortunate absence from the national helm." The theme of Fillmore's campaign had just been presented to him, with the tone that he wished to achieve. In the past, he had performed his duty to his country "and to all parts of the country, North as well as South." He pledged to do the same again if elected. Somewhat later, in an address to a Whig delegation, Fillmore stated that he expected the same support that he had enjoyed at the time of the Compromise of 1850. He should have "the old line Whigs of 1840, '44 and '52—but the support also of the old conservative elements of the Democratic party."[26]

At that time, it was very unusual for a presidential candidate to do any campaigning. Usually he remained discreetly in retirement, communicating with his supporters by letter, while others made the speeches and met the crowds. Fillmore broke precedent by making over twenty speeches and meeting endless delegations. All through his campaign, he stuck to his chosen theme—the Union must be saved from the dangers of sectionalism and he was the man of all the people.

The ex-President's speeches were not close to the Know-Nothing party line, for he seldom touched on their nativist or religious bias. At Newburgh, New York, he did refer, but very gently, to some of the party principles. He would be tolerant of all creeds, he asserted, "but if any sect or denomination ostensibly organized for religious purposes, should use that organization or suffer it to be used, for political objects, I would meet it by political opposition. . . . Church and State should be separate . . . religion and politics should not be mingled." In that same speech, he expressed some nativist dogma: "Americans should govern America because those who come from the old world monarchies are not prepared by education, habits of thought or knowledge of our institutions to govern America." Therefore, every American must resolve that "independent of all foreign influence, Americans will and shall rule America."[27]

Direct anti-Catholic statements were almost always absent from Fillmore's speeches. He did say, in one address, that he had seen much of Italy, "where priesthood denied the people Liberty and the

Bible." The word *Catholic* he used only once during the campaign. When he addressed an audience in Rome, New York, he mentioned that while in Rome, Italy, he had seen the pope but "had not become a Roman Catholic—far from it." Somehow, Bishop Timon of Buffalo was not concerned about Fillmore and anti-Catholicism. He pointed out that Fillmore's daughter had been a student at the Buffalo Academy for Young Ladies, which was run by the Sisters of the Sacred Heart, and that he had made a sizable contribution to the fund for the purchase of bells for St. Joseph's Cathedral.[28]

Despite his enthusiastic receptions wherever he went and his ardent speechmaking, Fillmore's hope for reelection was moribund by the fall. Instead of emphasizing their candidate's bid for sectional unity, the party managers preferred to dwell on their slogan Americans should govern America. The ex-President's chances dwindled as he was deserted by former supporters both in the North and in the South. "In the North I am charged with being Pro-slavery trying to extend slavery over free territory, and in the South, I am accused of being an abolitionist," he complained. He could not be the representative of either section, Fillmore wrote, and if he could not be accepted on those conditions, "I shall not complain."[29]

For a brief time, the American party had hopes that no candidate would receive a majority of the votes and the election would be thrown into the House of Representatives. If that happened, they speculated, Fillmore would have the best chance of being selected of any of the candidates. However, this was not the solution that many of Fillmore's friends sought. Fearful that John Frémont of the radical new Republican party might win, they voted for James Buchanan, the Democrat.

As it turned out, fear of Republican power was exaggerated. Buchanan won by 500,000 votes over Frémont and 960,000 over Fillmore. The American party candidate carried only Maryland, while Buchanan had the fourteen slave states, Pennsylvania, New Jersey, Illinois, and California. The new Republican party captured the eleven remaining Northern states. An analysis of the election does reveal that a change of about 8,000 votes in Kentucky, Tennessee, and Louisiana would have swung those states over to Fillmore, which would have deprived either of the two other candidates of the majority and forced the election into the House. But despite the opinion of the American party strategists, this would not have assured a Fillmore victory. It is interesting to speculate on what would have happened if the House had repeated its 1824 performance and given Fillmore, rather than the front runner, the presidency. Possibly the direct path to the Civil War might have been averted. Fillmore stated more than once, "For my own part, I know only my country, my whole country, and nothing but my country."[30]

The election of Buchanan proved disastrous to the nation, but Fillmore said only that he did not envy his successful rival. And if his successor restored "peace and harmony" to the nation, "he forgave" his enemies' slurs. At fifty-six, Fillmore put aside any further political aspirations forever. The uneasy alliance between the ex-President and the American party was dissolved by mutual consent. It had been no more than an empirical necessity. The party could use a man of some stature; the candidate needed a party to sponsor him. Only the unlikely possibility that the election would go into the House and the House would elect Fillmore could have turned him into a second-term president.

> When asked what state he hails from
> Our sole reply should be
> He comes from Appomattox
> And its famous apple tree.

With this atrocious but moving bit of doggerel, Senator Roscoe Conkling of New York started his nomination speech for ex-President Ulysses S. Grant at the Republican convention held in Chicago in June 1880. At this time, the General made a strong bid for a return to the White House and an unprecedented attempt to overcome the anti-third-term prejudice.

Although Grant had denied it to the public, his Cabinet, and his friends, talk persisted through the latter part of his second term that he wanted to be reelected. It was serious enough to cause the Democratic Congress of 1875 to pass a resolution declaring a third term unpatriotic, dangerous, and un-American. Finally, in order to kill the agitation, President Grant was forced to write a letter to the press in which he declined a third-term nomination. However, his aide and biographer, General Adam Badeau, did note that the General concealed his decision from Mrs. Grant, because she would have tried to change his mind. After some discomfort at the beginning of her tenure as First Lady, Mrs. Grant learned to enjoy her position and welcomed any suggestion that she might continue in that role for four more years.[31]

The Grant letter was not really decisive. It read: "I could not accept a nomination if it were tendered unless it should come under such circumstances as to make it an imperative duty—circumstances not likely to occur."[32] The statement left the door partly open, but Rutherford B. Hayes received the nomination in 1876 and, eventually, won the contested election.

Relieved of the presidency, Grant fulfilled a lifelong ambition by setting out on a trip around the world. While he was away, a substantial Grant boom was started. Among its most active promoters were a trio of Republican senators: Don Cameron of Pennsylvania, John A. Logan of Illinois, and handsome Roscoe Conkling of New York. President Hayes's difficulties in office and the unlikelihood of his renomination stimulated the Grant movement. Newspapers referred to the ex-President as a "man of iron" and to the incumbent as "a man of straw." Even Hayes's major achievement, the withdrawal of troops from the South, was claimed to have been Grant's idea. But not everyone had forgotten the scandals of the Grant administration. The Boston *Transcript* warned its readers that to revive it would be to "cast all Democratic errors in the shade."[33]

Grant had mixed feelings about the possibility of being President again. His many years of failure during his early life had always stayed with him, so he was unable to reject an opportunity to prove to himself that he could succeed again. Also, he needed the money. If he did not return to the White House, he would have to accept some sort of job. On the other hand, he wrote, "I dread getting back, the clamor of the partisan and so-called independent press will be such as to make life here unpleasant for a time." And then he made the mistake of returning to America too soon.

Grant's sponsors wanted him to make a triumphal reentrance on the American scene about six months before the election. They visualized a sensational reception followed by a cross-country tour that would rival the brilliant receptions that had been accorded the Civil War hero in his foreign travels. Unfortunately, Mrs. Grant's fretting about the children overcame the admonitions of the politicians, and the ex-President agreed to start for home, although he, personally, would have been content to continue his travels.

Aware of the brief interest span of the public, the Grant managers feared that enthusiasm over the General would melt away soon after his return. But since the Grants were homeward bound, there was nothing to do but to make it as spectacular a return as could be engineered. Grant's rather naive letter to Badeau describing his plans would be only partially fulfilled. "At the end of twenty-six months I dread going back," he wrote. "But I shall go to my quiet little home in Galena and wait there until the cold drives me away." Then he would go south, possibly to Havana and Mexico.[34]

General Grant, who had enjoyed a quiet voyage from Japan, was astounded when his ship, the *City of Tokio*, steamed into San Francisco harbor to the roar of welcoming cannonades. Thousands of wildly cheering citizens waited at the dock to see the ship arrive surrounded by a fleet of steamers filled with crowds and gay with flags. In the wake of the *Tokio*, a yacht squadron brought up the rear, festooned fore and aft with red, white, and blue bunting.[35]

Governor Irvin and his staff, Governor-Elect Perkins, Mayor Bryant, and other dignitaries formed a welcoming committee. The General was driven in a carriage up Market Street while the uproarious crowds pressed forward to get a glimpse of him. At each street corner bonfires burned, the windows along the route were lit with illuminations, and the skies were bright with fireworks.

The Palace Hotel, where Grant was to stay, was ablaze with lights, and when the hero alighted from his carriage, Mme. Fabri and a chorus of five hundred voices sang an ode of welcome. The enthusiastic San Franciscans were restrained by the police cordon with difficulty, agreeing to disperse only when they were promised that the ex-President would address them after dinner.

For the next few months, Grant moved across the country fêted and lionized by adoring crowds. He did not mention politics in his many addresses and adroitly avoided any leading questions on the subject. His political advisors were very hopeful that the Grant nomination would succeed, for many of them believed that only he could save the party. There was some modicum of truth to Badeau's exaggeration that the former President "had become a profound thinker and an international statesman" during his travels. It must be admitted that he was more fit to be President than before and understood somewhat his former errors in political administration. It was also significant that, strangely, he had become popular in the South and might have broken down the Solid South. Conkling echoed Badeau's judgment on this point. "If there be any one man on this footstool, whom the whites and blacks cherish in their hearts, that man is General Grant."[36]

After his successful continental tour, the Grant managers were relieved to see their prospect pack up for a trip to Cuba and Mexico. Unfortunately, however, his too-early reappearance already had had unfortunate results. The opposition was mobilizing to destroy the Grant boom. Anti-third-term forces formed anti-third-term clubs, and rivals developed their own organizations. James Blaine in the East, George F. Edmunds in Vermont, and John Sherman in Ohio were the strongest contenders. A number of newspapers, such as the New York *Tribune*, took a firm anti-Grant stand.

Upon his return from Mexico, Grant was advised to attend the Texas state convention and travel to Galena by way of Memphis, Tennessee. There he visited his former Civil War headquarters and then stopped in at the Arkansas state convention. Things did not go well for Grant in the state conventions, in which Blaine and Sherman were favored. The word got around that if Grant were nominated, he would lose the election; the *Tribune* announced that he was the only Republican the Democrats did not fear; and Thurlow Weed reported that, if nominated, Grant would lose New York and Pennsylvania. To add to his problems, in May the anti-third-term clubs held a convention in St. Louis that was attended by delegates from fourteen states.

Opposition to his nomination ignited Grant's will to succeed. Family pressure and the heightened self-esteem that he had acquired on his travels spurred him on to seek the second chance. Although he said little or nothing, his silence, Badeau asserted, was no more than a superstitious feeling that any effort on his part to secure his own advancement would ensure his failure.[37]

As the convention drew near, the Grant men were aware that their candidate did not have sufficient votes to win the nomination. Because of the unfavorable returns in the state conventions and the certainty of anti-Grant delegations that might contest seats at the convention, there was only one sure method to win. The convention must adopt the unit rule, whereby the majority of each state delegation would decide the vote for all the delegates. This, it was calculated, would give Grant 378 votes instead of the 224 that the *Tribune* allotted him, and the nomination. The ruse did not work. The first three days of the Chicago convention were spent in political maneuvering, but all that Conkling could achieve was the right to choose the chairman from among the three candidates whom the anti-Grant forces would select. George Hoar became the chairman, but the coalition against Grant succeeded in defeating the unit rule.

On the third day of the convention, the nominating speeches were made. New York Senator Roscoe Conkling, elegant and confident, mounted a reporter's table that was set in the center of the hall and, surrounded by 16,000 spectators, presented Grant's name in a stunning, dramatic speech. His theme was that Grant could carry the South as well as the North. "His services attest his greatness, and the country—nay the world—knows them by heart." He added, "His integrity, his common sense, his courage, his unequalled experience are the qualities offered to his country." In closing, Conkling repeated the theme that Grant alone could give the Republican party the next presidential election. He could "dissolve and emancipate a solid south" and thus defeat the Democrats. The Republican party could march "to certain and lasting victory with the greatest Marshal at its head."[38]

A forty-minute ovation followed the conclusion of the speech. The Chicago *InterOcean* said that the New York senator had presented "a gem of rhetorical finish." The address had "the warmth of eulogy, the finish of a poem, the force and fire of a philippic. Grant was in every line of it, his spirit breathed in every sentence." Benjamin Harrison, years later, wrote that although he opposed Grant's nomination, when he heard the nomination speech, he found himself "unconsciously applauding him as vigorously as his most sympathetic friend." However, he added, the address did not win over those who were opposed to Grant but, rather, "compacted his friends" into a phalanx that no acts or force could break. The "306," who were the solid phalanx of Grantites, became a legend in convention history, carrying a romantic aura that only a lost cause can invoke.[39]

James A. Garfield followed the famous oration with a nominating speech for John Sherman of Ohio. He said that the assemblage seemed to him "a human ocean in tempest." When "the hour of calm settles on the ocean," he said, then it would be necessary to appeal to the "thoughtful voters" who "sit by 4,000,000 Republican firesides." They will "make the choice of the Republic." Henry Stoddard wrote that it came into the minds of many delegates, as they listened to the masterful speech, that Garfield was the man to bring peace and success to the party.[40]

Brandegee of Connecticut, while seconding the nomination of

Elihu B. Washburne, raised the specter of the third-term controversy. Not even Conkling's "unmatched eloquence," he said, could persuade the voters that the third-term tradition was "all humbug and masquerade." Grant, "even with his magic name," would be on the defensive. "The name of Grant would carry this Convention through by storm, if there were not an invincible argument against his nomination."[41]

After the nominating speeches were over, a reporter from the New York *Sun* asked Roscoe Conkling, "How does Senator Conkling feel?" Referring to General Garfield's speech and to Senator Frye's speech on Senator Blaine, which pictured "a staunch old ship" in a storm, Conkling answered, "I presume I feel very much as you feel—*sea*-sick!" But he was seriously troubled about the outcome of the convention.

As soon as the first ballot was taken, the Grant men and their rivals knew that the former President would not get the nomination. Grant mustered 304 votes; Blaine 284; Sherman 93; Edmunds 34; Washburne 30; William Windom 10. Ballot followed ballot in wearisome succession. It was necessary for a candidate to get 370 votes to win. Grant hovered between 302 and 309 votes throughout, while the strength of the others varied from tally to tally. On the thirty-fifth ballot, the Grant forces rallied their greatest effort but were not able to get more than 313 votes.

On the second day of the balloting, the trend could be detected. Slowly but persistently, Blaine's strength declined and the dark horse, Garfield, gained votes. On the thirty-sixth ballot, Garfield achieved 399 votes, at the expense of Blaine. The faithful "306" supported their hero even at the end. Conkling, a master politician even in defeat, answered the call to make the nomination unanimous. In return, it was said, Conkling was allowed to choose the vice-president. The New York senator, however, denied that he had anything to do with the selection of Chester A. Arthur.[42]

Grant asserted that he had "grown weary of constant abuse" and was relieved that he had not received the nomination. He thanked Conkling for his "magnificent and generous support during and before the Convention." He was also grateful to the "three hundred and odd who stood with you through the week's labors."[43]

Grant's actions belied his words. He was bitter ever after about the Chicago convention for the role in it that he attributed to his lifelong friend Washburne. He believed that he had been false because he, too, ran as a candidate. Former supporters who deserted his cause in that last campaign were never again regarded in the same circle of friendship by the defeated hero. For Blaine and some who supported him, Grant also expressed violent acrimony. But only close friends such as Badeau knew how deeply wounded Grant was by his party's rejection. He who had been their darling was now discarded.

Doubtless, Grant's nomination was an attempt by the stalwarts to use the ex-President's fame and popularity. He was still the soldiers' candidate, and those who had been the recipients of his patronage during his two administrations were not ashamed "to wave the bloody shirt" again if it would get them the nomination. At the convention, it was the defeat of the unit rule that guaranteed Grant's failure. In order to succeed, the Grant forces had to seat their delegates, who were in contention, and to prevent the anti-Grant pockets in some of the delegations from voting. In the New York delegation, for example, there were twenty-two anti-Grant members. Grant did not realize that the fierce struggle that was going on in the convention of 1880 was not between him and other candidates but between Conkling and Blaine. Although the "Plumed Knight" could not get the election for himself, he succeeded in keeping it from Conkling, because Garfield was not a Conkling man.[44]

After the convention, Conkling strutted and sulked, refusing to call on the successful candidate. Grant overcame his disappointment and came out for Garfield, forcing the stalwarts, including Roscoe Conkling, to do the same.

Only honest, dull, portly Grover Cleveland succeeded in returning to the White House after vacating it for his successor. The anecdote is told that Mrs. Cleveland confounded Jerry Smith, an old White House servant, with a prediction. "Now, Jerry," she said as the Clevelands left the presidential mansion, "I want you to take good care of the furniture and ornaments in the house, for I want to find everything just as it is now when I come back again. We are coming back just four years from today."[45]

Cleveland, more conventionally, mouthed the usual truisms about being glad to leave as he had always felt like a prisoner. He seemed to be reflecting his honest opinion at the time, because he refrained from all political pronouncements for about a year. "Present personal interests are all against my appearing in the political field," he wrote.

Hence he refused many invitations to speak and concentrated on his law practice.[46]

Cleveland's notable speech on ballot reform given at a dinner of the Merchants Association of Boston in December 1889 has often been regarded as his first move toward the 1892 presidential nomination. The enthusiastic reception of his plea for honesty in politics was very flattering to the former President, but he enjoyed most some verses sent by James Russell Lowell, the poet. Unable to attend the dinner, Lowell asked that his poem be read to the audience.

> Let who has felt compute the strain
> Or struggle with abuses strong.
> The doubtful course, the helpless pain
> Of seeing best intents go wrong;
> We, who look on with critics' eyes
> Exempt from action's crucial test,
> Human, ourselves, at least are wise
> In honouring one who did his best.[47]

George F. Parker, an Indiana-born journalist who became Cleveland's publicity man for the years 1889–1892, asserted that Cleveland "neither suspected nor intended" the ballot reform speech to be the opening gun for his third nomination. On the contrary, Parker quoted the ex-President as saying "I do not want the office and, above all, I do not feel that I can take the risk involved in a second term after the intervention of one by another man and an opposing party. It would be necessary for me to start new again, and I do not feel equal to it."[48]

Cleveland believed that he had no support in New York State. Governor Hill and his friends were in complete control and wanted the presidential nomination for him. If it could not be obtained for Hill, said Cleveland, they were "determined it shall not come towards me."[49] However, the ex-President was encouraged by the election of 1890, even though he had refused to do any campaigning for any of the candidates on the grounds that he could not help them. The House of Representatives now had 235 Democrats, leaving the Republicans with only 85. Cleveland attributed this to national rejection of the McKinley tariff, a law that he detested.

Though he respected President Harrison's intelligence, Cleveland regarded his successor's administration as a series of blunders. He deplored the Dependent Pensions Act as much as the overwhelming support that was being given to powerful manufacturing interests both at home and abroad. His judgment was, however, that the Democrats should not counter the high McKinley tariff with a rival bill but rather let the Republicans "flounder. Then they would have to protect their own bill instead of throwing more dirt in the eyes of the public" by attacking a Democratic bill.[50] Cleveland was getting ready to engage in politics again.

In a strange twist of political fortune, Cleveland's famous silver letter, which should have ruined his chances for the Democratic nomination in 1892, instead enhanced his popularity. At this time, it looked as if the Democratic party would align itself with the bimetallists, who supported the unlimited coinage of silver. The Sherman Silver Purchase Act was a Republican piece of legislation that had come out of Harrison's campaign promise, but as Allan Nevins, Cleveland's biographer, notes, "the free silver virus had more deeply infected the Democratic than the Republican party," and its strength in the South was beginning to rival its strength in the North.[51]

Cleveland had opposed silver coinage in 1888 and was disturbed to read that the Boston *Journal* was spreading rumors that he was either favorable toward it or, at least, less opposed than he had been in the past. The matter came to a head in January 1891, when a free coinage bill passed the Senate with Democratic support. Cleveland could no longer be restrained. It was clear to him that if he had any intention of resuming the leadership of his party, he must state his views.

The opportunity presented itself when E. Ellery Anderson of the New York City Reform Club invited the ex-President to a meeting of businessmen whose purpose was to protect free coinage. Cleveland wrote a letter turning down the invitation and expressing his point of view. According to Parker, the controversial letter went through many drafts, its final length reduced by three quarters. With each draft, Cleveland strengthened his statement against free silver. The final version was brief, less than two hundred words, but carried a decisive statement. The "greatest peril" would result "if in the present situation we enter upon the dangerous and reckless experiment of free, unlimited and independent silver coinage."[52]

William C. Whitney, who later became Cleveland's campaign director, thought the declaration was "premature, unnecessary and impolitic." It would be fatal to Cleveland's hopes, he declared. At first his prediction seemed accurate, but gradually public opinion turned toward Cleveland. This made no difference to him, the former President said, although he admitted to being pleased when the Silver Bill failed in the House.[53]

New York politics, particularly the presidential ambitions of Governor David B. Hill, was the greatest obstacle to a Cleveland nomination. The New York State Democratic Committee met on February 22, 1892, which was two months earlier than ever before. The purpose was to exclude farm communities, whose representatives would be snowed in at that time of the year, and thus assure Hill's nomination. Many of the New York newspapers criticized the premature convention, but Cleveland, its intended victim, only commented wryly, "The State Committee has selected an historic day. I hope the weather is fine." The "Snap Convention," as it was nicknamed, instructed its delegates to vote for Hill at the national convention and imposed the unit rule to guarantee him all of the state's votes.

The opposition soon rallied under the name of the "anti-Snappers." Their convention was held in Syracuse and attended by at least one thousand delegates who were determined to show the nation that Cleveland was a formidable candidate with formidable support from his own state. The anti-Snappers had not neglected to send agents into all the states where conventions were being held to assure them that New York was safe for the ticket. The Cleveland boom quickly spread to twenty-four state and territorial conventions.

Cleveland's letters, at this time, express some ambivalence about resuming the presidency. His daughter Ruth, his first child, had been born in October 1891 and he was, he said, discovering other values in life than "fame, honor, place." The trials of the White House were plain to him. "My experience in the great office . . . has . . . impressed me with the solemnity of the trust, and its awful responsibilities," he wrote.[54] But the lure of the great prize did not allow him to reject a second chance.

Cleveland even made his peace with the city of Buffalo. Ever since the campaign of 1884, when a Buffalo newspaper had printed "A Terrible Tale," which detailed Cleveland's relationship with a widow named Maria Halpin, he had avoided his home town. The story stirred up a lot of gossip, because Mrs. Halpin accused Cleveland of being the father of her illegitimate son and of having placed the child in an orphanage. The truth was that Cleveland had had an intimate relationship with the woman but was not certain that the child was his. He had, however, taken the responsibility for his support. Trying to put his resentment behind him, Cleveland returned to Buffalo to celebrate the fiftieth anniversary of the German Young Men's Association and gave two speeches which were well received.

While Whitney and the coterie of business moguls who surrounded him worked for Cleveland's nomination, Cleveland himself claimed that he was doing nothing. His "inmost thoughts," which he revealed to Justice L. Q. L. Lamar, dictated that he could not refuse to serve his country and his party. "If I am given my discharge I shall thank God most fervently," he said, hoping that he might be disposed of by the selection of a more available candidate or the adoption of a position on the financial situation that he was not willing to accept. Neither event occurred. The Cleveland nomination effort moved on to its inevitable conclusion.

Whitney set up Cleveland headquarters in Chicago at the Palmer House and kept them open from early morning until after the meetings of the conference of supporters were over late at night. He handled all the problems brilliantly, gaining even the recalcitrant with his superb and contagious assuredness that Cleveland, and only Cleveland, could win the nomination and then the election.

The cost of the campaign to the ex-President was amusingly small. Parker, who was in charge, mentioned $2,000 for buttons, badges, flags, and souvenirs. Whitney spent about $5,000 on his and the group's expenses.[55]

The Hill bubble had burst long before the convention. He had outmaneuvered himself by forcing the legislature to elect him to the United States Senate, which infuriated Smith W. Weed, who thought that the job had been promised to him. Having antagonized the Weed machine, Hill was afraid to resign the governorship when he was elected to the Senate seat lest he lose his own machine as well. Consequently, he held on to both positions, which made his judgment suspect to many. Further, he nodded toward the Silverites, which antagonized conservatives, and tried to gain the support of tariff protectionists like Gorman of Maryland and Brice of Ohio because he knew they opposed Cleveland's nomination.[56] By convention time, there was no serious opposition to Cleveland. He was nominated on the first ballot, receiving 617⅓ votes, ten more than he needed. Adlai E. Stevenson of Illinois, who represented the agrarian Midwest as opposed to Cleveland's Eastern Bourbon affiliation, received the vice-presidential nomination. Stevenson's nomination was also a gesture toward the Silverites.

Seated quietly in the gun room at Gray Gables, his summer home in Marion, Massachusetts, the ex-President waited for the results. Mrs. Cleveland and her mother, Governor and Mrs. Russell, and Joseph Jefferson and his son Charles were present. Young Charles kept the tally of the votes. The others were somewhat anxious, particularly during a long and eloquent speech for Hill given by Tammany's Bourke Cochran, which delayed the convention for an hour. Cleveland, unperturbed, strolled out to dry his fish lines while New York was voting. But later, when Cleveland's nomination was made, Mrs. Cleveland saw the first ray of the morning sun break through the sky and illuminate her husband's head.

"One thing, I hope, will not be urged upon me and that is trip-taking and speechmaking," Cleveland said. He was spared because Mrs. Harrison became very ill and died that summer, making it unseemly for the President, the Republican candidate, to campaign. In deference, Cleveland announced that he would not take the stump either. Apart from his acceptance speech, delivered at Madison Square Garden to 20,000 cheering adherents, Cleveland limited himself to letter writing. He spent the greater part of the summer at Grey Gables closing his ears to his friends' pleas to make excursions to New York. He did participate in a kind of rapprochement with Tammany that Whitney had worked hard to arrange.

As reluctant as a balky child, Cleveland was cajoled into attending the Victoria Hotel conference with Tammany leaders in September. Whitney set the stage with great care, ordering an elegant dinner in a private dining room, which he hoped would ease the tensions. Not until coffee and cigars were served did the subject of politics come up in the conversation. William P. Sheehan, the most disgruntled sachem, spilled out his complaints against the reformers in the party and asked for patronage if Cleveland were elected. "No promises" was all Cleveland would say. The result of the conference was inconclusive, but the atmosphere was a little clearer between the two factions. Whitney wrote to Cleveland that he was certain that Tammany was now with them and Hill could do nothing to stop it.[57]

Cleveland told his friend Bissell, in confidence, that he had been consulted scarcely at all about the conduct of the campaign. It was an unusual experience for him to be running with all the politicians against him. What was even odder was that he was doing so well. Not having the politicians to worry about, he commented, meant also that there would be fewer obligations after the election.[58]

Though not touring the country, Cleveland spent a great deal of time writing to friends and associates asking for their support. The South, traditionally Democratic, was troublesome because of the former President's close association with Northeastern money interests and because, many felt, he did not understand their poverty. Whitney asked him to write some sympathetic statements about the tariff and silver to reassure his Southern supporters, but Cleveland refused. More than once Cleveland regretted his decision to run again. "Take my advice, my dear friend," he told Richard Gilder, "and *never run for President.*"[59]

Despite his protestations, Cleveland was a wise politician. When the news spread that the opposition was reviving stories about Stevenson having been a Greenbacker, the ex-President solved the problem. Since Stevenson had never written a letter accepting his nomination, Cleveland sent Parker to get on the train going south with Stevenson, carrying the draft of a letter that was decisive about sound money and the tariff. Parker did what he was told, presented the letter to the vice-presidential candidate, and was much relieved that it was accepted with no argument.[60]

Cleveland listened to the election returns at his house on Fifty-first Street, just west of Fifth Avenue in New York City. As the good news flashed in, friends flocked to the house and a crowd of well-wishers gathered outside in the street. After midnight, the ex-President went outside, made a short, dignified address, and then dismissed them. But party members and acquaintances continued to arrive until all hours of the morning. Finally, at about 4:00 A.M., Cleveland said to Parker: "Well, Parker, none of those men or all of them together know or realize as you or I do how this thing has been done." He referred to the simple, straightforward manner in which he believed his campaign had been managed, without machine connections, promises, or commitments. Therefore, he thought, he was perfectly independent. However, it was the Cleveland Conference, led by William C. Whitney, sometimes meeting secretly, that had really managed the campaign. The conference was composed of Wall Street bankers and financiers such as William F. Vilas, William L. Wilson, Josiah Quincy, Francis L. Stetson, and William F. Harrity. There were also trusted men from many states whose numbers increased as the campaign intensified. It was this nearly-three-year effort that triumphed on election night, 1892.[61]

Quite unexpectedly, the Cleveland victory was almost a landslide. He won New York, which was gratifying but not, as it turned out, essential. The Solid South remained obediently in the Democratic camp. In addition to the doubtful states of New York, New Jersey, Connecticut, and Indiana, he swept Illinois, Wisconsin, and California. The final popular vote count was 5,556,543 for Cleveland and 5,175,582 for Harrison. Cleveland got 277 electoral votes; Harrison, 145. The Populist party, led by James Weaver, polled a respectable 1,040,886 popular votes and 22 electoral votes. There were cries of a bargain between the Democrats and the Populists. In five Western States—Colorado, Idaho, Kansas, North Dakota, and Wyoming—which were traditionally Republican, it was said that the Democrats voted Populist in order to defeat the Republicans. This deal, however, would have been unnecessary, because the Populist party was cutting into the Republican vote anyhow, since the farmers were often Populists.

It was a glorious victory for Cleveland, the most decisive single triumph since Abraham Lincoln's in 1864. Much of it must be attributed to the feeling that many voters had that Cleveland stood for integrity and common sense. The American people have always enjoyed seeing defeat turn into victory, and Cleveland's quiet, dignified conduct during the campaign also won favor. As William Godkin said, here was "an example of Roman constancy under defeat, and of patient reliance on the power of deliberation and persuasion on the American people."[62]

Cleveland was pleased with his success, although a friend noticed that after the news of his election he did not share the boisterous enthusiasm of his colleagues but was, rather, pensive and grave. "I only wish God would put it in my power to make known to the Democratic Party what the last election means," he wrote. Even though he had enjoyed a remarkable comeback, he may have had an intuitive knowledge of the turbulence that lay ahead of him in his second four-year tour of duty.

No matter how much it annoyed Theodore Roosevelt to admit that his choice of a successor had been a poor one, by the time he had returned from his journeying year, it could not be denied that the former friends were irreconcilable foes. Matters personal and political had torn them apart. It was, however, the condition of the Republican party that angered TR the most. Taft's inept bungling had split it into two factions: the Conservatives, whose captive Taft had become, and the Progressives.

Roosevelt wrote to his son-in-law, Nicholas Longworth, who was the United States representative from Taft's home district in Ohio, that he was convinced "that we shall get beaten if we cannot get a common ground upon which insurgents and regulars can stand." The aim must be to try to get support from both wings of the Republican party.[63]

In August the ex-President went to Osawatomie, Kansas, to dedicate the John Brown Battleground at the site where the abolitionist, along with forty other Free-Staters, had defended the town against three hundred proslavery men. Roosevelt noted that he was "endeavoring to prevent the John Browns among the insurgents getting themselves into a position from which the Abraham Lincolns [could] not extricate them." However, the spirit of the old fanatic must have been hovering over the former President, because he then made the most radical statement of his New Nationalism. He declared that he supported such reforms as workmen's compensation, a graduated income tax and inheritance laws, the regulation of child labor and female labor, tariff revision, and increased power for the Interstate Commerce Commission. The judiciary must have more interest in human welfare than in private property, he asserted. Every man, he said, "holds his property subject to the general right of the community to regulate its use to whatever degree the public welfare may require it."[64]

Henry Cabot Lodge relayed to TR the reaction of the "startled" Eastern capitalists to his statements. In a phrase, they regarded him as "little short of a revolutionist." The conservative press did not spare the epithets, calling him a "fraud" who had indulged in "moral impudence." The New York *Sun* declared that he had just launched the third great crisis in the history of the nation.[65]

Unperturbed by the excitement, Roosevelt answered Lodge reasonably. What people thought most revolutionary in his speech was nearly a direct quotation from Lincoln: "Labor is prior to, and independent of capital . . . Labor is the superior of capital." As for his list of reforms, he had made them, in effect, in his messages to Congress. He did admit that "I may have here and there strengthened them or made them a little clearer."[66]

The Republican Old Guard squirmed at Roosevelt's New Nationalism, but the West rejoiced. The Progressives had found their St. George. "Roosevelt for 1912" was their battle cry, but they had reckoned without their newfound leader. Roosevelt's mission was party union, not an intensification of differences, so much to the disgust of the Progressives he started to endorse some of the administration policies. On his tour of the West and later in the East, he backed the middle-of-the-roaders rather than extremists such as the Progressive Robert La Follette of Wisconsin or the reactionary Senator William Lorimer of Illinois, who had been accused of buying his way into the Senate.[67]

Back in Oyster Bay, Roosevelt decided that he ought to put his own house in order by trying to reform boss-ridden New York State. With political dexterity, he defeated the machine politicians and was elected temporary chairman of the New York state convention. Henry L. Stimson, whom President Theodore Roosevelt had appointed United States attorney for the Southern District of New York and who had been a vigorous prosecutor of large companies, was persuaded by the ex-President to run for governor. Although Roosevelt knew that Stimson was a Taft man, he said that he was trying to put the Republicans in power in the state instead of turning it over to "Murphy of Tammany Hall, [who was] acting as the agent and ally and master of crooked finance."[68]

The fact was that TR was depressed with politics, even his own. "I have never had a more unpleasant summer," he complained to Elihu Root and said he would have much preferred to stay entirely out of politics. He was only doing what any decent citizen must do in 1910, "endeavoring to see that . . . control within the party was in the hands of sensible and honorable men who were progressives and not of a bourbon reactionary type." He was proud that he had praised "everything I conscientiously could of both Taft and the Congress" and refrained from condemnation of either, "strongly though I have felt."[69]

The Republican defeat in 1910 was a bitter one for the former President because, in New York, he felt it was a personal repudiation of him. The Stimson candidacy was so closely tied to his Roosevelt association that even the campaign songs revealed it.

> If Stimson came from Africa
> If he was a Zulu Chief

If he wore a feather in his hair
And dressed in a fig leaf
We'd vote for Henry just the same
And carry out the plan
Because he's Roosevelt's man.

In New York State, "the hatred of me amounted to a mania," TR wrote to his eldest son; "there was not a club in the neighborhood of Fifth Avenue, even including the Union Club, where I was not regarded as well-nigh a bomb thrower."[70] The Colonel had been caught between Scylla and Charybdis. The Progressives hated his endorsement of Taft and bolted the party. The Conservatives feared that the former President was campaigning for 1912 and formed Republicans for Dix (the Democratic candidate) leagues.

The election proved one incontrovertible fact. The signs for Taft in 1912 were portentous. The Democrats had gained enormous strength and now held power in the House of Representatives; perhaps more threatening to the President, the newly elected Progressives held the balance of power in the Senate. Theodore Roosevelt decided to fade into political oblivion and to let Taft be the candidate in 1912 and, inevitably, lose. "We have had a smashing defeat," TR informed Arthur H. Lee, but said he hoped for one result," and that is the elimination of me as a possible candidate in 1912."[71]

Several attempts had been made to bring Theodore Roosevelt and William H. Taft together and to end their estrangement, but without success. The President wrote to his former sponsor several times, asking his advice on the 1910 Annual Message and later on sensitive Japanese-American relations and a reciprocity treaty with Canada. Roosevelt's hearty replies were nothing but empty courtesy. And when a reporter, carried away by the spectacle of Roosevelt and Taft shaking hands enthusiastically when they met in Baltimore at Cardinal Gibbons's silver jubilee, gave the story to the Associated Press that the ex-President would support Taft's reelection, Roosevelt denied it. He wrote to Van Valkenburg of the Associated Press that he "seriously objected" to the AP's "faking news" and attributing to him "statements I never made."[72] After that, correspondence between Roosevelt and Taft stopped.

The old lion stayed in his Oyster Bay den and waited. Despite pressure from its founder and others, he did not join the National Progressive Republican League organized at the home of Robert

La Follette in early 1911. "At the moment I am very anxious not to seem to take part prominently in any political movement, in the sense of managing the details," he explained. However, he would "always fight for what I deem right but I do want to think very carefully to be sure that I don't make any error of judgment." He did not reject the league and offered to give it a "cordial endorsement" in the *Outlook*.[73]

La Follette, sick with a very bad case of presidential fever and suspicious of Roosevelt, tried to find out his plans. He sent two of his supporters, Ray Stannard Baker and Gilson Gardner, a Chicago newspaperman, to interview the ex-President. They reported that Roosevelt opposed the La Follette candidacy and were certain that he wanted the nomination for himself. All that was holding him back was his belief that Taft was sure to be the Republican choice.

In May 1911, TR wrote firmly that, as far as he could see now, "no situation could arise which would make it possible for me to accept the nomination next year." His friends could prove their friendship by refraining from starting a movement to get him nominated. Taft was stronger than ever before, Roosevelt believed, because his opponents had all gone to pieces. He felt also that he was young enough to wait for 1916, when the Republican party, purged of a defeated Taft, might be reformed under "capable and progressive" Roosevelt leadership.[74]

However, the political scene can change so quickly that a political man must be alert and ready to change his direction almost instantaneously. Although the exact moment when TR decided to try for the Republican nomination cannot be pinpointed, evidence shows that by the end of January 1912 he was ready to enter the race. On January 9, he said that under no circumstances would he lift a hand to get the nomination, but if it came to him "as a genuine popular movement," he would of course accept. By January 18, Roosevelt had concocted a plan to help create that popular mandate. He sent duplicate letters to Governors Glascock of West Virginia, Stubbs of Kansas, Osborn of Michigan, Hadley of Missouri, Bass of New Hampshire, and Johnson of California, saying that he had received letters from all of them asking whether he would run for president. He suggested that a group of four or five of them write him a joint letter or separate letters which would state briefly "the writer's belief that people of his State or their States, desire to have me [Roosevelt] run for the Presidency, and to know whether in such a case I would refuse the nomination." The letters were followed up by personal conferences or contacts made by Roosevelt friends.[75]

By the end of February, the Roosevelt campaign directors were selected: James M. Dixon of Montana to head the New York office, Truman H. Newberry to direct the financial headquarters in Chicago, and John C. O'Laughlin to handle the Washington office. The Roosevelt bandwagon was ready to roll.

One of the leading reasons for Roosevelt's decision was the elimination of Robert La Follette as a serious contender. Although completely exhausted from a lengthy speaking tour and apprehensive about his small daughter's illness, La Follette decided not to cancel an address to be delivered at the annual dinner of the periodical publishers held on February 2 in Philadelphia. La Follette followed Wilson, who had just given a brilliant speech before the eight hundred guests. The Wisconsin senator's subject was "Money in the United States and to Whom It Should Belong." Almost from the start of the address, it was apparent that something was wrong. La Follette was abusive about journalists and then started to ramble incoherently, sometimes rereading parts of his speech. Neither shouts from the audience of "Sit down" nor the attempts of the chairman to stop him had any effect. He continued for two and a half hours, while the audience gradually melted away until only the speaker and some embarrassed association officers were still in the hall.

"I wrote poor Senator La Follette at once," Roosevelt stated. But the unfortunate occurrence benefited the former President at once. Some Progressive leaders who, earlier, had declared for La Follette now had an excuse to leave his camp and join TR's. Among the deserters were William Flinn, Medill McCormick, and the Pinchots.

The letter from "the seven little Governors," signed and dated February 10, arrived opportunely. Alice Longworth admitted in her memoirs that it was "wicked," but her father preferred to continue the charade. He did, however, leak the news informally to a reporter in Columbus, Ohio, where he had arrived to give a speech before the state constitutional convention, by saying, "My hat is in the ring." Thus the Roosevelt candidacy was made public and the American political vocabulary was enlarged with a new phrase.

Having declared his candidacy in Columbus, he made a speech there that many believed immediately lost him the Republican nomination. The former President went over the list of reforms he favored, among them the initiative, the referendum, national primaries, and the direct election of senators, all of which were tolerable. Then he dropped a shocker—a proposal that there be review for judicial decisions. When a judge decides a constitutional question, Roosevelt advised, "the people should have the right to recall that decision if they think it is wrong." His rationale for this astounding reform proposal was that the people, though not infallible, had "shown themselves wiser than the courts" in such matters as the control of big corporations and the rights of workers. Roosevelt did make clear that his suggestion would apply only to the state's highest court, not to the Supreme Court of the United States. "Terrible Ted" had tossed a firecracker into the ring along with his hat. The country immediately split into those who cheered his proposal and those who were outraged. The politicians were stunned.

The former President was very understanding toward old friends who wrote that they were unable to accept his radical position. "[Nothing] would make me lose my warm personal affection for you," TR assured Henry Cabot Lodge; "of course you will stand by your convictions." But he insisted that there was nothing new in his Columbus speech, that "every single point" had appeared in his editorials for the *Outlook*. Lodge answered that the speech had made him "miserably unhappy" and that he had read all his friend's editorials but must have missed the one about the recall of judicial decisions.

"Heavens Sake! You have so often been right that it is perfectly possible that I am wrong," Roosevelt wrote to Stimson, who had come out for Taft. "I have always told you that you would have to be for him," he added to Taft's secretary of war. The loss of the support of old friends was a fact of political life that Roosevelt accepted. The most difficult conflict was that of Roosevelt's son-in-law, Nicholas Longworth, still the congressman from Taft's home district. Though fond of his father-in-law and aware of the clannish loyalty of the Roosevelts, he could not possibly support him. It was hard for Alice, but her father helped her to handle the situation.

Henry Adams predicted before the ex-President's decision that Theodore was "inevitable." He asserted that "the whole interest was in Theodore." There was no chance of keeping the convention "from voting Theodore by a general yell." He doubted that the former President could be elected, but "no one doubts that Taft will be defeated."[76]

The election of 1912 proved to be one of the most dramatic and imaginative of the quadrennial spectacles provided for the American voters. Theodore Roosevelt, who dominated it, was fifty-three years old and much too dynamic and vibrant to settle down into bucolic memoir writing and editorializing as the Sage of Sagamore Hill. Still the favorite of the cartoonists, his teeth flashed and his pince-nez twinkled, his chin jutted out as he emphasized a point, and he emananted what William Allen White called "ferocious nervous energy." The smell of danger, political or any other kind, galvanized his stocky frame into driving action. Henry Adams, among other of his friends, thought that he was insane to reenter the political arena. They also felt that he had left them behind with his new "radical" views. Adams noted that he did not know if Theodore had "a single backer of serious value." Half in jest, he added, "I see nothing for him but the Asylum."[77]

It was a mixed bag of adherents who rallied round the Roosevelt candidacy. The Progressives included such notables as ex-Senator Albert Beveridge of Indiana and California Governor Hiram Johnson. Political bosses William Flinn of Pennsylvania and William S. Ward of Westchester County, New York, backed him, and he had financial support from Frank Munsey and the controversial George W. Perkins. Newly resigned from the House of Morgan, Perkins was now devoting himself entirely to TR. The two men had first met when Roosevelt was governor of New York. Impressed by Perkins, he had appointed him to the Palisades Interstate Park Commission. William Allen White said that many Progressives disliked and distrusted Perkins even though he was efficient and able. His well-tailored, elegant New York look did not match White's idea of a suitable manager for the Roosevelt team. However, when some of the Progressives expressed their doubts about having a representative of "the malefactors of great wealth" holding a critical post on their team, as well as some political bosses, Roosevelt just waved away their protests with a hearty laugh.

The use of presidential primaries in the election of 1912 pleased Roosevelt because it was a reform he supported and because, as he expected, he made a good showing in them. Six states—Illinois, Maryland, Massachusetts, Ohio, Pennsylvania, and South Dakota—held primaries for the first time. The legislation to establish them had been supported by the Rooseveltians and opposed by the Taftites.

Once the Roosevelt strategy committee had determined that the concentration of effort would be in the states with primary elections, TR put aside his hopes that his campaign efforts would be limited to a few major speeches and set up an exhausting tour schedule. Starting at the end of March, the ex-President covered the midwestern states including Illinois, Indiana, Iowa, Missouri, Michigan, Wisconsin, and Minnesota. In April he made swings through the West, the Midwest, and New England. It was a grueling experience, Roosevelt declared. By the time he had finished up in Nebraska and Kansas, at the end of April, his voice was gone. He then had to confine his speechmaking to Boston and other cities, abandoning open-air speeches and "the cartail campaign."

The speaking tour did pay off. Roosevelt won the Nebraska primary handily and did well in Kansas. He was successful also in the Oregon primary, in both primaries in Washington, and in California. "Win or lose, we have made history in this campaign, and never again will the party be able to nominate its man by the old-time machine methods against the interests of the people," he said. His hopes would prove to be without substance.

Taft campaigned very hard also. In a Boston speech, he declared that the recall of judicial decisions was a revolutionary proposal and also attacked Roosevelt for attempting a third term. At the conclusion of the address, he said that to be forced to accuse Theodore Roosevelt of disregarding the constitutional principles of the United States was "one of the most painful duties of my life." Later, a reporter found the President sitting in his private railroad car alone and overwrought, his head buried in his hands. When he saw the newspaperman, he lifted his head and muttered hoarsely, "Roosevelt was my closest friend," and then wept uncontrollably.[78]

In its last stage, the campaign degenerated into name-calling and vituperation by both rivals. TR called the President a "puzzlewit" and a "fathead." Taft called the ex-President a "demagogue" and a "dangerous egotist." The public rather enjoyed the mounting tension between them, and when, on one occasion, the Roosevelt and Taft campaign trains accidentally stopped next to each other, the expectant crowd was disappointed that no confrontation between the two contenders or their followers occurred.

By June, it looked as if Roosevelt was going into the convention with a comfortable lead. The primary contests had yielded 278 delegates for him, 48 for Taft, and 36 for La Follette, now a forgotten man. To win the Republican nomination, 540 votes were needed. The New York *Tribune* gave the preconvention count as follows: 469½ for TR against 454½ for Taft. However, many of the Roosevelt votes were questionable, because the credentials of 252 pro-Roosevelt delegates were being contested. And on June 7, when the Republican National Committee met in Chicago, its first order of business was to rule on the disputed seats. Predictably, they awarded 238 of the places to the regular party favorite, President Taft.

As soon as the national committee's intention became clear, there was agitation in the Roosevelt camp to urge the former President to go to Chicago, but he did not want to if he could possibly avoid it. Finally, overcoming his reluctance and breaking precedent, Roosevelt set out to lead his faithful followers on the Chicago battlefield. He put on his wide-brimmed slouch hat, drove from Oyster Bay to New York City, and boarded the *Lake Shore Limited* for Chicago. En route, the irrepressible former President assured his well-wishers that he would fight to the finish and not stand for the theft of his rightful convention seats.

Teddy got a rousing welcome from the Chicago crowd, which was estimated at 50,000. Marching bands blared the Spanish-American War favorite, "There'll be a Hot Time in the Old Town Tonight," which was Roosevelt's campaign song, while the crowd sang along enthusiastically. He was surely the people of Chicago's choice but, a veteran of many political wars, TR knew that the decision would be made in the convention hall and not on the streets. A reporter asked the hero how he felt in the midst of all the popular acclaim. "I'm feeling like a Bull Moose," he replied.

The Roosevelt headquarters on the second floor of the Congress Hotel was the scene of frantic politicking conducted amidst noise and clamor. William Draper Lewis, dean of the University of Pennsylvania Law School, said TR was the least perturbed person there. He found the Colonel calmly seated in a rocking chair reading a volume of Herodotus.

The night before the convention started, a delegate who claimed to represent thirty-two southern delegates came to Roosevelt with a proposal. His bloc would vote for the former President's candidacy on the condition that they would be free to vote with the Conservatives on the platform. These votes would provide the amount needed for the nomination. While his friends waited in silence, Roosevelt answered promptly. "Thank the delegates you represent but tell them that I cannot permit them to vote for me unless they vote for all the progressive principles for which the progressive elements in the Republican party stand and by which I stand or fall," he said. Not even his oldest and closest friends could budge him on this decision. To two of them he said, "I have grown to regard you both as brothers; let no act or word of yours make that relationship impossible."[79]

The peak of emotion was reached when the ex-President spoke to his followers at the Auditorium. In a fiery oration intended to arouse them, he raged at "the usurpation of the sovereignty of the people by irresponsible bosses inspired by the sinister influence of moneyed privilege." Roosevelt was not a socialist radical but only a middle-class reformer. He was referring, of course, to the Republican National Committee and their robbery of his delegates. At the close of the speech, the tone of the Roosevelt campaign was struck. "We stand at Armageddon and we battle for the Lord," he said. St. Theodore had preached his crusade and his aroused followers were ready to set out on it.

From the start, the Republican convention held out little hope for success to the Roosevelt forces. With the Taft delegates seated and the election of the resolute Taftite Elihu Root instead of the pro-Roosevelt governor of Wisconsin Francis E. McGovern as chairman, Taft's nomination was assured. Cries and shouts of "We want Teddy" were all the effective opposition the Colonel's friends could manage while the steamroller moved on to the nomination of the President.

The decision that had to be made at the Roosevelt headquarters was whether to accept the Taft nomination or to bolt the party and form a third party with TR as the standard-bearer. It was a critical decision for many of the Republicans there. If the new party lost, their political careers would be finished for a long time. The Rump Convention met at Orchestra Hall while the dreary legitimate one gave Taft 561 votes and the nomination. Roosevelt received 107 votes and La Follette 41. Hiram Johnson presided over the bolters while they awaited the arrival of their favorite. Alice Longworth, who left the Coliseum to join the family at the second convention, noted the difference between "the sullen, shamefaced, obedient" regulars she had left behind and "the spirit, buoyancy and enthusiasm" of the Roosevelt crowd. "Everyone was chockablock with a sort of camp-meeting fervor, cheering and emotional," she observed.[80]

Roosevelt said that he would accept the new party's nomination if offered to him unless the delegates came up with another candidate. This offer was just a gesture of political politeness; the ex-President was the essence of the movement. He had no intention of moving over for anyone, least of all for his only possible rival, Robert La Follette. All evidence points to the conclusion that Theodore Roosevelt was in Chicago because the managers intended to arrange a bolt if their candidate did not receive the Republican nomination. Otherwise, why did TR stay on in Chicago once the convention had elected Root as chairman and thus guaranteed that the Colonel could not win. He stayed to rally his followers and well-nigh admitted it when he told them on June 20: "So far as I am concerned I am through . . . the real and lawful majority will organize as such . . . I went before the people and I won. . . . Let us find out whether the Republican party is the party of the plain people." Obviously TR did not want to compromise on some other liberal candidate such as Governor Hadley of Missouri. He wanted to fight his crusade and win it himself.[81]

The nomination of Woodrow Wilson as the Democratic party's presidential candidate was a blow to Roosevelt, because now he was no longer the only Progressive in the triangular contest. Though the New Jersey governor was an excellent man, individually, Roosevelt wrote, he could not support him, as was suggested, because his election would restore the Democratic bosses to power. The Colonel now believed his chances greatly diminished and the Democratic candidate correctly predicted that the split in the GOP would make his election certain.

The Bull Moose Convention met in Chicago on August 5 without some of the most prominent Roosevelt supporters, who had not followed the ex-President out of the party. Among these were Senators Borah of Idaho, Cummins of Iowa, and Bourne of Oregon. Six of the seven "little Governors" stayed safely at home, including Governor Hadley. Anyone who did not attend that Progressive party convention, however, whether he agreed with its principles or not, "missed a thrilling and memorable occasion," Henry P. Stoddard, veteran reporter, said. Each delegate was utterly free because each one had paid his own way.

The convention met on August 5, with Senator Albert J. Beveridge of Indiana as the chairman and opening speaker. The mood of the participants was inspired. Each delegation entered the hall singing and parading and worshipping TR as its patron saint. The California banner was emblazoned with the verse:

> I want to be a Bull Moose
> And with the Bull Moose stand
> With Antlers on my forehead
> And a Big Stick in my hand.

Michigan delegates led the convention in their song "Follow Follow./We will follow Roosevelt." Another convention favorite was the "Battle Hymn of the Republic," which had acquired a new verse:

> The Moose has left the wooded hill; his call
>   rings through the land;
> It's a summons to the young and strong to join
>   with willing hand
> To fight for right and country; to strike down
>   a robber band,
> And we'll go marching on.

The most startling entrance was made by the New York contingent. Led by Oscar S. Straus, the dignified Jewish diplomat, they snaked down the aisle singing lustily, "Onward Christian Soldiers."

Beveridge gave a memorable opening speech that set a very high standard for the convention. Its theme was that the government must be given back to the people, "so the first purpose of the Progressive Party is to make sure of the rule of the people." Roosevelt appeared on the platform on the second day. After an hour-long demonstration, he addressed himself "to you men who have come to spend and be spent in the endless crusade against wrong." Only the new party could effect reform, he postulated in his "Confession of Faith," which summed up the Progressive party's program. Among the social reforms proposed were social insurance for old age, sickness, and unemployment; the regulation of business by federal commissions; income and inheritance taxes; and a lower tariff. They were sound middle-class reforms most of which would have to wait for general acceptance until the Democratic Roosevelt's New Deal.

There was no voting or balloting at this convention of like minds. On the third day, Roosevelt was nominated for the presidency by acclamation and Hiram Johnson was chosen as his running mate. Jane Addams of Hull House made a seconding speech which was a mild gesture toward the convention's endorsement of women's rights.

As the two candidates walked side by side to the front of the platform, a banner with a verse adapted from Rudyard Kipling's "The Ballad of East and West" was lowered from the rafters.

> Roosevelt and Johnson!
> New York and California
> Hands across the continent
> For there is neither east nor west
> Border nor breed nor birth,
> When two strong men stand face to face
> Though they come from the ends of the earth.

The party platform was presented after the nomination. Some of the fervor for the candidates was clouded by a sharp struggle over the antitrust plank. The faithful reformers wanted the specific abuses clearly outlined, but Perkins, ex-associate of the House of Morgan, International Harvester, and United States Steel, preferred a more general statement. Roosevelt tried to be the mediator between Perkins and Gifford Pinchot, the most vociferous advocate of a strong statement. William Allen White, who was writing his news report in the hall of the Blackstone Hotel while the battle of the antitrust plank was going on, described the ex-President as "pendulating between Perkins' room and Pinchot's room." Looking over the top of his glasses, with the contested plank in his hand, he would enter one room, "and then in a few moments, like a faithful retriever, would come popping out . . . grinning at me like a dog wagging his tail as he tried to compromise the differences between the pinfeather wings of his new party."[82]

When the platform was presented, the trust issue caused consternation. Dean Lewis, the chairman of the platform committee, included in his presentation a paragraph that strengthened the Sherman Anti-Trust Act, one that Perkins believed had been cut out the night before. After the public meeting, a hasty meeting with an irate Perkins resulted in the removal of the controversial paragraph. White was not the only Progressive who regarded this reversal as a "disturbing disillusion."

The campaign that followed had its high and low moments for the starry-eyed Christian soldiers and their more practical cohorts. But the moving spirit of the party continued to be the Bull Moose himself. Though Henry Adams wrote catty letters about "our Theodore," calling him "an amoosin cuss" without much chance of being elected or "a rather droll Napoleon" who was "a dead cock in the pit," others saw him in an almost heroic light.[83] The ex-President rumbled and roared, expended his boundless energy without cease, and covered the country in his special train provided by the Bull Moose National Committee. Some two or three dozen reporters from metropolitan newspapers traveled with him. At first they enjoyed his friendly badinage, but soon they suffered from complete exhaustion.

Though he fought a gallant campaign, Alice Longworth admitted that the farther away "we got from the 'Rump' convention, the slimmer Father's chances looked for success in the election." The candidate also realized that his chances were poor. "For your private information," he wrote to Horace Plunkett in August, "I will say again that I think it probable at present that Wilson will win." He attributed this inevitability to the fact that "well-meaning progressives who do not think deeply or fundamentally" would support him. Since Wilson would carry the majority of the Progressive Democrats and some of the reactionary Republicans, who would desert Taft when they saw that he could not be reelected, "I shall only get the progressive Republicans," Roosevelt predicted, and though they made up the great majority of the party, "I shall not get any but those of strong convictions." The rest would vote the party ticket. He had some hopes still that as the campaign progressed his strength might grow, particularly among independent reformers, Democratic workers, and farmers. "However," he insisted, "win or lose, the fight had to be made and it happened that no human being could make it except myself." Even if the movement did not gain strength, TR was certain that he would do better than Taft.[84]

These private doubts did not stop Roosevelt's pace. In what was left of August, after the convention, he campaigned in New England. In September he left for a month's swing through the West. As the train moved westward to Seattle, Washington, he spoke in Illinois, Indiana, Missouri, Iowa, Minnesota, North Dakota, and Montana.

President Taft, apparently accepting defeat, confined his campaigning to a few speeches. Wilson, also, had planned to make only a limited number of major addresses in which he would present his principles and, perhaps, visit some doubtful states. But reports of the ex-president's permeating presence throughout the country forced Wilson into action. After September he, too, hit the campaign trail, traveling ceaselessly until election day.

Roosevelt had Wilson pegged as a prudish college professor, which was probably inaccurate but rather amusing. Some letters that allegedly involved Wilson in an affair with a divorced woman were being peddled to the highest bidder. Both parties' representatives refused them. TR wrote to Colonel J. Roosevelt, who had turned them down for the Progressive party: "Those letters would be entirely unconvincing. Nothing, no evidence could ever make the American people believe that a man like Woodrow Wilson, cast so perfectly as the apothecary's clerk, could ever play Romeo."[85]

The crusading hero almost met a martyr's death in Milwaukee, where he was scheduled for a major address. On October 14, Roosevelt left the Hotel Gilpatrick after a testimonial dinner to drive to the hall where he was to speak. He entered his car and stood up to greet the crowd that had been awaiting his appearance. From the crowd, at a distance of less than thirty feet, a man fired a bullet into TR's chest. Before the assassin could follow with another shot, Elbert Martin, one of Roosevelt's stenographers and a former football player, saw the glint of the pistol and hurled himself at its owner. Martin said afterward that he wanted to strangle the assassin, but Roosevelt, regaining his equilibrium, cried out, "Stand back! Don't hurt the man. I want to look at him." The ex-President scrutinized John F. Schrank, the would-be killer, a part-time bartender from New York, asked him why he had attacked him, and then, not waiting for an answer, told the police to take the man away. Schrank told police afterward that he opposed the third term and that McKinley had come to him in a dream and told him to avenge his murder by Vice-President Roosevelt.

The bullet had passed through Roosevelt's iron spectacle case and the thick manuscript of the speech he was about to deliver, both of which had been in his pocket. It did, however, fracture TR's fourth rib and lodge close to his right lung. Refusing to be taken to the hospital, the Colonel ordered the cavalcade to drive to the Milwaukee Auditorium. "Friends, I shall have to ask you to be as quiet as possible. I do not know whether you fully understand that I have been shot, but it takes more than that to kill a Bull Moose," he told the astounded audience. "The bullet is in me now, so that I cannot make a very long speech. But I will try to do my best." He then devoted the next hour to a discussion of the Progressive party's stand on labor.

After the speech, Roosevelt was disgusted with the unfeeling crowd that milled around him demanding to shake his hand and blocking his exit. He was taken first to a Milwaukee hospital and the next day to Chicago's Mercy Hospital, where he stayed until October 21.

President Taft immediately expressed the hope of the American people that Colonel Roosevelt would recover quickly from the effects of "this dastardly act." Wilson offered to halt his own campaign but did not follow through. Roosevelt was touched that so many of his old friends who had strayed from his fold wrote to him with great warmth. "It was fine to hear from you. I am practically all right again; and feel a little like the old maid who, when she at last discovered a man under her bed, seized him and said, 'You're the burglar I have been looking for these last twenty years,' " he wrote to Henry Cabot Lodge.[86]

Assassination was a subject TR had given a lot of thought to, he told the British historian Sir George Trevelyan, since he had become President as a result of McKinley's murder. "For the last eleven years I have, of course, thoroughly understood that I might at any time be shot, and presumably *would* be shot some time," he wrote. Any serious-minded public man had to be so absorbed in the great vital questions that he could exclude thoughts of assassination from his mind. It was not a matter of courage but "of the major interest driving out the minor interest." A private could have qualms, but not the general.[87]

Home at Oyster Bay again, the Colonel celebrated his fifty-fourth birthday and a few days later delivered a speech at Madison Square Garden. The crowds were out in large numbers to see the man who had just escaped the assassin's bullet. There was such confusion at the entrance of the Garden that TR's sister, Corinne Robinson, and her party had to climb the fire escape in order to get in. Alice Longworth was there too and was very moved by the ovation given to her father. Richard Harding Davis, the well-known reporter and novelist, had been following the Roosevelt campaign closely. He wrote that the mood of the crowd was one of "congratulations and thanksgiving." It was "a greeting from old friends to one who had nearly escaped them."[88]

Progressive party enthusiasts called the speech one of their leader's finest; others said it was trite and filled with platitudes. The audience was wildly enthusiastic. "We are for liberty," Roosevelt declaimed. "But we are for the liberty of the oppressed, not for the liberty of the oppressor to oppress the weak and to bind the burdens on the shoulders of the heavy laden." The rally was an exhilarating experience for the Roosevelts, but once back at Oyster Bay, the former President was aware that he might have reached the peak of the campaign. "We had the conviction and the vision, but alas not the votes," Alice Longworth observed. The "spirit, enthusiasm and the conviction of righteousness of our cause" would bow before the indifference or opposition of the majority.[89]

When the votes were counted, TR's original prediction proved to be accurate. Wilson won with a popular vote of 6,293,019 against Roosevelt's 4,119,500 and Taft's 3,484,956. Wilson's electoral vote was a sweep of 435 votes to the Colonel's 88 and Taft's pitiful 2. The President carried only Vermont and Utah. Roosevelt had destroyed his disappointing successor and had led what was probably the most exciting, dramatic, and idealistic campaign in American history. It had almost cost him his life.

After defeat, the losers must engage in soul-searching post-mortems. The Progressive party, running as a third party in a traditionally two-party system, had to ask itself if the campaign could be justified. Taft had been defeated, but the figures showed he would have been defeated even if Roosevelt had endorsed him. It had to be acknowledged, however, that the Progressive party, in one campaign, had become the second most powerful party in the nation. Though it had failed to win, its ideas would have to be taken seriously.

Why did its leader, Theodore Roosevelt, who seemed to know from the start that he would lose, decide to run? It was not enough, apparently, for the ex-President to be certain of Taft's defeat. Almost everyone had predicted it. He had the need to participate in that defeat and, at the same time, show that he could surpass him in the struggle. In Roosevelt's mind, the Taftites had stolen the Republican convention's nomination from him. This was true in the sense that TR had been clearly shown in the primaries to be the choice of the Republican party's rank-and-file members. Perhaps not all of the cases of rejected Roosevelt delegates were clear-cut. Historians grant only twenty-five to thirty of them as beyond question, the others open to interpretation. But had the thirty Roosevelt delegates been admitted, there would have been enough votes to keep Root from becoming chairman and this might have changed the convention's decision.[90]

The bolt out of the Republican convention raises other questions. As stated earlier, the fact that Roosevelt stayed in Chicago after it was certain that he would not get the nomination strongly suggests that he was preparing the bolt. Thus his suggestion that the bolted Republicans choose another leader before their convention lacked sincerity. Roosevelt put his position honestly when he said that he was in the fight "only on the principle, in the long run a sound one, that I would rather take a thrashing than be quiet under such a kicking."[91]

Sometimes headstrong and capricious, Roosevelt was neither naive nor foolish. He believed in the Progressive movement and certainly demonstrated that he had the courage of his convictions when he took the stand on judicial recall. He was pugnacious enough to enjoy a good fight and anxious to lay to rest his unfortunate statement of November 8, 1904, made just after his election: "On the fourth of March next, I shall have served three and a half years and this . . . constitutes my first term. The wise custom which limits the President to two terms regards the substance and not the form: and under no circumstances will I be a candidate for or accept another nomination."[92] In 1912, when he did run again, he had to give some explanation. In his letters, Roosevelt expounded often on his apparent change of heart about the third-term issue. His argument was that the 1904 declaration "had no application whatever to the candidacy of a man who was not at the time in office, whether he had or had not been President before." Therefore, if there were a strong popular demand for him, he would respond affirmatively. The earlier statement had had to do only with the next presidential election in 1908, he asserted, "and was universally accepted at the time as so referring." He clarified his new position with an anecdote. "Sometimes if asked to take a second cup of coffee, I say 'No, thank you. I won't take another cup.' This does not mean that I never intend to take another cup of coffee during my life . . . my remark is limited to that breakfast."[93]

The third-term issue surfaced occasionally during the campaign, though it never developed into the organized opposition of the anti–third term clubs and convention at the time of Grant's bid in 1880. The Taftites sometimes referred to saving "our liberty" and to the danger "of monarchy." There was also a popular jingle that appeared in anti-Roosevelt journals:

> Washington wouldn't
> Grant couldn't
> Roosevelt shan't.

In his own postmortem letters to friends and colleagues, TR assigned the cause of defeat to the odds being too heavy against them. The Democrats had chosen their strongest candidate and the Progressive party was too new. "We did not have half money enough," the Colonel insisted, using the argument to defend Perkins, "the Dough Moose." Finally, Roosevelt felt that had his Republicans won in New York in 1910, he would have carried the 1912 convention "and made the Republican party the Progressive party." But, as it happened, many of the Progressives in the Republican party did not leave it.[94]

Having once left the White House, Cleveland was the only ex-President whose party gave him a chance to win another four-year lease. Both Van Buren in 1844 and Grant in 1880 failed to get the nomination, although at first they seemed to be the favorites. This chapter has dealt only with serious attempts to regain the presidential office. There were feelers and boomlets for other former presidents, but they collapsed before they grew significant.

The question arises, then, of whether having been president enhances an individual's value as a candidate or lessens it. In the case of the major parties, it seems that realignments develop so quickly once a president steps down that party structure alters at once. A president in office, by necessity, makes enemies within his party through differences, slights, and misunderstandings. The politicos who regain power then do not want to reinstate their former chief. It is often the rank and file who remain loyal, as in the case of Van Buren in 1844. On the surface, it appeared that the Texas letter was his downfall but, as discussed, there were serious signs of defection before the letter was published.

Grant in 1880 ruined the plans of his managers by coming home too early and using up the resurgence of popularity that met his return. But it is doubtful that so fragile a commodity as personal glory could have survived a campaign that would have had to face the third-term issue and a revival of the Grant administration scandals.

As third-party candidates, the former Presidents did have something unique to offer—their prestige and the aura of the American presidency. No minor party could be considered without distinction that could point to an ex-President as its standard-bearer. In the cases of both Van Buren and Fillmore, the merging of party and candidate was almost entirely pragmatic. Van Buren was a Free-Soiler only as long as he was the party's candidate in 1844. Fillmore used the Know-Nothings to promote himself and his idea of a party for all the people. His identification with nativism and anti-Catholicism was only peripheral. Theodore Roosevelt, however, was another matter. He and the Progressive party seemed to be one, especially in the 1912 Bull Moose campaign. But even Roosevelt had ulterior motives. In addition to his desire for social reform, he wanted to beat Taft.

Cleveland, the exception, was fortunate in that he had a unique combination of circumstances in his favor. One might argue that Cleveland had never been a loser. In 1888, Benjamin Harrison took the election, but Cleveland won the popular vote and his loss of two key states, Indiana and New York, was almost surely due to fraud. There was a bargain, it appears, between the politicians of both the major parties in New York to give the governorship to the Democratic David B. Hill and the state's electoral votes to Harrison. In Indiana, the corruption was more blatant. Floaters were bribed and then escorted to the polls to vote Republican.

Cleveland had several assets that made him the Republican candidate in 1892 for the third time. He had a strong reputation as an honest man and attracted the youth vote. Harrison had been a weak opponent, and no Democrat had emerged during the four-year interval to challenge Cleveland. Furthermore, Cleveland had provided the issue for the election, which was the tariff. The elections of 1890 had repudiated the high Republican protective tariff, thereby making Cleveland the logical candidate, since he had supported lower tariffs during his administration.

Partisan Politics

S O FIRMLY is the ex-president identified as his party's leader that Barry Goldwater's statement in February 1975 hardly sounded absurd. The 1964 Republican presidential candidate reported that he had lunched with former President Nixon, who had said that he might like to be "a Republican Party spokesman." Though the Watergate scandal was still front-page news, Goldwater believed that this was a good idea, because Nixon's mail showed "no lessening of interest in him within the Party." After all, the senator observed, millions had voted for him. However, the statement caused such consternation within the Republican party that Nixon himself quietly announced that he hadn't meant it.[1]

Buchanan and Hoover both left the presidency in a thick haze of public disapproval and so did Lyndon Johnson, but no other chief executive, not even Andrew Johnson, who had been tried on impeachment charges, had equalled Nixon's situation. He was the only President in American history who had resigned from office, and it required a presidential blanket pardon to keep him from prosecution in the courts. Yet apparently even he had his defenders and advocates in the party that he had led to victory in 1968 and 1972.

The party use of ex-presidents occurs most often at election time, but there have been other occasions. The Federalist party turned to George Washington to stop President Adams from sending an embassy to the French Directory, because they did not want the United States to become an ally of revolutionary France. In the summer of 1799, England was triumphant over her traditional enemy, so it would seem to have been an ideal moment for an American withdrawal from an embarrassing entanglement with the Directory, which, the Feds believed, would soon be replaced by a restored monarchy. Honest John Adams, however, did what seemed best for the country; he ignored his party and sent the embassy to France, thus, according to the Federalists, playing right into the hands of Jefferson's Democratic-Republicans and setting them up for victory in the election of 1800.

Adams's motive was to keep the peace at all costs; he was even aware that the cost might be his reelection, which it was. Washington played an interesting role. Though he feared the result of the Adams mission, he decided to "remain mute." Disregarding Federalist pressure, he said: "The vessel is afloat or nearly so, and considering myself as a passenger only, I shall trust to the mariners whose duty it is to watch, to steer it into a safe port." By opting for inaction, the first President allowed the second to sacrifice his future while saving American foreign policy.[2]

It was a blow to the Federalists, who regarded Washington as one of them. It was his persuasiveness that forced John Marshall to enter politics against his wishes. The first President ordered Marshall to Mount Vernon "to converse on the elections." Reluctantly Marshall went and was very cool to Washington's proposal that he run for Congress from Richmond. The young lawyer tried to explain that he wanted to build up his law practice instead, but could hardly refuse to comply when the former President started to list his own personal sacrifices. Marshall yielded and was elected, though by a small margin.[3]

Upon his retirement, John Adams renounced politics and political parties. His interest now, he said, was academic and philosophical. He predicted that parties would alternate in power, twelve years conservative and then about twelve years radical. Parties, like people, could not stand success. It made them grow presumptuous and then break to pieces, he said.[4]

The Virginia succession had continued in power for twenty-four years when the last of the dynasty, James Monroe, was faced with the problem of the contested election of 1824. As President, he stated at the time, he had remained neutral, and in 1828 insisted that he was friendly to both President John Quincy Adams and his irate rival, Andrew Jackson. However, Monroe and the only other living ex-

President, James Madison, found that their wishes to be neutral had been ignored and that they both had been designated electors for Virginia on the Adams ticket. It was particularly awkward because the two men had been lifelong friends of the President and did not see how they could withdraw gracefully.

A somewhat anxious correspondence between the two ex-Presidents attempted to solve the problem jointly. Monroe wrote that to become partisans in an election would negate any useful service that might be rendered; "better they remain tranquil spectators." Finally, the two former Presidents resigned as electors. It was best for them to stay out of political activity, Monroe stated piously, although he had another motive for not being identified with Adams. Jackson was expected to be the victor, and Monroe knew that his suit with the government to recover his diplomatic expenses would have no hope of succeeding if Jackson were offended. Madison, who had no ulterior motive but was rather wearied with the political strife, said wisely that an ex-President's neutrality might not be appreciated by the incumbent.[5]

Since all the ex-Presidents opposed Lincoln's nomination in 1860, the muddle of candidates led naturally to proposals to submit the former chief executives as possible compromise candidates. No serious campaign was mounted for any of them, but there was some interest in the possibilities among the politicians. To John Tyler, the support of several party leaders, no matter how tentative, was gratifying because, as Julia Tyler said, it meant that he seemed "to have outlived the abuse of his enemies." There was a brief flurry for him about the time of the Harpers Ferry incident. New York's Tammany Hall considered him briefly, but when his friend Henry A. Wise lost the renomination for the Virginia governorship, the boomlet collapsed. Tyler wrote: "I have daily assurances from plain men of an anxious desire on their part to restore me to the presidency; but I receive them as nothing more than the expression of good will."[6]

Friends of Franklin Pierce saw him as a strong possibility for a harmonizing candidate. But Pierce refused and sent a strong letter to Caleb Cushing saying that he had suffered enough and that Mrs. Pierce's poor health required his full attention. A firm believer in party discipline, Pierce decided to follow his state convention's decision. However, he did not participate in the campaign except as an advisor, and there is no evidence that his suggestions were taken.

Millard Fillmore, who had learned from his 1856 experience, avoided the issue by staying out of the situation completely. He refused to give up his status as a private citizen.

In 1864, Pierce, who was now a widower and so unable to hide behind his wife's bad health, remained unmoved by his friends' assertions that he would be the ideal Democratic candidate to run against Lincoln. On the contrary, he saw no evidence that he was restored to favor in the public's heart. For his part, General McClellan, Horatio Seymour, or his secretary of the treasury, James Guthrie, would make a fine candidate. The platform that he preferred would advocate an end to the war.

Fillmore also favored McClellan at the Chicago convention. "I do not desire the nomination," he wrote, along with his endorsement of the general, "and I cannot think a great number desire me to have it." But, though very pleased with the McClellan-Pendleton ticket, Fillmore refused to attend political meetings, make speeches, or write letters for publication. "I regard myself . . . wholly withdrawn from party contests," he explained in August. By the following month, very reluctantly, he allowed the publication of a pro-McClellan letter, because he believed that the Democratic candidate held the only hope for "the restoration of the union, an honorable peace, and the security of personal liberty." He did not consider this statement partisan. "I do not consider myself as belonging to any party," Fillmore insisted. His only concern was the honor and welfare of "my beloved, but bleeding and suffering country." Without a change in administration, the country would be in bankruptcy and under a military despotism.[7]

The newest and most discredited ex-President, James Buchanan, was in virtual exile at Wheatland, and no one mentioned his name at the Chicago convention. McClellan was not his first choice as the party standard-bearer, he wrote to a friend, but "God grant he may succeed." When the Democrats failed again, Buchanan found consolation in the thought that winning would have posed "terrible difficulties & embarrassments for the party." Now it could be "a watchful guardian over the constitution." Lincoln's proper role, Buchanan felt, was to offer the Confederates conciliation so that they might return to the Union as they were before, leaving the slavery question to settle itself. If the President would do that, he would have accomplished the object of the war, and though the parties would not love each other, they would have mutual respect. "There would be no collision between them for a hundred years," Buchanan said.[8]

Vice-President Andrew Johnson became President after Lincoln's assassination and found that he, too, was to become a political victim of the Radical Republicans, who, now that the war was over, wanted to keep their power. They had no intentions of relinquishing it either to representatives from the defeated South or to the new President, who they believed was no better than a Southern Democrat. They almost succeeded in ousting their victim, but he escaped indictment at the impeachment trial by a hairsbreadth. After that there was no question of Johnson running on the party ticket in 1868. General Grant, political cipher and the hero of Appomattox, swept into office. But back in his home state of Tennessee, Andrew Johnson was still "the noble and heroic fighter" in behalf of constitutional liberty who had "sacrificed his personal ambition" for his principles.[9]

Andrew Johnson wanted his old Senate seat back, and all his energies were directed toward achieving that purpose. As a first step, he declared himself an independent candidate for congressman, making the announcement himself in Nashville's public square. He did not expect to win the congressional seat from the regular party candidate, but his campaign was energetic and courageous and served to remind his own people of his presence. A contemporary newspaper article said that he traversed the state "like a fighting apostle of loyalty" making "war to the knife on the attempt to glorify the Rebellion."[10]

Johnson lost the election, but his campaign was so memorable that he could be ignored neither by the people of the state nor by the legislators who, of course, were the ones to select the senator. Johnson's supporters were increasingly confident that he would be the choice as the time for the election drew near. Many of his old friends who were unable to support him for Congress because they were obliged to back the regular party men, "are your advocates of your election to the Senate," he was told. Only extremists would "be opposed to your reappearance in the U.S. Senate," another friend wrote. The ex-President felt that his prospects were good but, nevertheless, rallied his supporters so they would become better.[11]

Despite his optimism, Johnson had serious competition from three former Confederate major generals, among other contenders. The

balloting for senator went on for more than a week while Johnson
rallied and encouraged his thirty-five unwavering legislators, whose
support was loyal but inadequate. Finally, on January 26, the fifty-
fifth ballot delivered a Johnson victory. Nashville was ecstatic. Ten
thousand cheering natives merged on the public square to listen to
the ex-President deliver his victory speech. He promised that he
would return to Washington, not for revenge but to unite all men
in the country. Several other speakers that night suggested Johnson
for President in '76. It was a moment of happiness and vindication
for Andy Johnson. Telegrams and letters of congratulation came
from all parts of the nation.

When Johnson appeared to take his seat in the Senate at the special
session that President Grant had called to consider a treaty with
the king of the Sandwich Islands, the senators who had participated
in his impeachment proceedings were appropriately uncomfortable.
Appropriately also, the former President arrived in a driving snow-
storm to take the oath of office while a large crowd watched from
the visitors' gallery.

The presiding officer of the Senate, Henry Wilson of Massachusetts, vice-president-elect and a notorius Radical Republican, had
voted for Johnson's conviction on the impeachment charges and had
supported his disqualification from ever holding public office in the
future. It was, therefore, a tremendous satisfaction for Johnson to
enter the upper house a duly elected member from the sovereign
state of Tennessee and to confront head-on Wilson and such others
as John A. Logan of Illinois, who had been an impeachment manager,
as well as eight others who had supported his conviction, including
such luminaries as Frelinghuysen of New Jersey, Sherman of Ohio,
Cameron of Pennsylvania, and Roscoe Conkling of New York.

The New York *Herald* reporter observed that Johnson, at this
time, had changed less physically than many of those who had tried
to ensure his political demise. "There are neither hard lines nor deep
wrinkles in his face," the newsman wrote, "but his expression is a
mixture of sadness and earnestness—an expression which has been
habitual with him during the past ten years." With no apparent
embarrassment, the ex-President shook hands with Wilson, a gesture
that elicited wild applause from the gallery, and then went to his
seat, which friends had heaped with flowers. A page was waiting
there to hand the returned senator a bouquet. Overcome with emotion

and wishing to avoid any further demonstrations of support, ex-President Johnson escaped to the cloakroom. Even there he could not avoid the warm attentions of his fellow members, who wanted to shake his hand.[12]

During the brief session, Johnson had the opportunity to oppose the President and denounce the administration. Bitter factional strife during the Louisiana state elections culminated in violence. Grant sent General Sheridan to New Orleans to return the city to order, but the Northerner further inflamed the White Leaguers, whom he blamed for the bloodshed, by calling them "banditti." He also wanted to quell the White League militarily, which outraged the North as well as the South, although for different reasons. Their ire was particularly aroused when five members of the legislature, whose credentials were in question, were driven from the State House at bayonet point. Mass protest meetings were held at Cooper Institute in New York, at Faneuil Hall in Boston, and in other Northern cities. The theme of the protests was expressed by the aged William Cullen Bryant, who said that he feared federal rule over the state. How long before similar action might take place in Massachusetts or Ohio, Carl Schurz asked? "How long before a soldier may stalk into the National House of Representatives and, pointing to the Speaker's mace say 'take away that bauble,' " he added.[13]

At this interim session, a resolution was introduced to approve Grant's actions in Louisiana. Johnson, with fiery indignation, rose to defend constitutional freedom against the President's action to take over Louisiana and to keep it by military might. Grant's motive, the former President said, "was to inaugurate a system of terrorism" throughout the country and thus ride into a third term. "And when this is done, farewell to the liberties of the country," he proclaimed.

"That speech of Andy Johnson's," a Tennessee admirer wrote, "is the grandest speech that has been made in the U.S. Senate since the days of Daniel Webster."[14] The letter bag was full of similar sentiments. It was Johnson's swan song. He returned to Greenville when the special session was over and rested there until the summer. In late July he visited his daughter, Mary Stover, suffered a stroke, and in thirty-six hours was dead. His wishes, expressed in one of his speeches, that when he died he wanted "no better winding sheet than the Stars and Stripes and no softer pillow than the Constitution of my country" were carried out.

To his party's relief, Rutherford B. Hayes, "His Accidency" to many, refused to consider renomination in 1880 and took no part in the Garfield campaign. Three years later, when his party wanted him to run for governor of Ohio in order to save the state from going democratic, Hayes was not interested. "I inform everyone that *I would not under any circumstances accept the nomination if it were offered to me*," he declared. Once again, in 1888, the Ohio Republican party turned to Hayes as a possible candidate. Again he declared, "*under no circumstances* . . . and that is final." He was just as cool to the presidential flurries. "No more public life," he insisted.[15]

However, despite the fact that James Blaine had avoided him during his administration, Hayes supported the Maine senator in his bid for the presidency in 1884. The ex-President did not like the candidate as a person, calling him "a scheming demagogue, reckless and selfish," but conceded that he was an able man and would make a better president than a politician. Also, he had been fairly nominated and was the choice of the Republican masses rather than the machine and was therefore much to be preferred to Cleveland, his Democratic opponent.

During the campaign, Hayes met Blaine at Norwalk and introduced him at Fremont but did not electioneer for him. In return, Blaine praised the Hayes administration and talked about how the former President had gained in public esteem throughout his years in office. Hayes, who had endured a strong dose of unpopularity throughout his term in office, was pleased. But he was not surprised at Blaine's defeat at the polls. Another candidate, such as John Sherman or Benjamin Harrison, would probably have been elected, he said.

In 1888 Hayes supported John Sherman, although he regarded Benjamin Harrison as a good candidate also, and when he was nominated, wrote to him: "Very few households rejoice more sincerely than mine." Republican chances for victory were even that year, he predicted, even with Cleveland the incumbent, because the Republicans had not been so united since Grant ran in 1868. As a result of Harrison's victory, Hayes had an influx of visitors at Spiegel Grove who asked him to say a good word in their behalf to the new President. Hayes agreed to recommend those whom he knew would be worthy.[16]

Benjamin Harrison, like Hayes, served only one term, although his rivals in the 1896 convention, even William McKinley, regarded him as formidable. The press treated him well; therefore every appearance or statement he made was interpreted as having some political meaning. Harrison was rather amused, because another campaign or another term in the White House meant nothing to him but "labor and worry and distress."

In 1894, still a viable candidate, he was persuaded by the party leaders to make some speeches throughout Indiana in that interim election year. He agreed to make two appearances, one in northern and one in southern Indiana. They were so successful that he ended up making about twenty speeches on each trip. Although he had refused to leave Indiana, Harrison could not refuse to go to New York to campaign for his Vice-President, Levi Morton, who was running for governor. All of the candidates the former President supported won, which added to his popularity in the party and to speculation about his candidacy in 1896. Privately, Harrison confided to a friend that he saw no way in which his fame would be increased by going to Washington again.

Nonetheless, the party at least wanted Harrison to be willing to stand in the wings in case he was needed. The former President was adamant. It was undignified, he maintained, "to appear to be in the attitude of the little boy that followed the applecart up the hill, hoping that the board would fall out." And he did not swerve from that position despite many letters that asked that his name be used and the realization that his choice for the nomination, Senator William B. Allison, had little chance. He did not endorse Allison lest he be drawn into the party battles, and he continued to thwart a "Unite on Harrison" movement. When McKinley was nominated, Harrison wired his congratulations, predicted his success at the polls, and rejoiced that the heat was off him.[17]

Mark Hanna, McKinley's manager, did not let the ex-President escape that easily. He begged him to start the campaign with a keynote speech to be delivered on August 27, 1896. Though Hanna hoped to avoid the free silver issue, lest William Jennings Bryan crucify McKinley on a cross of silver, Harrison convinced him that it was the leading issue and had to be refuted, not dodged. Republicans, he said, must speak out firmly for a protective tariff.

At Carnegie Hall, not Madison Square Garden, where he disapproved of the acoustics, Harrison delivered a splendid speech that impressed his listeners and the press. Notwithstanding all his protests, after that speech, Harrison campaigned en route from New York to Indianapolis at Richmond, at Charleston, West Virginia, and, at the candidate's personal request, at Cincinnati. In Indiana, Harrison toured the state delivering forty speeches. "I think this ought to be regarded as my contribution to the campaign," he wrote to Hanna. After McKinley's victory, which Harrison never doubted, the former President disappeared from the political scene to devote himself to his law practice. He surfaced briefly after McKinley's second nomination, after having avoided the GOP convention by disappearing into the wilderness of Yellowstone Park and the Northwest, when he agreed to accept the President's appointment to the International Court. It was an honor for Harrison but also reflected well on the Republican President and his party. During the campaign, Harrison retreated to the Adirondacks and the following March died in Indianapolis.

The Democratic ex-President, Grover Cleveland, was in a difficult position at this time. At the close of the century, he was "disgusted" with the Silver Democrats, who had taken over the party; he distrusted them to the extent that he believed them to be no better than "influence sharks and swindlers" in their dealings with "the honest masses." Since he could not accept the Democratic program, he had to regard himself as a political outcast, merely a spectator. All during the period of Democratic Bryanism, Cleveland refused to participate in politics. Although he favored the platform and the candidate, he turned down an invitation to preside at a Democratic meeting in Trenton, New Jersey, in 1898. He feared that his interference would do more harm than good, and his political friends had to agree.[18]

Safely domiciled in Princeton, Cleveland's appearances were strictly academic. Each year, garbed in cap and gown, he led the academic procession at the commencement exercises. But when the Democratic national convention was taking place in Kansas City, he remained at Gray Gables, avoiding politics even in his thoughts. Mr. Bryan had not forgiven him for his failure to support him in 1896, so, Cleveland wrote to a friend, "*pending his pardon*, I have no standing in the new Democracy." The country's only hope, he wrote, was the rehabilitation of the party and the collapse of Bryanism. However, when that time should come, said Cleveland, "I shall remain only an intensely anxious looker-on."[19]

"Bryanism and McKinleyism! What a choice for a patriotic American," Cleveland wrote after the President's second nomination. And when McKinley asked him to accept an appointment as one of the arbitrators under the Hague Convention, he refused, although his Republican counterpart, Harrison, had accepted.

Hugging his disapproval of the candidate close to him, Cleveland resisted all appeals to come out for Bryan. Silence was all he could offer. It was hard because, as he understood, "there are millions of our fellow-citizens who believe that the organization now supporting Bryan is the same that on three occasions nominated and supported me." Even more disturbing was the letter he received from Vice-President Theodore Roosevelt right after the election. It praised him for his courageous stand against free silver. "I think now we have definitely won out on the free-silver business," TR wrote, "and therefore I think you are entitled to thanks and congratulations."

The defeat of Bryanism restored Cleveland to his party and rehabilitated him in the regard of the American people. He did not vote for McKinley, he said angrily to the editor of the Atlantic *Journal*, but he did believe that things looked brighter for "true democracy" now that Bryanism and populism would be "cut out of our party organization." Cleveland had been a political man and a Democrat all of his life. It was a tragedy to him to see the party in total eclipse and impossible for him not to blame himself for it in some way, since he had been the last successful presidential candidate. In 1904 he saw an opportunity to reassert his influence. Judge George Gray was his choice.

Although at every opportunity the ex-President insisted that his determination not to be a candidate was "unalterable and conclusive," conservative newspapers and conservative businessmen looked to him as the one who could save the country from the two radicals—Roosevelt and Bryan. But not Oscar or Nathan Straus or James Stillman or the New York *Herald Tribune* or the Brooklyn *Eagle* could convince Cleveland that a seventy-year-old rheumatic ex-President who disapproved of a third term should be anything more than "a dignified stalking horse," as Allan Nevins put it.[20]

Cleveland's friend George F. Parker went to the Democratic convention with a letter addressed specifically to Cleveland's southern supporters, especially the delegates from Georgia, who wanted to mount a Cleveland nomination. The letter said: "I want to do what I can to avoid a charge of permitting misapprehension of my position;

and so I say to you plainly as I can that all thought of my candidacy must be abandoned as absolutely and inexorably impossible." He also wrote to James Smith, a New Yorker, asking that his name not be used in connection with the presidential nomination at the convention. "I certainly would not accept," he stated firmly. Richard Olney's plea to the former President that only he could save the country from eight more years of Rooseveltism was ignored. It is possible that Cleveland might have been nominated if he had wanted to be. He had southern support, all of his old friends, and Tammany Hall.[21]

At the convention, there were frequent cries of "Three cheers for Grover Cleveland!" It was Cleveland democracy and not Bryanism that dominated the delegates. Judge Alton B. Parker, who became the candidate, came out strongly for gold, thus repudiating the Silverites and Bryan, which pleased Cleveland, who offered both his good wishes and his services to Parker. But the former President's activities in the campaign were very limited. He stayed at Gray Gables until October, after which he delivered only two speeches, one in New York and one in New Jersey. Efforts to lure him to nearby Connecticut and Massachusetts were futile. He did contribute an article about Judge Parker to *McClure's* magazine. In part, Cleveland's reluctance was due to poor health. Underneath, however, was the conviction that the Democrat could not win.

The tremendous Republican majority and terrible Democratic defeat disturbed Cleveland even though he expected it. "How the rejuvenation of the Democratic Party which seems to be absolutely essential is to be brought about, I do not know," he despaired. In due time, however, he was certain "a way [would] be made plain." It was not until 1912, more than four years after Cleveland's death, that the Democrat Woodrow Wilson was elected President. During the interim, Cleveland fretted over the persistence of Bryanism. In 1908 he saw no way to avoid another Bryan nomination unless some other candidate could be found and, during that winter before the convention, tried to influence anti-Bryan Democratic leaders to seek another candidate. He told Parker that if the party failed in 1908 it would "require an almost revolutionary popular resurgence to get the country's support again." In one of his last letters, Cleveland suggested the nomination of John A. Johnson of Minnesota, who could return the party "to our old creed and the policies and the old plans of organization which have heretofore led us to victory."[22] Cleveland was spared the third Bryan nomination and defeat.

Although Taft, the Republican candidate, failed in his bid for reelection in 1916, to no one's surprise, and the incumbent, Woodrow Wilson, was reelected effortlessly, possibly the most interesting aspect of the campaign was the role of the two Republican ex-Presidents. Fallen majesties worked out their rivalries and their personal styles in their joint reaction to the arch devil, President Wilson.

In June 1916, both Roosevelt parties met in Chicago to choose candidates. The Republicans held their convention at the Coliseum in a state of mass indecision. There were many possible candidates but no favorite. Available but weak prospects included such men as seventy-one-year-old Elihu Root, who was backed by Wall Street; a brace of Conservative senators, among them John W. Weeks of Massachusetts and Lawrence Sherman of Illinois; and ex-Vice-President Charles Fairbanks. The safest bet seemed to be Charles Evans Hughes, who had been in political limbo for the past six years as a United States Supreme Court justice and was, publicly and privately, a self-declared noncandidate. Hughes said he was antipathetic to politics; he preferred to ignore politics in deciding public issues. The presidency, he told Henry Stoddard, was "the greatest honor that could come to any man; it is also the greatest burden!" He could not refuse the gift if offered.[23]

Before the Republican convention there were moments when TR believed that he had a chance of being nominated. During the spring a machine worked at getting support for him, tapping certain possible sources. Negotiations were started with the Catholic Church because of his popularity in the past with the Catholic electorate. Even Robert La Follette was approached. And there were Rooseveltian promises made to defense societies and to job seekers. But the isolationist Middle West remained opposed to him even after, or because of, his swing through that area, not as a political candidate but as a "patriot" advocating universal military service and opposing the President's foreign policy, pacifism, and hyphenated Americans.

When the Republican and Progressive conventions met from June 7 to June 10, Theodore Roosevelt was not in Chicago, but he was connected by direct telephone line from Perkins's hotel room there to his library in Oyster Bay. He was in constant touch with the Chicago scene and although he told Arthur Lee that he did not have enough of a following to get the nomination and it looked as if Hughes would make it, he had not really given up. The Republican convention of 1916 was a very pedestrian one except for the possibility of a last-minute Roosevelt nomination, a possibility that was kept alive by the constant cries from the gallery for "Teddy."

In the meantime, the Progressive party convention was meeting. Their managers made some attempts to come to an agreement with the Republicans on a mutually acceptable candidate but without success. Finally, the Bull Moose was asked for his suggestion. He answered with the startling proposal of Senator Henry Cabot Lodge and then added the names of some other right-wing Republicans. William Allen White tried to convince the ex-President that the Progressive party convention was a gathering of "rather highly placed people" and not a "mob of irresponsibles," as Perkins and the Republicans had described the delegates. It was too late. Roosevelt had already sent his fateful letter to Perkins.[24]

On Friday night, June 9, the balloting began in the Republican convention. Hughes got 253½ votes on the first ballot, Roosevelt only 65. On the second ballot Hughes gained, but not enough to get the nomination, so the convention adjourned for the night.

The Roosevelt backers at the Progressive convention, particularly White and Bainbridge Colby, were determined to nominate the former President before the Republicans made their final decision. Ignoring parliamentary procedure, Colby in a hurried speech of less than one hundred words presented the Roosevelt name to the convention. White, a veteran convention-goer, said that the burst of spontaneous, exuberant cheering that convulsed the hall for ten minutes was unequaled in his experience. Within minutes, Louisiana's John M. Parker, a former governor, received the vice-presidential nomination.

Perkins had in his possession Roosevelt's letter saying that he would not accept the Progressive party's nomination. But he did not disclose it. Even after the Republican convention nominated Hughes, which was shortly after the Progressives finished, Perkins withheld the letter. Even after the exultant Progressives had started raising money for the campaign and the Republicans had gone home, Perkins held off. White, who knew about the letter, started to hope that by some miracle it had been withdrawn. Then, suddenly, it was read: "I am very grateful for the honor you confer upon me by nominating me as President. I cannot accept it at this time."[25]

Astonishment and then anger swept through the convention hall. White was not the only leader with tears in his eyes. Everyone felt betrayed and some, in despair and righteous indignation, ripped their

Roosevelt badges off their jackets and tore the Roosevelt pictures from the walls. Then, profoundly disappointed and disillusioned by the arrogance of power, the delegates left the scene of their brief moment of hope. Henry Adams's earlier comment had become a self-fulfilled prophecy: "Our friend Roosevelt and his following are disposed of. I suspect he is busted and done."[26]

The Progressives believed that Roosevelt had used them for his own personal ambition. Bainbridge Colby told Ray Stannard Baker that it was evident to him during the convention that the Roosevelt strategy was "to hold the threat of his nomination by the Progressive Party over the Republican Convention," hoping that the Republicans would capitulate and nominate him. White bears this out with his statement that "unofficial backstage bi-partisan caucuses were being held to bring the two parties together."[27]

Taft, who had been one of the Hughes backers, enjoyed the Roosevelt debacle, which, he felt, came to him as a result of his "dickering with the two conventions." Taft also commented that TR's proposal of Lodge's name for the nomination showed that, in his desperation "he was groggy." And with some satisfaction he concluded that his former friend was not a good loser but, rather, "a squealer with all his boasted sportsmanship." Obviously the stout ex-President was pleased that he had picked the winner, although he, too, had entertained some fleeting hopes that the Republican party would choose him again.

Taft doubted that his speechmaking would help the party effort. He differed from Roosevelt, Root, and Lodge, fearing that their jingoism might be overplayed. Labor's dislike of him also made him wonder whether he might hurt Hughes's chances more than enhance them.

Many thought that TR's campaigning did hurt Hughes. His violent denunciation of Wilson repulsed many. Colonel House observed to Wilson that newspapermen felt that Hughes was becoming increasingly irritable, probably due to Roosevelt's speeches.

In October, his throat irritated and swollen from constant speaking, Roosevelt made a swing through Kentucky, Iowa, Illinois, Indiana, New York, Maine, Michigan, Pennsylvania, Arizona, Colorado, Nebraska, and Connecticut. But no one could convince him to tone down his relentless anti-Wilson rhetoric. When Illinois Republicans tried to get him to modify his references to hyphenated Americans in ethnic Chicago, he refused. As a result, newspapers in that region carried headlines such as "Roosevelt Attacks Hyphens in Chicago." It hurt Hughes, but Roosevelt would not stop. "I must say what I believe the vital needs of this country at this time demand," he responded.

Unrestrained, the Bull Moose plowed through the country sparing no epithets. At Cooper Union in New York, his voice recovered remarkably. The audience received him with enthusiastic shouts of "Teddy! Teddy!" The orator was so carried away by his theme of Wilson's "incapable leadership when confronted by a great crisis" that he forgot to mention Hughes's name. "I thought I made a rather good speech," the indomitable ex-President wrote to Quentin.[28]

On election night at Oyster Bay, TR, overconfident because of the early returns which favored Hughes, declared that the Republican election was "a vindication of our national honor." Then he added that he would not make any recommendations for appointments or suggestions on political policy to the new President. In the next few days Wilson gained, but it was a week before the election was decided definitely in favor of the incumbent.[29]

Hughes was grateful to Roosevelt for his help and refused to agree with those supporters who maintained that his assistance had contributed to the candidate's defeat. On the contrary, Hughes blamed his failure on Wilson's slogan He Kept Us Out of War, and on labor. Roosevelt, however, blamed Hughes for his own defeat. He should have made "a straight-from-the-shoulder fighting campaign," TR said. Hughes and the Republicans "tried to beat skimmed milk with cambric tea, they earned their defeat."[30]

Roosevelt was out of kilter with his party after Hughes's defeat, but nothing is constant but change in party politics. By 1918, the *New York Times* and the *New York World* reported a boom starting for "Teddy in 1920." From his hospital room, Roosevelt remarked that it was foolish to pay attention to newspaper stories. He was particularly annoyed that his name was being mentioned among old-guard Republican machine politicians such as Boies Penrose of St. Louis. However, Roosevelt had been active in the 1918 campaign to elect a Republican Congress—regardless of the brand of Republican—in order to stop Wilson. He believed that any Republican was preferable to a Democrat committed to the administration.

Death took Teddy Roosevelt before the 1920 convention, but Taft lived on to support Warren G. Harding. By this time, Taft's hatred for Wilson had developed into disgust for the "mulish emperor, that mountain of egotism who lives in the White House." With some effort, he convinced himself that Harding was a more sincere friend of peace than Wilson and could be persuaded to accept the League of Nations. By the time that idea was thoroughly squashed, Taft was sitting on the Supreme Court as its chief justice, removed from the political arena.

Former presidents always have their faithful party supporters who believe that their favorite is always a potential candidate. The ex-presidents, especially when their careers have suffered an eclipse, sometimes listen to the siren songs. Wilson had behaved with great restraint during the Harding nomination and election, not even, at least publicly, commenting on his opponent's bad grammar or bad government. He had, however, interfered in New Jersey politics enough to write letters opposing the reelections of Senators Reed and Shields, who had voted against the League of Nations.[31]

An attempt to use Wilson's name to promote Cox, the defeated Democratic candidate in 1920, for the 1924 election caused a rift between the ex-President and his old friend Joe Tumulty. Tumulty asked Wilson to send a message of goodwill to the 1922 Jefferson Day dinner given by the New York Democratic Club. The former President's reply was that he did not find the occasion an appropriate one for breaking his silence. At the dinner, a message from Wilson was read from a piece of yellow paper with typing on it that looked like a telegraph form. It said: "Say to the Democrats of New York that I am ready to support any man who stands for the salvation of America and the salvation of America is justice to all classes." It was signed "Woodrow Wilson." The audience responded with cheers, and James Cox got up to speak. The following day, the *New York Times* carried the headline "Cox Boom Launched on Wilson Keynote of Justice for All."

No explanations, retractions, or protestations by the *Times* or Tumulty calmed either President or Mrs. Wilson. Tumulty was banished from the Wilson home and from their list of friends. Once again the Wilsons displayed their unforgiving natures. There was, however, another motive behind the Wilson reaction. Despite his illness and feebleness, the architect of the League of Nations had not abandoned the hope that he might have another chance, in 1924, to bring his beloved league to the American people.

Wilson's admirers had a touching devotion for their wounded

and fallen leader. On his sixty-sixth birthday, December 28, 1923, they presented him with a Rolls-Royce specially designed for him. It was black with a thin orange stripe (Princeton's colors) and had a mechanism that made it easier for the ailing man to get in and out of the car. It was a charming tribute but it came too late. The wartime President was so frail that he could not even sign his name legibly.

Cordell Hull told a moving Wilson story that took place at about this time. Hull was national chairman of the Democratic party during Wilson's last years. In this capacity, he was required by the ex-President to visit him at his S Street Washington home regularly to keep him informed of the progress of national and international affairs. Hull recorded that Wilson's "comments on men and measures, past and present, were highly interesting." The ex-President's main interests were foreign affairs and the rehabilitation of the Democratic party. Hull also wrote reports to Wilson and received in reply long typewritten letters containing suggestions about how to revive the party.

Among the Wilson proposals was one to break down the fiction, carefully nurtured by the opposition, that "citizens of the first class" in northern communities were men and women who voted Republican. "We must fill our seats with gentlemen and men of honor and let the politicians get used to good company," Wilson said. He also told Hull that if it was true that women were taking an active interest in the 1922 election campaign, it was surely to the advantage of the Democrats. "Our ideas are assuredly nearer their standard" than those of the Republicans, he said, and he would be disappointed if they did not support the party, because "they are chiefly indebted to me for the suffrage."[32] Wilson's optimism was rewarded. The Democrats won seventy-five new seats in the House of Representatives, for which Wilson hastened to congratulate Hull.

During the last months of his life, Hull remarked, Wilson reminded him of Andrew Jackson—pale, gaunt, lined, but determined. Just a few weeks before his death, the former President asked Hull to bring all the members of the Democratic National Committee, which was in session at the time, to S Street to call on him. It was a cold, rainy, bleak winter day when the 125 members arrived in a fleet of taxicabs. One by one, the party representatives filed into the library where Wilson sat huddled in front of a blazing fire. Mrs.

Wilson shook each member's hand before he entered the room, and Hull stood next to Wilson so that he could identify each member for him. It took an hour for the long file to go through the ritual of the handshake and the few words, and long before the last member was reached, Wilson's fatigue was pathetically apparent, but he refused to stop. It was his last effort to encourage and inspire his party.[33]

The tale of Hoover and the Republican party is a story of triumph over adversity. Having exited from the presidency in 1933 more of a detriment than an asset, his eventual emergence as a party symbol is a tribute to the healing powers of change or to the rewards of longevity. Nevertheless, long before his elevation to elder statesman, even in eclipse, Hoover represented the conservative elements of the party.

In 1936, still a controversial figure to most of his party, Hoover's speech at the Cleveland convention was one of its most exciting moments. He bade the party enter into "a holy crusade for liberty," after reviewing unfavorably the years of the New Deal. The most significant advice that he gave was to caution the Republicans against a "me too" strategy. During the Hoover address the audience applauded and cheered wildly until state delegations formed in a line and marched around the hall. For a moment it looked like a spontaneous move to nominate Hoover, but the convention managers moved quickly to stifle it. During a brief lull in the commotion, the presiding officer announced that Hoover had left the convention hall to catch a train for New York, which was untrue. The former President was resting in a room nearby, but the regulars had decided that Governor Alf Landon of Kansas was to be the candidate and they did not want to be challenged.

Hoover was annoyed at the story "that scum of Washington, Allen and Pearson," had printed about his participation in a "Stop Landon" movement during the Cleveland convention. Hoover protested that he had refused to see any fixers or candidates who wanted to talk to him, because such action "would have torn the party apart."[34] However, there was awkwardness between the ex-President and the party candidate. John D. M. Hamilton, chairman of the Republican National Committee, wrote to Hoover asking for his assistance in the campaign. Hoover answered that he would be glad to discuss the situation with Governor Landon if he would write to him and ask for his participation.[35] Finally, Hamilton got Hoover's consent to accept an invitation from Landon to be extended over the telephone.

On September 2, Hoover finally got the call from Landon at his house in Palo Alto, California. In a stilted conversation, it was decided that after Hoover, who was leaving for the East Coast, saw Hamilton in Chicago, he would stop off in Topeka, Kansas, on his way back to California, to discuss his appraisal of the political situation in the East with the governor. Early in the conversation, Hoover referred to "gossip going about that I am not wanted in the campaign," which, he said, was "a little hard to bear. It would be settled instantly if you make some statement," Hoover suggested. Landon answered: "There is no question in my mind about your being in the campaign. When the time comes I will be very glad to do anything along these lines." In a letter to confirm the conversation, Hoover mentioned that he would indicate at some point that Landon had made such a request, because certain members of the Republican publicity organization were "giving a contrary color and are damaging the party and your interests."[36]

Hoover's apprehension proved to be valid. He was shown an Associated Press dispatch in which members of Landon's staff had denied that Hoover had spoken to the candidate. Angrily, the former President said that if Landon's staff persisted in the denial, he would have to publish the transcript of the telephone conversation, which his secretary had taken down on an extension phone. The governor's staff retracted their statement.

This contretemps was an indication of the real feeling of the party regulars toward Hoover. At the Chicago headquarters he found a cool reception, and there was deliberate delay in arranging for his speeches. He was told that local politicians were reluctant to arrange meetings for him. In response, Hoover set up his own staff to take care of his speaking arrangements and broadcasts. Obviously the Republicans were wary of any references to the Hoover administration, and the party candidate avoided any mention of the last Republican presidency throughout his campaign. Instead, Landon concentrated on FDR's failures. A dissenting Republican wrote that this created the impression that "we ourselves were ashamed of the Hoover record and that we are now going to offer the people something entirely different." The Republican party, therefore, showed no courage and appeared to "run away from its own record."[37]

Herbert Hoover was a candidate in the election of 1940. By November 1939, there was ample evidence that he was lining up delegates, and at least two national committeemen, Colonel R. B. Creager of Texas and Harrison P. Spangler of Iowa, were working for him. On November 16, the Chicago *Daily News* revealed that the ex-President had been there for a week conferring with important men in politics, finance, and industry. Hoover said nothing, but a trial balloon proposing a Hoover-Lindbergh ticket was sent up in the East. It collapsed and was discarded, and then there was gossip of a Hoover-Dewey combination.[38]

A Gallup poll issued just as the delegates were arriving in Philadelphia for the Republican convention revealed Dewey in the lead as the presidential hopeful with 47 percent of the vote; Willkie was next with 29 percent; Taft and Vandenberg had 8 percent each; and Hoover had 6 percent. It was significant that part of Dewey's own delegation was leaning toward Hoover.[39]

Though at the start of the convention it looked as if Taft would be the man Wendell Willkie had to beat, there were persistent rumors that Hoover had people canvassing votes for him. His drive for the nomination, it was believed, would take place on Tuesday, the second night, after he made his speech to the delegates. This time he would not leave the convention floor as he had in Chicago four years earlier. To some analysts it appeared that Iowa's favorite-son movement for Hanford MacNider, led by Verne Marshall, publisher of the Grand Rapids *Gazette*, was a holding action for Iowa's *favorite* favorite son, Herbert Hoover.[40]

For Hoover, this was the moment for him to succeed. He was already sixty-six years old; by 1944 it would be too late to try again. This was his last chance to get back at Franklin Roosevelt and challenge the New Deal from the chief executive's chair. All his opponents' camps were fearful that Hoover's speech would overwhelm the convention as it had in 1936, except this time the Hoover contingent—the conservative Republicans—were ready for Hoover or, if need be, for Taft.

On Tuesday, June 25, the packed convention hall was called to order by Joe Martin, who had delayed until 9:20 for the nationwide hookup scheduled for 9:30. After the audience sang "God Bless America," the band struck up "California Here I Come" to herald the entrance of Hoover flanked by John Hamilton and the rest of the committee of escort. They filed down the center aisle to the rostrum. Volley upon volley of applause, feet stamping, and wild cheering delayed the start of the ex-President's speech. He stood on the platform waving to all sides of the auditorium and basking in the public adulation so long withheld from him until Joe Martin, mindful that the radio audience was waiting for the speech, hushed the delegates.

Most of Hoover's speech was no surprise. He said that there could be no isolation "from wars which envelop two-thirds of all the people in the world." German aggression was wrong, he told his audience, and the Allies must be helped, but we must not become combatants. "The three thousand miles of ocean is still a protection," he reminded the Republicans. Then he turned to the third-term issue, saying that this would be tampering with tradition.

After the speech the multitude applauded vociferously, but their enthusiasm did not match the 1936 response. The stampede for Hoover just did not occur. "Well, he didn't make it," the Willkie managers said with great relief. But, undeterred, Hoover at his press conference answered the question of whether he would accept the nomination crisply. "I have no further comment," he said, thereby convincing the press that he was indeed a candidate.[41]

On Thursday, when the balloting was to begin, Hoover was operating from his eleventh-floor suite at the Bellevue-Stratford. He was simultaneously rounding up delegates for himself and meeting with the other candidates. Each candidate hoped for the ex-President's support in case he decided not to run. Hoover polled thirty-two votes on the third ballot, the maximum he achieved, and on the sixth ballot, Wendell Willkie, ex-Democrat, an unknown, unsupported by the party regulars, won the nomination. "My congratulations. The result of a free convention and a free people will carry you to victory" was Hoover's message to the candidate, which Joe Martin read to the convention. Although Willkie was not Hoover's choice (he would have preferred Taft or even Dewey), the former President campaigned for him, especially in the Midwest. Willkie lost, which did not surprise Hoover, who had warned all along that "me tooism" would not defeat Roosevelt.

Judge Charles W. Fisher of California, in an interview, described an interesting organization whose aim was the nomination of Hoover for the presidency. He called it "the Hoover circle." It had got started at a Masonic retreat in the Santa Cruz Mountains, where about forty Republican leaders were invited to meet Hoover. The circles were organized on the state level first and then worked down to the city and community levels. Fisher became the executive secretary for the northern California circle and so could comment with authority on their difficulties. Hoover circle workers found that there was a lot of opposition from old-line Republicans who resented the existence of an organization whose direction was the promotion of one individual. Other Republican leaders thought that Hoover was the most qualified candidate but were certain that he could not win. They disapproved of the activities of the circle members, believing that if Hoover got the nomination against Roosevelt, the circle would have succeeded only in making a martyr of him. Eventually, after a few years, the organization of Hoover circles died a natural death.[42]

Hoover was disappointed again in 1944, for neither Robert Taft nor General MacArthur, his preferences, received the nomination. Governor Dewey, who won the candidacy, was not a close political friend of Hoover's for several reasons. At that time, according to Herbert Brownell, Dewey believed that the Republican party as well as the country at large was more liberal than Hoover. Dewey also feared that Hoover, who had become the party's oracle, might dominate him. Nevertheless, Hoover supported Dewey and encouraged his friends to do the same.[43]

By 1948, Hoover was seventy-five. At the Republican convention he made another of his inspirational speeches warning against increased collectivism and was, once more, received with tremendous bursts of enthusiasm. Hoover said that this was probably his last appearance before a convention. The crowd responded with "No! No!" The old gentleman was to have the opportunity to make that same prediction three more times. Dewey was nominated, as previously arranged, and Hoover, due to ill health, took only a minor part in the campaign.

As early as 1949, attempts were made to interest Hoover in an Eisenhower candidacy for 1952. Ward Bannister wrote to the former President that he and his wife had dined with the Eisenhowers in Denver and found that the general "believes much as you do." Bannister also suggested that Ike had intimated that he would like to sit down and talk to Hoover.[44] But Hoover had old ties with Robert Taft which made him cool to others.

At first, somewhat puzzlingly, Hoover remained neutral in the Taft-Eisenhower struggle in 1952. It was as late as July 9, right before the convention, that Hoover said that his "conscience" demanded that he speak out. By his leadership in the Senate, Hoover said, Taft, whom he had known since World War I, had "provided the Republican party with a fighting opposition to the current of collectivism in the country." At the convention, Hoover tried to play the part of honest broker in resolving the Taft-Eisenhower struggle. And after Ike was nominated, he offered to give a major TV and radio speech for him. "If you believe it better that I stay out of a public part in the campaign, it will in no way dim my prayers for your success," Hoover wired in October. Obviously, Eisenhower wanted the speech, and it was a huge success. There were over 150,000 applications for reprints, 90,000 from individuals, Hoover reported to the candidate. Several thousand requests came in daily.[45]

Four years later, Hoover again preferred Taft but accepted Ike with good grace. The former President's unpopularity during the FDR period was now almost forgotten. The President was expressing the opinion of many when he said that Hoover represented "the dignity and the spirit of the Republican party." If he did not appear at the convention, every delegate would be disappointed.[46] Hoover's speech at San Francisco had lost all of the spirit of partisanship. He was now only the elder statesman of conservative persuasion who advocated that the convention make "a resounding declaration of the principles of American life." Again in 1960, Hoover's convention speech avoided specifics and emphasized patriotism and compassion.

Hoover played a small part in the controversial matter of the Nixon-Kennedy debates in 1960. He was opposed to the decision that Nixon enter into the debates. "That's the biggest mistake he could make," Ellen Brumback quoted him as saying. He recalled that they had tried to get him to debate when he was running for president. "It's a mistake. He shouldn't do it," Hoover repeated prophetically.[47]

Hoover saw other signs of mismanagement during that campaign. A day or so before the election, there was a Republican rally at the Coliseum in New York to which Nixon and ex-President Eisenhower came. Watching it on his home TV, Hoover observed that about twenty minutes of the half hour of TV time was taken up with applause for Ike. When Nixon finally got up to make his speech, he had little time. Hoover thought that this was overdoing the idea of support and that the time would have been better used by the candidate in placing his program before the public. Hoover did try to get Nixon press support from his friends who were associated with the big newspapers but he did not succeed, and the Vice-President continued to have terrible press coverage.[48]

The aged former President was too feeble to go to San Francisco for the 1964 Republican convention. Instead, Everett Dirksen was delegated by Hoover to present his message, which was received with great emotion. "Regret I cannot take part actively in campaign but will be glad to make a statement when it will best help you if you will let me know time in due course," Hoover wired to Barry Goldwater, but he did not live to see the Republican defeat.[49]

In an interview not long after he had stepped down from the presidency, Harry Truman made it quite clear that he was not through with politics. His retirement, he explained, was just tempo-rary—until the 1954 elections—when he would "be in there pitching." He would not run for political office, though he admired John Quincy Adams for his post-presidential career in the United States Congress. But he would stump for the Democratic candidates in 1956.[50] Though he had been President of the United States, Truman said that he was willing to work in the ranks if the party would let him. No special privileges accrued to him, he insisted. Adlai Stevenson was the leader of the party, because he was the Democratic nominee. Despite Tru-man's modest statements, the Democratic National Committee knew that the dynamic, outspoken ex-President had to be reckoned with. He was the elder statesman of the party, its only living former President, and "his experience provides a bridge between the past and the future." Hence his counsel about the future direction of the party was important and had to be given strong emphasis.[51]

The Truman protestation of support for Stevenson was not quite sincere. The intellectual's delight had little charm for Truman, who could have done with less wit and more will to win. As a strong party man, Truman did the right things, such as meeting with Stevenson wherever and whenever he was asked. But when it came time for the Democratic convention of 1956, Truman announced his support for Governor Averell Harriman. The New Yorker Truman said, was the best-qualified man, whereas Stevenson had proved he was not a "fighting man," not really qualified for the big job. Some of Steven-son's supporters felt that he was well rid of the burden of Truman and Trumanism and would be able now to express himself freely. Stevenson, however, tactfully expressed his gratitude for past favors.

In this instance, Truman met his match in Mrs. Eleanor Roosevelt. She, too, was a symbol of the Democratic past, of its finest hour in modern times, and she was a staunch friend of Adlai Stevenson. As soon as her plane landed in Chicago, worried Stevenson managers rushed to tell her that Truman had endorsed Harriman and she must immediately attend a press conference and deal with the setback. They hurried her to the waiting pressmen and she deftly punctured the Truman position. In her high-pitched, refined voice, never abandoning her gracious, ladylike manner, Mrs. Roosevelt asked all the right questions. How could Truman accuse Stevenson of not being a "fighting candidate" when his choice, Averell Harriman, had not even entered the primaries? As to Adlai's preparation for the presidency, surely the governor was no less prepared than the ex-President had been at the time of FDR's death, and was probably better equipped than Truman had been in the field of foreign affairs. In defense of Stevenson's moderation, Eleanor Roosevelt maintained that "being a moderate did not mean standing still." With a gentle ruthlessness, Eleanor reminded Harry that they were both seventy-two and must turn over the party reins to younger people. Though the voters were fond of the former President, she continued, he would not influence their votes, for he was part of "the old tradition when the professional politicians had more influence than they should have."[52]

The two elderly protagonists lunched together without referring to their differences and mentioned the coming struggle but once. Truman said that any action he would take would be because he thought he was doing the right thing. Mrs. Roosevelt said her motives were identical. "What I want to do is make the convention do some real thinking about the issues," the ex-President stated smugly. Students of the political scene were not convinced. As early as 1955, Truman had started to promote the Harriman candidacy. His strategy was to garner the votes of the unpledged delegates and the favorite-son delegates and thus stop Stevenson. Some observers thought that Truman's support of Harriman was merely a front to use him as a stalking horse for his real favorite, Stuart Symington.

Truman had to accept the convention's renomination of Stevenson and the nomination of Kefauver, whom he disliked and referred to in private conversation as "cowfever." He had opposed the possible nomination of John F. Kennedy for the vice-presidency because he was against having a Catholic on the ticket.[53]

The nominations completed, Truman addressed the convention on the theme of party unity. "I am here to give my full support to Adlai Stevenson," he said. "Governor Stevenson is a real fighter and I ought to know. . . . He's given some of us here a pretty good licking, and he's going to give Eisenhower a better one."[54] The old man had been set aside, it appeared to many. A new Democratic leadership had emerged, but the old war-horse continued to ride into battle.

Truman hit the campaign trail with his usual energy, covering a good part of the country, particularly the Midwest. So adept at arousing controversy that those he supported often wondered if he were really helping them, Truman attacked President Eisenhower. In Pittsburgh, he implied that Ike had "run out" on General George Marshall, who, the former President reminded the audience, had been the "great architect" of our victory in World War II. And, he added, "You can not elect Ike without electing Tricky Dicky."[55]

Some party managers shuddered at Truman's no-holds-barred technique, but he was most valuable in many ways. A Utah committeeman, for example, informed the Democratic National Committee that labor in his state would listen to only one man and that was President Truman. His speeches in Salt Lake City, which all the labor leaders in the area attended, helped not only the presidential candidate but also the chances of electing a Democratic governor in that state.[56]

After the second defeat of Stevenson, members of the urban-intellectual wing of the Democratic party, led by Stevenson and Thomas Finletter, a New York lawyer, established the Democratic Advisory Council. Its purpose was policy making in the interest of developing a responsible party government that would prepare a party platform responsive to the current needs. It would also issue policy statements on significant national and international issues.

For any hope of success and influence, the DAC needed the support of ex-President Harry Truman. The council invited him to become a member and he accepted. The founders were not so successful in recruiting congressional leaders and southern leaders. Despite its limitations, however, the organization survived until the election of a Democratic president in 1960.

From the start, differences on foreign policy divided the council into two factions; one led by Stevenson, the other by Truman. Although not active in the DAC, Truman's membership ensured that his role would be important. He was a link with the congressional Democrats, especially Lyndon Johnson and Sam Rayburn. He also brought the council prestige, and his presence ensured the interest of the press in the organization.

Truman, on his part, was willing to lend his name and occasional presence to the council for several reasons. Most important was his need to justify continually his administration's foreign policy. If the former President served on the DAC, Dean Acheson's seat on the committee was assured. The question of Truman's link with the congressional party can be looked at in two ways. Either he was working to make the DAC more acceptable to the congressional party or he was trying to keep the DAC in line. Opinion on this differs among Truman watchers. The answer might be somewhere in between. Truman did both, in a sense. As a member of the council, he wanted to lessen the differences between the DAC and the congressional leadership, but he also tried to persuade the council to modify its position so that it would be acceptable to the congressional leadership, some of whose members resented this extraofficial body. Johnson, in a memorandum to Sam Rayburn, said that he feared such a committee would cause a rift in the party and that the American people would "bitterly resent" the supervision of elected congressmen by "appointive professional politicians." Truman, said Leon Keyserling, did much to keep their resentment in check.[57]

In 1960 the Democrats chose a winner, but once more he was not Truman's choice. This time the ex-President came out openly for Stuart Symington, the handsome, liberal senator from his own state, whose manager, Clark Clifford, was Truman-trained. Clifford had been a speech writer and the general counsel for President Truman. Because Truman knew that Symington would have a chance only as a compromise candidate, the senator did not declare his intentions to enter the race until the spring of 1960, when it was too late, because the Kennedy machine was already rolling.

Hardly able to stand the idea that neither Symington nor his second choice, Lyndon Johnson, had a chance at the convention, and sensing that he was now nothing but an old-timer, Truman absented himself from the Los Angeles convention. However, on July 2, before the delegates met, the former President repeated his 1956 performance by blasting the front-runner. Once again, Truman repeated his support for Symington and then followed with a list of further possibilities, including Johnson, Chester Bowles, and Meyner. The convention, he accused, was being controlled by one candidate and the results had been prearranged. Addressing himself to Kennedy, he said: "Senator, are you certain that you are quite ready for the country or that the country is ready for you in the role of President?" A man with "the greatest maturity and experience" was needed. "May I urge you to be patient?" To many Kennedy supporters, implied in those words was Truman's unspoken question about the religious issue. Sorenson said that Truman's personal opposition to a Catholic candidate had been told to the Kennedy men by more than one Democrat. It was a very hot issue. The Pickwick bookshop in Hollywood noted that before and during the convention they sold out on Paul Blanchard's *American Freedom and Catholic Power*.[58]

Two days later, the young candidate answered the former President. "Mr. Truman regards an open convention as one which studies all the candidates, reviews their records and then takes his advice," JFK said. He then pointed to fourteen years of active service in elective office, more than Wilson, Roosevelt, and Truman had had. Continuing the history lesson, Kennedy added that six previous presidents had served in their forties. "Mr. Truman asks me if I think I am ready. . . . Today I say to you that if the people of this nation select me to be their President, I believe that I am ready."[59]

After his nomination, Kennedy sought Truman's support. He called on him at the Truman Library and received the desired pledge. Stuart Symington and Harry M. Jackson of Washington, the Democratic national chairman, were also present at the rapprochement.[60]

There were several times during the campaign when Kennedy may have wished that Truman had stayed quietly at home in Independence, although he was in demand in some areas, particularly the Midwest. The Democrats of Iowa asked for him, saying "It is just what we need to bring about a Democratic victory," but the Republican candidate seemed to bring out the worst in "Give 'em hell Harry." He disliked Nixon. In a taped interview with Merle Miller not long after the campaign, Truman expressed his views on him. "Nixon is a shifty-eyed goddam liar and people know it," he said. The root of Truman's hatred went back to an episode in the 1952 campaign that took place at Texarkana, Arkansas, when Nixon was campaigning there. As Truman interpreted his statement, Nixon called "General Marshall and me traitors." The Associated Press reported the Nixon speech somewhat differently. In their version, Nixon said that Truman, Acheson, and Stevenson were "traitors of the high principles in which many of the nation's Democrats believe."

The latter version, of course, accused Truman and the others of being traitors to their party and not to the nation. To the peppery ex-President, it was all the same. "You can't very well forget things of that kind, and that's why I don't trust Nixon and never will," he said.[61]

In view of the many deletions in the now famous Nixon White House tapes, the 1960 Republican candidate's sanctimonious complaints about Truman's colorful language seem laughable. In a San Antonio speech, Truman said that Texans who voted for Vice-President Nixon ought to go to hell. Nixon criticized the former President's "gutter language" and, in his second debate with Kennedy, tried to make the candidate responsible for the Truman language. Kennedy treated the matter with the lightness that it deserved. "I really don't think there's anything I can say to President Truman that's going to cause him to change his particular manner. Perhaps Mrs. Truman can, but I don't think I can."[62]

A more serious use of Truman's talents was his schedule of speeches to his fellow Baptists. In Waco, Texas, for instance, the ex-President confronted the heavily Baptist central Texas audience on the Catholic issue. To a cheering crowd, Truman said that the time had come "to bury once and for all this question of religious bigotry" in presidential campaigns. "One reason I am glad I am a Baptist is that nobody dictates to me as a Baptist," he added. The worst part of the anti-Catholic campaign, he pointed out, was that it was not discussed publicly but, rather, was an "underground campaign of defamation."[63]

Kennedy, whatever private doubts he had about the balance of Truman's efforts in his behalf, publicly displayed his gratitude to him and thanked him for his part in the Democratic success. Truman, on the other hand, had reservations about the way in which the young President had achieved his victory. But he blamed mostly "the Pop [Joseph Kennedy]," who, said Harry Truman, was "as big a crook as we've got anywhere in this country, and I don't like that he bought his son the nomination for the Presidency." According to the former President, he bought West Virginia so "his boy" would win the primary from Humphrey. He didn't buy the election, Truman conceded, but he did not have to. Anyone could have won running against Nixon.[64]

The campaign of 1960 was Truman's last hurrah. Age and failing health kept him from further marathon campaign trails. It didn't hurt Lyndon Johnson's chances, of course, to visit Truman's hospital room in October 1964, when the old man was recuperating from injuries sustained in a fall. About 30,000 people lined the streets to see the Johnsons travel to the hospital, where the President told Truman how proud he was to have known him since he was a young man in the House of Representatives.

Dwight D. Eisenhower, who might have run for a third term had there been no constitutional amendment to stop him, had been disturbed by Nixon's defeat in 1960. It "upset my calculations, revised my expectations and exploded my plans," he said. Consequently, Eisenhower and his former presidential aides formed a group to watch the Kennedy administration. He would not dictate to the party, Ike explained, nor did he regard the group as the same as the DAC, but he would make appropriate intelligent criticisms of Democratic action in the field of foreign policy.[65] As he promised, Eisenhower tried to remake the Republican party "in his own image" by seeing a steady stream of visitors, handling a tremendous volume of correspondence, and making occasional public appearances. He wanted the party to be freed of its identification as the party of wealth and big business.

Eisenhower commented on foreign affairs frequently. The Cuban invasion was "a stupid blunder," he judged, and the President was running the presidency as if it were a "one-man show." The Republican party must win in 1964 by a program of "responsible progressivism." Therefore, he ignored the reactionaries in the party and concentrated on those more appealing to him. In 1961 he seemed to prefer Rockefeller, although as long as Nixon was a possibility, he couldn't say so. Goldwater, he stated, would not be a serious candidate by convention time. [66]

The General campaigned in 1962 by attacking Kennedy's "dreary foreign record of the past 21 months. It is too sad to talk about," he said. In a six-state tour, he blasted the administration, pointing out that during his presidency, "no walls were built [referring to the Berlin Wall]. No threatening foreign bases were established. One war was ended and incipient wars were blocked [referring to Vietnam]." He labeled Kennedy's Camelot as an administration of "sophisticated nonsense."[67]

The Republican ex-President started to have some "mystical value" in Republican circles, Cabell Phillips maintained, as the country went into the election year. Though Eisenhower did not say so, it was generally known that he did not want a Goldwater nomination because the Arizonan was too right-wing for him and did not fit his criteria. To succeed, the party needed a low profile to overcome the southern gap and its unpopularity in the big cities. Lodge, Scranton, Romney, Rockefeller, or any other Eisenhower Republican would be more appropriate, but Ike was not ready to support a "Stop Goldwater" movement. [68]

After the California primary, which Goldwater won, there was a meeting between Eisenhower and Scranton. The Pennsylvania governor had said in a TV appearance that he would accept the vice-presidency if Goldwater offered it, which, Theodore White said, was only a polite gesture even though it appeared to be a capitulation to the California primary winner. More significant was Scranton's visit to Gettysburg, which took place on a miserable rainy day. The governor motored down from Harrisburg and met Ike at his office in the town of Gettysburg for an hour-and-fifteen-minute talk, chiefly about the Goldwater nomination, which, it appeared, Eisenhower deplored. When Scranton left the conference, he believed that if he opposed Goldwater openly at the Cleveland convention, he could expect Eisenhower's endorsement. The press and other media picked up the story, saying that Eisenhower had finally made his selection and that Scranton was his choice. The next day, which was Saturday, June 6, Scranton was scheduled to be at the governor's conference in Cleveland and to appear on *Face the Nation*, which was to be televised direct from the conference. Eisenhower said that he would be watching.

Expecting to reveal his open candidacy, Scranton landed in Cleveland with his wife, Mary, and three aides and went immediately to the Sheraton-Cleveland Hotel, where a message awaited him. He was to call ex-President Eisenhower at once. Ike said that he wanted "Bill to know that he could not be part of any 'cabal' to stop Barry. Bill was on his own."[69] Scranton's eagerly awaited television appearance was a disaster. Confused, disappointed, and overwhelmed by Ike's change of heart, all the unhappy Pennsylvania governor could do was to make stumbling answers that added up to a feeble announcement that he was available for the nomination but would not go out to defeat Goldwater. Eventually Scranton regained his equi-

librium, but both Milton Eisenhower and Malcolm Moos, Eisenhower's advisor, felt that Ike had made a muddle and suggested that
he should reconsider supporting Scranton.

Then in mid-June Goldwater voted against a civil rights bill, which
was a repudiation of the Eisenhower administration, which had sponsored civil rights legislation. Ike called Scranton to tell him how
furious he was about it. Scranton answered that he was, too, and
would run for president after all. Eisenhower replied that he was
pleased at his decision and hoped that the governor would support
his views on civil rights. Scranton ran a bold campaign, but it was
too late to defeat Goldwater.

At the Republican Convention held at the Cow Palace in San
Francisco, Ike abandoned Scranton just when his support seemed
sure. It seemed that the ex-President was about to endorse the Scranton resolution on nuclear control when he backed away again. At
lunch, he announced that he had second thoughts about the correct-
ness of his taking a stand on a matter of national defense and had
decided to say nothing.

During the campaign, Ike's health was too poor to allow him to
make speeches. He did, although reluctantly, agree to appear on TV
with the candidate on September 22 to try to lay to rest a response
made by Goldwater in 1963 to Eisenhower's statement that six
NATO divisions in Europe could be cut to one. They could be cut
one-third, Goldwater had said, if NATO generals were allowed to
use tactical nuclear weapons in an emergency. Whatever he meant
by the statement, to millions of Americans in 1964, "A vote for
Goldwater was a vote to go to war," and wherever he went, the
Republican candidate was met with placards carrying such slogans
as "Welcome Dr. Strangelove."

A depressingly small audience watched the Eisenhower-Goldwater
program. Dutifully, the former President said that he supported
Goldwater and that the notion that the senator favored the use of an
atomic bomb was "tommyrot." Goldwater, however, continued to
equivocate on the issue.[70] And eventually he lost to a Johnson sweep.
It is certain that no amount of Eisenhower support could have saved
him.

After his 1964 experience, Ike was even more reluctant to be a
kingmaker. He would go to the Miami convention in 1968, if he were
well enough, because he wanted to avoid any misunderstanding.
For the same reason, he would make a speech on party unity and

then go home. There had been, earlier, a slight misunderstanding over George Romney, who had been an early front-runner. Eisenhower was suspected of having eliminated the Michigan governor as a candidate but did not like it when news broadcasts quoted him as writing off Romney's presidential aspirations. The *New York Times* quoted Eisenhower's friends as saying that Ike had told them that Romney sounded "like a man in panic." Abashed at the publicity his alleged comment made, the former President said on CBS, "I could earnestly endorse any candidate, including the governor, who has long been a good friend of mine along with the others." That tortured sentence convinced Ike that he had better stay out of it.[71]

Just before the convention, Eisenhower changed his mind and endorsed Richard Nixon. From Walter Reed Hospital, where he was recovering from another heart attack, Ike said that he had changed his usual pattern of reserving judgment on candidates before the convention. This endorsement was not only in appreciation of Nixon's services during his two administrations but "for his personal qualities. He is a man of great reading, a man of great intelligence, and a man of great decisiveness. He's had great experience over the years and he's still quite a young man." Nixon was pleased but not surprised. The former President had told him earlier of his support, because he felt that Nixon would win against any opponent and that "further neutrality on his part would only damage" his Vice-President's chances of getting the nomination.[72] Nixon got the nomination and, in his acceptance speech, used Ike's name and influence to endear himself to the convention. "This time we're going to win . . . for a number of reasons," he said. "First a personal one. General Eisenhower, as you know, lies critically ill in the Walter Reed Hospital tonight. I have talked, however, with Mrs. Eisenhower on the telephone. She tells me . . . there is nothing that he lives more for and there is nothing that would lift him more than to win in November. And I say, let's win this one for Ike."

During the Democratic convention in Chicago, Eisenhower was on the critical list, and some consideration was given to the question of how his death would affect the convention. Already there had been suggestions that the convention should be moved from Chicago to confuse the plans of the disrupters, and the death of Eisenhower might have provided the necessary excuse to postpone it and thus avoid the confrontations that resulted in Democratic defeat. However, the General survived, although he was ill throughout the entire campaign period. Nixon made ostentatious visits to his bedside to get "some good advice," he said. And Nixon was elected.[73]

One of the most artful politicians in American history, Lyndon Johnson, left the presidency in full retreat from the Vietnam War and remained in exile from his party, even on the local level, refusing to be lured into Texas politics. He stayed out of the primary contest between Senator Ralph Yarborough and former Representative Lloyd M. Bentsen. He did, however, hope to attend the Democratic convention in 1972. He felt that it was his due as the last Democratic President, but word came that Larry O'Brien, the national chairman, and others thought it best for him to stay away.

The convention and its choice were completely indigestible to Johnson, a bitter reminder that he had no influence on the national party. The George McGovern nomination was the final proof that no Johnson influence remained. Although the senator had endorsed all of LBJ's Great Society legislation, he was violently opposed to the President's war policy and had been for seven years. Already a dove in April 1965, President Johnson had tried to convince McGovern of the seriousness of his desire to win the war, but any credibility of the President's position was negated for McGovern when, at the same time, he increased American bombing of North Vietnam.

Before the convention Johnson favored Edmund Muskie, but he was not surprised when he failed. "Muskie will never be President," Johnson had predicted several years before, "because he doesn't have the instinct to go for his opponent's jugular."[74] Prior to the convention, Johnson had spoken to Muskie and Mayor Daley about the possibility of stopping McGovern, but he refused any active part in the process lest his opposition have the effect of increasing the senator's chances instead of weakening them.

Above all a party man, Johnson endorsed the McGovern ticket and suffered a meeting with him at his ranch. The nomination of Sargent Shriver for vice-president helped make the ticket a little less painful, although the ex-President made clear that he and the candidate were miles apart on Vietnam. The party had room to accommodate differences, Johnson stated, and he favored "the growing participation in the Democratic party by the young, by women, by blacks, by Mexican-Americans and others who have too long been outside the political system."[75]

The meeting at the ranch between a smiling McGovern and ex-President Johnson, who looked old and somewhat unfamiliar because of his long white hair, was eased by the presence of Shriver. The party hoped that this friendly picture would reassure Democrats who were being frightened away by McGovern's extreme antiwar position. Johnson made no promises to campaign or to raise money for the team. He offered only a détente. However, the meeting did achieve one purpose. It separated LBJ from former Texas Governor John Connally, Johnson's protégé, and other Texas friends who were involved in Connally's Democrats for Nixon organization.

The McGovern campaign was depressing and frustrating for Johnson. It was based on a rejection of his foreign policy and, to make matters worse, was inept and doomed to failure. Johnson was ill and suffering from constant chest pains during this time. Two months after the second Nixon victory, he died.

Though no one can become president of the United States without his party, once the former president is completely retired, his interests and those of his party are not always identical. A phenomenon of the American party system is that each party exists nationally, in a serious sense, only every four years when its fifty state parties get together to elect a president. Otherwise, though the individual state parties carry the same generic name, they are very different from each other. The former president, on the other hand, has been president of all the people and has acquired a national outlook that becomes permanent and that he does not want to relinquish. This was seen in the cases of the pre-Civil War presidents who were cool to the development of sectional parties.

The president also develops a world view which separates him from local partisan politics. Particularly in modern times, their foreign policies are the aspects of their administrations that ex-presidents guard most carefully. Witness Truman, whose chief interest in the DAC was the preservation of his foreign policy. Eisenhower, in his turn, felt just as strongly, and Johnson, though it destroyed him, never budged on Vietnam.

Logically, then, the ex-president would tend to promote as candidates those in the party who are closest to his policies and most likely to continue his programs. The good of the party is not the primary consideration for the former president, but the protection of his administration's policies.

The party, realizing this, will use the ex-president for its own purposes. He is the symbol of its past success. As such, he is displayed like a victory banner at the convention and is expected to endorse the party nominees. He is usually, however, not included in the party deliberations or has minimal influence. His prestige is useful to the party but, at the same time, threatening to the politicos. He can become an embarrassment to the party managers but cannot be controlled. To his political party, then, the ex-president is a mixed blessing.

Tools of the Incumbents

T HE POLITICAL USE of ex-presidents is an obvious inevitability. There were times in many administrations when the president found it expedient to solicit the advice and counsel and even the action of a former chief executive. The exiles, finding themselves needed again, were usually happy to perform the role of elder statesman. And so, with something of noblesse oblige, they would good-humoredly lend their prestige.

As noted earlier, Washington acceded to John Adams's call to emerge from retirement and resume martial duties. The first President, then, although reluctantly, set a precedent for the future. In the case of Jefferson, there was fear that James Madison, his heir and his successor, in a philosophical as well as a political sense, would rely too heavily on the Sage of Monticello. Jefferson realized this and, for the most part, stayed meekly in the background. He wrote but seldom to his close friend in the White House, and when he ventured to mention his views on current situations, was becomingly discreet. The two Virginians so agreed in spirit that it was not necessary to be explicit. Jefferson was certain that Madison's presidency would be eight years of "wise administration." However, it must be admitted that the two gentlemen met annually. Each September, President Madison made a pilgrimage to Monticello, where he and Jefferson spoke at great length to each other. There are no records of their conversations.

Ex-President Jefferson did effect a reconciliation between his two friends Madison and Monroe that had significant consequences. It reunited the Democratic-Republican party and it molded the future of Monroe. The estrangement had started when Madison was Jefferson's secretary of state and Monroe was in Europe negotiating his unsuccessful treaty with England. It reached its peak when Monroe opposed Madison in the presidential election of 1808.

Shortly after his return to private life, Jefferson wrote to the President that Monroe was leaving Richmond to return to his farm and was, therefore, leaving his "undesirable" friends and supporters behind. As a first step to a rapprochement, Jefferson arranged that Monroe be invited to a banquet given in Richmond in honor of the President. Monroe attended the affair and offered a toast: "National honor is national property—its protection among the first duties of Free men."[1]

In return, Madison made a friendly overture. He had heard that Monroe would accept the governorship of Louisiana if it were offered, so he asked Jefferson to broach the subject to him. Jefferson did so in a letter to which he received a clear answer. Monroe wanted no office in which he would be subordinate to anyone but the President. When Jefferson mentioned that the death of General Hampton would make a military post available, Monroe replied that he "would rather be shot" than serve under General Wilkinson. On the whole, Jefferson wrote to Madison, "I conclude he would accept a post in the Cabinet or a military command dependent on the executive alone and very likely a diplomatic mission."[2] A couple of years later, Monroe was offered, and accepted, the top Cabinet post in Madison's administration.

President James Monroe consulted both Jefferson and Madison before presenting his famous doctrine. "The moment is peculiarly critical as respects the Present state of the world, our relations with the acting parties in it, in Europe, & in this hemisphere," Monroe informed Jefferson. He wanted "your [Jefferson's] sentiments" on the situation. "Can we, in any form, take a bolder attitude in regard to it, in favor of liberty," than they had taken at the time of the start of the French Revolution, he asked. A few months later, in October 1823, Monroe wrote again to tell his friend of the startling proposal that George Canning, the British minister, had made to Richard Rush, the American minister in England. The Englishman had suggested that the Holy Alliance had designs on the independence of South America and that the United States and Great Britain should cooperate in support of South America and against the members of the Alliance. After stating his own position, Monroe wrote, "I am sensible, however, of the extent and difficulty of the question, and shall be happy to have yours and Mr. Madison's opinions on it." He did not want to trouble the two retirees "with small objects, but the present one is vital."[3]

Jefferson responded quickly, saying that the question was "the most momentous which has ever been offered to my contemplation since that of Independence." He advised that the United States should never "entangle ourselves in the broils of Europe" or "suffer Europe to intermeddle with cis-Atlantic affairs." The American system of keeping all foreign powers out of American nations must be established and if, to facilitate this, it were possible to divide the European powers and draw England, its most powerful member, to our side, "we should do it." Therefore, the President should encourage the British government. Then, with diffidence, Jefferson pointed out that he had been so long away from political subjects, "and have so long ceased to take any interest in them, that I am sensible I am not qualified to offer opinions on them worthy of any attention." Only the fact that the question proposed would have such a decisive effect on the nation's future induced him to hazard an opinion.[4]

Madison, after receiving Monroe's letter from Jefferson along with the pertinent Canning-Rush correspondence, gave his opinion. He believed that it was necessary for the United States, because of its sympathy and friendship for "the revolutionized colonies," to "defeat the meditated crusade." He was quite certain that Great Britain's motives were "different from ours," but nevertheless "our cooperation is due to ourselves & to the world."[5] His views were similar to Jefferson's.

Undoubtedly the vote of confidence as to general support for Latin American independence from his Virginia colleagues helped Monroe to solidify his own thinking. However, Secretary of State John Quincy Adams was unalterably opposed to an alliance, no matter how tenuous, with Great Britain. The United States must never "come in as a cock-boat in the wake of the British man-of-war," he declared. And when the Monroe Doctrine was enunciated, it was as strong as the ex-Presidents wished, but it was independent of a British alliance. Jefferson was pleased that the doctrine included his principle of closing the Western Hemisphere to European colonization. Madison said to Monroe, "One thing is certain, that the contents of the Message will receive very close attention everywhere, and that it can do nothing but good everywhere."[6]

Though old, sick, and often bedridden during the Jackson administration, Madison was able to render the President an indirect but appreciated service during the nullification controversy. Through an extensive correspondence with Nicholas Trist, Jackson's private secretary and a grandson-in-law of Jefferson, Madison was kept informed of the administration problems. The ex-President answered questions on nullification with arguments and historical data that Trist then published anonymously in Washington and Virginia newspapers.[7]

A typical letter from Madison to Trist had enclosed in it a paper on "The Great Complaint against the Tariff" which delineated the question of the unequal burden placed by the tariff on the planting states. Madison suggested an equalizing arrangement while cautioning that "it is impossible to do perfect justice in the distribution of burdens and benefits, and that equitable estimates and mutual concessions are necessary to approach it." Madison told Trist that his views "may be suggested where it is most likely they will be well received," but this must be done without "*naming* or *designating* in any manner the source of them." It was best now, the aged statesman told all his correspondents, that he should be before the public as little as possible, "to give way to others with the same love of their Country, who are more able to be useful to it."[8]

Madison felt some sense of responsibility for South Carolina's defiance, because the advocates of nullification, although erroneously, used the Virginia Resolutions of 1798, of which he was the author, as a precedent for the right of a state to refuse to carry out a federal law. South Carolina resolutely appealed to the Virginia Resolutions and their rejection of the Alien and Sedition Acts "as expressly or constructively favoring this doctrine." Madison was further impelled to oppose nullification in order to defend his dear friend Jefferson, author of the Kentucky Resolutions (also written at the time of the Alien and Sedition Acts), who was no longer alive to defend himself. "It is remarkable how closely the nullifiers who make the name of Mr. Jefferson the pedestal for the colossal heresy, shut their eyes and lips, whenever his authority is ever so clearly and emphatically against them," he wrote to Trist. "It is high time that the claim to secede at will should be put down by public opinion; and I should be glad to see the task commenced."[9]

In a similar fashion, ex-President Jackson urged President Tyler to take action on the annexation of Texas. A fierce Anglophobe, Jackson was aroused by reports of British intrigue in Texas and wrote letters frantically urging annexation. Tyler asserted that he took the initiative in urging Texas annexation without consulting Jackson but admitted that the hero of New Orleans gave the President "his zealous and cordial support," so he would be "the last to deny him the full measure of honor which his patriotic advocacy implied." A. V. Brown of Tennessee was more insistent in a letter to Sam Houston: "general Jakson [*sic*] more than any man, is the basis of whatever has been proposed to your government."[10]

There was little indication of ex-presidential influence on administrations during the period of intense sectional strife that preceded the Civil War. The retirees wrote letters of congratulations to incumbent Presidents, occasionally asked for the favor of an appointment for a friend or relative, but otherwise confined their comments to their friends and diaries. John Tyler, for instance, was pleased that when he met President Franklin Pierce at White Sulphur Springs, he was received by him "with generous extolling language."

Sometimes an ex-president made a spontaneous gesture in behalf of the incumbent. Jackson regarded Polk as his friend and protégé and, in that spirit, warned him that his secretary of the treasury, Robert J. Walker, was involved in land speculation that "might blow you and your administration sky high." Polk was touched by the letter because it was Jackson's last, written just two days before he died. This indication that Old Hickory had been so concerned with the success of his career, plus the confidential nature of the letter, moved Polk to tell his diary that he would preserve it "as a highly prized memorial of the dying patriot."[11]

When James K. Polk became the first dark-horse presidential candidate in American politics, he felt that he owed an explanation to ex-President Van Buren, who had expected the nomination. He wrote that when they had met in the spring of 1842, he had anticipated that "you would now occupy the position in which I have been placed." He added that his nomination at the Baltimore convention in 1844 had been unsought. Now he wanted Van Buren's advice on the selection of his Cabinet. Since Silas Wright of New York had just refused the treasury post, the President-elect would like the name of another New Yorker. Van Buren's choice would, of course, be kept in the strictest confidence.[12]

Van Buren answered immediately that Azariah C. Flagg or Churchill C. Cambreleng would be suitable for the treasury. For secretary of state, he advised, the President would want "a man of bland manners, good temper, great quickness of perception, industry & high personal character." Only someone who has had the experience, he explained, can appreciate the increased facility with which an administration can get along when it has a person with such qualities in the top Cabinet post. Van Buren suggested that Benjamin Butler would be "a very fit man."[13]

However, Polk's sense of obligation to Van Buren cooled quickly. Just a month later, he wrote that he preferred a secretary of the treasury from the South but was thinking of George Bancroft, the historian, who had been Van Buren's collector of the port of Boston. For the War Department he had in mind Butler or William L. Marcy, a former governor of New York. This last suggestion disturbed Van Buren, because Marcy, formerly an ardent Van Burenite, had thrown New York support to Polk in the past convention. Polk concluded his comments with the smug truism that there were many difficulties in Cabinet-making.[14]

Van Buren, a practiced politician, ignored what he did not like in the Polk correspondence and continued to urge him to give first place in his Cabinet to a New Yorker. He heard that Polk had offered Butler the War Department, which he refused, suggesting Cambreleng or Flagg instead. Mrs. Butler wrote to Van Buren that it was not her doing that her husband had refused the post, but had he been President it would have been a more pleasant offer. Still undaunted in his Cabinet-making efforts, Van Buren wrote to Polk that he would try to make suggestions that would be acceptable and that he had no unkind feelings toward the President because they disagreed. As for Bancroft, the allegation that he was an impractical person was untrue. He had run the custom house perfectly.[15]

At this period of time, Polk recorded in his diary that he believed that Van Buren had become offended with him because he exercised his own judgment in the selection of the Cabinet. He wrote that he "would not be controlled by him and suffer him to select it for me." Then he referred to Van Buren's "most extraordinary letter addressed to me on that subject" to which he had made no reply, but which he kept. After that, the *Diary* said, Polk had no direct correspondence with Van Buren except for sending him two annual messages that had been acknowledged.[16] Which of the several Van Buren-Polk letters that have been preserved on the question of Cabinet formation offended him, it is impossible to say. It is likely that Polk got tired of Van Buren's persistence in giving advice, when Polk's request for it had perhaps been no more than an insincere gesture of reconciliation. Of the letters available, none of Van Buren's seem "extraordinary," but, rather, polite and helpful. It seems that the President chose to forget that he had written asking for Van Buren's advice.

Finally, Polk did not give the State Department to a New Yorker, but, rather, to James Buchanan of Pennsylvania. The treasury post also went to a Pennsylvanian, Robert J. Walker, a strong advocate of Texas annexation who had been in charge of the 1844 Democratic campaign. William Marcy, the renegade Van Burenite, was made secretary of war, but had to wait for Pierce's administration for the top Cabinet post. Bancroft was appointed secretary of the navy and served for a year, during which he pushed for the formation of a United States naval academy and ordered General Zachary Taylor to cross the United States-Texas border, thus activating the Mexican War. He then became the American minister to England.

A similar situation arose after Grant, who was expected to get the Republican nomination in 1880, was outrun by dark horse James A. Garfield. Although Grant supported Garfield during the campaign, he was not consulted after the election on the choice of Cabinet members. On the contrary, the ex-President was dismayed when his archenemy, James F. Blaine, was chosen to be secretary of state. Even worse, William A. Robertson, who had been active in bringing about Grant's defeat, was given the coveted job of collector of the port of New York without the President's consulting Roscoe Conkling, the senator from New York, as was customary. After considering the possibility of denouncing the administration, Grant relented and visited the President at the White House, receiving from him assurances of his gratitude and a desire to please him with his appointments. However, instead of honoring Grant's request that General Adam Badeau, his former aide, be retained as the consul general in London, Garfield started to play musical chairs with the positions of a number of the ex-President's closest friends and relatives. Badeau was removed from London to make room for Dudley Merritt, the former New York collector. General Grant's brother-in-law, M. J. Cramer, who had been chargé d'affaires in Copenhagen, was moved to Berne to make room for Badeau. The odd man out was Nicholas Fish, the son of Hamilton Fish, Grant's secretary of state. This operation, which displeased all the people involved, was carried out without warning to Grant only two days after Garfield had assured the former President of his wish for recommendations for office.

Though recognizing fully Garfield's right to appoint whomever he pleased, Grant felt that Garfield's acts were deliberately offensive. However, he tried again in Badeau's behalf, providing him with a letter to Garfield asking that he be given either Italy or the naval office in Washington. Ironically, Badeau met Merritt on the White House steps engaged in a similar errand because he did not want to change his post. Ultimately, after further correspondence with Grant, Badeau refused Copenhagen despite Garfield's attempts to convince him to take it. His reason, Badeau said, was that it would "relieve him from the appearance of disregarding General Grant's personal wish."

Thoroughly disgusted with the dark-horse President, Grant wrote that he would never again support a presidential candidate "who has not strength enough to appear before a convention as a candidate" and gets into office because, "being outside," he is preferred to either of the candidates before the convention. By June, Grant told Badeau to accept the Copenhagen mission rather than leave the public service. But before the appointment could be made, Garfield was shot.[17]

At this point, Grant's situation was a strange one. He had mended his relationship with Garfield enough to call on him when they were both at Long Branch, but his real sympathies were known to be with Conkling and Arthur. Consequently, the hero of Appomattox was so out of favor with the people that it was rumored that he was not displeased at the President's assassination. Therefore, it would seem that the accession of Arthur to the executive seat would assure Grant significant influence in the new administration. Arthur had gone to Chicago in 1880 a Grant-for-a-third-term advocate and, of course, owed his position as Vice-President to Grant and Conkling. Hence when Arthur and Grant met at the Garfield funeral, it was logical that the new President should ask for Grant's advice in structuring his Cabinet.

Badeau claimed that Arthur's appointment of F. T. Frelinghuysen as secretary of state was due to Grant's influence. However, the former President's proposal of John Jacob Astor first for the treasury, which flattered the financier but did not interest him, and then for the Court of St. James, did not appeal to Arthur. He preferred to keep James Russell Lowell there although the poet had been one of his detractors.

Grant's attempt to promote the candidacy of General Edward F. Beale, a personal friend, for the navy post also fell on deaf ears. Arthur seemed to be satisfied that the Frelinghuysen appointment had paid off his obligations to the former President and he cooled off toward him. It was not long before Arthur, who had been so grateful to have Grant by his side at the inauguration, wanted to stand alone with no attachments from the past. Furthermore Grant still suffered from his inability to say no to the countless office seekers—friends, relatives, former army officers, and others—who plied him with requests. As a result, the President started to avoid Grant's company.

The final blow to Grant was Arthur's appointment to the Cabinet of William Chandler, the anti-third-term leader at the Chicago convention. The purpose of the appointment was to forge amity among all the factions of the Republican party, but to Grant it was a knife in the back, particularly since the post awarded was the navy department, which the former President wanted for Beale. Arthur, Grant felt, had gone over to the enemy.

President Arthur made one conciliatory move toward Grant, undoubtedly prodded by his secretary of state. He appointed him a commissioner to negotiate a commercial treaty with Mexico. At first Grant hesitated about accepting because he was critical of the administration and also because he felt that the appointment was made for the purpose of placating him, as well as to give the appearance of complete harmony in the party. However, he accepted. The treaty that was signed by the two nations provided for reciprocity between them, a tariff concept that Arthur promoted because the United States already had excessive revenue and wanted more trade. Twenty-eight Mexican articles would be admitted free of duty, including tobacco and sugar, in return for American articles, mostly manufactured goods. Congress did not debate the Reciprocity Treaty until March 1884, at which time it was ratified. However, in order for it to go into effect, legislation was required of Congress, and by this time Arthur had failed to be renominated by his party. Consequently, the reciprocity program, which included countries other than Mexico, was rejected, and the Mexican Treaty never went into effect.[18]

Grant suffered accusations and abuse over his treaty. There were allegations that both he and the Mexican negotiator, his friend and later benefactor Matias Romero, would benefit by it. Utterly without any basis as the accusation was, Grant felt that the President had used him and then callously ignored his honest attempt to promote his American system for the American continent.[19]

On October 4, 1902, on the spur of the moment, ex-President Cleveland wrote to President Theodore Roosevelt proposing a temporary solution for a strike in the anthracite coal fields that had started in May. Cleveland was impelled to write ("I promise never to do it again," he said) when he read in the newspaper that a White House meeting with the representatives of management had been unsuccessful in settling the strike.

Cleveland's suggestion was that, first, enough coal should be produced to satisfy consumer needs and that then both sides could resume the dispute, "without prejudice," and the "dangerous condemnation now being launched against both their houses might be delayed." The ex-President noted that in his experience "when quarreling parties are both in the wrong," they will do strange things to save their faces.[20]

Roosevelt, telling the strike story in his autobiography, ignored the Cleveland letter and its suggestion for handling the strike. Instead he recorded that "even so naturally conservative a man as Grover Cleveland" had expressed sympathy "with the course I was following" and indignation at the conduct of the operators. Then, said TR, he wrote to Cleveland that the mines must be run and that if there were no voluntary agreement between the owners and the workers, he would appoint an arbitration commission to force terms on both parties. Cleveland would be asked to accept "the chief place on the Commission," and he had indicated that he would be available.[21]

The Roosevelt account was a not quite accurate rendering of the Cleveland part in the maneuvering that went on. Elihu Root met with J. P. Morgan on his yacht and apparently convinced him that the President would use federal troops to run the mines if the strike were not settled and then would invoke a commission to settle it. Consequently, Morgan pressured the mine owners to come to terms. Cleveland became an issue because the operators did not want the ex-President on the arbitration board, preferring, according to Roosevelt, General Wilson and, according to some reports, someone who was a less dangerous radical. In March 1903, the commission, without Cleveland on it, met and decided that the miners should receive a ten-percent wage increase but denied recognition of their union.[22]

"I appreciated so deeply your being willing to accept that it was very hard for me to forego the chance of putting you on the commission," TR wrote to Cleveland. But after the settlement Cleveland learned that Roosevelt planned to "make quite a general exhibition of my letter, which should have been regarded as strictly personal." It was to be published in the press "when in the opinion of Roosevelt's tenters the psychological moment arrives—if it ever does." Cleveland was annoyed but said that he was not sorry that the incident had occurred, because it put him on his guard against writing letters "of any description to Mr. Roosevelt."[23] However, Cleveland was not ashamed of his "coal letter," as Roosevelt called it, nor did he want to retract any part of it. His motive, he claimed, was to spare the people from the effect of a coal shortage and nothing else. Furthermore, he asserted, he would never have accepted a place on the arbitration board even if it had been offered to him. The Chicago *Record-Herald* had a different interpretation. The newspaper reported that an eyewitness had told them that the President refused to appoint Cleveland because he would then be in such a prominent position that he would become TR's Democratic rival. Roosevelt thought these newspaper rumblings were nonsense.

Doubtless Theodore Roosevelt believed that the incident occurred as he had described it. The perceptions of both participants may well have been inaccurate. However, the major benefit, if any, surely would accrue to the President, who could show support from an ex-President who was also a member of the opposition party.

William Howard Taft always wanted to be chief justice of the Supreme Court. In 1910, when he was President and had to appoint a chief justice, he said to Justice Moody, "It does seem strange that the one place in the government which I would have liked to fill myself, I am forced to give to another." He then made a statement that proved an embarrassment to him when he became a contender for the position later on. In answer to Senator Murray Crane's proposal, backed by Joseph Choate, that Elihu Root be appointed chief justice, Taft answered emphatically, "I am not going to put him on the bench at all and certainly have no idea of making him Chief Justice. . . . He is sixty-five years old. What the country needs for

Chief Justice is a man young enough to devote his strength and years to getting the Court out of the slough of despond it has fallen into of late years."[24] Instead, Taft appointed Edward D. White of Louisiana, an associate judge who had been put on the bench by Cleveland in 1894. He was the first judge of the court promoted to become chief justice since 1796. It was thought that Taft had an understanding with White that he would remain on the bench until a Republican president was elected who would appoint Taft chief justice.

Warren Harding, a Republican, was elected in 1920, but to Taft's dismay, Chief Justice White made no move to vacate his seat although his health was very bad. On the day before Christmas, 1920, Taft arrived in Marion, Ohio, to keep a breakfast appointment with President-elect Harding. While the two men and Mrs. Harding, known as the Duchess, dined on waffles and chipped beef, they discussed the domestic affairs of the White House. The ex-President feared that the new tenants were planning to be too informal in their behavior there, so while Harding was out of the room, Taft warned the Duchess that it was most important that her husband realize that now his friends must call him Mr. President—the dignity of the office demanded it.

Once alone, the two leading Republicans discussed the future Cabinet. Harding mentioned that he had offered State to Hughes. Surprisingly, Taft suggested that Hughes would like to be chief justice instead, and proposed Root for the Cabinet post. Harding rejected Root as too old. Taft then proposed Charles Hilles for the Treasury Department, but Harding had already chosen Dawes and Hoover for Interior and Commerce. Impressed by Harding's choices so far, Taft also went along with Senator Harry S. New for War and H. M. Dougherty for attorney general. The ex-President thought that Dougherty's choice was reasonable since he and the President-elect were such close friends. Harding asked Taft for several other suggestions, such as a good possibility for governor general of the Philippines. Taft suggested Charles R. Forbes.

Suddenly Harding turned to Taft and said: "By the way, I want to ask you, would you accept a position on the Supreme Bench? Because if you would, I'll put you on that Court." Taft was amazed but kept his head. He replied that it was his life's ambition to sit on the Supreme Court but since he had, as President, appointed three of the justices still sitting on the court and firmly opposed the ap-

pointment of Justice Brandeis, he could only accept the position of
chief justice. He then pointed out that White was deaf and ill and
contemplating resigning, so the position would be open soon. Harding remained silent after Taft's statement, so the former President
switched the subject to the appointment of Negroes below the
Mason-Dixon line.

Taft advised Harding not to appoint any Negroes there, because
it did neither the whites nor the Negroes any good in communities
where "the leading element was white." Harding replied rather
bitterly that he would consider this carefully "because of his reputed
ancestry," referring to the gossip that was circulating that he had
some Negro blood. He believed in a lily white Republican party,
Harding said ironically, not a black and tan.[25]

Once President, Harding distributed appointments major and
minor, including the post of assistant secretary of the navy to Theodore Roosevelt, Jr. But senile, ailing Chief Justice White made no
move toward fulfilling his promise to Taft even after Attorney General Dougherty visited him several times and hinted broadly. What
was worse for Taft was that there were persistent rumors that when
White finally succumbed, Hughes would resign as secretary of state
and become chief justice. It was also rumored that Senator Sutherland wanted the job and Harding had promised it to him.

"Presidents come and go but the court goes on forever," Taft once
said. He had dreams of court reform and the chance to mitigate his
humiliating defeat in 1912 by brilliant leadership there. Now his
ambition was being threatened by Harding's familiar technique of
trying to please everyone. The President hoped to accomplish this
by getting a brace of Judges to resign—White and William R. Day
or White and Oliver Wendell Holmes—thus freeing two spots, one
for Taft and one for Sutherland. When he got wind of this, Taft
was not above suggesting that the bench be freed of "the great dissenter" by offering him a place on the Disarmament Commission.

Gus Karger, Taft's former campaign manager, managed the
former President's campaign for the chief justiceship with the help of
instructions from the candidate. The Senate Democrats were to be
reminded that of Taft's six appointees, three were Democrats and
therefore they should support his appointment. Taft worried that
Senators Borah and Norris, both on the Judiciary Committee, regarded his selection with disfavor and that Reed would go along
with them. He also feared that he would be accused of not having

had enough experience on the bench to warrant his appointment. He had served three years on the state bench, two years as solicitor general of the United States, eight years as presiding judge of the United States Circuit, four years on the Court of Appeals, Sixth Circuit, and eight years as Kent Professor of Law at Yale University. He also fretted that because he was sixty-four years old his comment about Hughes's age might be resuscitated, although despite that pronouncement, he had appointed Associate Justice Linton when he was over sixty and White at over sixty-five.[26]

The path to the appointment did not run smooth. Harding told Karger that Taft's age was not the issue but Sutherland was, and then proposed the possibility of having Day named chief justice, serve for six months, and then resign in favor of Taft. Wearily, Taft told Karger that he hoped Harding would not do that, because it was too important an office to go into with that obligation. Remembering White's promise, he said, "Day's memory of the understanding will grow as dim."[27]

Taft's champion turned out to be Harry Dougherty. It was his influence that persuaded Harding to appoint the former President and discard the Day plan. The President told Karger that the appointment would be made in early July, but thanks to Dougherty's prodding, by June 30 Taft's nomination was confirmed by the Senate, although not without some opposition. Taft was overjoyed. "I have come back from the status in which the campaign of 1912 left me," he said, and he could not return to Washington fast enough. He bought a seventy-five-thousand-dollar house at Twenty-third Street and Wyoming Avenue and took long walks to preserve his health.

On the surface it looked as if Taft had made handy use of the restoration of Republican power to the White House. He demanded and eventually received the reward that he wanted. However, it is just as true that Harding had kicked upstairs the only living Republican ex-President and had rendered him politically impotent, since a member of the court is, by definition, nonpartisan.

The story of Hoover's food missions for Truman and Eisenhower has already been told. But some further consideration of Truman's motive for resurrecting the only living ex-President at the critical time of the closing days of the European war may throw some light on the nature of ex-presidential use by the incumbent. Hoover wrote a candid and thorough memo about his first meeting with Truman at the White House, concluding somewhat cynically that he had little confidence in the President's sincerity about using his talents and experience. Truman, on the other hand, recounted the episode very differently, recalling a highly emotional response on the part of the elderly former President.

In a taped interview fifteen years after the event, Truman said that while he and Hoover were sitting together in the Oval Room just after he had told him that he would be delegated to feed hungry Europe, great big tears ran down the ex-President's cheeks. Then, Truman said, Hoover excused himself and went into the other room. In a few minutes he returned, entirely recovered, and resumed the conversation. At the end of the meeting, according to the President, Hoover agreed to participate in the United States relief program for Europe. "I knew what was the matter with him," Truman commented. "It was the first time in thirteen years that anybody had paid any attention to him."[28]

Apart from Truman's genuine respect for Hoover's expertise in this area, his appointment of Hoover was politically astute. Now that the war was coming to an end and isolationism was no longer a factor, the possibility of the ex-President's emergence as an important Republican figure might have to be dealt with. Also, Truman was scornful of FDR's pettish refusal to overcome his prejudice against his predecessor or to give him any opportunity to display himself in a more popular role. Truman said, self-righteously, that he differed from Hoover on economics and politics but, nonetheless, he was a "man of character, capacity and talent." He asserted that Roosevelt could have invited him to join the bipartisan group that he had set up to administer the war effort.[29] Also, Hoover was still a magic name in hungry Europe, and his reappearance as Truman's emissary of mercy could only enhance the American President's image there.

Truman had not finished utilizing Hoover's talents even after he completed the foreign missions successfully. He then asked the former President to use his organizational and administrative talents to head a commission to reorganize the executive branch. Hoover agreed to do it, though he was not in good health and was suffering from a severe, painful case of shingles that temporarily paralyzed his right arm and shoulder. For twenty months, the aged ex-President shuttled back and forth between New York and Washington, working indefatigably at the task.

The twelve-man bipartisan committee that comprised the Hoover

Commission, as it became known, included Dean Acheson as vice-chairman, Secretary of Defense James Forrestal, Joseph P. Kennedy, and several Republicans other than Hoover. All of the members worked hard but none as hard as the chairman. Truman launched the project at the White House with a speech that advised open-mindedness and a nonpolitical approach. The commission, he said, should bring back "the most honest findings you can get and don't worry whom it might or might not please."

Congress passed the Reorganization Act of 1949 which provided for the commission, but, as Hoover wrote to Truman, only some of the reforms could be included in it; other needed changes would require special legislation. Therefore, the former President recommended "special privilege" bills, which the commission had drafted and which he hoped that Truman would propose, thus assuring the widest public support.[30]

The Hoover Commission Report was a massive survey of the administrative structure of the United States government, distilled into an orderly arrangement of information and opinion that proposed about three hundred reforms. Among them were: elimination of rival agencies in the same department, such as, for example, the Forest Service and the Soil Conservation Service, which were both doing some of each other's jobs and were both part of the Department of Agriculture; establishment of a Department of Health, Education and Welfare; and the removal of the Post Office from politics. All down the line there were suggestions for increasing efficiency that would save millions of dollars by avoiding duplication of efforts and demanding accountability.

Truman considered the work of the commission one of the most valuable contributions of his administration, and eventually about seventy percent of its proposals were accepted. Hoover must be given a sizable slice of the credit both for his work on the commission and for getting support for it from the people. He organized a citizens' committee to lobby for the reform, calling it "a crusade to clear the track for competency . . . a job for citizenship rather than partisanship."[31] Truman reaped the short-term rewards of Hooverian bipartisanship, but the former President was looking at the long-range objective. He saw the work as done to benefit the next administration, which he was certain would be Republican.

President Eisenhower revived the Hoover Commission, because by 1953 the cost of government had increased again due to large spending for war and armaments. He was able to convince Hoover, now almost eighty, to resume leadership of the project. In describing the more difficult assignment of the second commission, its editorial director, Neil MacNeil, explained that the first commission's job had been vertical, "concerned with the structure of government," while the second commission's job was horizontal, "concerned with function."[32] Hoover's twenty task forces, now empowered to subpoena witnesses, dealt with how things should be structured as well as what should be done by government. The most fundamental change was that both the Democratic and the Republican members of this new commission were more conservative.

Attorney General Brownell, a commission member, said that he "really admired" Hoover, who worked like a Trojan. His recollection centered on how hard and how continuously he worked, begrudging every minute taken out for a sandwich or coffee. "We used to joke with him a little about it and he would laugh about it but he'd go right on with business during the lunch," Brownell said.[33]

In March 1955, the second commission started to release its findings. Again there were hundreds of precise recommendations that promised to save roughly six billion dollars annually. Hoover expected and got a great deal of opposition, which he blamed on the bureaucracy which would lose out if the changes were made. "Old reformers never die; they get thrown out," he quipped. As Brownell pointed out, in the second Hoover Commission, matters of policy were gone into more than in the first. Therefore some of the issues were, eventually, political issues, upon which Congress divided, usually along party lines. "I think that would account for the fact that some of the recommendations were not accepted," Brownell said.[34]

At first Hoover hoped for as high a percentage of acceptance as the first time, although this was totally unrealistic under the circumstances. The ultraconservativeness of the organization, its relentless drive to save money, and its disapproval of many government services foreshadowed its rejection by many in Congress. For example, it was so wholeheartedly against government in business that it questioned the TVA, which to many Americans was the New Deal's noblest experiment. Some liberals charged that Hoover was using the commission to justify his presidential policies by restoring the executive department to what it had been when he was in the White House.

Others, for other motives, resented the commission's assault on the Defense Department.

Hoover was disappointed that the legislative members of the commission did not push its recommendations more firmly. He blamed Joseph Kennedy, a member of both commissions, for not prodding his son Senator John Kennedy to take some action. He admired the youth and energy of young Kennedy and felt that it should be utilized for the commission's work. The chairman also felt that the President did not throw enough influence into it. "President Eisenhower's heart is in the right place, wouldn't you think he would do more to implement the recommendations?" Hoover was quoted as saying. However, in May 1956, Ike did refer to the Hoover Commission in his message to Congress. He mentioned its "important and desirable objectives for the improvement of federal administration" and expressed his appreciation to ex-President Hoover and his associates, but he did not push hard for acceptance of its proposals.[35]

In October Eisenhower wrote to Hoover telling him that the department and agencies of the executive branch were studying the relevant recommendations and their implementation. "I am encouraged by what seems to me to be a satisfactory degree of progress, but obviously a great deal more needs to be done." Some of the measures required congressional action, the President observed. Hopefully, the modest start made with bipartisan support in the last Congress would continue. In conclusion, Ike patted the old gentleman on the shoulder. "Your own contribution to the betterment of Government over the years, and particularly through the two Commissions which bore your name and profited by your leadership, has earned the deep appreciation of the Nation as well as my own."[36]

No doubt Eisenhower used Hoover's abilities in the work of the commission, but even more tellingly he used the rising prestige of the old Republican standard-bearer, particularly in conservative circles. Criticism of the commission's conservatism could also be conveniently borne by Hoover alone. Hoover, in his expression of dissatisfaction over Ike's halfhearted effort to push for the commission's conclusions, indicated that he suspected the motives but still hoped to be able to effect the changes through his own efforts.

Bearing out the suggestion above is the persistence with which Hoover continued to urge the commission's findings and recommendations. He wrote to President Kennedy suggesting that there was a sharp need for reforms in the budgeting and accounting of government funds. Kennedy's answer was that bills had been introduced by senators but no action had been taken for the past ten years because of differences of opinion between the two houses. "I am sure that you realize that separation of powers makes this a sensitive issue," he said. However, the former senator, who had failed to push action on the Hoover proposals, wrote: "We will do everything possible to ensure House consideration of the measure." He assured the ex-President that within the executive branch, "we are continuing to make budget improvements along the lines recommended by your Commission."[37]

Just six months before his death, Hoover wrote to President Lyndon Johnson suggesting the activation of a third commission on organization, because there were still many economies that could be effected in the government and much more efficient methods of operation that could be developed.[38] Earlier, Johnson had assured Hoover that he was studying the reports of his commissions for the purpose of cutting the costs of government administration. For Hoover, the work of his commissions was his last attempt to repudiate New Dealism and his final contribution to his country.

When Eisenhower became President, there was more than one ex-President for the first time in twenty years. After Ike's inauguration ceremony, Truman went over to Hoover on the inaugural platform. Hoover greeted him and said: "I think we ought to organize a former Presidents club." Truman answered, "Fine. You be the president of the club and I will be the secretary."[39]

The mutual respect and cordiality that characterized the relationship between Truman and Hoover did not carry over to Eisenhower-Truman relations. Truman felt that the careful preparations he had made for an orderly transfer of government were spurned by the President-elect. His invitation to Ike for an informal lunch at the White House on inauguration day was also refused, contrary to custom. On that day, Eisenhower remained in his car at the portico of the White House instead of calling on the outgoing President before they both left together for the ceremonies, also contrary to custom. Truman reported a hostile exchange in the car going down Pennsylvania Avenue. "I did not attend your Inauguration in 1948 out of consideration for you, because if I had been present I would have drawn attention away from you," the President-elect said. "You were not here in 1948 because I did not send for you. But if I *had* sent for you, you would have come," Truman rejoined. During the rest of the drive the two Presidents remained silent.[40]

It was not their only exchange that day. Before going out to the inaugural platform, while sitting in the room of the sergeant at arms in the Capitol, Eisenhower suddenly asked Truman who was responsible for ordering his son John to Washington from Korea. "I wonder who is trying to embarrass me," Ike asked. Truman answered: "The President of the United States ordered your son to attend your inauguration. The President thought it was right and proper for your son to witness the swearing-in of his father to the Presidency. If you think somebody was trying to embarrass you by this order then the President assumes the full responsibility."[41]

Truman attributed their bad feeling toward each other to his having lectured Ike during the campaign for his failure to defend General George C. Marshall after he was called a traitor by Senators McCarthy and Jenner. He should have been upset about this, Truman felt. The Washington *Post-Times-Herald* attributed the feud to Eisenhower's anger because Truman had called him a demagogue, thus spoiling his image. Truman's attitude toward the new President persisted. He always referred to him as "the fellow that succeeded me in the White House" and consistently refused his invitations. In December 1958, when Eisenhower invited the ex-President to accompany him to Arlington Cemetery for the dedication of the Tomb of the Unknowns, Truman declined, saying that he was leaving on his European trip. The following year he sent his regrets again, saying that a previous engagement would keep him from attending the dinner that the Eisenhowers were giving for Sir Winston Churchill.

The Man from Missouri did not relent until Eisenhower joined the ranks of the ex-Presidents. Then he sent his best wishes for a long and useful life and an interesting and satisfying retirement. To Truman the club of ex-Presidents was so exclusive that no member could be ignored.

Truman often said that a former president had to be careful about commenting on current events and about offering advice to the administration. He should wait until his advice was sought and then express it quickly, behind closed doors, leaving any public statement to be made by the President. Truman did not always follow his own advice, but he did support Ike's position occasionally. He and Hoover both endorsed the policy of sending American soldiers and marines to Lebanon in 1959. They declared that the President had no other choice "if the freedom of nations is to be protected from militant conspiracies," as Hoover's statement expressed it.[42]

Hoover served the Eisenhower administration whenever possible. "I hope you will feel that my job is to aid the success of this Administration and, therefore, I would be glad to participate with you in any helpful way," he wrote to Sherman Adams when the Hoover Commission was activated. Eisenhower reciprocated by providing such conveniences as a plane to transport the elderly former President from New York to Washington, thus relieving him of long commuting hours on the train. Eisenhower and Hoover occasionally found time to fish together.

John Kennedy, some of his closest admirers admitted, had a talent for constantly wooing his opponents and a sense of history. These two characteristics influenced his relationship with the trio of ex-Presidents who were living during his thousand days in office. None of them were among his admirers at the beginning of his administration: two were Republicans and Harry Truman, the sole Democrat, was a doubtful ally.

Even before he took office, President-elect John Kennedy used the services of a former president. JFK's father, Ambassador Joseph Kennedy, had worked with Hoover on both commissions and was able to enlist the ex-President's help. After the election, narrowly defeated Vice-President Nixon went with his family to Key Biscayne, Florida, to recover from his disappointment. About two days after his arrival, while at dinner in a public restaurant, he received a phone call from Hoover. "The Ambassador [Joseph Kennedy] has just called me and suggested that it would be a good idea for you and the President-elect to get together for a visit," Hoover said. Kennedy was in Palm Beach and would like the Vice-President to phone to make an appointment. Surprised and somewhat reluctant, Nixon asked Hoover what he thought he should do. Hoover answered quickly that "some indications of national unity are not only desirable but essential" in the situation the world was in. Nixon had no choice but to reply that he would talk to Kennedy and that Hoover could so inform the ambassador.

Losing no time, Nixon phoned President Eisenhower at his farm in Gettysburg. Again he was told to talk to Kennedy. "You will look like a sore-head if you didn't," Ike remarked. Nixon hardly had hung up before the phone rang again. It was the President-elect, who made arrangements for a meeting but mentioned neither Hoover nor his father. Afterward, Nixon mused that in less than ten minutes he had talked to "a former President of the United States, the present President and the President-elect." It would have consoled him to know then that these three men had just talked to a future president.[43]

With more deliberate thought, undoubtedly, than any of his predecessors, Kennedy systematically kept in touch with the ex-Presidents and tried to employ their services. As far as he was concerned, all past differences were forgotten. He seemed genuinely pleased by Eisenhower's careful attention to an orderly transfer of executive responsibility. The President's offer to meet with Kennedy at any mutually convenient time was followed up with two appointments, one on December 8, the second on January 19. During these meetings the two men revised their opinions about each other. Eisenhower told a friend that Kennedy had "tremendously impressed him." Kennedy admitted that Ike was "better than I had thought" and very cooperative. However, the young President ignored his predecessor's farewell recommendation to establish a first secretary of the government to supervise all foreign affairs agencies and quickly eliminated the Eisenhower military method of chains of command in favor of informal meetings and more candid relationships with his staff.[44]

Kennedy's first visitor at the White House after the inauguration was Harry Truman. This was the first time that the former President had visited the White House since he left it as President. After a cordial exchange of greetings, Kennedy invited Truman to call on Jackie, and the three of them had a delightful half-hour visit.

Hoover was unable to come to the Kennedy inauguration because bad weather had closed the airport, but he sent "every blessing of the Almighty." He was "confident of your great success as our President."[45]

On his first day in office, JFK sent a thank you note to Ike for his "many acts of cordiality and assistance" during the interregnum. "I am sure that your generous assistance has made this one of the most effective transitions in the history of our Republic," he wrote. Kennedy showed his gratitude by providing Ike with a relief staff to take care of the volume of mail still pouring in for the former President. He also urged legislation to restore Eisenhower to his former military rank. When it was approved, Kennedy informed Ike at once. "The legislation constitutes a reaffirmation of the affection and regard of our nation for you," the President wrote. He then arranged to have an exact copy of the bill made and enclosed. A few days later, Ike made a statement supporting Kennedy's firm warning against communist intervention in the Laos crisis. It was the ex-President's first statement on foreign affairs since leaving the White House and was made at a press conference in Palm Springs, California. Eisenhower had received a phone call from Washington that morning, after the President had read in the newspaper that a statement would be made. Kennedy asked if it was about Laos and the ex-President said yes.[46]

Hoover was not as cooperative. Kennedy asked him to serve as honorary chairman of the National Advisory Committee to the Peace Corps. "Your acceptance of this position will rally millions of Americans and people all over the world who remember and respect your own pioneering leadership in this field of human assistance and constructive service," Kennedy wrote cajolingly. Hoover turned it down, pleading his many commitments "to educational and charitable institutions." He then said, almost as an afterthought: "Also, I think you will agree that it would not be fitting for me to be intervening in the organization you have set up. Some day you will find yourself in the same predicaments." It was a disappointment, because it would have helped the administration to have a distinguished conservative Republican former President backing a project that many Republicans in Congress regarded as somewhat quixotic and dangerous. But Hoover understood too well what his involvement would be if he accepted. When a former President accepts an honorary position, he wrote, "the American public holds him responsible for the activities of the organization." Eisenhower called the Peace Corps "a juvenile experiment," clarifying his complete rejection of Kennedy's notion that his idea would provide an outlet for the idealism of American youth.[47]

President Kennedy took full blame at the time and later for the Bay of Pigs disaster. This attempt by anti-Castro Cuban exiles to recapture the island from the Communists, using a plan of attack developed by the CIA, failed in April 1961 and prematurely ended the glorious Camelot period for many of Kennedy's liberal supporters.

Lest the setback stimulate Republican attack, Kennedy invited Ike to Camp David on April 23 to discuss Cuba. The administration was

George Washington, the
First Ex-President.
*Courtesy of the
National Archives*

Mount Vernon, George
Washington's Virginia
estate. *Courtesy of the
National Archives*

John Adams. Painting by
Gilbert Stuart. *Courtesy
of the Library of Congress*

Peacefield, the Adams home in Quincy, Massachusetts. *Courtesy of the Adams National Historic Site, United States Department of Interior*

James Madison at age 82. *Courtesy
of the Library of Congress*

James Madison's home, Montpelier, Virginia. *Courtesy of the Library of Congress*

James Monroe. Painting
by Gilbert Stuart.
*Courtesy of the Library
of Congress*

Andrew Jackson. Painting by P. A. Healy. *Courtesy of the Library of Congress*

The Hermitage, home of Andrew Jackson. *Courtesy of the Library of Congress*

Martin Van Buren by
Mathew Brady. *Courtesy
of the Library of
Congress*

John Tyler. *Courtesy of
the Library of Congress*

Millard Fillmore, Know-Nothing candidate. Campaign poster for the election
of 1856. *Courtesy of the
Library of Congress*

James Buchanan by Mathew Brady.
Courtesy of the Library of Congress

Franklin Pierce, from a Mathew Brady
daguerreotype. *Courtesy of the
Library of Congress*

The Death of Andrew Johnson, 1875. Courtesy of the Library of Congress

conscious of the fact that the training and arming of the Cuban army of liberation by the CIA had been originated and authorized during Eisenhower's term of office. Over a lunch of fried chicken, served in the presidential cabin, Kennedy and Eisenhower talked for an hour and a half. The President told the press that he had summoned his predecessor to brief him on the latest developments in Cuba and to get "the benefit of his thoughts and experience." No doubt he reminded him of the origin of the Cuban attack plan. Eisenhower agreed to support a policy of national unity on the Cuban fiasco. "I am still in favor of the United States supporting the man who has to carry the responsibility for our foreign affairs," Ike said.[48]

At the end of April, Kennedy visited Hoover in his Waldorf Towers apartment. Consequently, Hoover stated that he supported any action that must be taken to defend the country. "The existence of a communist country ninety miles from our borders is an intolerable menace to the safety of our country; it is a center of conspiracy to overthrow all free governments in this hemisphere by violence," he asserted. Kennedy was grateful for this endorsement by the senior ex-President and for his kindness in "sharing his thoughts on the current world crisis with me."[49]

Through the next few critical weeks, Eisenhower continued his support of Kennedy. He cautioned against any "witch hunting" investigation of the Cuban failure and advised bipartisan national support for Kennedy, who was occupied with "the most important question in the world, preventing the establishment of a communist stronghold in this country." Because of this situation Ike announced that he would not criticize the domestic policies of the administration at this time.

The support from Eisenhower was firmly sought by Kennedy, but his private view of Ike, at least in many instances, rather belied his public and political stance. When he was shown a Gallup poll on the Bay of Pigs, which indicated that 82 percent of the American people were behind him, he commented unkindly, "It's just like Eisenhower; the worse I do, the more popular I get." The Republican ex-President's support, however, helped to calm a vicious Republican attack. In this case, need for the Democratic ex-President's support was not regarded as critical. Consultation with Truman was assigned to Vice-President Johnson.[50]

To Kennedy's relief, Ike's support of his foreign policy continued. The General approved of his action in the Berlin crisis, foreign trade discussions, and foreign aid. "Your important support and judgment are readily at the nation's command, for which I am truly grateful," Kennedy wrote. He was willing to accept the eventuality that Eisenhower pointed out, that there would be differences on domestic matters but that "in matters of national concern, especially in foreign affairs, we will see eye to eye."[51]

Kennedy carefully worked at assuring Eisenhower approval for his foreign policy moves. He included congressional leaders from both parties in his briefings and appointed some Republicans to top posts in his administration. He was also not above publicly reminding the opposing party of his own and his party's support during the Eisenhower years.

Occasionally, however, neither Kennedy wiles nor Kennedy charm moved the two older ex-Presidents. An administration plan to name Truman and Hoover honorary coadvisors to the American Food-For-Peace Council was foiled jointly. Truman sent a copy of his refusal to Hoover, who replied that he was grateful for the letter and had also refused. "Apparently we have avoided this one," he wrote.[52]

Some attempts were made by the busy Kennedy PR men to exploit the existence of four living Presidents by trying to get them together on television. One effort, made in connection with a show on the trade program, was flatly turned down by Hoover, Pierre Salinger admitted. The distinguished three all refused an invitation to the Churchill citizenship ceremony. And when the National Historical Publications arranged a report to President Kennedy at a Washington's Birthday luncheon in 1963, they also proposed inviting the three ex-Presidents, a possibility that Kennedy thought might be explored. Truman responded that he would come, and Eisenhower said that he would come if Hoover did, and Hoover's physician said that he might be well enough to attend. The plan did not materialize but it pointed out the publicity value of the former Presidents even in terms of ceremonial appearances.[53]

Eisenhower's willingness to discuss foreign programs with Kennedy—giving them the aura of Republican approval that the administration craved—was sought by the President in periodic meetings. Prodded by Kennedy's reminder that he had indicated support for foreign aid and the necessity for long-term financing provisions, Eisenhower sent JFK a long telegram. He "emphatically" reaffirmed his support of the mutual security program, which he said strengthens peace through "reinforcing the combined power of the non-communist world." The part of the message that served the President best said: "I join you in urging congressmen of both parties to approve adequate funds for this crucially important undertaking."[54]

Though there were those observers who believed that Eisenhower's public criticism of the Peace Corps and fiscal policy had injured the relationship between the two men, Kennedy never ceased to be exceedingly cordial and appreciative of all that Ike did. He wrote to him agreeing with his television remarks on the extremists and praising him for "his very instructive and helpful" piece on Berlin in the *Saturday Evening Post.*[55]

All three ex-Presidents were circularized about the trade expansion program with the expectation that they would send their endorsements. Hoover wrote from the Florida Keys, where he had been fishing, that he was in agreement "with both the gravity of our situation in foreign trade and with your major proposals for legislation." He also noted that at the time he was President he had requested the same sort of authority to change tariff rates (the "flexible tariff") but that the worldwide depression "from the economic collapse of Europe rendered it an insufficient remedy in that storm."[56]

Eisenhower had been supportive already, but the President asked for his "continued support as we go into the debate stage." Kennedy dropped in to see Ike at Palm Desert, California, in early spring for a "cordial" fifty-minute discussion on the situation around the world, and in May Eisenhower wired his support for the trade extension bill. He could not come to Washington but would be willing to send a message to be read at the luncheon he was unable to attend. "As you realize I have publicly generally supported the measure and assure you I want to be of assistance," he said.[57]

While in the decision-making process for the most terrifying confrontation of the Kennedy administration, the Cuban Missile Crisis of October 1962, the President talked by telephone to Eisenhower, Truman, and Hoover. Kennedy had discussed the influx of Soviet arms and technical military aid to Cuba with Ike in September, because the Republicans had been urging administration action against Castro. Since Eisenhower's support of Kennedy after the Bay of Pigs had tempered Republican criticism, JFK hoped that once again the ex-President would be willing to moderate his party's temper. And the General did try to halt criticism by saying that Cuba should not be a partisan issue. As to Kennedy's request to Congress for standby authority to call up 150,000 reservists, Ike said that none of us were in a position to know the situation as the President did. "As Americans we must all back our President."[58]

In these matters, Kennedy had no problems. All the ex-Presidents were rabidly anticommunist. Truman had blamed Eisenhower for Castro's turning to the Soviet Union for support. When Castro came to power, he said, "Ike sat on his ass" and acted as if "Castro might go away or something." Then the Russians got him lined up on their side, "which is what you have to expect if you got a goddam fool in the White House."[59]

The last support from the elder statesmen that Kennedy sought in his brief administration was for his treaty limiting nuclear tests. Truman gave his unqualified approval. Hoover excused himself from giving his opinion because of his recent illness. Ike was for it, with the reservation that the Senate make clear that the United States retains the right to use nuclear weapons to repel aggression. Fulbright agreed with Eisenhower, but some of the administration supporters feared that the General had given those senators who were on the fence about the treaty a weapon with which to kill it. They might now require the reservation and add others until the treaty became unacceptable to the Soviet Union.[60]

Kennedy's success in using the ex-Presidents was manifested mainly in the international field. Eisenhower did not cease to assail Kennedy's domestic program. In one article that he wrote, he called the crash program to put a man on the moon "a mad effort to win a stunt race." He said, also, that as a farmer he would prefer jail to compliance with the cattle-production controls advocated in Kennedy's farm bill. All in all he was outspokenly unhappy with JFK's internal policies and with his "apparent thirst" for increasing the power of the federal government, particularly the executive branch.[61]

In public, Truman loyally went along with the Democratic President. Kennedy, for his part, was meticulous about congratulating the Missourian for the honors and awards that were constantly being given to him. They kept up a ceremonial exchange of birthday greetings, both of them being May babies. In answer to Truman's 1963 greeting, Kennedy said that the former President was the one most capable of judging the toil and the reward of the years in office. "It is my hope that forty-six will rest as lightly on me as seventy-nine do on you." However, because Truman hated Joe Kennedy, there was some distrust for "the boy in the White House." He was critical of the amount of money that the Kennedy family had spent to put

John F. Kennedy there. "The minute you can buy an *election*," he said, "this country is in trouble."[62]

Lyndon Johnson acknowledged that his accession to the presidency after the assassination of Kennedy was eased by the support of the former Presidents. Hoover, who was very old and ill, sent a message through Richard Berlin of the Hearst papers. "I am ready to serve our country in any capacity from office boy up," he said. Truman, who had experienced a similar catapulting into office, also gave his advice and support. He likened Johnson's stand on Vietnam to his own firm position on Greece, Turkey, and Korea. Though opinion polls had showed a drop in popularity from 87 percent to 23 percent because of his aggressiveness, the ex-President said, these stands represented "his proudest achievements."[63]

On the day after Kennedy's death, ex-President Eisenhower drove from his farm in Gettysburg to the White House. He visited with the new President in his office in the Executive Office Building and gave him his ideas. Then he went to the outer office and wrote "Confidential Notes for the President" in longhand on a sheet of legal-size yellow paper. He then asked Alice Boyce, a secretary whom he trusted, to help him. He dictated his note to her and asked that she make no more than two copies of it—one for the President and one for himself. In *The Vantage Point*, Johnson included the Eisenhower memo. Among the ex-President's notes were suggestions to confer with Robert Anderson, ex-Secretary of the Army Gordon Gray, and General Goodpaster, assistant to the chairman of the Joint Chiefs of Staff. He also suggested that Johnson call a joint session of Congress and make a short speech of no more than ten or twelve minutes. In it he should stress that no revolution in purpose or policy "is intended or will occur"; rather, the "noble objectives" of his predecessor would be implemented. He would want the close co-operation of Congress and to achieve it would "go more than half way." Also he should offer a prompt tax cut and reduce expenditures for 1964. In conclusion, he should say that the people of government and the entire nation would join together in order to further world peace. Johnson told the press that he had incorporated some of these suggestions in his speech to the joint session.[64]

Throughout his administration Johnson courted the ex-Presidents. In a speech given a month after his inauguration, the new President specifically told reporters that he was going to "keep the ex-Presidents informed." He was true to his word. On his first presidential visit to New York, he went to the Waldorf Towers to see the ailing Hoover.

Of course, courtesy was not the prime motivation for seeking Ike's advice. The former President had solid influence with his party and the public. Whether the subject was the Vietnam War or his gallbladder operation, Johnson consulted Ike. Before going into Bethesda Naval Hospital for surgery, the President talked for an hour with Eisenhower, during which they discussed Eisenhower's White House illnesses and the problems of disclosing health information to the public.

Much of what was discussed during meetings between the past and present Presidents was kept secret. When Eisenhower was at Walter Reed Hospital in December 1966, Johnson visited him to ask about two or three decisions that he was considering. "Now I know what I am going to do about them," Johnson told reporters, but would only reveal that they were matters concerning defense and international politics.[65]

President Johnson dramatized the signing of the Medicare bill into law on July 30, 1965, by traveling out to the Truman Library. He chose that site so that the ex-President could be a participant, because he had started the national health program during his presidency. It was a proud day for old Harry Truman, who was genuinely touched by the President's gesture. It was also an impressive spectacle for the public to see the two Democratic Presidents together.

Six months later Johnson traveled to Independence again so that he could present President and Mrs. Truman with Medicare cards No. 1 and No. 2. "The Social Security boys asked me to bring along your new Medicare card," Johnson drawled to a smiling Truman. "If you wish to get your medical insurance, you will have to sign this form." Truman signed the card and LBJ witnessed it. The President continued: "This is to show you we haven't forgotten who is the real Daddy of Medicare. Because of the fight you started nineteen years ago, nineteen million Americans will benefit on July 1 and . . . will have another cause to bless Harry S. Truman."[66]

Whatever reservations of a private nature Eisenhower may have had about his Vice-President and his grandson's father-in-law, publicly he appeared pleased with Richard Nixon's election. His son reported that the President-elect visited Ike several times in his hospital room, and told the story that as Nixon appointed each future member of his Cabinet, the General would invite the new appointee to the hospital to be interviewed and advised, a procedure that amused everyone.

Richard Nixon was not a man that Lyndon Johnson could adjust to. He was too partisan, too cool, and too insensitive. For example, Johnson could not see how the President could fail to invite a single member of Congress to his daughter Tricia's wedding. He deplored the Republican's domestic policies and predicted an inflation-recession before his first year in office was over.[67]

Continuing the pattern of the post-FDR Presidents, Nixon made diplomatic overtures to his predecessors that were accepted in the same spirit. He invited Johnson to attend the Apollo launch at Cape Kennedy and arranged that the dedication of the Lady Bird Johnson Grove in the Redwood National Forest, California, take place on the ex-President's sixty-first birthday. The Johnsons were invited to attend as his guests.

When the Johnson family arrived at San Clemente in August 1969 for the dedication, the Nixons welcomed them with an eight-man Mexican mariachi band that played "Happy Birthday" and "The Yellow Rose of Texas." After the serenade, the two Presidents got into a green golf cart with a white fringed top that carried them to Nixon's office, a new building which had just been erected. There they had their first serious conversation since the inauguration.

In his dedication speech at the park ceremonies, Johnson reciprocated by saying that he wanted to help his successor achieve "the single greatest objective of any President, peace among the nations of the world." More important in the speech was a statement that reveals the real bond between all Presidents, past or present, of whatever party. "One never knows what it is to be President until you are a President."[68]

It was to Nixon's advantage to keep Johnson informed about the Vietnam War. It had put him in the White House, and Johnson, he realized, was the only person in the world who really understood that dilemma. Every Friday, therefore, a jet carrying briefing papers on foreign policy prepared by Kissinger's office landed at the LBJ ranch. These documents were augmented by telephone calls from Cabinet members and, occasionally, President Nixon. Henry Kissinger came in person to discuss the peace talks with the ex-President and so did General Westmoreland. In September 1970, Vice-President Agnew flew to Johnson City to brief LBJ on his five-nation tour of

Asian trouble spots. Newsmen were allowed to travel with the Vice-President on the plane but were not permitted to go to the ranch. The impression given was that Nixon had begun to rely on Johnson on Vietnam matters. Johnson liked the attention but was astute enough to sense that he was told what Nixon and his advisors wanted him to know. President Nixon phoned just a few weeks before Johnson died to tell him that a cease-fire was very close. The ex-President immediately asked his speech writer Horace Busby, to get a statement ready for that occasion, using the theme that "no man worked harder or wanted peace more than I." Two days after Johnson's death, the Vietnam cease-fire was declared. The speech was never made.[69]

The Watergate scandal had not really reached its peak before Johnson's death in January 1973. However, it had revealed itself enough for the ex-President to make a pronouncement. "Nixon has made a terrible mistake surrounding himself with amateurs," he judged.[70] At the time of Johnson's death, Nixon was at the top of his popularity, celebrating his smashing second-term victory. His predecessor did not witness his exit from the White House, less than a year later, dishonored and deserted by his party and the electorate. There were no former presidents at the time whose ranks he could have joined. Probably the big Texan would have had more compassion than satisfaction over Nixon's fall. The bond of the presidential experience has become a tight one.

The services rendered by ex-presidents to their successors were often more ceremonial and supportive than truly significant. Yet their presence added some feeling of continuity and needed confidence in times of stress. There is a proper use of ex-presidents as elder statesmen. However, they should not be exploited for their former power and influence in order to enhance an administration or to cover up some blunder. Happily, this has never been seriously the case. On the contrary, the hardy survivors of the toughest job on earth have more often behaved like gadflies than like pawns.

PART II

Post-Presidential Citizens

Making Ends Meet

D O YOU THINK that the presidential retirement bill will pass the house?" Harry Truman asked Sam Rayburn in a confidential, handwritten letter written to the Speaker in August 1957. If the bill passed, the ex-President explained, he wanted to make a program of educational appearances at small colleges and schools at no charge to give the students "an historical background on what they have, how it was obtained, and what they must do to keep it."

"Sam, I'm not lobbying for the bill," Truman continued. But if it did not pass, he wrote, "I must go ahead with some contracts to keep ahead of the hounds."[1] The bill passed, although similar legislation had failed to get through more than one of the houses of Congress. Hence the two ex-Presidents alive at the time were the first to be provided for by an ungrateful public that had elevated them to the highest office in the land and then, almost innocently, tossed them aside to manage as best they could.

Interestingly, much of the credit for the passage of the bill was owed to Lyndon B. Johnson, then the Democratic leader in the Senate. "You put the proposition with eloquence and very cogently," Charles J. Murphy, Truman's aide, wrote to Johnson. "This is not the first time that I have seen what you can accomplish in the Senate, of course, but I am constantly impressed with the way you do it."[2]

Lyndon Johnson's argument for the bill was based on the thesis that the President of the United States "remains a public figure after he retires from office . . . the American people still look to an ex-President for advice, for counsel and for inspiration in their moments of trial." The bill, he said, represented "a modest recognition" of these services. It provided for an allowance of $25,000 a year, an allotment for an office staff, the franking privilege, and a pension of $10,000 for the widow of a chief executive.[3]

Editorial opinion around the country agreed with Lyndon Johnson and the Congress, although the term *pension* was unacceptable and *lifetime salary* preferred. The Washington *Post* pointed out that any former president can make a comfortable living easily, if necessary, but the country should not want its former chief executives "to be forced into business or a profession or any kind of money-making venture." They could be used to better advantage as elder statesmen.[4]

The Presidential Retirement Bill was long overdue, for money had only too often been a pressing problem for retiring presidents. Some also had been tormented by doubts as to what was an acceptable way of earning money and, in some cases, what constituted a proper dwelling place for a former White House tenant. The early presidents, all landowners, did not have that problem, since they all had homes, but difficulties arose about the means to maintain them.

Mount Vernon has been a national shrine for almost as long as the United States has existed. Its pillared portico has been copied so often that ridiculously scaled-down versions of the first President's home can be seen all over the country. However, when Washington returned to the family acres after the wearying presidential years, he found his "last retreat" in deplorable condition. The first few months of ease were spent "in a litter of dust occasioned by joiners, masons, and painters working in the house, all parts of which, as well as the outbuildings, I find upon examination to be exceedingly out of repairs." His eight-year absence, the ex-President lamented, had not only "despoiled my buildings but also deranged my private affairs."[5]

The tremendously high cost of running the Washington estate was one of the reasons why Washington had accepted the second term. He needed the money to keep up his existing life-style, but the presidential salary was not enough and he had to sell off some of his land to make the necessary repairs. Absentee landlordism was very expensive.

Nevertheless, despite Washington's protests that his estate was an "unproductive one," his will valued the property at about $488,137, a very considerable sum of money at that time. The other Virginia planter ex-Presidents did not fare so well.

Though Jefferson's Monticello was a magnificent reflection of his good taste, artistic and creative gifts, and personal philosophy, its owner suffered mightily trying to keep it for his descendants. One of Monticello's greatest glories is its situation at a height of 580 feet. The land slopes gently down for one and a half miles to the Rivanna River. From the northern terrace, there is a sublime view of the surrounding mountains and valleys. One of Jefferson's grandchildren wrote that the President and his guests would sit there in the summer evenings until bedtime, free from the annoyances of dew or insects. "Here, perhaps, has been assembled more love of liberty, virtue, wisdom, and learning than on any other private spot in America," Colonel Jefferson Randolph noted.[6]

Margaret Bayard Smith, the charming gossip who recorded Washington's first forty years, described a visit to Monticello not long after Jefferson's retirement. She, too, was thrilled by the view from the top of the mountain where the house stood. She observed also how much the ex-President loved the house and how extensive his plans were for improving it. "My long absence from this place has left a wilderness around me," he said. Mrs. Smith wrote: "I looked on him with wonder as I heard him describe the improvements he designed in his grounds; they seemed to require a whole life to carry into effect, and a young man might doubt of ever completing or enjoying them." She realized, however, that he had "transposed his hopes and anticipations" to his children. "It is in them he lives," she said.[7] No doubt Margaret Smith, a close friend of Jefferson and a great admirer of his accomplishments, was right, but the burden of the family was too heavy for a retired patriarch.

There were twelve in the family at Monticello, including Jefferson's daughter Martha, her husband John Randolph, and their numerous children and grandchildren. Randolph was a neurotic given to depression and rages, and Jefferson worked at sparing his daughter from "the heaviest of misfortunes," a split between her father and her husband.[8] But Jefferson's most serious problem was his ever-increasing debt, which the care of this large family added to considerably. Even before leaving Washington, he had to borrow eight thousand dollars to pay off the debts he had incurred while President.

Then, at an emotional cost that only a book lover can understand, Jefferson was forced to sell his library.

When the British burned the American capital during the War of 1812, the Congressional Library was destroyed. "I presume it will be among the early objects of Congress to recommend replacing the collection of books," Jefferson wrote to Secretary of State Samuel H. Smith. But since war in Europe continued and communication with that continent was risky, it would be difficult to accomplish. "You know my collection, its condition and extent," Jefferson continued. He had spent fifty years building his library, sparing no expense or effort to bring it to its present point. While in Paris, he recalled fondly, he had spent his summer afternoons searching out every book that related to America and every scientific work that was rare and valuable. He had standing orders with the booksellers of the principal European bookmarts—Amsterdam, Frankfort, Madrid, London—for books relating to America that could not be found in Paris. Now the collection was between nine and ten thousand volumes. He enclosed a catalogue and added that eighteen to twenty wagons could carry his collection to Washington in one trip.[9]

After some disagreement, a committee of Congress decided to buy Jefferson's library. Objections were made by some of the Massachusetts Federalists, who insisted that the collection was too large and, worse, contained many works whose philosophy and theology were insulting to the nation and useless to congressmen. They were overruled by the majority, who dismissed Federalist obstructionism on the grounds that it was only a desire to get even with Jefferson for the Embargo.

Joseph Milligan, a Washington bookseller, who was sent to Monticello to appraise the collection, valued it at $24,000, based on an arbitrary formula that he had devised. Ten dollars was allowed for a folio, six dollars for a quarto, three dollars for an octavo, and one dollar for a duodecimo. This ridiculous method, which allotted an average price of three dollars and fifty cents per volume, underestimated the value of the collection and spared Milligan from the need to know anything about book values. But Jefferson, who needed the money badly, accepted the offer of $23,950 that Congress subsequently made.

The bittersweet task of labeling the books, getting back those he had loaned, and finally, arranging them according to the catalogue was exhausting for the former President. "It is with real regret that I inform you the day of delivering the library is close at hand," Jefferson wrote to a friend. He watched eleven wagons loaded with his beloved volumes wind down his mountain for the journey to the capital. Unfortunately, the collection was doomed, for in 1851 the Library of Congress had a fire that destroyed two-thirds of it.

"I cannot live without books," Jefferson wrote to his friend and fellow bibliophile John Adams, "but fewer will suffice where amusement and not use is the only future object." Without realizing that he was doing so, Adams sent his colleague the very person to purchase his new library for him. George Ticknor arrived at Monticello with his friend Francis C. Gray, armed with glowing letters of introduction from Adams, who wrote, "as you are all Helicones Librorum [gluttons for books] I think you ought to have a sympathy for each other."[10]

Jefferson was very impressed with Ticknor, whom he called "the best bibliographer I have met with." Since, opportunely, Ticknor was leaving for Europe to continue his studies, Jefferson commissioned him to procure "some part of the literary treasures which I have ceded to Congress."[11] For that purpose, Jefferson had set aside five hundred dollars from the money he had received. When the new collection was completed, it came to about a thousand volumes.

In his last years, Jefferson's fortune collapsed completely. The panic of 1819, a series of crop failures due to natural causes, and deteriorating health combined to hasten the probability of bankruptcy. Expenses had mushroomed through the years as the Jefferson family increased. Also, the Sage of Monticello extended royal hospitality to the many friends and admirers who came to his door, and then fretted anxiously about how he would pay the bills for their entertainment. By the 1820s, Jefferson owed more than one hundred thousand dollars.[12]

Thomas Jefferson Randolph, Jefferson's favorite grandson, tried to relieve his grandfather by taking over the operation of the estate, but it was too far gone to be salvaged. Through his friend J. C. Cabell, a member of the Virginia legislature, the ex-President applied to that body to allow him to dispose of his property in a lottery, "which, bringing a fair price for it, may pay my debts and leave a living for myself in my old age, and leave something for my family." He cited the sale of the estate of the late Colonel Byrd in 1756 as the historic precedent for the state to make an exception to the law against lotteries. He did not seek remuneration from the treasury or from the earnings of his fellow citizens, Jefferson stated, but only permission to sell his own property and pay his own debts. Lest the objection be made that his case would set a precedent for others in a similar predicament, Jefferson wrote: "Have they, as in this case, devoted threescore years and one of their lives, uninterruptedly, to the service of their country? Have the times of those services been as trying as those which have embraced our Revolution, our transition from a colonial to a free structure of Government?"[13]

In a poignant letter to his old friend ex-President James Madison, Jefferson spoke frankly. If refused the lottery, "I must sell every-thing, perhaps considerably in Bedford, move thither with my family, which I have not even a log hut to put my head into, and where ground for burial will depend on the depredations which, under the form of sales, shall have been committed on my property." Despairing, he concluded, "To myself, you have been a pillar of support through life. Take care of me when dead, and be assured that I shall leave with you my last affection."[14]

There was strong opposition to Jefferson's request in the Virginia legislature, but finally it admitted the bill by a "disgraceful" majority of four. "I blush for my country, and am humiliated to think how we shall appear on the page of history," Cabell said.[15] The bill passed in February 1826, by a vote in the Senate of 13 to 4. In Richmond and other parts of the state, resolutions were passed endorsing the bill, but Virginia gave Jefferson no financial aid.

Washington was shocked by the news that Jefferson was obliged to sell his home. President John Quincy Adams's youngest son, Charles Francis Adams, wrote to his grandfather telling him the sad news that Monticello would be sold at lottery if Virginia allowed it. The young man echoed the feelings of all decent people in his letter to ex-President John Adams, Jefferson's friend and occasional enemy. Someone so long exposed to the harms of the world "surely might expect a comfortable repose in his old age. But such it seems is not his lot." John Adams, comfortable though not wealthy, grieved for Jefferson but said nothing to him in his letters. Were it not for his grandson's letter, there would be no evidence that he knew the truth.

Jefferson's financial plight was discussed by the President and his Cabinet. James Barbour, secretary of war, proposed to JQA that on the Fourth of July, the fiftieth anniversary of the Declaration of Independence, after the ceremonies at the Capitol, he should address the audience and ask for an immediate subscription for Jefferson. Adams thought that the endeavor would be more successful if the subscription were raised elsewhere.[16]

Ex-President James Monroe wrote to Jefferson immediately upon hearing that he had applied for a lottery. He expressed his concern and revealed that he was in a similar financial bind, though not quite so severe. "[I] can readily conceive the causes which led to it," he said ruefully. A few weeks later, after recovering from a bad attack of influenza, Monroe wrote again, pointing out how clear it was that Jefferson's long public service had been detrimental to his large private fortune. He promised that he would communicate with friends in New York, especially his son-in-law, Samuel Gouverneur, to promote his cause.

Outside of Virginia, prompt action had been taken to relieve Jefferson's financial embarrassment. Mayor Philip Hone of New York raised $8,500, which was sent to Monticello on behalf of the people of New York. Philadelphia and Baltimore sent $5,000 and $3,000, respectively. Jefferson was very touched, and happily he died without realizing that these sums and the sale of his property failed to cover his debts. Martha Jefferson Randolph, Jefferson's "dear and beloved daughter," had to leave Monticello completely penniless. The legislature of South Carolina, upon hearing of this, voted her $10,000, which was promptly matched by Louisiana. Ungenerously, Jefferson's native state did nothing.

James Madison, to whom Jefferson had appealed in his desperation, answered with a description of his own financial woes. Since his return to private life, he said, "such have been the unkind seasons & the ravages of insects that I have made but one tolerable crop of Tobacco, and but one of wheat." He reminded his friend that he had no resources "but in the earth I cultivate" and had been living on borrowed means. If his debts were called in, he confessed, his situation would be as grave as Jefferson's.[17]

Montpelier, the Madison family estate in Orange County, Virginia, had been expanded and remodeled in 1800 and in 1809, with the help of the presidential salary. By the time Madison retired, the house had an elegance and splendor that made it look very different from the original four-room brick dwelling that had been built by Madison's father. The history of the birth of the United States was reflected in the house. The vestibule had a semicircular window divided into thirteen parts that symbolized the thirteen original states, and the large drawing room was called "the hall of notables" for it housed portraits of Jefferson, Washington, Franklin, John Adams, Lafayette, and others. Outside the house was a sixty-foot-long piazza supported by six tall pillars and large enough for the Madisons to take their walks on when the weather was bad.

Madison's mother lived at Montpelier in her own separate establishment. At ninety-nine she said, "I have been a blest woman . . . I have no sickness, no pain, excepting my hearing, my senses are but little impaired. I pass my time reading and knitting." Margaret Smith said that her face was not as wrinkled as her son's, though he was only seventy-seven.[18]

James and Dolley Madison and the ancient Mrs. Madison were the only permanent residents at Montpelier. Its most irksome visitor was Payne Todd, Dolley's son by her first marriage. When he was young, his gambling debts and drunken sprees constantly drained Madison's cash, and bailing out Todd made Dolley anxious and Madison miserable. As Todd grew older, he started to invest in get-rich-quick schemes that failed, and once again his parents had to come to his rescue. From 1813 to 1836, the President spent about $40,000 on his worthless stepson. The necessity to sell his Kentucky lands and his stocks and to mortgage his property can be blamed in large part on Todd.

Madison was a serious working farmer who hoped to make his plantation a financial success. However, the combination of circumstances already discussed made it an impossibility. And, like Jefferson, he suffered from the cult of Southern hospitality, which was extended to an army of nieces, nephews, and relatives as well as friends and visiting dignitaries.

In 1825, Madison asked Nicholas Biddle of the Bank of the United States for "a modest loan" of $6,000 at the lowest allowable interest rate. He explained his temporary embarrassment in terms of "the unfavorableness of the season for the staple productions in the quarter" and the markets and, consequently, the difficulty in collecting debts. Madison offered unencumbered real estate as collateral, but Biddle answered stiffly that the bank had a rule that forbade advancing money on real estate for indeterminate periods.[19]

Although Madison never suffered the disaster that Jefferson experienced, he was forced to halve his property and often lived on borrowed money. Finally, in 1844, eight years after Madison's death and five years before Dolley's, Montpelier had to be sold.

James Monroe, the last of the Virginia dynasty, had his share of financial disaster also. When he left the presidency, it was well known that he had a debt of $75,000 which, if not paid, might result in the loss of his property. The sale of nine hundred acres of some of his best land for twenty dollars per acre devalued his property but lessened the debt by one-third. He tried to save Oak Hill, his Virginia hilltop in Loudoun County, by selling off his Albemarle acres. When that failed, he looked to the only cash source that he could tap, the collection of claims against the United States that dated back to his last European mission in 1794. This included expenses incurred in England after his return from Spain and during the special mission in which he was associated with Pinckney. A congressional bill was necessary to grant him the money.

While still President, Monroe had pointed out that he had been denied an outfit [expenses] on his French mission and the money that he had had to lay out had forced him to sell 950 acres that he owned above Charlottesville. At the time, a House committee took up the claims, looked at all his bills and records, and concluded that he had a valid claim of $53,000, which included interest. Questions were then raised as to whether the $30,266 interest accumulated was really owed, because it was not unusual for diplomatic accounts to take a long time to be settled and Monroe had been in the government and receiving a salary during much of the time.[20]

The matter was still unsettled when Monroe left the presidency, so not only was a great deal of his time spent gathering further evidence to bolster his claims, but also the political factor became important. President John Quincy Adams offered Monroe a position on the American mission to the Panama Congress of 1826, and there was talk of the vice-presidential spot on the Adams ticket for 1828. Monroe refused both offers, partly for fear of antagonizing the Jacksonians in Congress. His gestures did not help his cause much, because according to Monroe's friend Tench Ringgold, many Jacksonians and Crawfordites blamed Monroe for supporting Adams in the election of 1824. Monroe's protests that he had maintained strict neutrality during the contest and that he had stood up for General Jackson after his unauthorized raid into Florida were disbelieved.[21]

After Jackson's election to a second term, Monroe and his supporters tried once more to arouse interest in his claims by publishing
and distributing a memoir which described Monroe's financial sacrifices in the public interest and told about the house he had bought
in Paris in 1795 with the understanding that the American government would buy it from him to serve as a permanent residence for
the American minister. The house was not purchased by the United
States, and Monroe lost $10,000 because he had had to leave Paris
before he was able to collect the balance of his money from the
purchaser. Three thousand copies of the pamphlet were distributed
to friends and politicians. Congressman William Cabell Rives, a close
friend of Monroe's, was made chairman of a committee to review
his demands. The committee recommended a settlement of $60,000
based on acceptance of the new claim and some others that had been
rejected previously, such as money advanced to Thomas Paine that
had never been repaid. However, the report was again postponed
because of the vengeful Jacksonians.

A series of personal tragedies in the summer of 1830 overshadowed
the claims battle in Monroe's life. George Hay, his trusted son-in-law,
died in Washington, and when Eliza Monroe Hay was returning to
Virginia with her husband's body, she was summoned to Oak Hill
to take care of her mother, who was fatally ill. After Mrs. Monroe's
death, the ex-President was so shaken that his daughters, Eliza Hay and
Maria Gouverneur, decided that he was too feeble to live at Oak
Hill alone. He agreed and went to live with the Gouverneurs, cared
for by his widowed daughter Eliza.

James Madison was sorry to read that Monroe's estate in Loudoun
County was up for sale. He deduced correctly that it was "an omen
that your [Monroe's] friends in Virginia were to lose you" and
feared that the New York climate would be "unsuited for your
period of life and the state of your health." However, he was happy
that the sum voted by Congress even after "the loppings to which it
was exposed from the accounting process at Washington" would
relieve some financial worries.[22]

In February the House of Representatives granted Monroe $30,000,
not so much because of the virtues of his case as because of public
pressure. It was not done, however, until the grief-stricken, ill, old
gentleman had written to remind the Speaker of the House that his
bill had been postponed. The opposition of North Carolina's Lewis
Williams reflected arguments that had been offered and continued

to be offered in later years against pensions or amelioration for former presidents. Since Monroe had known what his salary would be for all the posts he held, why then should he receive any further monies just because he had been President of the United States? Fortunately others, more generous, were touched by the idea that a former chief executive had to be supported by relatives. Although eccentric Silas Burrows, a wealthy New York banker, and Samuel Gouverneur went to Washington to support Monroe's claims, it must be noted that Monroe's supporters did not include the Virginia delegation, which was ardently pro-Jackson and critical of Monroe's nationalism while he had been in office.

The money finally granted was not as much as Monroe had hoped for, nor did it satisfy his need for vindication. He still had to sell Oak Hill, because he was not well enough to manage it alone and his son-in-law did not want to leave New York. Perhaps being displaced was too much for the ex-President. When John Quincy Adams visited him in New York, he found him "extremely feeble and emaciated." Monroe's hope that he would be able to make a trip to his Virginia home and join his colleagues on the board of the University of Virginia "once more at least," as Madison had requested, seemed doubtful to his former secretary of state. Adams's gloomy but accurate prognosis that he would not be able to leave his room again proved to be true. Monroe had enjoyed a splendid career in public service, "received more pecuniary reward than any other man in the existence of the nation," and was now dying "at the age of seventy-two in wretchedness and beggary," JQA noted in his diary.[23]

On July 4, 1831, James Monroe died, the third early President to succumb on the nation's anniversary. The plan for the sale of Oak Hill had fallen through, so "the good old man" had been spared that last blow. Tench Ringgold insisted that a trip to his estate, even in a litter, might have saved Monroe's life.

Anxiety bred of family troubles and business difficulties, was the lot of the nation's hero, Andrew Jackson, when, at the age of seventy and in chronic bad health, he retired from the presidency. Like the other planter Presidents, he was the victim of the business cycle— in this case the panic of 1837 and the subsequent necessity to sell off part of his lands. Jackson's enemies rather meanly rejoiced at his financial difficulties, saying that the panic was his fault and therefore it was poetic justice that he should suffer from it.[24]

The original log dwelling that Jackson had built on his land eight miles from Nashville, Tennessee, had been replaced by a handsome brick house. The estate, called the Hermitage, now one of the most famous historic homes of America, is not the original, which was burned to the ground in 1834 and then rebuilt according to the original plan.

Jackson returned to the Hermitage poorer than when he had left it for the presidency. He brought five thousand dollars to Washington and returned home with ninety dollars, half of which he gave to his secretary, Jack Danielson, who said that he needed the money to buy corn. The nation's hero had not been enriched by the nation's exchequer.

In 1838, still stubbornly opposed to banks, Jackson sold his land in western Tennessee to free himself from debts. Most of the money went to relieve his adopted son, Andrew Jackson, Jr., his wife's nephew, who, despite his father's warning, endorsed notes for others. Always anxious to make allowances for his indulged child, Jackson wrote, "Andrew was inexperienced, and he happened to fall into the hands of men who pretended to be his friends."[25]

When the Independent Treasury Bill was passed, Jackson, who had advocated the removal of the nation's funds from the hands of the banks, was given as much credit for it as President Martin Van Buren. The ex-President's popularity rose so dramatically that his successor invited him to be present at the observance of the twenty-fifth anniversary of the Battle of New Orleans. There was no doubt that the President had in mind the fact that Jackson's appearance would be good for the Democratic party, but it was hard for the aged former President to take the trip in midwinter. Jackson had all kinds of other problems, too. He was out of funds, the water was too low to take down his cotton, and he could not "bear to travel as a pauper." He realized fully the political value of his appearance and he had not forgotten that he had already sacrificed both health and property to the "salvation of New Orleans"; he still chafed at the thousand-dollar fine that he had been forced to pay there and at the ingratitude of the city, which had never attempted to have "the unjust sentence" removed. Further knowledge of Andrew Jr.'s indebtedness forced Jackson to reconsider his decision on New Orleans, but finally he decided to go, convincing himself that he could attend to business on the way south. "Recollect, my son, that I have taken this trip to endeavour to relieve you from present embarrassments," he wrote.

General Jackson endured the orgy of celebration under the most trying circumstances. He suffered a hemorrhage the morning before he reached Pittsburgh and "struggled against pain and sickness for ten days and nights." Nevertheless, he was "highly gratified" at the reception he was given on the journey.[26]

Jackson believed that part of the hounding for debts that his son suffered was inspired by political enmity toward him. In September 1840, the former President wrote that in the past two months he had paid more than $12,000 in cash and was not clear yet. "Every whigg he [Andrew Jackson, Jr.] owed has either sued or warranted him," Jackson said. The young man went to bed with chills and fever and seemed to show no signs of recovering. It was the debts preying on his mind, Jackson believed, and was quite right, no doubt, because the sickness was followed by a very brief recovery and then a relapse. Meanwhile the aged father, ill and suffering from old, unhealed wounds, struggled to meet the creditors' demands. The debt far exceeded Andrew Jr.'s calculations. "Every dollar I could raise since I came from Washington has been applied to them," Jackson wrote.[27]

The Hermitage also suffered from the assaults on its owner's purse. There was no money for repairs or paint or the General's saddle horse, and the debts incurred by young Jackson never let up. The young man who had shown great early promise was now incapable of coping with any responsibility. When he was cornered, he tried to lie his way out. However, Jackson could not bear to allow him to go into bankruptcy, and as his patience with his son gave out, he found solace in his many grandchildren and in the belief that when Andrew was finally disentangled from his debts, he would have learned a lesson.

Since the Whig newspapers never lost an opportunity to report on Jackson's financial difficulties, his friends were aware of them and tried to help him. Major Jean B. Planché offered his former commander $6,000 to be used when needed to pay his engagements. Jackson accepted the loan with the stipulation that Planché consent to take a mortgage on the Hermitage. Reluctantly, Planché agreed. Meanwhile, Jackson's supporters in Congress worked to get a bill passed that would refund the fine that New Orleans had imposed on Jackson because of his imposition of martial law there after the battle. Jackson agreed to accept the refund as compensation for the unjust accusation and as vindication for his actions, which might serve as a precedent for future officers who could find themselves in similar situations. Since he had acted "in the interest of the successful defense of the country," officers in the future might be protected from "the tyranny and oppression of vindictive judges."[28]

Jackson was infuriated when the nature of the congressional bill was changed from an exoneration of his acts in New Orleans to a gratuity for his public services. "I would starve before I would touch one cent of the money under that odious & insulting amended bill," he raged. He wrote to Louis Linn, who had introduced the bill in the Senate, that "as an act of justice the passage of that bill would have been gratifying" but he would not sink to accepting money in any other way. Congress eventually passed the bill erasing the New Orleans fine. A Treasury draft arrived at the Hermitage, sent by President John Tyler, for $2,732.90, the original fine plus the interest calculated from 1815. New York celebrated the repudiation of Jackson's sentence with a transparency hung across Broadway inscribed with the legend Justice to the Brave.[29]

The money came just in time. Old Hickory was in desperate financial trouble again. He had shipped his 1842 cotton crop to England with the expectation of better profits than he could get selling locally only to find that he had sustained greater expense and would have done as well in New Orleans. The following year his cotton crop was drowned by floods, and Andrew, Jr., signed notes again, which his father covered, in part, by selling some excellent colts cheap.

The firm of Blair and Rives, which had been advancing money to Jackson and waiving his accounts for many years, made a gallant gesture in 1845. They authorized General Andrew Jackson to draw any sum between "one and one hundred thousand dollars and his draft will be honored." This opportunity to consolidate his debts in the hands of "our noble and generous friends" was, Jackson hoped, the panacea for his reckless son. The young man continued to make promises to reform, but even approaching death did not save Jackson from the pressure of his son's debts. Propped up in bed because he was too ill to lie down, his face swollen, well aware that he had only a short time to live, the former President still struggled to secure the future of his son and his family. In June 1845 he borrowed $2,000 against his maturing cotton crop. "You may rest assured that A. Jackson, Jr. will never again draw unless covered by assets," he wrote. A week later, utterly exhausted, Old Hickory died.

At the time of his death, Jackson owed $26,000, mostly to Blair and Rives, and though their repayment was provided for in the will, neither Blair and Rives nor the other major creditors claimed their money. By 1856 Andrew Jackson, Jr., had increased the debt to $48,000, at which time the state of Tennessee bought the Hermitage, allowing the Jacksons to continue to live there as long as they lived. Andrew Jackson, Jr., died in 1863 and his wife, Sarah, in 1888.[30]

Being landed and seemingly wealthy magnified, rather than lessened, the problems of the planter ex-Presidents. Jefferson described some of their difficulties in his *Thoughts on Lotteries*. "Everyone knows how inevitably a Virginia estate goes to ruin when the owner is so far distant as to be unable to pay attention to it himself; and the more especially when the line of his employment is of a character to abstract and alienate his mind entirely from the knowledge necessary to good and even to saving management."[31] Added to these ills, partly to be blamed on lives devoted to the nation, were instances of spoiled or incompetent sons and the expense of constant and elaborate hospitality.

The Massachusetts ex-Presidents, John and John Quincy Adams, had an easier time financially. John Adams lived in Quincy at the Adams family home, which he called Peacefield, or Manzillo, surrounded by a respectful family. His only regret of a monetary nature was his lack of funds to build the library he wanted for his collection, which he had gathered in Europe and then added to with books that JQA found for him while on his European missions.

"If I was not poor I should plague you to death in hunting Books for me all over Europe," John Adams wrote to John Quincy in London when he was American minister at the Court of St. James. "Oh! What a building I should erect of Quincy North Common granite, capable of holding the Library of Alexandria!" The former President continued: "This is a rage; a mania; a delirium or at least an Enthusiasm which I desire you to correct in me and in yourself, and in your son George."[32]

John Quincy Adams had little money when he retired from the presidency. Due to a bad investment that he had made for his father, the younger Adams had undertaken the responsibility of making it up to his parents and thus drained his own resources. Besides, a diplomatic career was very expensive. Part of JQA's motivation for returning to public life as the congressman from the Plymouth district was the need for money to support himself and his family. The library that both the presidential Adamses dreamed of was built only after their deaths, by John Quincy's son, Charles Francis, who became wealthy through money that he and his wife inherited from her father, Peter Chardon Brooks, the owner of the largest fortune in Boston.

On the positive side, these stately, though sometimes heavily mortgaged, homes were places of pilgrimage where many citizens came to pay their respects to the aging patriarchs. But Martin Van Buren, whose estate at Kinderhook, New York, was called Lindenwald, never achieved that dignified status. Money was not Van Buren's problem. It was more a case of displacement. Little Mac served only one term as President, very reluctantly left Washington, and considered the return to his acres more of an exile than a welcome release. He spent a good part of his time trying to escape from Lindenwald and return to public life.

Van Buren expected that Lindenwald would become, at the very least, a second Hermitage. To prepare for this, he enlarged the original red brick farmhouse and made it more elegant with a stuccoed facade painted bright yellow and a semicircular driveway flanked by two gatehouses at the entrance. A pagoda with an Italian summit crowned the house, making it visible from a distance as well as providing a view of the Hudson River. To accommodate the expected flock of visitors, the stables were enlarged, a new well dug, wines laid in the cellar, and the supply of cattle and chickens increased. The new library was equipped with sets of the classics shipped from New York, and portraits of Jefferson and Jackson were hung in the dining room. But not all these additions or the beautiful wallpaper or the marble fireplaces attracted distinguished callers. Van Buren had to content himself with his sons and their families in his out-of-the-way estate.[33]

As the possibility of a return to public office receded, Van Buren's loneliness increased. It was not until his return from Europe that he accepted his life at Lindenwald. Among other reasons, the fact that the club of ex-Presidents was increased to five and he was no longer its only one-term member seemed to make him feel better.

In a complete reversal of attitude, Van Buren became a model farmer who raised prize potatoes and invented a revolving bookcase. He shed all his affectations except for his gilded English coach. Nonetheless, Lindenwald never became a national shrine. It was sold after Van Buren's death and remained in the hands of strangers. The one happy note was the phrase in the former President's will that read: "I, Martin Van Buren . . . for the last and happiest years of my life a farmer in my native town. . . ."

Millard Fillmore was the first ex-President who had neither a gentleman's estate nor a family home to which he could return. Moreover, he had to find a way to earn a living. The $75,000 he was worth upon retirement would not be enough to support him in a manner suitable to his station, he felt. After some uncertainty, he rejected a sinecure as a bank president and decided to practice law. At first nothing worked out. He had second thoughts about returning to the law because of his conviction that for a man in his position to function in any field other than public affairs would be improper and a practice limited to such cases would not earn him a living. It was a national disgrace that former presidents were "cast adrift" after their administrations were concluded, he complained.[34]

Fillmore's situation changed when he married Mrs. Caroline C. McIntosh, a fifty-two-year-old childless widow with a comfortable fortune. Though the ex-President refused to take his wife's property, he did accept an annual retainer of $10,000 for managing her estate. The Fillmores bought a huge mansion on Buffalo's Niagara Square, a pseudo-Gothic structure complete with parapets, towers, and balustrades. It was lavishly furnished and became a haven for Buffalo society. One of its amusing features was a large collection of portraits and busts of Fillmore—whom Queen Victoria called the handsomest man she had ever seen—that Mrs. Fillmore placed in every room.

Franklin Pierce, a careful New Englander, had prepared for his retirement. With $78,000 saved from his salary, he made judicious investments so that he could enjoy "a dignified and idle" retirement without having to return to his law practice. The Pierces traveled part of the time and maintained a house in Concord, New Hampshire, and a summer dwelling at Little Boar's Head on the coast. Pierce's finances flourished, so he was able to help many nieces and nephews with their education as well as Nathaniel Hawthorne's son Julian.

The most touching example of sudden impoverishment unrelieved by governmental aid concerned Ulysses S. Grant, hero of the Civil War and twice President of the United States. The Grants left the White House with savings of about $100,000, which they invested in railroads bonds and stock such as Consolidated Virginia, which paid very well. Money that had been given to Grant from public subscriptions collected for him from a grateful people had been invested in government bonds, and the Grants also had real estate consisting, in part, of homes the General had been given and, in part, of land that he had bought in Washington. Among the gifts that the victorious Union leader received was a completely furnished mansion in Philadelphia which had come from the Union League Club. The citizens of Galena, Illinois, Grant's home town, had refurbished the modest home that he had left to go to war and presented it to him along with a cash gift of $16,000.[35]

With these resources, Grant decided to satisfy a lifetime desire to travel and went on a trip around the world. Upon their return in 1879, the Grants lived in a hotel in New York City, occupying a two-room suite. Since the income from his $100,000 was not enough to support an ex-presidential standard of living, Grant decided to invest his money in his son Ulysses's banking business and become an inactive partner of young Grant's colleagues, Ferdinand Ward and James D. Fish.

Grant never participated actively in the business, displaying the same negligence in this endeavor that he had in the White House. After making some small effort to determine that the firm was honest, he declared that he knew nothing about banking. He did stipulate that he could not tolerate any dealings in government contracts because, in his position, this would be improper. For a time profits from the company were enormous, which pleased Grant, particularly since both of his sons were also in the business.

On May 6, 1884, Grant left his house on Sixtieth Street for his Wall Street office. He was met at the door of the office by his son Ulysses, who said, "Father, you had better go home. The bank has failed." Adam Badeau found the General later that day, sitting alone in his empty office. "We are all ruined here," he told his former aide. Then he went home and never returned to Wall Street.

A few days prior to the collapse, Ferdinand Ward convinced Grant that if he could secure a loan from the Marine Bank, in which

Grant and Ward had large deposits, the business could be saved. Once again gullible, Grant went to William A. Vanderbilt and secured a loan for $150,000 without security. The General did not realize that the business was already lost and that nothing could save it. When the business failure was certain, Grant and his wife made over all their property to Vanderbilt, including the house, in which Mrs. Grant had a dower right. Grant's trust fund of $250,000 was lost also, because the interest had been invested in Grant and Ward. The entire family was ruined—Grant's youngest son, who had deposited all his money in the family bank just a few days before its fall, Grant's daughter, a sister, and a nephew.

At first the former President's financial distress was acute. He and his wife had only $210 in cash between them. Two friends offered immediate help: Charles Wood, an unknown benefactor who sent $1,000, and Matias Romero, the Mexican minister, who came from Washington immediately to be with Grant. Romero and Grant had been close friends since the French had been driven from Mexico.

The family ruin was complete. No one could go into business until released by the creditors. The entire family stayed with the Grants except for the eldest son and his family, who went to live with the Chaffees, their wealthy in-laws.

Since the end of 1883, the editors of the *Century Magazine* had been trying to convince Grant to write some articles about his Civil War battles. Grant was not enthusiastic, because he did not know whether he could write. After the bank failure, the editors tried again.

At first Grant shrank from any publicity, but when he was offered a sizable sum for his efforts, he felt that he had to accept. The General was surprised to find that he had the ability to write clearly and felicitously, which pleased his editors so much that they begged for more. Grant, now bitten by the literary bug, agreed immediately. The distraction of literary production relieved him of some of his anxieties about his financial distress.

General Adam Badeau, who guided Grant through his first article and acted as his literary agent, encouraged the former President to continue the work. After the first article, an account of the Battle of Shiloh, appeared, the public assumed that Grant was working on his memoirs. Publishers immediately made offers which were quietly ignored. However, Grant sent for Badeau to stay in the household permanently to work with him. The Shiloh article was succeeded by accounts of Vicksburg, Chattanooga, and the Wilderness campaign. With the consent of his publishers, Grant now planned to incorporate them into his memoirs.

On Christmas Eve, 1883, Grant fell on the ice and injured himself severely. Though he was able to get around by himself, he needed crutches and had to give up driving his own carriage in the city. In October, the ex-President started to complain about continual pain in his throat. It had started in the summer but was now much worse. Unwilling to give in to the ailment, which was diagnosed as having cancerous tendencies, Grant traveled alone by streetcar on his many visits to the doctor for treatment. Badeau described the scene that he had to make in order to get the obstinate General to agree to use his carriage for these visits. Badeau would rise from the breakfast table and declaim dramatically that he would rather have the General stick a knife in him than go on the streetcar.

By December, Grant could not swallow without suffering exquisite pain. He neither wrote nor talked. For hours he just sat in a chair, his arms folded, staring at the blank wall. Adam Badeau begged him to try to overcome his depression, if not for himself, for his family, whose future depended on him. "I am not going to commit suicide," the tortured General answered. And they returned to work.[36]

Grant now seemed to live only for his work, which he pursued with enthusiasm. He wrote for five or more hours and then, in the evening, read the day's output to the assembled family. The publishers of the *Century Magazine* were so delighted with the increase in circulation that Grant's articles had caused that, unsolicited, they sent him a thousand-dollar bonus. Though the former President said that he would have liked to spend the money on Christmas presents for his daughter-in-law, he dutifully returned the loan from Charles Wood instead.

The creditors of Grant and Ward were still not satisfied with the settlement that they had received. Some of the lesser ones eyed Grant's collection of swords and the presents that he had received after the Civil War from grateful states and cities, from Congress, and from admiring foreign rulers. To avoid their getting them, Vanderbilt was prepared to claim the lot as the main creditor, to deed all the former Grant property to Mrs. Grant and make her the guardian of the General's trophies during her lifetime, and, after her death, to have them transferred to the government. Grant agreed to the arrangement for the souvenirs but refused a similar arrangement for some of his property. Vanderbilt refused to take no for an answer and persisted until the exhausted ex-President acquiesced. Then, an hour later, Mrs. Grant, to her husband's relief, retracted the acceptance. The Grants lost everything, and the entire world knew of their humiliation. No doubt this further ignominy increased the rate at which Grant's illness devoured him. The intense pain that had been absent at times now returned with increased intensity.

Mark Twain, or, rather, Mr. Samuel Clemens, met General Grant in 1866 at one of the receptions given to the Civil War hero in Washington. At that time they only shook hands, but subsequently met on several occasions. As early as 1881, the author recorded in a memoir that was part of his autobiography that he had tried hard to persuade Grant to write his memoirs, but was turned down because the former President did not want to present himself publicly as an author. He did not consider himself a good writer and was certain that such a book would have no sale. He cited the undeniable facts that General Adam Badeau's military history of Grant's exploits had sold poorly and that John Russell Young's account of Grant's trip around the world had hardly sold at all. Clemens insisted that these books were not to be compared with a book written by General Grant himself. It would have an enormous sale, the successful author turned publisher declared. The memoirs should be in two volumes, he advised, and sell for three dollars and fifty cents per volume, and sales ought to reach about a half a million sets. At that time Grant did not need the money and answered that he would leave full notes behind so that after his death his children could write the book.

When Mark Twain learned that Grant was writing articles for the *Century* and being paid the paltry sum of $500 for each of them, he went right to General Grant's house and told him what he had heard. Grant acknowledged the rumors and admitted that he was about to sign a contract for his memoirs with the Century Company at a ten-percent royalty. The offer was "simply absurd," Clemens protested. If he asked for better terms he would surely get them, and if the Century editors, who had little experience in the book field, refused, any publishing house in the country would be glad to have the book. Then, the famous author said later, he had an idea. He remembered that he was a publisher himself. "Sell *me* the memoirs," he said. "I am a publisher. I will pay double price." Grant was reluctant at first, certain that Clemens would be running too much of a risk. It took a lot of persuading to convince him that his memoirs would make a large profit. Eventually Mark Twain's publishing company, which went under the name of the Charles L. Webster Company, got the book.[37]

The financial arrangements decided upon provided that General Grant would be paid an advance of $25,000 as each volume was completed. If the volumes did not earn the advance, it need not be returned. Grant still thought the offer too generous. He would not take an advance that the publisher might lose and he refused a twenty-percent royalty. Instead, he opted for seventy percent of the profits. As he had promised, although it was not in the contract, Mark Twain advanced $10,000 to Grant before the book was issued. Colonel Fred Grant was told that he could draw on the money whenever it was needed.

Clarence Seward, the son of Grant's secretary of state, represented him in the drawing of the contract. The book was transferred to Mrs. Grant and then from her to Charles L. Webster Company for $1,000 in order to save the book's earnings from the creditors. Webster thought that the arrangement was a formality until Grant's lawyer told him privately that *"the General's family have not a penny in the house and they are waiting at this moment with lively anxiety for that small sum of money."* This account appears in Mark Twain's *Autobiography*. Badeau, in his long and moving description of Grant's last days in *Grant in Peace*, never mentions Twain, although Twain mentions Badeau's presence at the negotiations.

The *Memoirs* sold well over the estimated 300,000 sets. Mark Twain wrote that in a hundred consecutive days, subscriptions for Grant's books averaged 3,000 per day.[38]

By the beginning of 1885, Grant was so ill that he was unable to visit his doctors. The tearing pain in his throat was increasingly present, and after a biopsy was performed, a diagnosis of a malignant cancerous growth was made. Grant had been aware that his disease was serious but not that his death was imminent. With a wanton cruelty that the press is frequently guilty of, an announcement of the General's fatal illness was published in the newspapers. Grant read the articles and the sympathetic editorials and thus learned the truth. As usual, he said nothing, but General Badeau wrote that the thought of dying and leaving his family in humiliating poverty tormented him even more than the excruciating pain he was enduring.

The public, always maliciously pleased when it could mock the famous and successful, was shocked now into a recollection of how much it had idolized General Grant after Appomattox. Letters and telegrams arrived inquiring about the General's health. Visitors came to pay their respects. The sons of Robert E. Lee and Albert Sidney Johnston and Jefferson Davis, ex-President of the Confederate States of America, sent their good wishes. Messages of sympathy arrived from the state legislatures, from the queen of England, and from American schoolchildren.

This surge of mass sympathy was reflected finally in the passage of a bill to restore Grant to his rank of general, with the retirement pay that went with it. Similar bills had been proposed several times before but had failed each time due to President Arthur's refusal to sign them for political reasons. As Mark Twain put it, the bill had been lagging in Congress "in the characteristic contemptible and stingy congressional fashion." Congress wanted to "avenge on General Grant" President Arthur's veto of the Fitz-John Porter bill. General Porter, who had been blamed for the Union defeat at the Second Battle of Bull Run and dismissed from the army, was prohibited from holding office in the United States. When President, Grant had refused to open the case, but President Hayes, who succeeded him, agreed to set up a commission, which, after looking at new evidence, exonerated Porter. Congress introduced several bills to waive Porter's punishment, even getting Grant's support in an article printed in the *North American Review* called "An Undeserved Stigma." Grant wrote: "If Porter had been in command . . . the fighting would have ended then and there." President Arthur was willing to remove the part of the penalty that forbade Porter to hold office in the United States, but he would do no more; vetoing a bill that offered further relief, he thus continued his party's position on the issue.[39]

The Grant bill was passed under dramatic circumstances. Minutes before the end of the congressional session, just before Cleveland's inauguration, Samuel J. Randall, the Democratic floor leader, asked that the rules be suspended so that the Grant Relief Bill could be taken up. With the galleries filled with visitors awaiting the inaugural and the entire hall enveloped in emotion, the bill was passed. "The piercing rebel yell mingled with the applause of the Northern men," Joe Cannon reported. Arthur, as his last executive act, signed it. Cleveland, as his first executive act, restored Grant to his military rank.[40]

General Grant was gratified. He wrote his own telegram of acceptance and took pleasure in filling out the monthly report to the adjutant about his address so that his money could be sent to him. "My post office address for the ensuing month will be—3 East 66th Street, New York," he wrote.

The country could restore his commission to Grant but not his health. It was worsening so rapidly that his daughter Nellie came from England in March. By this time her father was not in such intense pain but had constant insomnia and spells of weakness.

As sick as he was, Grant insisted on giving testimony about James D. Fish, one of the partners of Grant and Ward, who was standing trial. The lawyers and stenographers came to his bedside to hear the hour-long declaration. The General spared neither Fish nor Ward and spoke with such feeling that the others in the sickroom feared that the effort would kill the dying man. The exertion did take its toll. He began to fail so rapidly that two physicians stayed in the house around the clock.

In the spring, however, almost miraculously, Grant started to improve. He was able to come to the dinner table and to participate in the celebration of his sixty-third birthday on April 27. He also began to go out for drives and to dictate and sometimes write. His interest in his book revived and with it his determination to complete it. The remission was, of course, part of the progress of his fatal malady, but General Badeau believed it was the result of his renewed popularity with the American people.

On June 16, General Grant was taken to Mount McGregor, near Saratoga Springs, to escape the heat and humidity of a New York summer. During the eight weeks after the first of May, Badeau recorded, Grant produced more material for his book than at any other period. He seemed to have total recall and to be able to write or dictate with intensity and ease. He saw almost no visitors, just worked and followed his doctor's orders. He drove himself to finish the book because the future of the family depended on its sale. Since the army pay would stop as soon as he died, the family resources would dwindle to the income from the trust fund, the mortgaged house on Sixty-sixth Street, and a few small properties, not enough to keep the three dependent families.

When Grant stopped work in the winter, about half of the memoir was completed. He knew that if it had to be finished by others, it would not make anywhere near as much money as the half a million dollars that Mark Twain had estimated. Grant finished his book before he died. Perhaps it would be more exact to say that he kept himself alive until he had finished the book.

Each American president as he became a plain citizen again tangled with the problem of a suitable dwelling and a suitable job. Rutherford B. Hayes returned to Spiegel Grove, his home in Fremont, Ohio. Fremont, named after Frémont the Pathfinder, who was the first and unsuccessful presidential candidate of the Republican party, was a country town of about ten thousand people, mostly of New England origin. Spiegel Grove had been enlarged from a simple house to an impressive brick mansion almost twice its original size. The new rooms included a library decorated with portraits of the presidents of the United States, a state dining room, a curio room to house the presidential mementos (called "the Smithsonian" by the family), and twenty guest rooms. The house was set in a twenty-five-acre park that boasted a miniature ravine and two small lakes. The tall trees that dotted the many acres were named after presidents. Grover Cleveland had one named after him and, as time went on, so did William Howard Taft. An impressive eighty-foot-long piazza provided Hayes with an area in which to take his daily walk on rainy days.[41]

Rumor said that Hayes left Washington with $20,000 which he had saved during his term in office. Hayes denied it, claiming that he left office with less than a thousand dollars. Actually Hayes had made excellent investments in real estate, and though he denied that he was a millionaire, he admitted that he was in comfortable circumstances and that all his boys were earning their own living. He said that he was worth about fifteen to twenty percent of the amount reported.[42]

Hayes did not work during his retirement but spent a lot of time writing, speaking, and devoting himself to humanitarian causes. Among them were the Peabody Education Fund, the Slater Fund, the Lake Mohonk Conferences, and the National Prison Association, of which he became president.

The last few years of his life Hayes worried about money. He said that he was heavily in debt and hard up because his real estate holdings were unproductive. "I earn nothing by my services or operations. I do not try to earn money and for the most part pay my own expenses," he recorded in his diary in 1891. However, he admitted that despite his debts, which now exceeded his income, his real estate was worth $300,000 and that in time its value would increase faster than his debts, although at the moment his financial state was embarrassing.[43]

Since Grover Cleveland had no private fortune, after he was defeated for reelection in 1888 he needed a job. Buffalo was ruled out as a place to return to and Washington would be awkward after the defeat, so Cleveland accepted an offer to join the firm of Bangs, Stetson, Tracy and McVeagh in New York City. He was to be permitted to do whatever he wished and would not be expected to go to court.

Though the ex-President received an overwhelming number of offers of houses, he decided to stay at the Victoria Hotel until he could make up his mind. He finally moved into 816 Madison Avenue, near Sixty-eighth Street, a four-story red brick and brownstone structure.

In order to protect himself from any unpleasant or unsuitable involvements, Cleveland did not become a partner in the law firm. He had the use of one of the best offices in the suite, the office staff, and the library, for which privileges he paid one-tenth of the office expenses. Occasionally he was called into consultation by the firm, but most of his income was earned as a referee appointed by the courts. There were several advantages. The work could be done in his own office or by correspondence, and since it corresponded with the court sessions, it left Cleveland with the summers free. His finances improved considerably after he sold Oak View, his twenty-seven-acre country house outside of Washington on Georgetown Heights, which he had bought in 1886 and used as the summer White House. It sold for about one hundred thousand dollars more than he had paid for it.[44]

In 1892, the lease on Cleveland's Madison Avenue house expired and he had to move. Among the chores that had to be done was the clearing out of a large room into which the White House papers had been dumped. George F. Parker assisted Cleveland in the process of sorting the material. When it came to personal correspondence and private papers, obviously much of it of historical value, Parker could not persuade Cleveland not to destroy them. "Mr. Cleveland, full of sentiment as he was, did not permit it to operate where he was himself concerned," Parker wrote. The ex-President had no regard for anything in his own handwriting and saw no reason why anyone else should. Most of the letters and papers were destroyed "in spite of the pathetic pleadings of a fellow worker," Parker lamented, though he was able to wheedle a few items from Cleveland. Unencumbered by the memorabilia, the former President moved to 12 West Fifty-first Street.[45]

At this time Cleveland bought a cottage in Marion, Massachusetts, called Gray Gables. It was located in the Buzzards Bay area on a peninsula with a view of the Monument River and the Cohasset Narrows, a quiet spot where Cleveland could enjoy fishing and privacy. Most of his time was spent with close friends who also summered there, such as actor Joseph Jefferson and Richard W. Gilder, editor of the *Century*.

After the interregnum was over and Cleveland returned to the White House for a second term, he left New York behind him permanently. His second retirement found him searching for a residence again. He wanted a place that was countrified for his three small daughters. Andrew F. West, professor of classics at Princeton University, convinced Cleveland to move to Princeton. They chose a large colonial house made of stucco set in a wide lawn, which was named Westland, after the professor. The university town suited Cleveland. He attended general university meetings and in 1901 was made a trustee, in which capacity he served until his death.

Cleveland's permanent retirement was financially much easier than his first, despite the addition of two sons to the family. His fortune, estimated at more than $300,000, consisted of savings from his presidential salary, earnings from his law practice, and the sale price of Oak Hill. Successful investments increased his estate, and his financial situation became more and more comfortable.

Cleveland earned some money from an occasional legal consultation, but the larger part of his earnings came from writing. Between 1900 and 1906, he wrote eighteen articles for the *Saturday Evening Post*, receiving as much as $250 an article. He wrote occasionally for such other publications as the *Atlantic*, the *Century*, the *Youth's Companion*, *Ladies' Home Journal* and *Collier's*.

Cleveland's most lucrative endeavor during these years was his involvement in the reorganization of the Equitable Life Assurance Company, which he undertook because he considered its work a public service. In order to be useful, he had to learn the insurance business in a very short period of time. As a result of public hearings, it was revealed that the insurance companies had a very negative image. Consequently Cleveland, who had been paid $12,000 to work on the reorganization of the Equitable, was now offered the same amount to act as a referee for the Equitable, Mutual, and Prudential insurance companies. Since a large part of the work could be done from his Princeton office, Cleveland accepted. He also agreed to serve as the head of the Association of Presidents of Life Insurance Companies, whose chief purpose was to resist governmental regulation. All in all, the former President's most valuable contribution to the insurance business was the restoration of public confidence in the companies.[46]

By the end of the nineteenth century, the alternatives open to an ex-president seemed clear. If the former chief executive did not have a suitable estate to which he could return, he must acquire one. If he did not have the means to support his new status, there were a few possibilities open to him. Although a return to politics was sometimes feasible, this was outside of his control. Therefore, his most likely option was an academic post or writing for magazines or newspapers. The public is always interested in what these elder statesmen have to say, even if their opinions were not so acceptable while they were in office. It was also all right to return to a law practice, if it was discreetly limited to important cases and restricted court appearances.

Benjamin Harrison returned to his Indianapolis home, which, he complained, had been neglected by his tenants during the White House years. He immediately refurbished it with a new stable and a new front porch. At first, Harrison was content to settle down and unpack his books, papers, and china. "I find myself exceedingly lazy, unable yet to do much work," he confessed to John Wanamaker, who had just sent the ex-President's grandchildren a burro. He was glad "not to be under the spur" but was not rich enough to be permanently idle.[47]

There were always institutions and businesses that were eager to acquire the prestige of the ex-President's name. Harrison received many offers, including the presidency of a bank and a well-endowed chair at the University of Chicago. Harrison refused them all in favor of the freedom inherent in his own law practice. He did, of course, limit it severely. He would not accept a retainer of less than $500 and would work only as the associate counsel. He kept to the self-imposed rules rigidly, appearing in court only in the most outstanding cases.

Harrison also wrote. *The Ladies' Home Journal* paid him $5,000 for nine three-thousand-word articles which were later turned into a book called *This County of Ours*. To Harrison's delight, it sold well in the United States and was translated into five languages.

One of the most famous of the presidential homes is Theodore Roosevelt's Sagamore Hill, located in Oyster Bay, Long Island. Roosevelt bought the land shortly after his marriage to Alice Hathaway Lee, his first wife. Four years later, in 1884, he drew up the plans for the rambling, solid, twenty-two-room house with eight fireplaces. But before it could be built, Mrs. Roosevelt died in childbirth. Grief-stricken, TR signed a contract for the construction of the house so that his daughter Alice would have a place to live and then fled to the Badlands and the rigors of ranch life in order to try to forget his despair in the wild Dakota Territory. A few years later, Theodore Roosevelt married Edith Kermit Carow, a childhood friend, and settled down at Sagamore Hill, where three of the couple's five children were born. It was the summer White House during TR's administration and the scene of some of the peace negotiations between the Russians and the Japanese. A popular ballad by a local bard, Wallace Irwin, went:

> And oysters frolic noisilee
> All over Oyster Bay
> The graybeard tells his little niece
> How Theodore did trek
> To drag the gentle Bird of Peace
> To Portsmouth—by the neck.[48]

Roosevelt loved Sagamore Hill. It raised his spirits and renewed his energies. The story is told that an old Chinese mandarin, an emissary from the empress dowager, dressed in a yellow jacket and peacock feathers, stood on the lawn at Sagamore Hill absorbing its ambiance. He finally pronounced his judgment on it. It has "a better *feng shuey*, indeed, than any other house I have seen in America, except Mount Vernon." A house's *feng shuey*, he explained to President Roosevelt, is "its capacity to attract good spirits and repel evil ones."[49]

After he left the presidency, Roosevelt returned to Sagamore Hill, which was just as he had built it except for the North Room, or Trophy Room, an impressive, high-ceilinged chamber two steps down from the rest of the house, which had been added at TR's expense to provide a suitable place to receive distinguished visitors. Despite the large house with ample grounds and a comfortable income from his father, the former President needed to earn some money to support his large family. During his retirement, he earned $12,000 a year from the *Outlook* and sizable royalties from his books, especially *African Game Trails*.

In 1917, a chance meeting on a train from New York going west resulted in a new writing assignment for TR. Irwin Kirkwood, the editor and general director of the Kansas City *Star*, visited the former President in his stateroom to discuss with him the fast-fading hope for a Roosevelt division. Roosevelt was discouraged and anxious about the administrations's sluggish attitude toward the war effort.

"Colonel Roosevelt, wouldn't it be fine if you could get your ideas on the war to the people before they were twenty-four hours old?" asked Kirkwood. "The only way that could be is through a newspaper." Kirkwood was referring to TR's monthly contributions to the *Metropolitan Magazine*, which, of course, had to be written long in advance. Roosevelt's immediate reaction to the proposal was favorable because he liked the idea that the *Star* was published in the heart of the progressive West.

After some weeks of consideration and Roosevelt's candid reminder to Kirkwood that many people disliked his ideas and that "probably many of your subscribers will be perfectly furious at the *Star* for printing my editorials," the deal was arranged. At TR's suggestion, the contract would run for only two years, until October 1919. Since 1920 was a presidential year and there was a good chance that Roosevelt would be the Republican candidate, the 1919 cutoff seemed appropriate. No contract was signed, but there was a mutual understanding.

Ralph Stout, the managing editor of the *Star*, went to New York to discuss the details with Roosevelt. The ex-President was willing to have his five-hundred-word biweekly articles circulated throughout the county except to newspapers that had been hostile to him and his principles for a long time. Eventually, about fifty newspapers printed the editorials, most of which were telegraphed from Oyster Bay. As Roosevelt predicted, his criticism of the administration was not widely popular, nor was his vigilant prodding for more militant action, particularly among isolationists. Some of the southern papers discontinued his articles, deeming them "undesirable in our territory." Even the *Star* did not carry some of his articles because of "local conditions," but they were published in other newspapers. The Kansas City paper editorialized in July 1918 that it was proud "to belong to the little group of constructive critics, including pre-eminently Colonel Roosevelt, who worked to get wrong conditions changed."[50]

The *Star* paid TR a salary of $25,000, which was augmented by $5,000 from his monthly articles for the *Metropolitan*. But all this scribbling seemed "trivial" to Roosevelt, who only wished that he were with his four sons at the front. "About all I can do is earn what money I can for Archie, & perhaps Quentin, during the war, and have things ready for them to start after the war," he wrote to Theodore Roosevelt, Jr. "My real task is done," he added, referring to the raising of his children. He did not live long enough to see his sons launched on their careers. Only Archie was home, invalided out of the service because of his wartime injuries, when his father died at Sagamore Hill. "The old lion is dead," he cabled to his brothers.[51]

Eventually William Howard Taft achieved his heart's desire, which was to be chief justice of the Supreme Court, but first he had to make other accommodations. He accepted an appointment as pro-fessor of law at Yale University. "Being a dead politician, I have become a statesman," Taft observed wryly. "I am on the tower of St. Simeon Stylites, or up a tree, to use a more homely expression, where I witness the passing show with continued sympathy, with freedom from the sense of responsibility that I have had to have for nearly twenty-five years, and with a sense of freedom that I have never had before."[52]

Taft was quite satisfied with his financial situation upon leaving the presidency. He informed his successor, Woodrow Wilson, that he had been able to save about $100,000 from his salary. The letter, a frank piece of advice, said: "You will find . . . that Congress is very generous to the President." His expenses would be only those of feeding his family and "a large boarding house of servants," be-sides personal expenses such as clothing. Therefore, he advised, the $75,000 salary plus the $25,000 for traveling expenses is "very much more than is generally supposed."[53]

The proper limitations of an ex-president's law practice almost ruined Bainbridge Colby, Wilson's last secretary of state, who, after the presidency, became his law partner. The partnership was to have law offices in New York and Washington, with Colby scheduled to spend most of his time in New York and about one day a week in the capital. Wilson, having been granted a license to practice law by the District of Columbia bar, expected to work about an hour a day in his law office. But the ex-President's health was so precarious that Dr. Grayson forbade any visits to an office and insisted that Colby consult with Wilson at home.

Wilson's physical limitation was not the only obstacle facing the partnership. Political clients were ready to pay outrageous fees to be represented by an ex-president and an ex-secretary of state, but Wilson's scruples forbade accepting them. Nor would he touch any case that was concerned with government. Thus such potential clients as the Western Ukrainian Republic, which wanted recognition from the League of Nations; Harry F. Sinclair and E. L. Doheny of the Teapot Dome scandal; and the government of Ecuador, which was seeking a loan from the United States, were sent away. Colby said to Mrs. Wilson: "Day after day I sit in my office and see a procession walk through—thousands and thousands of dollars—and not one to put into our pockets."[54]

In a moneymaking sense, therefore, almost no cases were possible. Regretfully, the partnership had to be dissolved. In a year, Wilson had earned $5,000, which he spent on an electric automobile, while Colby, who had paid all the bills, had lost a sizable sum of money. Too ill to work anyhow, Wilson had appeared at the office only once.

Wilson decided to live in Washington rather than in Baltimore, Richmond, Boston, or New York after his retirement, because he wanted to be near the Library of Congress to work on the book he was never well enough to start. Also, Washington was Mrs. Wilson's home town. Before leaving the White House, the couple planned to build a house, but although looking at property and cutting out plans from architectural magazines amused Wilson, they found, instead, a house in the 2300 block on S Street that seemed just right and bought it.

Because of his poor health, Wilson spent most of his time in his bedroom. His bed was a copy of Lincoln's bed, eight and a half feet long and six feet two inches wide, with a long silk banner decorated with the American flag and the American eagle that had been presented by the state of New York hanging over it. The original of the popular World War I Red Cross poster "The Greatest Mother in the World" hung over the door, and on the mantelpiece was the empty brass shell that had held the first shot fired in the war by

United States troops. Wilson often entertained his friends in the room while he had lunch.

Calvin Coolidge, the last unpensioned President, whose simple tastes were supposed to exemplify the Puritan spirit, returned to Northampton after his term in office. At first he lived in his modest duplex apartment at 21 Massasoit Street, for which he paid thirty-six dollars a month. The taciturn New Englanders who lived in town respected the ex-President's privacy, so he could move around freely. But the tourists, fascinated by the sight of a real ex-president of the United States sitting on his front porch in an old-fashioned rocking chair, drove him into hiding. There was no answer but to find another, more secluded residence.

The Coolidges bought The Beeches, a large, ostentatious estate of nine acres with a swimming pool and eight hundred trees. A fence ensured the required privacy and the freedom to sit on the porch and admire the magnificent view. Coolidge was proud of his twelve-room house and enjoyed inviting his friends and former associates to stay with him.

Money was not a problem for Coolidge. He exited from the White House with substantial funds as a result of having made first-rate investments. His holdings were estimated at about $200,000. The former President had been on J. P. Morgan's list of favored subscribers along with such other men in public office as Newton D. Baker, William Gibbs McAdoo, and Charles Francis Adams. This favored-person status meant that he and others were in a position to buy stocks before they were put on the market for the general public and to pay less for them.[55] Coolidge saw nothing wrong with this activity. After all, he was the man who had said that the business of America was business. Therefore, when he could, he took advantage of the main chance. He would have been surprised to know that such a practice would, in the future, be suspect as possibly constituting a conflict of interest.

Since idleness was a sin, Coolidge had to seek a job, although he did not really need one. He was a director of the New York Life Insurance Company, for which he was paid fifty dollars a month, but most of his income was earned writing articles for magazines.

In April 1929, Coolidge finished his autobiography in a record three and a half months of intensive work. It appeared first as a series of articles in *Cosmopolitan* and later in book form. Though the book was characteristically both reticent and dull, unrevealing except for what could be gleaned from reading between the lines, it sold well and earned a sizable sum. This public response immediately resulted in countless offers for more from his pen. He wrote for the *Ladies' Home Journal*, *Collier's*, and the *Saturday Evening Post*. In 1930 Coolidge wrote a syndicated column for the McClure papers. He commented on the American scene, avoiding with great skill the worsening financial straits of the country. The articles were devoid of literary style, flair, or any particular point of view, but about a hundred papers around the country carried the banal material. His avoidance of serious political issues was, no doubt, deliberate. He wrote "like a humorless David Harum," Donald McCoy said about the daily "Thinking Things Over with Calvin Coolidge" paragraphs. After earning $203,045 from the column, the former President let his contract expire.[56]

Various proposals made over the years to provide a pension for American ex-presidents elicited many responses. Congress often adopted a dog-in-the-manger attitude. The legislators did not want to undertake the expense on behalf of their constituents but were outraged when a private citizen offered to do it for them. Andrew Carnegie offered a pension of $25,000 to ex-presidents and their wives, naming Taft as the first recipient. "I can't take the pension for obvious reasons," Taft wrote, but he believed that Carnegie was well intentioned. He was amused that irate lawmakers, "some of our cheapest statesmen," thought the Carnegie offer an insult to the nation.[57]

Eisenhower was the first President to step down from office after the Presidential Retirement Act was passed. John Eisenhower, Ike's only child, said with disarming honesty that "a President in recent times has been well taken care of by the nation when he leaves office." However, Ike was in an unusual position. He had been a five-star general, which carried with it the privilege of keeping the rank for life. In 1952 he resigned from the army for political reasons but later wanted to get his rank back. Again John Eisenhower explains. His father wanted it back in order to be able to retain in his employ Colonel Robert Schulz and Sergeant John Mooney. An obliging Congress, more grateful to a hero of World War II than an earlier body had been to successful Union General Ulysses S. Grant, made a special arrangement whereby President Eisenhower was given back his military rank but could retain only his presidential pension. He was allowed to keep the military personnel he wished on his staff, but their expenses were deducted from his official office allotment. President Kennedy signed the bill for his predecessor, which placed him behind General Douglas MacArthur in rank but ahead of General Omar Bradley.

The Eisenhower transition from President to squire of his Gettysburg estate was quiet and orderly. The Eisenhowers had purchased the Gettysburg property, which adjoins the battlefield, in 1950. Over the years they had altered the original simple farmhouse into a Georgian-style two-story brick mansion. Washington columnist Drew Pearson spread the gossip that Ike received substantial gifts for his Gettysburg home. His story was that three Texas oilmen had contributed $500,000 for the farm. "Nobody has ever built any part of my farm," Eisenhower told newsmen. He denied that anyone at all had ever put money into it. In 1967, the Eisenhower farm was deeded to the United States as a national historic site.[58]

When it came time for Lyndon Johnson to benefit from the pension bill he had sponsored, he did not need its benefits. He was probably the wealthiest ex-President this country has yet seen. Though his retirement was only of four years' duration, it has been reported that he almost doubled his already sizable estate. The Johnson holdings, some of which belonged to Mrs. Johnson and were inherited from her family, included television interests in Texas, Louisiana, and Oklahoma; real estate in the Caribbean, Mexico, and five counties in Texas; and a photographic supply company in Austin. The sale of the television station, KTBC, in Austin to the Times-Mirror corporation of Los Angeles brought nine million dollars. When Johnson split up with his lifelong business partner, Judge A. W. Morsund, apparently over the purchase of a bank, just a year before Johnson died, their joint holdings were divided. The ex-President received a four-thousand-acre ranch and 214 subdivision lots along Lake LBJ in Austin. And before he died, Johnson was negotiating the sale of the working part of his ranch on the Pedernales. It was arranged that the National Park Service would take the ranch as a national historic site if and when Ladybird Johnson decided to live elsewhere.[59]

Johnson adopted the ex-presidential habit of memoir writing, but otherwise his retirement was a contrast to that of his two predecessors. Since the curse of the Vietnam War followed him into retirement— actually caused his retirement—Johnson became a very private citizen. In the months after their retirements, Truman and Eisenhower had been much in the public eye. Johnson said little except off the record. He did participate in TV interviews conducted by Walter Cronkite for CBS, but this was linked with his contract for his book, to be published by Holt, Rinehart and Winston. The former President's energies were devoted to his 330-acre farm, on which he planted experimental grass, developed his cattle herds, and exhausted his ranch foreman. "I want to talk Democratic politics, he only talks hog prices," a political friend complained. But he still lived like a President, summoning an air force helicopter to take him from the ranch to Austin and his extravaganza of a library, which has a landing pad on its roof. In his brief time as the ex-President, Johnson may not have had the popularity of an Eisenhower, but he lived like exiled royalty.

When Richard Nixon was forced to resign from the presidency in disgrace, he returned to private life with serious financial problems. Within a year most of them were resolved, however, for the pension system and the public's insatiable interest in all things presidential combined to bail him out. The exile of San Clemente may not be restored to grace in the eyes of most Americans, but the probability of his being comfortably solvent, if not wealthy, is fairly certain.

During the winter of 1974, while still President, Nixon estimated that he had amassed about one million dollars during his term in the White House. Most of the money derived from tax deductions he had taken for his presidential papers. By the time he retired, thousands of dollars in these tax deductions had been disallowed and he owed the government for the back taxes. Hence the former President returned to La Casa Pacifica, his San Clemente estate, owing taxes and mortgage payments. He also had staggering legal fees, and more to come. His lawyer, Herbert Miller, estimated that the legal costs for the fight to recover his presidential tapes and papers would run to about $500,000. There were also at least thirty civil suits not covered by President Ford's blanket pardon that had to be defended. The most serious one was brought by Morton H. Halperin and Anthony Lake, both former members of the National Security Council, whose places were tapped by the government between 1969 and 1971. Mr. Halperin was asking for damages including $100 per day for each day the wire tap was in place. The most unexpected additional expense was Nixon's phlebitis, which turned out to be a serious, almost fatal, illness. His surgery, hospitalization, and medical fees amounted to about $33,000, and due to some "staff foul up," Ronald Ziegler said, Nixon had no health insurance.[60]

These large debts caused a cash bind that made the ex-President look like an impoverished victim, or so he liked to have it seem. However, the financial crunch was temporary. The back taxes were paid before he left office, which depleted Nixon's cash reserve, but the $148,000 underpayment on 1969 taxes, for which the statute of limitations had run out and which Nixon promised to pay, seemed to have been forgotten.

At first, all emphasis was placed on Nixon's liabilities. Realistically, his assets were always present. Shortly after the resignation, President Ford asked the Congress for an $850,000 package to cover the ex-President's transitional needs until June 30, 1975. Arthur F. Sampson, the administrator of the General Services Administration, provided an itemized account for the astounded lawmakers. The money, he said, would be allotted in the following way:

$4,000 — travel
$8,000 — personal benefits such as health insurance
$5,000 — office supplies
$65,000 — furnishings and office supplies
$21,000 — communications
$10,000 — printing
$100,000 — miscellaneous

The miscellaneous category was for "contingencies," Mr. Sampson explained, such as security beyond what is provided by the Secret Service. Upon being pressed, he admitted that Lyndon Johnson had spent only $370,000 of his allotted $450,000 for transition expenses.[61]

Debate in the House was sharp, particularly on the part of the Democrats. "What function does the ex-President who left under less than honorable conditions perform for the people of the United States?" asked Representative John E. Moss, a California Democrat. Republican members were much more generous. A representative from upstate New York argued that "a valid and natural service" was performed "by providing an adequate amount for transition purposes." The House cut the figure requested, but the sizable amount remaining went to Nixon, who used it for salaries and office expenses, which were very high due to the voluminous mail that had to be answered about the resignation and the pardon.

Nixon real estate represents a valuable investment. The former President has equity in San Clemente and his two houses in Key Biscayne, Florida, all of which have increased in value since he bought them. The final mortgage payment for La Casa Pacifica, the California ex-White House, was due on January 4, 1975. Apparently Nixon could not have met it at the time, but a secret benefactor paid it for him and arranged much easier installments and a longer time to pay them in. Though the benefactor's name was kept secret, Nixon's lawyer gave assurances that "the people involved are not criminal or secretive interests. It does not involve campaign fund sources. . . . There is no taint and no sort of impropriety."[62]

The greatest asset that all recent presidents have is the marketability of their memoirs. The expectation that Richard Nixon will finally reveal the whole truth about Watergate will assure record sales for the book he is now working on. According to the ex-President's agent, Irving Lazar, Nixon will receive a total advance of 2.5 million dollars from his publisher, Warner Paperback Library, New York. He received $350,000 upon signing the contract and will receive a similar sum upon completion of the first two hundred pages.[63] It is not certain how the problem of the impounded presidential tapes and papers will be handled by the author. However, since it has been customary from the days of George Washington for the president to have full power to take his papers away with him at the end of his administration, it would seem that Nixon has a good case.

Though the fight to recover the papers will be an expensive one, Nixon said that he would take it to the Supreme Court if necessary. He has financial help for the effort. Rabbi Baruch Korff, a fanatically loyal Nixon advocate, formed the Nixon Justice Fund to raise money to cover the legal expenses connected with the recovery of the papers. He has collected $200,000, with every expectation that the remainder will be forthcoming. The quantity of pro-Nixon mail that pours into the Nixon compound indicates that the besieged ex-President has a sizable number of sympathizers.

The presidential pension of $60,000 per year plus up to another $96,000 per year for office expenses is considerably less than the presidential salary of $200,000 annually with an additional $50,000 for office expenses, but under the circumstances, Richard Nixon has no cause for complaint. If he had been removed from office by Congress, an almost certain assumption, he would have forfeited all pension rights for himself and his wife. President Ford's pardon also protected him from some suits connected with Watergate that he would have otherwise had to defend.

The story of presidential retirement from Washington to Nixon has been one of progress from laissez-faire to ultraprotection. This is literally true, for the former President and his wife are provided with lifetime Secret Service protection. Also, there are fringe benefits: free office space, free mailing privileges, free use of government planes, and up to $18,000 in civil-service retirement benefits. Only with disastrously bad management could a modern ex-president suffer the loss of his beloved library as Jefferson did, become a burden to his family as James Monroe did, or have to write out his life to leave his family provided for as Grant did.

Ex-Monarchs Abroad

ILLARD FILLMORE was the second ex-President to go abroad but the first to bring up the question of how a former chief executive of the United States should be treated by foreign heads of state. In a letter to Hugh Maxwell, the former collector of the port of New York, who had suggested Fillmore's trip so that he and other supporters could arrange the ex-President's candidacy on the Know-Nothing ticket, Fillmore expressed his quandary. Would his position in relation to titled dignitaries subject the United States to any indignity, he asked Maxwell, who had just returned from Europe. Should he refuse invitations to festive entertainments to avoid the problem? Should he, perhaps, travel incognito? How many servants should he take? "You will understand," Fillmore said, "that while I have no personal pride for any social distinctions in Europe, I would not knowingly place myself in any position where my country would be degraded or insulted through me."[1]

Apparently all doubts were resolved, for the Fillmores sailed in May 1855 on the Collins steamer *Atlantic*. Or at least positive motives outweighed objections to the trip. Concealing the political reasons, Fillmore cited his wife's poor health and his own need for a change while he made the transition from an active to an inactive life. "It is better to wear out than to rust out," he observed. And since he had been deprived of his profession, politics, which he loved, he would diversify his talents by traveling.[2]

The voyage across the Atlantic was pleasant except for a thirty-six-hour storm, during which the ship was surrounded by icebergs, a wheelhouse was destroyed, and some sailors were injured. Many years later, the former President told a meeting of the Buffalo Historical Society that at the height of the storm he had thought only of how much he wished he were at home. "If I *ever* reach Buffalo, I shall remain there," he had vowed.[3]

Handsome Millard Fillmore was a great success in England and on the Continent. He was entertained by kings and emperors, ambassadors and distinguished men of all kinds. Charles Leslie, the painter who met Fillmore at a Fourth of July dinner given by George Peabody, an American financier who had settled in London, said: "What a noble looking man. . . . He reminds me of Sir Robert Peel." Fillmore's popularity pleased Peabody, who was very concerned with the improvement of Anglo-American relations.

The story was often told, although there is no documentary evidence for it, that when Fillmore was presented to Queen Victoria, she commented that his manners were the most elegant of any American's who had been presented to her. If Fillmore heard these stories, he was undoubtedly delighted, for enemies always insisted that he was an extremely vain man.

Ex-President Martin Van Buren was in London at the same time Fillmore was. The first former President to leave his native land, Van Buren had sailed from New York in April 1853 with his son, Martin. After taking the grand tour, Van Buren had decided to spend the rest of his life abroad. He had settled down at the Villa Falangola in Sorrento, Italy, and begun to write his autobiography. He abandoned his plans to stay when his son died in Paris in March 1855. He was in London recovering from his grief and getting ready to return to the United States.

The two former Presidents met frequently. London was rather intrigued with the spectacle of two American ex-Presidents in their midst. John Bright, upon seeing them both sitting in the visitors' gallery of the House of Commons, mentioned it on the floor of the House.

After several months in England, during which he refused an honorary degree from Oxford University on the grounds that he lacked a classical education, Fillmore left for France to visit the International Exposition. While there, he was presented to Napoleon III and, according to some reports, arranged for Horace Greeley's release from jail. The editor had been arrested as a result of charges brought by M. Leschene, a Paris sculptor, who demanded $2,500 in gold for a statue of his that had been broken at the New York Crystal Palace Exhibition. This ridiculous accusation was acted upon because of Greeley's offensive behavior to the arresting bailiffs, who felt that his wild oaths constituted an insult to France. Neither Greeley nor his biographers acknowledged Fillmore's intercession. They only conceded that, along with other curiosity seekers, Fillmore and Van Buren visited the irascible editor in his jail cell at Clichy prison to convey their "good wishes and good will."[4]

In Rome, Fillmore had a near brush with the Papal State. Van Buren had been received by the pope with no problem, but Fillmore had some reservations about whether he should go through with the audience. Presumably his dilemma had no connection with the Know-Nothings, his new party. He claimed that he was worried that he would be expected to kiss the hand or the foot of the pope. "I could only consent to be presented to the pope as the sovereign of the State, not as High Priest of a religious sect or denomination," he explained. At the audience the somewhat naive former President was surprised that the pope received him sitting down, graciously asked him to sit, and then talked familiarly for ten or fifteen minutes about his great interest in helping the common people. "He has a very benevolent face and must be a good man," Fillmore conceded, but still remained critical of the system that the pope administered. The Catholic Church was "entrenched in political and ecclesiastical despotism" and hedged in "by a numerous and selfish priesthood," he said.[5]

Accompanied by Elam R. Jewett and Thomas M. Foote, two editor friends, Fillmore left Rome for a tour of Naples, Cairo, Jerusalem, and Constantinople, and then returned to Trieste. Thus he satisfied all of his original travel plans except for his wish to go to St. Petersburg. He did, however, visit Berlin, where the king of Prussia was much taken with him and told the American minister that, given the opportunity, he would most certainly cast his vote for Fillmore for president.

One of the highlights of the German tour was a visit with white-haired, dignified, eighty-six-year-old Baron von Humboldt, the scientific explorer. Fillmore called on him at his rooms in one of the king's palaces in Potsdam, where he found the old man reading proofs of his five-volume treatise called *Kosmos*. The sage reminisced about his visit to the United States in 1804, during which he had spent some time with President Jefferson. Later, Fillmore met von Humboldt again at the palace of Sans Souci and was pleased to note that the king, the queen, and all the court treated the scientist with the greatest respect. In 1869, when Buffalo celebrated the centennial of von Humboldt's birth, about 45,000 residents gathered to hear ex-President Fillmore speak of his meeting with the explorer of the Orinoco, the Amazon, and the peaks of the Andes.[6]

At the end of his year-long journey, Fillmore declared that he had no cause for complaint about his treatment by European officialdom. "That they should not like our government is neither strange nor unnatural," he said. For himself, he was content that he was not expected to like theirs. However, his travels convinced him that the people of Europe were unfit for the republican form of government. If they ever could reach that stage, he concluded, "it must be by slow degrees through a constitutional monarchy."[7]

Fillmore proved to be a huge success as an American goodwill ambassador without portfolio. His good looks, dignity, and old-fashioned courtliness helped to dispel the idea of the stereotype American abroad as a bustling, uncouth, materialistic barbarian. In the United States, especially in Washington, he was often pilloried for being vain and second-rate, but abroad his bland good humor was much admired.

George Bancroft tried to persuade former President Van Buren to accept President Polk's offer to send him as minister to the Court of St. James. In Europe, the historian pointed out, prime ministers were often selected to go to foreign missions, particularly in critical times such as the United States was experiencing with England. For example, he said, Metternich went to Napoleon and Guizot just lately was sent to England. "You love society," Bancroft told Van Buren, and you owe it to your country. Van Buren refused even though he would have welcomed a means of escape from Lindenwald. "Prince John" was opposed to the appointment as incompatible with his father's dignity.[8]

Poor Mrs. Franklin Pierce was not at all well when she and the President left the White House in March 1857. She had never recovered from the death of her son, Benny. A couple of months before the inauguration, the Pierces and their twelve-year-old son had boarded a train in Andover to return home to Concord, New Hampshire. They had traveled for about a mile when the car they were riding in snapped free and pitched over the embankment. The two elder Pierces escaped with minor cuts and bruises, but their youngster's brains were dashed out by a fragment of the train's framework that struck him on the forehead. General Pierce picked up the child, unaware of his terrible injury until he took his cap off. Mrs. Pierce was carried away from the tragic spectacle utterly distaught. None of the other passengers were hurt.[9]

The President-elect had to continue with his commitment to the country, but he was much saddened, as he had always said that the only reason he stayed in politics was to help his son's future. Once the four-year term was over, Pierce felt that he must devote himself to his sad and ailing wife. They spent the spring and summer in New England, but in the fall it became obvious that the former First Lady could not endure the harsh New England winter. After considering several alternatives, they decided to go to the Island of Madeira, and President Buchanan graciously offered them passage on the *Powhatan*. For the first time in their lives, the Pierces had the opportunity to move out into the world.

After resting in Madeira for the winter, the Pierces traveled through Europe, visiting all the countries on the tourist route. They saw Spain, Portugal, France, Germany, Austria, Belgium, and England. During the summer of 1858 they stayed at Lake Geneva, and in the winter went on to Rome, where there was a reunion between Pierce and Nathaniel Hawthorne. Unfortunately it was not under the happiest circumstances; Una, the author's young daughter, was suffering from Roman fever and had been in critical condition for four months.

When Hawthorne first saw Pierce he was struck by "the marks of care and coming age in many a whitening hair and many a furrow." Even more distressing was "something that seemed to have passed away out of him, without leaving a trace." His voice was sometimes strange and old. The writer's observant eye noted that the former President remarked on how stout a lad Julian Hawthorne had become with something of melancholy in his voice. "Poor fellow! he has neither son nor daughter to keep his heart warm," Hawthorne told his journal.

The two old friends visited St. Peter's and all the other Roman landmarks together, renewing their friendship with enthusiasm. As time went on, Hawthorne decided that Pierce was not really as much changed as he had first thought. They were able to exchange views on politics and the future with a great deal of candor. Pierce seemed "fairly resolved" not to run for president again, the author said, and seemed sincere in that resolve.[10]

Pierce proved to be a great help while Una was still desperately ill. Sophia Hawthorne wrote: "I think I owe to him, almost my husband's life. He was divinely tender, sweet, sympathizing and helpful." Hawthorne was touchingly grateful also. He had never before known any trouble "that pierced into my very vitals. I did not know what comfort there might be in the manly sympathy of a friend; but Pierce has undergone so great a sorrow of his own, and has so large and kindly a heart, and is so tender and so strong, that he really did me good, and I shall always love him the better for the recollection of those dark days."[11]

Although over the fever, Una could not be moved for another month, so Hawthorne was not able to accompany the Pierces when they left Rome for Venice and Trieste. The author was disappointed that they had to part but pleased that he had found in Rome "the whole of my early friend, and even better than I used to know him." He observed that Pierce had always been unsatisfied with his former successes no matter how great, always restless and striving. Hawthorne could not decide when Pierce had first begun to look forward to being President, but observed, "I believe that he would have died a miserable man without it." Now Pierce was happier than he had ever seen him since their college days at Bowdoin. "I do not love him one whit the less for having been President," he concluded charitably.[12]

When the Pierces returned to the United States in August 1849, the former President told the crowd of friends gathered to welcome them that the object of his trip had been partially fulfilled. Mrs. Pierce's health had improved but, unfortunately, it was only a respite, for within a short time her melancholia became even more aggravated. Obviously the Pierces had chosen to travel quietly as ordinary American tourists and had succeeded in doing so, but ever after an American ex-president abroad was denied that choice.

Silent, unpretentious ex-President Ulysses S. Grant was an unlikely candidate for the title of the world's greatest traveler, yet by the time he had completed his two-and-a-half-year trip around the world, he had earned it. He had, as his dear friend and biographer,

General Adam Badeau, noted, "visited more countries and [seen] more people from kings down to lackeys and slaves, than anybody who ever journeyed on this earth before."[13]

Van Buren and Fillmore had been received with attention as distinguished American citizens, but General Grant, the hero of the Civil War as well as the ex-President, must, according to Lord Beaconsfield, be received as a sovereign. Grant did not care much for protocol, but when he was in England the serious matter of whether he would call first on the Duke of Cambridge or vice versa was discussed with suitable gravity by the London press. President Hayes directed Secretary of State William M. Evarts to notify all United States representatives abroad that the former President had sailed for Liverpool and it was expected that they would "find patriotic pleasure" in giving him every attention.

Grant had always wanted to see the world, so finding himself financially able, he allotted $25,000 for the trip, hoping that it would be enough for two years. As it turned out, it would have been much too little, but fortunately Grant's son Ulysses ("Buck") made some successful investments for his father and was able to add $60,000 to the travel fund.

On May 17, 1877, accompanied by their young son Jesse, the Grants departed on the *Indiana*, a government vessel put at the disposal of the ex-President for as long as he wanted it. John Russell Young of the New York *Herald* was sent by his newspaper to feed a constant stream of dispatches home. Thus the trip became an experience in which all the American people could participate and resulted in restoring General Grant to his former popularity.

While the Grants' ship was making a stormy passage across the Atlantic, their reception in England was being masterminded by Edwards Pierrepont, Grant's attorney general, who was the American minister in England. His chief, he vowed, was not going to go into dinner at the end of the procession and without a lady on his arm. Not General Grant. The objection raised by the British that ex-presidents had no official status in their own country was set aside by Pierrepont. Ex-kings received honors, he pointed out, and would not listen to the argument that former monarchs were of royal blood. After much discussion with Lord Derby, the minister of foreign affairs, it was agreed that General Grant would be received as an ex-king. He must pay the first visit to members of the royal family but otherwise would take precedence over all other Englishmen.

The only unresolved problem was how to determine the ex-President's rank in relation to ambassadors, who were, of course, the direct representatives of their sovereigns. The solution was to omit Grant from the guest list of those invited to attend the queen's birthday, an occasion on which ambassadors had to be present. Instead, it was arranged, Grant would meet the queen another time and the Duke of Wellington would have him to dinner on that night.

All this fuss over etiquette was worth the effort, because Grant's reception in England set the precedent for his reception around the world. He would have been deprived of many interesting experiences without the exalted rank he was given. And it was a compliment to the United States to have a former President treated with such unusual honor.

Receptions and speeches dotted Grant's path through the cities of Liverpool, Manchester, and Leicester on his way to London. Once there, the queen extended the courtesy of waiving the usual court presentation and issuing a blanket invitation to all the court festivities. An English lady commented that whatever England's feelings were toward America, toward General Grant there was the greatest friendliness. "Thus far the journey of the hero of Appomattox has been as triumphant as Sherman's march to the sea."[14]

Despite the elaborate arrangements to establish semiroyal status, there were slights that got into the papers and supplied table talk. General Badeau, who was something of a social climber, exacerbated the episodes by reporting them exhaustively. For example, he was not satisfied with the Prince of Wales's behavior to the Grants. He reported that at the prince's dinner, the general and his wife were seated at the bottom of the table and ignored. The Grants preferred not to resent the insult or even to acknowledge it, but according to Badeau, some of the English people who were present noticed it and talked, and eventually the American newspapers took up the battle. The prince wrote to the American minister justifying his actions by pointing out that the emperor of Brazil was present at the dinner and he could not be expected to give General Grant precedence over an emperor. The prince could have avoided the problem by not inviting Grant and the Brazilian at the same time. Besides, the English government had promised the ex-President precedence over dukes, and the Prince of Wales had placed him below earls. Further, the fact that the prince did not speak to Grant proved that he was displaying royal arrogance and a distaste for democracy.[15]

Badeau was certainly involved in, if not responsible for, a tempest in a teapot over the queen's invitation to the Grants to dine at Windsor Castle. Nineteen-year-old Jesse Grant was not to be seated at the royal table but was to eat with the royal household in a different room. Mrs. Grant recorded in her diary: "Mr. Pierrepont sat pale and anxious, as though this were a very serious international question indeed. I tried playfully to pacify Jesse, but only made matters worse by suggesting that they only looked upon him as a boy." General Grant solved the problem calmly. He sent for the proper person and said to him: "We fear there has been some mistake. My son, Mr. Grant, came down here under the supposition that he was invited to dine with Her Majesty. Will you make inquiry. . . ." Almost at once, the gentleman returned with an invitation for Jesse to dine with the queen.[16]

England treated Grant royally. The City of London presented him with the full freedom of the city at a dinner given at the Crystal Palace. After a sumptuous meal, a fireworks display including Grant's portrait aflame in the sky was followed by a sketch of the United States Capitol. Grant immensely pleased, a scarcely perceptible grin on his poker face, remarked to his dinner companion, "They have burnt me in effigy, and now they are burning the Capitol."

Though many English workers had suffered severely during the American Civil War because the northern blockade kept cotton from reaching the English mills, it was the common man who supported the Union cause. Now they welcomed "the most distinguished citizen of the United States." To a delegation of forty English workingmen, each representing a different trade, Grant spoke with emotion. He had had "orations, handshakings, and presentations from different classes, from the Government . . . but there has been no reception which I am prouder of than that of today."[17]

King Leopold of Belgium avoided the problem of protocol when Grant arrived in Ostend by calling on him alone. The king discussed the problems of the Congo with him with such candor that, later on, when stories of Belgian atrocities in Africa were exposed by the press, Jesse Grant said that having met the king and listened to him, he could never accept their validity. King Leopold gave Grant the royal railroad car to bring him to Brussels, where he was formally entertained at a banquet.

For the next two months Grant toured the Rhine valley, the German cities, and the Black Forest before proceeding to Switzerland.

Everywhere he received enthusiastic public welcomes. At Geneva he told the crowd gathered to hear him dedicate the cornerstone of an Episcopal church that he had long wanted to visit the city where the Alabama Claims had been settled peaceably by international arbitration.

The majestic glory of the Alps so impressed the phlegmatic general that he interrupted his schedule to stay three days at Chamonix. Fanny Kemble came to see him at Thursis and reminded him that Algernon Sartoris, Grant's son-in-law, was her nephew. Richard Wagner called on Grant at Heidelberg, but they could communicate only through interpreters. However, Wagner wanted to meet a warrior whose deeds resembled those of his operatic heroes.

Rome was not Grant's cup of tea. The pictures, the statues, and even the Sistine Chapel bored him. Badeau, at his wit's end to find something to interest the General, took him to see the famous equestrian statue of Marcus Aurelius, hoping that he might like the Roman emperor's horse. Grant was unenthusiastic, liking it no better than the Gothic splendor of the cathedral at Milan. His admiration was reserved for the massive Egyptian pyramids which he would see later on.

Unable to speak the language, Grant spent most of his time in Paris with the American colony or sightseeing. He was entertained by President MacMahon, however, and met him frequently at formal dinners. A reporter from the *Figaro* interviewed Grant and found him silent and imperturbable. Wellington was called the Iron Duke, he quipped, Grant might well be titled the Steel General. The interviewer was unable to persuade the General to give any opinions on French politics. Instead, Grant spoke of the pleasure he had got from his sympathetic reception in England and of his plans for future travel.

The American steamship *Vandalia* met the Grant party at Villefranche to carry them to Egypt. The beauties of Naples left Grant cold, but he wanted to ascend Vesuvius. He was disappointed, however, because official calls delayed him until there was not enough daylight to reach the top and look into the crater. Pompeii was not a great success either. It was the custom when a distinguished visitor came to see the ruins to uncover a new house and name it after the guest. The Grants were placed in chairs before the mound and work was started. To the chagrin of the Italian official in charge, only some bones, a few bronze ornaments, and a loaf of bread were uncovered. Hungry, tired, and annoyed, Grant managed to turn down politely the offer to excavate another mound.

After an American Christmas celebration abroad the *Vandalia*, at which Grant presented his wife with a beautiful coral handle for her parasol which he had bought at Naples, the ship stopped briefly at Sicily. Passing Scylla and Charybdis and other Homeric landmarks, the General was completely uninterested in following the adventures of his namesake, but Mrs. Grant enjoyed the classical references.

The former President's reception in Egypt was as thunderous as the one in Europe. Upon his arrival in Alexandria, the khedive, through the governor, offered him a palace in Cairo and a steamer to take him up the Nile. A boring reception by the pasha was succeeded by an interesting meeting with Henry M. Stanley, the man who found Livingstone. The famous explorer had just returned from one of his African journeys and regaled Grant with fascinating tales about his adventures.

Grant got his first glimpse of the pyramids from a special train that carried him to Cairo. It whetted his appetite for more, so the khedive placed a steamer at his disposal and sent one of the directors of the Egyptian Museum to accompany him. Grant did not miss a ruin. He was ready early every morning, wearing an Indian helmet wrapped with silk to guard him from the sun. When there were no ruins to see, he sat silently on the deck reading Mark Twain's *Innocents Abroad* or entertaining the party with anecdotes about the Civil War or his administration. All along the Nile, the former President was received with great ceremony.

At Luxor, where he was welcomed with a gun salute and flying flags, a miniature expedition had been prepared to carry him by donkey caravan over the desert to visit the two statues of Memnon and then cross-country to the temple of Medinet Haboo, which has rooms in which Rameses lived. At a state dinner given by the Arab vice-consul after the desert journey, Grant was ignored by most of the guests, who did not realize that the short, plain man was the "King of America."

The party pushed up the river to Aswan, the frontier of old Egypt, and the boundary of Nubia. The black governor, dressed in the latest Paris fashions, received Grant and arranged a visit to Philae, a small island in the Nile just above the first cataract, which was the Holy Land of Egypt. Then the boat was turned around to return to Cairo. Some missionaries came on board with the news that Russia had taken Adrianople and England was ready to go to war. Someone suggested that since Grant was to visit Turkey soon, he might offer the sultan his services. "No, I have done all the fighting I care to do," he said, "and the only country I shall fight for is the United States."

After visiting the Holy Land, the *Vandalia* took the Grants to Constantinople. Fortunately, they arrived after the treaty ending the war between Turkey and Russia had been signed. The sultan's situation spared Grant from another tiresome military reception, but to make it up to him, the sultan's master of ceremonies presented the General with an Arabian horse from the royal stables and, later, with a second. Both horses were transferred to the American legation for shipment to the United States. One was dappled gray with small, well-set ears, pink nostrils, large soft eyes, a waving mane, a long tail to the ground, and delicate skin. The other stallion was iron gray with a white star on his forehead and white hind feet. Grant, who loved horses, was delighted. He was disappointed, however, that he could not visit a Russian camp still positioned about eight miles outside of Constantinople. But having enjoyed Turkish hospitality, he felt it would be rude to visit with their enemies.[18]

With restless energy, Grant moved back and forth across the European continent, fêted and entertained by royalty all along the way. In Berlin, Grant and Bismarck met several times. "Good to welcome General Grant to Germany," Bismarck said, seizing the American cordially by the hand. They discussed General Philip Sheridan, whom Grant called "one of the greatest soldiers of the world." Bismarck, who had met Sheridan when he was an observer of the Franco-Prussian War, commented on his quick eye. They talked at length about the assassination attempt on the German emperor, which had delayed Grant in Holland for two weeks while he waited for the old man to recover from shock. Grant had been invited to be his guest. The only way to deal with an assassin, Grant said, "is by the severest methods." A crime like that "not only aims at an old man's life, a ruler's life, but shocks the world." Even though there was strong sentiment against the death penalty at home, Grant continued, "I am not sure but it should be made more severe rather than less severe. Something is due to the offended, as well as the offender, especially where the offender is slain."[19]

Of all his encounters with the great that Grant experienced during his travels, he considered his meetings with Bismarck the freest and most comfortable. Even the chancellor's dog, his constant companion, took to Grant. Bayard Taylor, the American minister, seeing the rapport between the two men, proposed a toast—"eternal amity between Germany and the United States"—to be sealed with a glass of schnapps. Smiling, the two dignitaries touched glasses.[20]

A brief trip to Scandinavia provided a short escape from official receptions when the Grant party took an inland trip toward the land of the reindeer. They did not get there, because they had to return for a gala reception planned by King Oscar. Russia was the next stop. The czar received Grant cordially and provided him with a yacht to take him to Peterhof, the Versailles of St. Petersburg. Once again, after visiting Moscow and the Kremlin, Grant crossed Europe, and this time traveled to Spain to visit King Alfonso.

The Spanish king solved the problem of rank by deciding that the ex-President would be received as a captain-general of the Spanish army. The arrival of General Grant caused a great deal of anxiety and preparation at the American ministry. James Russell Lowell, the American minister to Spain, was pleasantly surprised to find the Grants "simple-minded and natural people," and was rather impressed with the General's skill at handling the endless ceremonies with "a dogged imperturbability." He endured the visit to the opera, however, with somewhat less aplomb. After about five minutes, he asked Lowell if they hadn't had about enough, explaining that he could not tell one tune from another except for bugle calls and he had some difficulty with them.[21]

The king of Portugal came to Lisbon to meet General Grant. He discussed the possibility of commerce between their two countries and presented him with a copy of *Hamlet*, which he had had translated into Portuguese. He wanted to bestow the Cross of the Tower and Sword on Grant, but the former President refused the decoration on the grounds that it was against the law for American officials to receive foreign awards and he preferred not to break the precedent.

The Grants next returned to England. Mrs. Grant stayed in Southampton with her daughter, and the General visited Ireland as he had promised. The American man-of-war that was scheduled to take the ex-President to India was still in the United States when he returned from Ireland. Since he had been told that it was not healthy to visit India after the beginning of April, Grant booked passage on a French steamer leaving Marseilles for Alexandria. In a week the Grant party, which now included their son Colonel Frederick Grant, reached Alexandria, where they caught a train that carried them across the desert toward the Red Sea.

For once Grant thought that he had moved quickly enough to avoid a reception party but he was disappointed. He was met by the military aide to the governor of Bombay and other officials as well as a large crowd awaiting his arrival at the pier. The continuous round of dinners and receptions kept him from seeing the sights of Bombay and from contact with the people of India. The enthusiastic welcome granted to the Civil War hero was interesting, because he was responsible for the economic ruin of Bombay. England had imported most of its cotton from India and Egypt while the American war was going on. When Lee surrendered in April 1865, Bombay collapsed, and before the year was out, not one of the hundred companies that had mushroomed during the war survived.

At Jaipur, the maharajah staged a grand reception, which proved to be an ordeal for Grant, who had to sit next to the gloomy maharajah through an endless sacred dance that lasted for many hours. Grant avoided a tiger or leopard hunt by pleading lack of time, but he did participate in a boar hunt that the maharajah arranged. It was a strange ritual. He was driven in an oxcart within range of the boar; after he had killed it, he was rewarded with two pairs of boar tusks.

When they reached the sacred city of Benares, to Grant's horror he and the others were provided with sedan chairs in which to tour the city. The former President refused to get into the elaborate conveyance, heavily ornamented with gold and brass and carried by four bearers. Instead, he preferred to walk through the narrow alleys lined with shrines and open temples and the stalls of sacred cows. One of the beasts, which walked about freely as they all do, made a dive for the garland of flowers that some well-wisher had draped around Mrs. Grant's neck. A policeman came to the rescue, but he had to wrestle with the cow before he could separate her from her dinner.

The *Richmond*, which was supposed to meet the Grants at Calcutta, was delayed, so plans to visit Ceylon and Madras had to be canceled. However, the king of Siam, who did not want to be bypassed by "General Grant, late President of the United States," sent a letter inviting him to Bangkok. Grant accepted the invitation, and the king sent a steamer with his aide aboard carrying a letter that welcomed "the most eminent citizen of that great nation which has been so friendly to Siam, and so kind and just in all of its intercourse with the nations of the Far East." The party was housed in the Saranrom Castle close to King Chulahlongkorn, who had been educated by an English governess.

The king and Grant met in a magnificent audience hall decorated in the French style. The entrance hall had busts of contemporary rulers, including a dark bronze of General Grant that was a very poor likeness. The two men talked formally, and Grant suggested that the king should send some of his young subjects to America to be educated. Later, at the state dinner, Grant repeated this suggestion and added that he had been away from home for nearly two years and seen many capital and other large cities but nothing interested him more than Siam.[22]

The former President was not surprised that when he reached China, he was immediately asked to explain the United States law restricting Chinese immigration. At Penang, a deputation of Chinese merchants asked that he use his influence to have the law changed. Grant explained that the bill had been passed since he had left the United States, but that it must be understood that the Chinese came to the United States in a different way than the other immigrants. They came as slaves of companies who imported them like merchandise, and surely the Chinese gentlemen must realize that emigration under such circumstances was of no benefit to either party.[23]

Although Grant was honored in Canton by being granted the privilege of a green chair, a highly esteemed color in China, the public was disappointed that "the King of America" was dressed in plain evening clothes instead of diamonds, embroidery, and peacock feathers. Shanghai outdid itself in the effusiveness of its welcome for the former President. One hundred thousand Chinese stood quietly at the landing when the ship arrived, and the night of the General's reception, the sky was alight with colored bursts of fireworks, transparencies, and illuminations. One theme was "Washington, Lincoln and Grant—Three Immortal Americans."

At Peking, Grant met with the regent, Prince Kung (the emperor, his nephew, was seven years old), who sought his advice on a problem that had arisen between China and Japan over the Loochoo (Ryukyu) Islands, situated in the West Pacific Ocean between Formosa and Kyushu Island, Japan. The regent understood that Grant was "merely a private citizen journeying about like others, with no share in the government and no power" as the former President hastened to explain, but he still insisted that his influence at home and among

General Grant Writing His Memoirs. Engraving after a photograph by F. L. Howe, 1885. *Courtesy of the Library of Congress*

Rutherford B. Hayes (standing) at Spiegel Grove with the Hon. William Henry Smith, c. 1888. *Courtesy of the Library of Congress*

Cleveland cartoon, "The Free Silver Controversy in the Democratic Party," by Jacob A. Riis. *Courtesy of the Library of Congress*

Ex-President Harrison's Second Marriage, 1896. *Courtesy of the Library of Congress*

Theodore Roosevelt in
Africa, April 9, 1910.
*Courtesy of the Library
of Congress*

Roosevelt and the Bull
Moose Convention.
Drawn by Clifford Berry-
man, August 1912. *Cour-
tesy of the Library of
Congress*

Chief Justice William Howard Taft.
Courtesy of the Library of Congress

Ex-President Wilson and Mrs. Wilson on Armistice Day, 1921. *Courtesy of the Library of Congress*

Calvin Coolidge.
*Courtesy of the
Library of Congress*

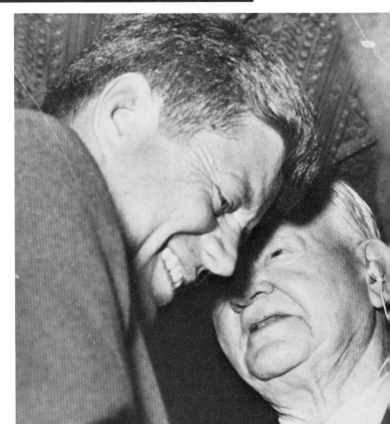

President-Elect John
F. Kennedy and Ex-
President Herbert
Hoover, 1961. *Wide
World Photos*

Former President
Harry S. Truman in
his office in his home,
December 3, 1971.
*Courtesy of the Harry
S. Truman Library*

Ex-President
Eisenhower, Mrs.
Eisenhower, and Prime
Minister Harold
Macmillan on the steps
of Admiralty House,
London, England,
August, 10, 1962.
Wide World Photos

Ex-President Lyndon
Johnson and Democratic
presidential candidate
George McGovern at the
Johnson ranch, 1972.
Wide World Photos

Richard Nixon on the
beach near his San Cle-
mente, California, estate,
July 28, 1975. *Wide
World Photos*

nations was great. Since Grant was to be the guest of the emperor of China, he would be able to present China's views.

The difficulty was that the king of the Loochoo Islands, who had paid tribute to China for generations, was now paying tribute to Japan. Further, it had been learned that the king of Loochoo had been taken to Japan and deposed and a Japanese official had been put in his place. Prince Kung knew of no provocation on the part of Loochoo for such an action, and the Japanese minister in China offered no explanation. Grant said that he knew very little about the matter but promised that while he was in Japan he would discuss it with the authorities; of course, he added, he could have no opinion until he had heard both sides of the case.

China was willing to rest its case with Grant's decision, Prince Kung asserted. Grant answered cautiously that in the Alabama Claims case, for example, which was settled by arbitration, neither side was wholly satisfied. For the world, of course, Grant added, this must become more and more a means of adjusting disputes. What, then, did China want, Grant asked. Japan must restore the captured king, withdraw her troops, and give up her claim to exclusive sovereignty over the island, Kung replied. Grant promised to discuss the matter further with the viceroy, read the documents in the case, and meet with the Japanese authorities. He would be very pleased if he could be instrumental in securing peace. This unusual exchange between the Oriental potentate and the Westerner was considered very significant by the China experts. "General Grant's visit has done more to break down the great wall between her civilization and that of the outer world than has ever been done by diplomacy," one expert said.[24]

Both Chinese immigration to the United States and the Loochoo Islands were discussed by Grant and the viceroy when they met at Tientsin. Grant advised that the Chinese government should halt emigration for five years and stop the slavery system so that emigration would be free as it was from European countries. Concerning Loochoo, the ex-President asked several pertinent questions. How did the islanders feel toward China? What was their racial makeup? The viceroy assured him that the islanders preferred "the Chinese connection." But Japan had made no reply to Chinese remonstrances. Further, the Japanese occupation of the islands was a threat to Chinese commerce and brought Japan within a step of Formosa, which was but a step to mainland China. The viceroy blamed the militant Japanese party that included the princes of Satsuma, but not the mikado, for the aggressive policy toward China. Once again Grant gave assurances that he would confer with Mr. Bingham, the American minister to Japan, study both sides, and try to see the Japanese authorities. The viceroy expressed his gratitude and his hope that when General Grant was President again he would not forget them. Grant replied that he did not wish to resume the heavy burden of the presidency again.

The Grant party traveled on the *Ashuelot* from Peking to the mouth of the river, where the *Richmond* awaited them. All along the route, forts fired salutes, troops paraded, and the boats on the river were decked with flags. Through this scene of oriental splendor, Grant sat quietly on deck, his mind on the next stage of his voyage, just a little disappointed that the very hot weather had forced him to abandon plans to see the Great Wall of China and Tartary. On the way to Japan, the navigator of the *Richmond* managed to find the end of the Great Wall, where it reached the seacoast. Lieutenant Sperry spotted through his glasses "a thick, brown irregular line that crumbled into the sea." A large contingent went by small boats to the shore, accompanied by a sailor with a pot of white paint who inscribed the legend that the *Richmond* had visited the Great Wall. Grant observed that the labor expended on the wall could have built "every railroad in the United States, every canal and highway, and most if not all of our cities."[25]

Nagasaki was the first Japanese port of call, and from the moment of the former President's arrival in Japanese waters, it was the government's intention that he would be the nation's guest. At the landing the steps were covered with red fabric, and Grant passed through an aisle of troops to a rickshaw that waited to draw him to his residence. All along the route, which was hung with American and Japanese flags and had arches of green boughs and flowers across the road, the people stood and bowed as the General passed. For six days there were feasts and dances and fireworks displays that lit up the city at night. Before departing, General and Mrs. Grant each planted a tree in Nagasaki Park to commemorate their visit.

After a brilliant reception in Tokyo, Grant was conducted in the emperor's private carriage to the emperor's summer palace. It was a simple and tasteful building with wood ceilings, walls decorated with natural scenery, and sparse but elegant furniture. The palace grounds were spacious and landscaped to give wide vistas, because the emperor seldom went outside of the walls.

The formal presentation to the emperor was scheduled for July 4, selected by the mikado as the most suitable for his audience with General Grant. The three Grants, some naval friends, and Mr. Bingham made up the American party. Waiting for them was the Japanese cabinet including the prime minister, who were to accompany the Americans into the throne room. Mrs. Grant looked elegant in a mauve silk gown made by Worth, demitrained and trimmed with beautiful Brussels lace. Her hat was a charming cluster of flowers and lace. At the far end of the room, the emperor stood with the empress. He was a young, slender man of medium height with a striking face and a Hapsburg mouth, black-haired with a black mustache and beard. The empress wore a court robe of ruby velvet over a white silk skirt. Her hair was in wide plaits arranged in a bow on the back of her head, and on her forehead was an aigrette resembling a peacock feather. The emperor shook hands with the former President, a gesture that had never been seen before in the history of the Japanese monarchy. They then exchanged short, formal speeches of greeting. "While holding the high office of President of the United States, you extended toward our countrymen especial kindness and courtesy," the emperor said through the noble lord who read his speech. Grant answered: "America is your next neighbor, and will always give Japan sympathy and support in their efforts to advance. I again thank your majesty for your hospitality."[26]

After reviewing the emperor's troops, on a later date, Grant and the mikado met in a little summerhouse on a lake for a personal talk. In the two-hour conversation, Grant gave his opinions freely; he was entirely at ease with the emperor of Japan, whose subjects regarded him as a god, who had no family name because his ancestry was eternal, and who was never photographed because his people were not allowed to look at his face. With candor, Grant advocated an elective assembly for Japan, with gradually increasing power and an expanding electorate as a first step toward representative government. "Every nation should control its own commerce and she is entitled to all the profit that can be derived," Grant said. The United States wanted complete independence for Japan, and therefore she should avoid incurring debts to Europe. He pointed to Egypt, which had fallen so heavily in debt that her creditors had made her dependent on them.

After these preliminaries, the ex-President opened up the subject of the Loochoo Islands. He explained that he realized that his was not a proper diplomatic channel, but he could not refuse China's plea to broach the subject in the name of peace. China and Japan should both make sacrifices to settle disputes between them, he advised, and become allies so that they could both become independent countries. War between them would surely bring in foreign nations, "who would in the end suit themselves." The emperor took the "American Mikado's" advice with good grace and arranged further discussions of the matter with his ministers.

Grant sincerely felt that European treatment of the East was disgraceful. He wrote to Badeau that he was struck by the heartlessness of nations as well as individuals. "But a day of retribution is sure to come," he predicted. "These people [Japan] are becoming strong and China is sure to do so also."[27]

For two months the Grants and their party enjoyed the emperor's hospitality. Other monarchs had been courteous and generous, but no one had lavished such splendid care as the mikado. Grant had been made to feel that his advice had political significance and influence, and when the time for the farewell audience arrived, the ex-President wrote out his speech carefully so as to say exactly what he felt to his imperial host. "I now take my leave without expectation of ever again having the opportunity of visiting Japan," he said sadly. The emperor, whose speech was instantaneously translated into English, answered that he had enjoyed their "very pleasant and personal acquaintance" and was pleased with the strengthening of friendly ties that the visit had achieved.

After a series of farewell ceremonies, the Grants embarked on the *City of Tokio* in Yokohama harbor. A Japanese man-of-war, the same one that had met the party at Nagasaki upon their arrival, kept the steamer company for an hour. As they parted, the warship fired a twenty-one-gun salute while the Japanese sailors climbed on the rigging to cheer their departing American friend. The steamer answered by tooting her steam whistle. Japan was the favorite part of the former President's travels. China was pleasant, he said, but he wouldn't want to go there again. However, Japan was a beautiful country with charming people, and, he noted, "My reception has been the most extravagant I have ever known, or even read of."[28]

General Grant was equaled as a traveler by only one other ex-President, and that was the naturalist-explorer Theodore Roosevelt. As soon as the Colonel's White House stint was over, he started to consider his options. "Of course I would like to have stayed on as President—any strong man would have liked to continue to be President," he confessed to "Springy" (Cecil Arthur Spring Rice). But he was certainly not ready to settle down at Sagamore Hill a fifty-year-old has-been. Under the auspices of the Smithsonian Institution, he headed a scientific expedition to Africa to collect flora and fauna, particularly big game. Kermit Roosevelt, a freshman at Harvard, eagerly accepted the opportunity to accompany his father, along with three professional naturalists—Lt. Col. Edgar A. Mearns, Edward Heller, and Alden Loring. They would be joined abroad by R. J. Cunninghame and Leslie Tarleton, two famous hunters.

The pier at Hoboken was filled with frenzied crowds who wanted to see the ex-President, dressed in a khaki uniform with a colonel's insignia and carrying his famous black slouch hat, before he embarked on the *Hamburg*. President William Howard Taft sent Archie Butt, his military aide, to represent him and to bring his farewell present. It was a gold ruler with a pencil at one end that was inscribed "Theodore Roosevelt from William Howard Taft, Goodbye—Good Luck—and a safe return." Accompanying it and an autographed picture of the President was a long emotional letter that indicated one of the reasons that TR thought it best to go away. "I want you to know that I do nothing in the Executive office without considering what you would do under the same circumstances and without having, in a sense, a mental talk with you over the pros and cons of the situation," the successor to the Roosevelt throne wrote. "I have not the facility for educating the public as you had . . . I am under obligation to see to it that your judgment in selecting me as your successor and in bringing about the succession shall be vindicated."[29]

Roosevelt was neither embarrassed nor surprised at the tone of the letter. "Am deeply touched by your gift and even more by your letter. Everything will surely turn out all right, old man," he telegraphed. Two hours later, he sent another telegram: "Greatly appreciate your greetings and the autographed picture which hangs in my stateroom."[30] There are records of the telegrams plus Archie Butt's letter to his sister-in-law Clara saying that he had seen Taft to tell him how much the former President appreciated his gift and messages. Yet either the President did not receive the telegrams or was dissatisfied with them, because there were serious repercussions later.

The ship, which left Hoboken on March 23, 1909, took six days to reach the Azores. TR was restless and homesick for his wife, as he expected to be, but he had resolved to treat himself to this last great adventure. Edith Roosevelt told Archie Butt that the day her husband left for Africa was one of the most dreadful in her life. She had been calm in front of her husband and son, but, as Kermit sensed, "her heart was almost broken."

From Naples, where the *Hamburg* deposited them, the Roosevelt party embarked on a German ship for Mombasa in British East Africa.* The German kaiser sent flowers to TR and a telegram wishing him luck in the field. En route, the ship stopped at Messina, the scene of an earthquake and tidal wave that had occurred several months earlier and caused terrible damage. The king of Italy, who was there on a battleship surveying the rather ineffective efforts to rebuild the city and relieve the people, sent for Roosevelt to come aboard his ship, which he did. TR was pleased to observe that a small group of American naval people who were helping had accomplished more than the Italians themselves and all the other Europeans combined.

Mombasa was only the jumping-off place for Roosevelt's journey "through the Pleistocene," his title for the first leg of the African adventure. Here the enormous retinue of native bearers and porters gathered. Once the animals were killed (and the specimens sought were to include such large beasts as elephant and rhinoceros), they would have to be skinned, their hides cured, and the bones cleaned and packed immediately. The meat of the animals would be used to feed the members of the expedition.

Roosevelt traveled with his own tent with bath and about a dozen pairs of pince-nez eyeglasses, because his eyesight was very poor. His slouch hat was replaced by a white sun helmet, and he wore heavy hobnailed boots, a khaki shirt, and khaki trousers buttoned tightly at the ankles. Included with the weaponry was an elephant gun presented to him while he was still in the White House by some English zoologists and sportsmen in recognition of his services "on behalf of the preservation of the species" in founding national parks and forest reserves.

Most unusual of all the impedimenta was Roosevelt's pigskin library, which had been given to him by his sister, Corinne. This was a selection of books, bound in pigskin for durability, that was carried in a light aluminum and oil cloth case. It weighed about sixty pounds, or a load for one porter. The original pigskin library con-

_____
* At present the independent republic of Kenya.

tained a selection of classics, histories, and novels. The Bible, Dante, Shakespeare, Spencer, and Milton were included along with Keats, Shelley, and Browning. American writers were represented by Emerson, Longfellow, Poe, Mark Twain, Cooper, Bret Harte, and Oliver Wendell Holmes. There were five novels of Sir Walter Scott, two each of Dickens and Thackeray. Bunyan's *Pilgrim's Progress* traveled with Euripides's *Hippolytus*, the *Chanson de Roland*, and the *Nibelungenlied*. Five books of George Borrow went along, including his travels in Spain as an agent of the Bible Society and his works on gypsy life. Roosevelt explained that this selection did not necessarily represent his favorite books but, rather, those that he wanted on that particular trip.

The newspaper fraternity considered Roosevelt prime copy and were disappointed that they were banned from the expedition. An exception was made for Francis W. Dawson of the United Press, who acted as editor for the Scribner articles TR had contracted to write. He received the weekly scrawled messages that came from the Roosevelt camp by native runner, then relayed the news to the waiting outside world, and returned the runner with messages for the Colonel.

Roosevelt started from the Kapiti Plains station on April 24 and moved eastward, hunting and killing zebra, hartebeest, wildebeest, impala, steinbok, and dik-dik. Into the record went a description of the contents of the slain animals' stomachs and the number of bullets it took to kill them. But as the former President pointed out, he killed only for science and food, not for sport. "Death by violence, death by cold, death by starvation—these are the normal endings of the stately and beautiful creatures of the wilderness," he wrote. Only sentimentalists ignored nature's mercilessness.[31] One of the expedition's major aims was to bag big game, and in the first five weeks over seventy skins, including twenty-two species from dik-dik to rhinoceros, were prepared and sent back to the Smithsonian.

TR grew attached to his gun bearers and other native helpers but referred to them as "boys" while he enjoyed the title of "bwana Makuba" (great master, or chief). He approved of the work of the American Industrial Mission, which regarded industrial training as the foundation stone to raising "ethical and moral standards" among the natives. East Africa, Roosevelt concluded, would be a suitable country for white settlement as well as an ideal playground for sportsmen and travelers.[32]

Kermit was the expedition's photographer. His father was proud of his work, particularly one picture of a hippo charging at TR with his mouth open. Roosevelt asked his Scribner editor to include the photo in his article. "I hope Kermit's photos of wild wildebeests will be used . . . from the zoological standpoint they are the most important of all," the former President noted.[33]

Hunting elephant entailed more hardship and fatigue than any other kind of hunting in Africa, Roosevelt observed. He had a close call when he shot a big bull elephant with good ivory, hitting the beast's small brain with his second bullet so that he came crashing to the ground. But at that moment, before he could reload, another great bull charged out at him from the bushes. The animal was so close, the Colonel said, that he could have touched his trunk. The Colonel leaped to one side, threw out his empty shells and loaded his rifle. Meanwhile, Cunninghame fired twice, hitting the elephant, who stopped, turned, and fled into the forest with one shrill trumpet. The first elephant was dead on the ground. "I felt proud indeed as I stood by the immense bulk of the slain monster and put my hand on the ivory," Roosevelt wrote.

After keeping a rendezvous with the Carl Akeleys, the husband and wife naturalist and big-game hunter team, that had been planned the year before at a White House luncheon, Roosevelt was ready for the next lap of his safari. A reduced party traveled by rail to Port Florence on Lake Victoria and then by ship across the lake to Entebbe, the headquarters of the British in Uganda. Though the native population was now mostly Christianized, the ex-President felt that Uganda could never be white man's country. Therefore the chief task of the British should be to train the natives to develop industry and self-government.

On Christmas Day, the expendition was on the march since, TR said wistfully, "there is not much use in trying to celebrate Christmas unless there are small folks to hang up their stockings on Christmas Eve." At each camp along the trek, the head chief of the district would have gifts waiting for the American chief, such as eggs, chickens, sheep, a bullock, bananas, and pineapples. The chief himself would appear in flowing robes, dignified and courteous, but usually, the Colonel noted, too servile. Roosevelt would invite the chief to tea, where he would always enjoy bread and jam. He would then be presented with a return gift.

On January 5, the party reached the shore of Lake Albert after a 160-mile trek from Lake Victoria. From there the expedition boarded boats to go down the Nile to the wild, uninhabited Lado country to hunt the white rhinoceros and supply the Smithsonian and the Museum of Natural History with promised specimens. The beast being sought was the square-mouthed rhinoceros, erroneously called white, larger than the familiar African variety, with a hump over its withers and a large misshapen head.

Success in meeting the grass-eating rhinoceros was almost immediate. Following the trail of its footprints, the Roosevelt party sighted a rhinoceros asleep near the foot of a tree, "looking like an enormous pig." The ex-President fired at it, knocking it off its feet. It fell over with a squeal not ten yards from where it had been resting. Shortly after, Roosevelt killed a calf, possibly the cow's child, and Kermit got a bull, thus completing the group for the Smithsonian. To celebrate the last day on the Lado, the Roosevelts shot a dozen bucks to provide a feast for the porters and sailors. The next morning, the members of the expedition boarded the boats and floated down the Nile to Nimule, where they were greeted by the English officials and several elephant hunters.

On February 7, a regrouped safari set out on a ten-day march to Gondokoro (now Juba),* "a barren and thirsty land" where the heat at noon was 112 degrees in the shade and the ground burned the porters' feet so that the day's march had to begin at 3:00 A.M. All the members of the party except the two Roosevelts had fever and dysentery by the time they reached Gondokoro. They then crossed into Belgian territory to hunt the giant eland. These large, handsome, little-known African antelopes were very elusive. "It took me three days before I got my eland," Roosevelt recorded. The skinners had to work particularly hard in that climate to save the eland skins. TR enjoyed enormously a chant that one of the natives improvised at a feast that ended the hunt. He sang of "Bwana Makuba," who had come from his own far country and killed a giant eland.

The last of February, the Roosevelt expedition started down the Nile, stopping along the way to say farewell to friends. The hunting was not quite over; some species, such as the white-eared kob and the handsome saddle-marked antelope, had not been obtained. However, they were successful in bagging some specimens along the way. As they traveled down the Nile with the wind blowing hard and

* A town on the White Nile in Sudan.

steadily in their faces, the health of all the companions improved so that by March 14, 1910, when the expedition reached Khartoum, everyone was well. There was a sad parting from "our faithful black followers," Roosevelt said, but it had been an interesting and happy year. Now it was time to be with his own people and turn toward home.[34]

Mrs. Roosevelt and Ethel joined TR and Kermit at Khartoum, and in a few days Lawrence Abbott arrived to be the Colonel's volunteer secretary. It was obvious that the former President would not be allowed to roam over Europe as an ordinary traveler. Invitations from the great and near great had been flooding into Khartoum. As he said at the end of his tour, while staying at the Dorchester House in London: "Confound these kings; will they never leave me alone."[35]

Theodore Roosevelt's volatile personality fascinated his European hosts. He was a refreshing combination of high-mindedness, energy, a broad knowledge of many subjects, experience in politics, and an almost boyish enthusiasm. His tour of Europe was "a missionary journey in behalf of political and social morality, yet full of the gayety and vivacity of life," Lawrence Abbott said.[36] Kings and commoners enjoyed talking to him and responded to his personal magnetism.

Even before the European travels began, there was an awkward difficulty over an invitation from the German kaiser. TR was invited to stay at the German monarch's palace, but Mrs. Roosevelt was excluded. "I will not go to stay with anyone while Mrs. Roosevelt is with me and is not asked," he wrote to David Jayne Hill, the American minister to Germany. Tell His Majesty, TR said, that one of the things "I most desired in coming abroad was to meet him." However, under the circumstances, he must stay at the embassy with his wife.[37] Breaking royal tradition, the kaiser asked Mrs. Roosevelt to stay at the palace.

A serious diplomatic tangle with the Vatican was not so easily resolved. The "elegant row" that developed over the former President's proposed visit to Pope Pius X started when Merry del Val, the pope's secretary of state, informed Ambassador Leishman that Roosevelt's audience could take place only if he refrained from seeing the Methodists who were, at the time, agitating in Vatican City. Respectfully but firmly, TR responded that "it would be a real pleasure to me to be presented to the Holy Father, for whom I entertain a high respect both personally and as the head of a great Church," but he could not accept any conditions.[38]

An attempt to intervene was made by John C. O'Laughlin, a young newspaperman who had attached himself to the Roosevelt staff as a secretary, but his talk with del Val was fruitless. TR fumed that del Val was a "bigoted reactionary" who had been a "worthy but narrowly limited parish priest" and now had Pope Pius under his control. Consequently, the presentation did not take place and Roosevelt visited neither the pope nor the Methodists. When the Methodist missionaries indiscreetly publicized their triumph by issuing "an address of exultation," the Colonel canceled his meeting with them, thus declaring his independence from the Roman Catholic Church and its powerful Protestant rival. Had he been a candidate, Roosevelt confided to Henry Cabot Lodge, he would have had to regard his actions as "gravely compromising" his usefulness, but since he never expected to be a candidate again, he felt that he had rendered "a small service to the cause of right-thinking in America." He did, however, make his correspondence with the Vatican public and published a statement in the *Outlook*. "Among my best and closest friends are many Catholics," he wrote. "I most earnestly hope that the incident will be treated in a matter-of-course way, as merely personal."[39]

There were several indications during Roosevelt's European trip that Catholic dignitaries regretted the papal incident. In Vienna, the papal nuncio appeared at the ex-President's reception in official ecclesiastical robes and later received him at his palace. The newspapers discussed the possibility that the nuncio would be disciplined by the Vatican, but nothing happened. At Porto Maurizio, where the Roosevelts were visiting Emily Carow, Mrs. Roosevelt's sister, TR lunched with Antonio Fogazzaro, author of *The Saint*, a book that had been denounced by the Church as heretical. The author had just been taken back into the faith and had been given permission by his bishop to visit the former President. However, although Roosevelt received cables supporting his action from many American Catholic priests, he also learned that Archbishop O'Connell of Boston and Bishop James McFowle of New York were heading an attack against him. "I will give them a bellyfull," he promised upon getting the information, for he sincerely believed that the majority of the American Catholics supported him.[40]

President Taft, who had been criticized during the campaign of

1908 for supposed sympathy toward the Catholic Church, was completely supportive of his predecessor. "I do not see how Roosevelt could have done other than he did," he told Archie Butt. Cardinal Gibbons met with Taft for about half an hour at this time, which caused much press interest. When asked if the Vatican incident had been discussed, Taft answered that Roosevelt would have "every reason to feel aggrieved" if any public comment had been made. The reporters then told Taft that the cardinal had told them officially that the Vatican matter had been discussed, so they would have to use the story. Taft then demanded that his denial be printed at the same time and he dictated a flat contradiction to Gibbons's statement.[41]

Theodore Roosevelt's whirlwind tour through Europe's palaces read like a roster of ruling monarchs. Clearly, royalty liked him and valued his opinions. TR enjoyed them, too, but with something of the curiosity that a naturalist reserves for a rare and vanishing species. In various letters and conversations, he expounded and explained their foibles, revealing that he had no illusions about royalty. During the Progressive campaign of 1912, he was accused of wanting to be the king of America. "I know kings and I don't," he answered. A king, he said, is a cross between a vice-president and a leader of the Four Hundred. He had been vice-president and knew how hollow an honor that was, and he had no desire to be the leader of society. Roosevelt believed that it was not that the various monarchs wanted to see him so much as that they did not want him to see other rulers and pass them by. The monarchs, who were all related, corresponded frequently with each other. There was constant competition among them. Regarding himself as a sort of American ambassador, TR dutifully visited all those who invited him except the czar of Russia. Thankful that he could decline Nicholas's invitation because of previous commitments, Roosevelt wrote that he would hate to go to Russia as a guest of the ruling authorities, for that would keep him from speaking out in behalf of Finland, the persecuted Russian Jews, and the oppressed Russian liberals.[42]

Roosevelt's favorite among the crowned heads was Victor Emmanuel III, the king of Italy. He was an agreeable man, TR wrote, who sympathized with many of the purposes and doctrines of the socialists and who was training his son so that he could be the first president of the Italian Republic. He was the strongest man in Europe, the ex-President told Taft, with the greatest insight into his nation's problems, but he suffered from lack of confidence because of his size. "If I were in his place, I would not care a hang about my height," the Colonel asserted.[43]

The one monarch Roosevelt disliked was Queen Wilhelmina of Holland, who, he commented, was excessively unattractive and commonplace, conceited and bad-tempered, and reminded him of "a puffed-up wife of some leading grocer" in a small town. Furthermore, she henpecked her husband. The prince, who had been to Ceylon, wanted to show the former President his hunting trophies. "Take Mr. Roosevelt into your room," the queen commanded. He did not hear and turned around to ask her what she had said. "I said, *take Mr. Roosevelt into your own room*," the queen snapped, her face red with anger. The prince escorted Roosevelt into the room in gloomy silence. "I am glad your daughter, the little princess, seems so well," TR said to change the subject. "Yes, I hope she has a brother; otherwise I pity the man who marries her," he answered with awful frankness.[44]

At Christiania (now Oslo), where he was the guest of King Haakon and Queen Maud at the royal palace, Roosevelt delivered his long-delayed Nobel Prize speech, thus fulfilling the obligation he had incurred when he accepted the prize for his work in settling the Russo-Japanese War. He had been told that no American was being considered for a Nobel Prize because he had not yet given his speech.

The German press had been carrying stories that Roosevelt planned to lecture the kaiser on peace and disarmament, which, they said, would be in bad taste for a visiting private citizen. The Colonel blamed the German Foreign Office for planting the stories, but he was secretly relieved, because it gave him an excuse not to push the peace plan that Andrew Carnegie and others had urged him to broach to the German emperor. Instead, TR restricted his peace proposals to those he had made in his Nobel Address—arbitration treaties, armament limitations, particularly in the field of naval armaments, a "League of Peace" to be governed by the world powers, and an international court.

Roosevelt met the kaiser at Potsdam. Later, when he visited Taft at the White House, TR gave his opinion on Wilhelm to a very interested President. "I found him vain as a peacock," TR said. "He would rather ride at the head of a procession than govern an empire." As to whether he contemplated war with England, Roosevelt said he asked him that point-blank. The German's response was that there was nothing further from his mind or that of the German people.

He loved England next to Germany and was hurt that the English people were unkind to him when he visited there. The Colonel was not deceived by the kaiser's confidences. He saw no hope for the universal peace plan or naval disarmament. Only bankruptcy would stop Germany, he warned. Taft tried to persuade TR to be the head of the next peace commission, but was turned down. "I would not feel justified in throwing so much of myself away, for that is what it would amount to," he said.[45]

The emperor liked Roosevelt and showed him a number of unprecedented courtesies. He invited him to review German troop maneuvers during which they both sat on horseback for five hours, and the kaiser "talked steadily." The ex-President wore a khaki riding suit and his black slouch hat, and as the troops marched by, being only a civilian, he did not salute but raised his hat. He was the only private citizen ever to review German troops, Kaiser Wilhelm assured "mein freund," a form of address that constituted an unusual intimacy on the part of the monarch.

While Roosevelt was in Stockholm, King Edward VII of England died and Taft appointed the former President a special ambassador to represent him at the funeral. "I wonder whether Kaiser Theodorus will like being chief mourner to his great and good friend?" Henry Adams wrote. Archie Butt observed that with TR and the kaiser present, it would be a wonder if the poor corpse got a passing thought. There was some substance to their comments, for on May 15, 1910, the first page of the London *Daily Mail* gave almost as much space to the ex-President's arrival as it did to the dead king's funeral arrangements.

Because of TR's official capacity, the Roosevelts could not stay with the Arthur Lees as planned but had to go to the Dorchester House, the residence of Whitelaw Reid, the American ambassador. Alice Longworth joined the family there, and after fourteen months of separation, the reunited Roosevelts sat together far into the night exchanging news.

At the "veritable wake" given by King George V in Buckingham Palace the night before the funeral, Roosevelt and French Minister of Foreign Affairs Stephen Pichon were the only ones who were not either sovereigns or of royal blood. The assorted royalties were very interested in TR's opinions and sought him out constantly throughout the evening. Ferdinand I, the Bulgarian king, thanked him for what he had done for Bulgarians. The German kaiser, who was angry with Ferdinand because he had sided with the Austrians in a quarrel over protocol that had erupted on the way to the funeral, interrupted the conversation. "Roosevelt, my friend, I want to introduce you to the King of Spain; *he* is worth talking to," the German said rudely. Then Alfonso XIII immediately thanked TR for his consideration toward Spain while he was President. He admired his military career, the Spaniard told Roosevelt, "though I am sorry that your honors have been won at the expense of my countrymen." The Colonel answered with praise for the gallantry of the Spanish soldier in battle, "although frankly I cannot speak as highly of their leadership." The king then complimented Roosevelt on his position with the Vatican, because, he said, attempted encroachments there had become intolerable. The anarchists were no more "dangerous to my country than are the ultraclericals." The king of Greece, "a nice old boy, but a preposterous character as a King," Roosevelt said, wanted something done for his country about Crete and Thessaly. On a later day, he visited the former President and begged him to say something for Greece against Turkey; he would not be convinced that this was a matter about which Roosevelt could not say anything.

M. Pichon, who was in a constant state of anger about some real or imagined insult, regarded Roosevelt, the only other Republican in the funeral party, as his natural ally. They were scheduled to travel to Windsor in the same carriage. That morning, TR found Pichon, so furious that he looked like a gargoyle, standing outside their magnificent carriage complaining vociferously that they did not have a glass coach like those for the royalties. The Colonel, who said he had never heard of a glass coach except in "Cinderella," could not get upset about it or fret, as Pichon did that "ces Chinois" were placed ahead of them in the procession. The Frenchman's fury peaked when he discovered that a shy, inoffensive-looking, somewhat intimidated Persian prince was to ride with them. When the coach drove up, Pichon leaped in to make sure that "ce Perse" did not get the seat of honor. En route to the funeral, Pichon sputtered that they were behind the coaches of all sorts of little royalties, even the king of Portugal. To TR's sensible observation that to make a fuss about such things only showed a lack of self-confidence, Pichon answered that in Europe these things were important. With some effort, Roosevelt persuaded the Frenchman to wait and see how they were treated at lunch at Windsor Castle. Fortunately, the ex-

President was seated at the king's table and a slightly mollified Pichon was observed seated at the queen's table.[46]

Roosevelt made the most controversial speech of his European tour at the Guildhall in London. It was based on a discussion he had had with British officials while at Khartoum. Just prior to TR's arrival in the city, the Coptic prince, Boutros Pasha, had been assassinated by a member of the Egyptian Nationalist party, an extremist group that advocated immediate freedom from British rule. At a dinner, given for the Colonel at the governor's palace, he was asked what he would do with the assassin. Without hesitation, Roosevelt answered that he would take him out and shoot him so that, if the vacillating Home Office advised waiting before taking action, he could wire back: "Can't wait; the assassin has been tried and shot." The home government could then recall or impeach him, but *"that assassin would have received his just desserts."*

Most of the British officers and officials at the table had been delighted with Colonel Roosevelt's strong stand and had begged him to tell the people in London how important a decisive approach to Egypt was. He had agreed to do so and during his European travels worked on the speech. Before it was delivered, the former President showed it to Sir Edward Grey, Lord Cromer, Mr. Asquith, and, probably, Lord Kitchener and sought and accepted suggestions for changes.

At the Guildhall, the lord and lady mayoress of London presided over the city aldermen, dressed in their red robes, and the many distinguished guests. Confident that his cause was just, TR delivered his address, which supported the colonial administration of Egypt and criticized the home government for its "weakness, timidity, and sentimentality" in handling the fanatical Egyptian Nationalist party. With astonishing boldness, he told the gathering that England either had the right to be in Egypt or it did not. "If you do not wish to establish and keep order there, why then, by all means get out of Egypt." But if England, as he hoped, wanted to stay in Egypt, "it is your first duty to keep order, and . . . to punish murder. . . . Some nation must govern Egypt. I hope and believe that you will decide that it is your duty to be that nation."[47]

The Conservative press agreed with Roosevelt's advice. The address "A Plain Talk on Egypt" was tonic, the *Daily Telegraph* said, accepting his "govern or go" position. "We have no intention of going," the paper said. The London *Spectator* called the speech "one of the greatest compliments ever paid to a people by a statesman from another country." In a personal letter, an anonymous writer addressed the ex-President as "His Excellency Govern-or-Go Roosevelt." The Liberal press was less complimentary, and some critics felt that the speech was an abuse of England's hospitality.

Both Oxford and Cambridge universities bestowed honors on Roosevelt. At Cambridge he was given an honorary LL.D. and was received with enthusiasm by the students. As soon as the degree was bestowed, a teddy bear was lowered from the ceiling to the amused delight of the recipient. At Oxford, Roosevelt received an honorary degree and delivered the Romanes lecture which he called "The World's Development: Biological Analogies of History."

Just twenty-four hours before he was to leave from Southampton, TR went off with Sir Edward Grey. In a delightful article that he wrote for the *Outlook*, the ex-President explained his disappearance. He said that he knew a great deal about English birds from books—Shakespeare and Shelley's lark, Milton and Keats's nightingale, and Jenny Wren and Cock Robin of the nursery books—but he had never seen and heard them in real life. Sir Edward Grey agreed to be his guide, and for several hours the two statesmen tramped through the valley of the Itchen, then drove to the New Forest and wandered there. At the end of their walk, they listed the birds they had seen and heard. After this bucolic interlude, Roosevelt sailed back to the reality of waiting crowds and nervous politicians and the wedding of Theodore, Jr., to Eleanor Alexander.

The final adventure was still to come for the intrepid ex-President. Like a prima donna who must give just one more last performance, TR was not finished with courting danger and hardship. After delivering speeches on such Rooseveltian subjects as "Character and Civilization," "American Ideals," and "The Democratic Movement in a Republic" at the invitation of the governments of Argentina and Brazil, he would travel north through the center of the continent to the Amazon valley. At first the expedition was planned as another collecting trip for New York's Museum of Natural History, but Lauro Müller, Brazil's minister of foreign affairs, had a better idea. He saw the possibility of using the ex-President's prestige and popularity to promote an interest in his country abroad. He proposed that the government of Brazil mount an expedition to be jointly led by Roosevelt and Colonel Candido M. da S. Rondon, an explorer for the Brazilian Telegraphic Commission, who knew the Amazon Basin.

Rondon had discovered the headwaters of an unmapped river which he named Rio da Duvida ("River of Doubt"), and the purpose of this Expedicao Scientifica Roosevelt-Rondon would be to descend this river.

"Of course this is a feat worth doing, and I accepted," TR wrote to William Allen White. The American team of naturalists who were scheduled to go with the Colonel had the option of forgoing the trip into the unknown, but Father John A. Zahm, Frank Harper, Leo Miller, and George K. Cherrie all accepted eagerly, expecting to get worthwhile specimens for the museum in this undiscovered country.

At the end of November 1913, Roosevelt said good-bye to his wife and niece Margaret, who had traveled with him during the speech-making part of his South American trip, and with Kermit, set out to face the wilderness again. Kermit, now engaged to Belle Willard, considered this his final fling as a bachelor. His father had some misgivings about taking the young man along, but Kermit would not get married in his father's absence and "moreover felt that this semi-exploration business was exactly in his line." On his part, TR was fully aware of the probable discomforts and certain dangers that he was about to face. He predicted mosquitoes and insect pests, fever and dysentery, but was certain that Colonel Rondon, his full-blooded Indian co-explorer, would make the trip "a success of note." He told Henry Cabot Lodge, "There may be unpleasant surprises for us when we get over the ridge and come down some affluent of the Amazon," yet he "was inclined to think we shall come through all right."[48]

On December 12, Roosevelt met Colonel Rondon on the Brazilian boundary, and for the next month the expedition hunted and collected specimens from Corumbá to Tapirapoan. On Christmas, the party was aboard the river boat *Nyoac*, chugging up the upper Paraguay, jammed in with dogs, rifles, partially cured skins, and provisions and supplies of all kinds including photography equipment, tools, and ammunition. Whenever they reached a settlement of any size, there was a reception ready for the ex-President, with flags and bands and serenades.

The expedition collected some 250 mammals, including the jaguar, giant anteater, and marsh deer, as well as several species of tapir and bush deer and a thousand birds. Roosevelt suggested in a letter to Frank Chapman that the Museum of Natural History mount the three white-lipped peccaries that he and Colonel Rondon had shot and give them both credit, a gesture that he felt would be appreciated by the government of Brazil.

At Tapirapoan, the headquarters of the Brazilian Telegraphic Commission, pack mules and pack oxen were waiting for the next lap of the trip, an overland safari. The Brazilian government had a gift waiting for the Colonel, a handsome silver-mounted saddle and bridle, which pleased Roosevelt but, he noted, was an incongruous contrast to his rough and shabby clothes.

Roosevelt planned to write a book about his trek through the Brazilian wilderness, so after breakfast each morning, before leaving camp, he would sit down somewhere and write until the mules were ready. Then he would put his writing materials in his duffel bag and start the day's journey. He said: "The true wilderness wanderer . . . must be a man of action as well as of observation. He must have the heart and the body to do and to endure, no less than the eye to see and the brain to note and record."[49]

In February the company entered a very wild area, the land of the Nhambiquara Indians, who were hostile and naked. Another hazard in the area was the big nocturnal spiders, but most serious was the scarcity of fodder for the animals. The pack animals grew so weak that they could carry only light loads. All luxuries had to be discarded. The torment from insect pests was constant. The many different small flies did not hurt when they bit but left an itching scar. Head nets and gloves were some protection, although the stifling heat made them uncomfortable; at night, mosquito netting was essential. Carnivorous foraging ants just missed destroying the camp; their column marched between the kitchen tent and the sleeping tents in a stream that took several hours to pass by.

When the expedition reached its destination, the headwaters of the River of Doubt, the Roosevelts, Rondon, Lieutenant Lyra, Cherrie, and Dr. Cajazeira, with sixteen paddlers and seven dugout canoes, prepared to make the descent. They had to determine whether the river led to Gy-Parana, the Madeira, or the Tapajós. Provisions for fifty days were taken, only part rations, for they planned to live on the country—fish, game, nuts, and palm tops. Personal luggage was cut down to the minimum, except for a fly to sleep under and a light tent for anyone who got sick. Food, medicine, bedding, and some instruments went along. TR took the last two volumes of Gibbon, the plays of Sophocles, More's *Utopia*, Marcus Aurelius, and

Epictetus. All were armed, but cartridges were not to be used for sport—only for collecting specimens, repelling attack, getting food. "We were about to go into the unknown, and no one could say what it held."[50]

On February 27, after midday, the expedition started down the River of Doubt; Roosevelt, the doctor, and Cherrie were in the largest canoe with three paddlers. It pleased the ex-President to note that no civilized man, no white man, had ever seen the country they were about to explore. From the start the voyage was filled with hardships, fatigue, and danger. Huge flies bit them, drawing blood and leaving scars for weeks. Roosevelt did his writing in a head net and gauntlet to get some protection. The necessity for portaging around the rapids made constant toil necessary. At the Navaite Rapids, it took two and a half days of incessant labor before it was possible to move on. Day after day they descended the river, twisting, portaging when necessary, their hands and faces swollen with bites, watching the tall rubber trees in the forest on either side of the river. Roosevelt was somewhat comforted by Kermit's copy of the *Oxford Book of French Verse*.

All through March the party made slow progress. Two of the old canoes were waterlogged and one of them broke in rapids, so the expedition had to halt while the men hollowed out the hardwood of a big tree with axe and adze to provide a replacement. By this time the food supply was limited. TR, Kermit, and Lieutenant Lyra went hunting, but Roosevelt caught nothing and the others were not much more successful. Now the heavy rains were drenching them and their clothes were constantly damp.

The Colonel was grateful that Kermit was with him but worried that some accident would overtake him and he would have the anguish of bringing the bad tidings to the young man's fiancée and to his mother. On March 15 Kermit almost drowned when his canoe tipped over in the rapids. It was a very narrow escape. Simplicio, one of the rowers, was not so fortunate and drowned in a similar mishap. On an expedition such as they were embarked on, TR wrote, "death is one of the accidents that may at any time occur, and narrow escapes from death are too common to be felt as they would be felt elsewhere. We had to continue with our work."[51]

The unknown river that the expedition had been seeking was discovered on March 18 and, to the Colonel's "pleased surprise," christened Rio Roosevelt. He was "much touched" when Colonel Rondon, with all the others present, read the orders of the day, which included the naming of the river. It was now three weeks since the company had started descending the River of Doubt. They had come about 140 kilometers and hoped that the worst obstacles had already been encountered. They were wrong.

A week later the going became even tougher, with many waterfalls slowing their progress. Half of their provisions were gone. If there were still a long distance to go before they reached the rubber plantations, they would have to face a shortage of food. They did not know where they were or how far they had to go. They now sighted low mountains and a gorge about three kilometers long. They were forced to reduce their load drastically, because everything had to be dragged over the rough land. They kept all the food and the fly for the six of them to sleep under. TR took the clothes he was wearing, one set of pajamas, a spare pair of drawers, a spare pair of socks, a half-dozen washcloths, a washkit, a medicine kit, a spare pair of glasses, needle and thread, fly dope, and a purse and letter of credit to be used when they reached civilization. All this went into the bag containing the cot, blankets, mosquito netting, and gauntlets. The others also cut down.

The country was beautiful, but its mountains and rapids promised further hardships and delay. The dwindling food was particularly worrisome, because there seemed to be little life in the woods; tapir and deer tracks were seen, but the voyagers did not dare to take a few days for a hunt that might yield nothing. Miseries small and large beset them. Termites ate the Colonel's boots, extra drawers, and handkerchiefs. The succession of rapids made the *camerados* despondent and sullen. One day a hostile Indian's arrow killed a dog, just missing Colonel Rondon. And since the river was unexplored, there was no way of judging when the recurring canyons of rushing water would give way to calmer water.

All this hardship touched off a tragedy when Julio, a crew member who had been stealing food from the others, killed Paishon, a huge black man in charge of the *camerados*. Everyone feared that Julio would run amok and pick off the others, but he fled into the forest in a panic, hoping to reach some Indian village before he starved to death in the wilderness. The leaders of the expedition decided not to follow Julio, since he could not be executed legally and they were not near enough to civilization to deliver him to the proper authorities. "Whether the murderer lived or died in the wilderness was of no moment compared with the duty of doing everything to secure the safety of the party," TR judged.[52]

Everyone was growing weaker. Kermit had an attack of fever. Lieutenant Lyra and Cherrie suffered from dysentery. While Roosevelt was in the water trying to help with an overturned canoe, he smashed against a sharp stone and got a deep gash in his thigh, the same one that had been injured in 1902 when the carriage in which he had been riding hit a trolley car and hurled him forty feet, injuring the thigh bone, which required surgery and gave him recurrent trouble ever after. The Colonel's wound became infected; the leg swelled and started to drain. An abscess formed, followed by some dysentery and a high fever. The doctor cut open the abscess and inserted a drainage tube—"an added charm being given the operation, and the subsequent dressings, by the enthusiasm with which the piums and boroshudas took part herein," Roosevelt wrote.[53]

Roosevelt in his account said that the worst part of the trip was over by the time his "serious trouble" occurred and that he had only to ride in the canoe, which, he admitted, was not ideal for a sick man, particularly to lie on boxes in the bottom of a small open dugout enduring either the heat of the sun or the drenching rains. Other members of the party in their accounts of the descent of the River of Doubt described vividly the agonies of the delirious ex-President. During the night, when Kermit watched anxiously over his stricken father, he heard him recite poetry such as Coleridge's "In Xanadu did Kubla Khan/A stately pleasure dome decree." But more often his ramblings expressed his fears for the dwindling supplies and his belief that since he could not work, the others should have his food ration.

Both leaders of the expedition had moments of despair on the last terrible lap. Colonel Rondon considered the possibility of leaving the river and striking out overland through the jungle. During one feverish period, the ex-President said that he was a burden to the others and should be left behind or should end his life with the morphine he carried in his medicine bag. But he knew that Kermit would never abandon him in the jungle and he was a most unlikely candidate for suicide. Once lucid, he decided that he had to "come out myself."

On April 5 the expedition reached the first rubber plantation. "It was all child's play compared to what we had now gone through," the Colonel recorded optimistically. Actually, there were two more weeks of difficult downstream canoeing until, on April 27, they arrived at Sao João, the first real settlement since Tapirapoan. From there they traveled by river steamer to Manaus. TR sent a long, triumphant telegram to General Müller, noting briefly the perils and tragedies of the voyage and concluding with its achievement. "We have put on the map a river about 1500 kilometers in length whose upper course until now has been utterly unknown to everyone and whose lower course was known for years to rubbermen but not cartographers." To the Arthur Lees he wrote, "We have put upon the map a river as long as the Rhine or the Elbe." In answer to doubters, TR added, Sir Clement Robert Markham, a former president of the Royal Geographical Society, might doubt his achievement, but to him and others he had to say only that the river was nearly a thousand miles long, it would stay there, and anybody could go and verify it for himself. During their sixty days of travel it was impossible to get down in any way except by the river and "we have the diaries, the photos, and the astronomical observations" to prove it.[54]

A much thinner, weaker Roosevelt arrived in New York on May 19, 1914, via Barbados, where the ship stopped and the ex-President bought fifty books, all of which he read on shipboard. The price that TR paid for the discovery of Rio Roosevelt was, according to William Roscoe Thayer, ten years of his life, which was probably accurate, medically speaking. The injured thigh never healed, was chronically infected, and sometimes brought on severe attacks of infection and fever, as it did on the Colonel's western trip in 1918. The jungle dampness aggravated his chronic rheumatism and reactivated the jungle fever first contracted in Cuba during the Spanish-American War. No doubt TR realized the toll this last adventure had taken on his severely tried body. He admitted to Hiram Johnson in July that he was far from recovered from his Brazilian fever and his throat was in such a condition that it was hard to speak. "I could handle the jungle fever all right, and the Progressive Party all right, but the combination of the two is a trifle beyond me," he said.[55] Nonetheless, it had been a grand adventure.

Harry Truman, on his way to Europe in May 1956, referred to the European trips of his two predecessors who were famous travelers. Grant, he said, toured with an "increasing baggage train of gifts and souvenirs," while Theodore Roosevelt, after his African trip, attended the funeral of Edward VII and "had the time of his life." Truman, who enjoyed great popularity in Europe because of his part in World War II, had no official role. When asked if President Eisenhower requested that he perform any mission on the trip, Truman laughed. "Why should he? I wouldn't be worth a dime to him. I don't know what's going on."[56] Truman's principal reason for traveling abroad was to receive an honorary degree from Oxford University. He also wanted to renew his acquaintance with old friends and visit and dine with a number of kings, queens, and heads of state. It was the ex-President's first trip abroad since leaving office, but he had been overseas with the army during World War I and as President had attended the Potsdam Conference.

The trip was carefully planned to allow for sight-seeing as well as state occasions. The official itinerary specifically stated: "In some places plans have been left vague on purpose to provide as much freedom as possible." However, it was very difficult for Harry Truman to preserve the status of private tourist or to remain silent. As soon as he arrived in France, he announced that he did not trust the Soviet leaders, who, he reminded the press, had broken thirty-two agreements during his first years as President.[57]

The public also refused to ignore the former President. Tourists gathered while he drank a nostalgic cup of coffee at the Café de la Paix, a favorite Parisian oasis for United States servicemen during the First World War. He was not quite up to his famous walks, so exhausting to reporters during the White House years, because he was still using a cane owing to a recent injury to his ankle. The Truman visit to the pope at the Vatican was uneventful and amiable. A source close to the Vatican revealed that the two men agreed that the West must use great circumspection in dealing with the communists. But at Salerno Truman got involved in an unnecessary, somewhat ridiculous exchange over a gratuitous comment. He said that the Battle of Salerno and the Anzio Beach landing during World War II were "utterly unnecessary and planned by some squirrel-headed general." There were easier beaches, he suggested.

American newspapers picked up the comment at once. In Washington, Murray Snyder, Eisenhower's acting press secretary, was asked if there would be any comment on Truman's remark. "I refer you to the squirrels," he answered facetiously and pointed to squirrels on the White House lawn. At a press conference, the President defended Anzio, calling it a "holding operation." In his book *Crusade in Europe*, General Eisenhower had said that a landing at Anzio, a hundred miles beyond the front lines, was risky and possibly costly in terms of troops. But, Eisenhower continued, Churchill was determined to carry out the operation. In the end, Ike concluded, "the Anzio operation paid off handsomely."[58]

Back in Naples, Truman tried to deny his awkward statement about "squirrel-headed generals" by explaining that he had been listening to some people who had been there. "I am sorry about it," he said, and hoped it would be cleared up. A reporter who had been accompanying the party asserted that Truman had been quoted correctly, so the matter did not drop. In Rome the ex-President tried again to quiet the ruffled waters by saying that, in his considered opinion, the landings at Salerno were made to win the war and that that objective had been attained.[59] For the rest of the trip Truman exercised greater care, although, as usual, he had to have the last word. The newsmen had blown up the Salerno incident, he protested. He would take care of it when he returned from Europe.

Truman's good intentions to avoid comment on European events past or present lasted only to Salzburg, Austria, where he received a traffic-stopping ovation from five hundred admirers. At first he refused to make a statement to the press on the resignation of Molotov as Soviet foreign minister, but the next day he pronounced that Molotov's resignation would make no change in Soviet policy. "I don't trust them if you want the facts," he said.[60]

On June 9, still using a cane, Truman was back in Paris, where he laid a wreath on the Tomb of the Unknown Soldier at the Arch of Triumph. After a tour of the Loire valley and its glorious châteaus, the Trumans went to Brussels, where they were received by King Baudouin. At The Hague a week later, Truman was still following his resolution to say nothing about the world situation. "My principal interest right now is the President's health," he told reporters. He said that he was happy to hear that morning that Eisenhower was on the mend from his ileitis operation. But he did allow himself the comment that the new Soviet line was "not a failure but a fake."[61]

At Oxford University, Harry Truman, who had never earned a college degree, received an honorary Doctor of Civil Law. His citation read: "Truest of allies, direct in your speech and in your writings and ever a pattern of simple courage." In his speech, the public orator referred to the 1948 election with an adaptation of a verse from the *Aeneid*. Vergil could have described Dewey's plight, he said, in the following way:

> The seers saw not your defeat, poor soul;
> Vain prayers, vain promises, vain Gallup Poll.

In his after-dinner speech, Truman called for a new Magna Carta. "If we are wise, we will not limit the benefit of our democratic way of life to ourselves." The Oxford students cheered him, and as he passed New College, some of them leaned out of their windows shouting "Harricum! Harricum!" When he looked up, they added: "Give 'em hell, Harricum."[62]

The Trumans visited all the tourist sites in London. When he saw the stately homes, the ex-President's only comment was that he preferred his own house in Independence. He did enjoy the reunion with Churchill at Chartwell. "Just like old times," he said. And the dinner at 10 Downing Street with three British prime ministers—Churchill, Eden, and Attlee—impressed him. While gazing at the tombs of England's greatest in Westminster Abbey, Truman announced that he wanted a short epitaph. "Yes, sir, I want them to put on mine, *He done his damnedest.*"[63]

The fifty-three-day trip was enjoyable. The Trumans were received with proper dignity and consideration by Europe's rulers and cheered by Europe's populace, but they were not lionized as Grant and Theodore Roosevelt had been. An American ex-President was no longer an oddity.

In 1958, the Trumans returned to Europe with Judge and Mrs. Samuel Rosenman as their traveling companions. They had no definite itinerary, only to land in Italy and then go to France if the political situation was quiet enough. Other than the mild statement that de Gaulle was the man to "save France" and he was certain that Frenchmen would resolve their differences, Truman dodged reporters' questions on European politics. His only comment was that the United States was handling them.

At Villefranche, 4,000 inhabitants turned out to greet Truman, but on the whole it was a quiet trip. While sight-seeing in Naples, Genoa, and Venice, Truman displayed admirable control of his agile tongue. However, once off foreign soil, while returning home on the *Constitution*, he talked to reporters about the Sherman Adams case. The people of the United States knew the facts now and would not be "mislead and fooled as they once were by Mr. Nixon, his little dog and a Madison Avenue script with Hollywood overtones," he commented. He also talked about Eisenhower's "disastrous" foreign policy. As for his trip, he had been treated "wonderfully" but was always happy to get home.[64]

In the summer of 1962, ex-President Eisenhower sailed to Europe on the *Queen Elizabeth* with his wife, his grandchildren David, age fourteen, and Barbara Anne, a year younger, and a party of ten others, including staff and friends. They took fifty pieces of luggage. It was to be a "grandfatherly" trip, Ike explained, during which he would call on old friends, travel as a private citizen, and have fun with his family. His last trip abroad, while he was President, had been to Paris for the ill-fated summit meeting.

Eisenhower's only formal engagement was to speak at the International Teachers Conference held in Stockholm on July 31, where he would appear as the chairman of the People-to-People Corporation. His message would be that the United States wanted peace but would not be pushed around.

As was to be expected, the former Supreme Allied Commander in Europe was not allowed to enjoy privacy by the public, the press, or officialdom. In Paris, crowds gathered calling out "Vive Ike" as the Eisenhower party left the railroad station to enter cars for a sight-seeing trip around the city. Denmark extended a very warm welcome to the General, under whose command Denmark had been liberated in May 1945. At a luncheon, the acting premier called Eisenhower "a great American who had won the war and built the peace." Eisenhower received a tumultuous welcome in Stockholm. He publicly apologized for "having wrongly criticized the social security conditions in Sweden" while President, but his reception demonstrated that those words had been forgotten. In his address to the Teachers Conference, which was telecast over NBC and ABC, he proposed to the 400 delegates and 100 observers from eighty countries the founding of an international school for global understanding to teach young people "the objective truths" about the "issues that divide the world." He suggested a student body of from 2,000 to 3,000 young people and a two-year college-level course in "the things that separate nations and tend to prevent them from living peacefully and securely together." The curriculum should lay special stress on world history, diplomacy, and politics. The United

Nations might direct the gathering of a staff for such a school. On their last day in Sweden, the Eisenhowers were entertained at lunch by the king and queen.

In Bonn, Ike met with Chancellor Adenauer, his associate during the war. In Paris, General de Gaulle gave a luncheon for Ike at the Elysée Palace. In London, Eisenhower visited eighty-seven-year-old Churchill, who was confined to a hospital with a fractured thigh. "He looks the same old Winston to me," Ike told reporters. Earlier Ike and Mamie had dined with Queen Elizabeth at Buckingham Palace, where a crowd of 2,000 waved and cheered the visiting American.

For a brief rest, the Eisenhowers went to Culzean Castle at Ayr, near Prestwick in Scotland, where they occupied the sixteen-room suite that had been given to the General for his lifetime by the grateful Scottish people. They traveled north in the Pullman car *Joan*, which had been Ike's mobile wartime headquarters. British railways and the Pullman companies made the car available as a gesture of Anglo-American friendship.

On board the liner *America* en route back to the United States, Ike remarked that the progress since he had left Europe after World War II was revolutionary. The people seemed happy and hopeful. He enjoyed the fine tour, he told reporters, but had discovered that "a former President is endowed with a celebrity that he cannot escape." Millard Fillmore's fears that he might be ignored by Europe and thus bring disgrace on his country had changed to Eisenhower's complaint: "It's been a lot of fun but it was not quite as free an existence as I thought it would be when I started. I thought I was going to have more time to wander around and look at statues and things."[65]

The change in the nature of the American presidency from the time of Van Buren, as well as the change in the power of the United States, has come to bestow on the contemporary ex-president traveling abroad the status of exiled royalty. No solicitous ambassador has to make demands for an ex-president abroad as Mr. Pierrepont once did for General Grant. The faces and deeds of American ex-presidents are well known abroad and their policies are sure to have affected life overseas. Van Buren and Fillmore were deposed leaders of a faraway republic coming to a continent ruled by autocrats. Truman and Eisenhower arrived as world leaders already familiar with

Europe's rulers. No matter how much a former president argues that he is just "Mr. Citizen" now, he has been anointed and the imperial aura still hangs over him. He need no longer wait to see if he will be invited to the palace. If there is a glass coach to be had, the American ex-president will surely ride in it.

The Perfect Careers

WHAT TO DO after the presidency was obvious for the planter presidents, but for most of the others it was a problem that had to be resolved. Since all of the ex-Presidents were in the twilight of their lives, not all were healthy and vigorous enough to continue an active life. Some farmed; some practiced law, limiting their practice to suitable cases; some wrote; some taught; some served on the boards of corporations, philanthropic institutions, social reform organizations, and universities. Some accepted retirement as a way of life. But only John Quincy Adams and William Howard Taft had careers that equaled their presidential ones in stature.

John Quincy Adams admired perfection. It was a virtue that he pursued all his life but never expected to attain. Demanding much of himself always, he lived by some lines of Pythagoras that he translated and paraphrased and put on the flyleaf of volume six of his valuable *Diary*:

> Let not thine eyelids close at parting day
> Till, with thyself communing thou shalt say,
> What deed of good or evil have I done
> Since the last radiance of the morning sun?[1]

This was written while Adams was secretary of state—the best the United States ever had, it can be argued. But although he is given full credit for the Adams-Onis Treaty, which gave the United States Florida, the master policy that became the cornerstone of American foreign policy was called the Monroe Doctrine, and historians now give the lion's share of credit for it to President Monroe rather than to his secretary of state.

The presidency of the second Adams was a tragic failure that was doomed from the start because the House of Representatives, not the electorate, placed him in the presidential chair. Further, the suspicion of a bargain between Adams and Clay to wrest the election from Andrew Jackson, recipient of the highest number of electoral votes in 1824, hung over the one-term administration. All the experience and ability that JQA brought to the presidency could not cancel out the suspicion that surrounded his accession to office.

Andrew Jackson spent the years between 1824, when he was "robbed" of the presidency, and 1828 ensuring his election and was successful. Adams quietly withdrew to a house he bought on Meridian Hill. "It was my intention to bury myself in complete retirement as much as any nun taking the veil," John Quincy stated. Nothing could have been further from the truth. At sixty-one, the ex-President thought he had resigned himself to a life of literary pursuits and gentlemanly seclusion, but several factors were operating against this. The suicide of George Washington Adams, the oldest son of John Quincy and Louisa, made his father despondent, and the family finances were worrisome. Release came unexpectedly when Richard Joseph Richardson, the United States congressman from Plymouth, decided to give up his seat and the National Republicans offered it to the former President. Charles Francis Adams, JQA's youngest son and always a bit of a snob, felt that his acceptance of the job "diminished the man" and was generally opposed to it. Mrs. Adams called it a "silly" plan and confessed that it was not to her taste. Unimpressed by his son Charles's final argument that he would be setting a bad precedent for all future ex-presidents by accepting the nomination, Adams was delighted to return to the real world. The situation in Europe was "a typhoon raging" and South America was in a "hurricane," JQA noted. The United States had the elements of revolution in its multitudinous problems—the Indians, the tariff, the railroads, and nullification. The times were too exciting to miss out on. Having missed the first Revolution because of his youth, he did not want to miss the second.[2]

Adams was elected by 1,814 votes out of 2,565 by the residents of the twenty-two towns in the Plymouth District, beating the Jacksonian and the Federalist candidates by taking nearly three votes out of every four. He was delighted, although he admitted wryly that his dearest friends, meaning, of course, his family, "have no sympathy with my sensations."

John Quincy Adams's perfect career started on December 5, 1831, when he attended the first session of the Twenty-second Congress, the first ex-President to sit in that chamber. He regarded his election to Congress as a "call" which had been unexpected and unsolicited. He predicted, with accuracy, that he would experience "slights, mortifications—insults—loss of reputation—and perhaps, exposure of myself by infirmities of temper unsuited to the trials."[3] He went through all those only to emerge as "Old Man Eloquent," spokesman for the truth no matter how unpopular.

JQA's greatest fight in the House was for the repeal of the "gag rule." Like many of the ex-Presidents who came after him, Adams had a strong sense of the need to preserve the Union. He loathed slavery, but he was afraid to take a position that would split the nation into its two factions. However, he was unable to swallow the Pinckney resolution, known as the "gag rule," which said that all petitions that related to the subject of slavery or the abolition of slavery, "shall, without being printed or referred, be laid on the table, and that no further action whatever shall be had thereon."[4] This coup of the slavocracy was the first of a procession of "gag rules," each stricter than the last.

Efforts to silence Congressman Adams when he rose to read the forbidden antislavery petitions on the floor of the House were coolly ignored. He was willing to risk formal censure by the House after he presented a petition that purported to come from slaves but was a hoax devised by the Southern bloc to embarrass him. Adams knew that the paper was spurious but stood by the principle of his right to present it even if it came from slaves, who, according to the slave-holders, were not people and therefore not entitled to the right of petition. This 1837 resolution against Adams failed to pass by a vote of 21 to 105, but the resolution that slaves did not have the right to petition swept the House, 163 to 18. Adams was not made happy by this personal exoneration, because the controversy proved to him that "henceforth the question of slavery would mingle with every conflict in the union." It was some consolation that during the summer, while he was vacationing at his Quincy home, a delegation from the Massachusetts House of Representatives came to visit him to read an address approving of his activities in Congress and to present him with a cane made of timber from the *Constitution*. The ex-President accepted the cane, after a struggle with his conscience, since it was not "of sufficient pecuniary value to be declined." This did not mean that the Adams constituency favored abolition. JOA's family and friends tried to wean him away from his abolitionist friends such as Samuel C. Webb and Benjamin Lundy. "Between these adverse impulses my mind is agitated almost to distraction," he complained. "I walk on the edge of a precipice in every step that I take."[5]

Adams's house in Washington was deluged with petitions. Many of his evenings were spent assorting them and entering them on a list. On February 14, 1838, he presented 350 petitions, including 158 for rescinding the "gag" resolution, 65 for the abolition of slavery and the slave trade in the District of Columbia, and 17 for the prohibition of the internal slave trade. This barrage of petitions enraged the slave bloc. As the former President spoke, frenzied cries of "Order! Order!" rang through the House, the Speaker's voice among the loudest.

As time went on, John Quincy's position on slavery hardened. He now declared freely that he believed "slavery to be a sin before the sight of God." The abolitionists, sensing this, tried to force him into a more militant position by threatening to challenge his reelection if he refused to present the test question in the House—immediate abolition of slavery in the District of Columbia and Florida. Consequently, Adams almost lost his seat as a result of a ruse whereby the Democrats supported a last-minute abolitionist write-in candidate, hoping that, since Adams had no formal opponent, his supporters would not come out to vote. This ploy angered Adams, who could not understand the willingness of the abolitionists to strengthen the administration whose principles they abhorred if they could not have things exactly as they wished.

However, the ex-President continued to be unruffled either by congressional displeasure or by the threatening letters that he received about his "d——d abolition petitions." If he did not stop presenting them, a Virginian promised, "I will let loose the reign of my Vengeance and the consequences will be that the life of our once beloved President will be no more." A Georgian, more colorfully, promised that the former President would "be shot down in the street, or yor [sic] damned guts will be cut out in the dark."[6]

Adams developed his own program for gradual, legal abolition of slavery. He presented three amendments to the House of Representatives in February 1839. He had no hope that they would be adopted and was not surprised that their advocacy of nonviolence and justice, even to the slaveholder, offended the abolitionists. They were as follows:

1. From and after the 4th of July, 1842, there shall be, throughout the United States, no hereditary slavery, but on and after that day every child born within the United States, their territories or jurisdiction, shall be born free.
2. With the exception of the territory of Florida, there shall never be admitted into this Union any State the constitution of which shall tolerate within the same the existence of slavery.
3. From and after the 4th of July, 1845, there shall be neither slavery nor slave trade at the seat of government of the United States.[7]

Like all compromise solutions, the modest proposal infuriated its opponents. But Adams could not condone immediate abolition without compensation, because it would have to be abolition by means of force. He wrote, in answer to an invitation to the National Anti-Slavery Convention that he was unable to regard the problem in any other way.

John Quincy Adams's annual battle to defeat the "gag rule" suffered defeat year after year. In 1839, he presented 511 petitions on slavery that were tabled at once but served to keep the issue before the House. At a summer session of Congress in 1841, Adams tried a ploy to fight the reinstatement of the hated rule that almost worked. But Henry Wise, who led the fight against it, worked himself up into such a rage that he became deathly pale, said that he was ill, fell back into his chair, and fainted. After a weekend of rest, he returned to the House and delivered a six-hour hysterical tirade against the former President, whom he called the archfiend and leader of all abolition. The anti-Adams victory was assisted by support from congressmen from New Hampshire and Maine.

Continual suppression of his adamant position that the right to petition was a constitutional one inevitably moved JQA closer to the abolitionists. Their very near merger was practical rather than ideological, but it gave Adams some outside support. How much working together there was between the former President and the antislavery clique at Abolition House, Mrs. Sprigg's boardinghouse where they lived, cannot be precisely determined. But Adams did entertain Theodore Weld at his Washington home and did meet with about a dozen members of the group, including Seth M. Gates and Joshua Giddings, to develop a plan to save the right of petition.

The Southern bloc, somewhat diminished in size at the moment, presented Adams with his opportunity. Determined to press his advantage, the ex-President, told Weld a day in advance that he would present some petitions that would set the slavocracy aflame. Consequently both Theodore Weld and Lord Morpeth, an English abolitionist, were in the gallery to see the fireworks. Adams presented a petition from Habersham County, Georgia, which asked that he be removed as chairman of the Committee on Foreign Relations because of his abolition bias. The Southerners tried to have the petition tabled because of its reference to slavery, but JQA insisted that he had a right to be heard in his own defense.

By the House rules, the Speaker was forced to give Adams the right to speak. Old Man Eloquent rose and with "a voice like a trumpet" spoke until "slaveholding, slavetrading, and slave breeding absolutely quailed under his dissecting knife." The Southern bloc, raging and shouting, surrounded the seat of the embattled old man, screaming for the Speaker to "*put him down.*" When, finally, he was stopped for a moment, the ex-President said, "I see where the shoe pinches, Mr. Speaker, it will pinch *more* yet." He pointed out that there was an alliance between the Northern Democrats and the Southern slaveholders to remove him from his Foreign Affairs Committee chairmanship while the House voted 91 to 76 to shut him up.[8]

A few weeks later, Adams gave the Whigs, now disenchanted with his obstinacy, their opportunity to suppress him. He presented a petition from forty-six citizens of Haverhill, Massachusetts, asking Congress to immediately and peaceably dissolve the Union because it did not offer reciprocal benefits but, rather, a vast proportion of the resources of one section of the Union was drained annually to sustain the views of another section without adequate return and the result must be that the whole nation would be dissolved in destruction.[9] All hell broke loose on the head of the aged patriarch. The moment, long awaited, had come for the slave interests to expose him before the whole nation. Thomas Walker of Virginia presented a resolution to censure John Quincy Adams. In offering a petition asking for the dissolution of the Union, he had offered "the deepest indignity to the House of which he is a member; an insult to the people of the United States," it said. If it went unrebuked and unpunished, it would be a disgrace to the country in the eyes of the whole world. It might well merit expulsion "and the House deems it an act of grace and mercy, when they only inflict upon him their greatest censure."

The small, bald, gray ex-President, his hands trembling with age, was now the storm center of Washington. Galleries packed with visitors and senators who had left their own chamber waited to hear the former President's defense. He turned to his chief prosecutor, Thomas Marshall, handsome and young nephew of the great Supreme Court chief justice, who accused him of having asked the House of Representatives to commit high treason by reading a petition that advocated the dissolution of the Union.

"I call for the reading of the first paragraph of the Declaration of Independence," Adams commanded.

The clerk read, urged on by Adams's cries of "Read it! Read it! And see what that says of the right of a people to reform, to change, and to dissolve their government."

Twice Adams insisted, before he would continue with his argument, that the clerk read from the Declaration: "But when a long train of abuses and usurpations, pursuing invariably the same Object evinces a design to reduce them under absolute Deposition, it is their right, it is their duty, to throw off such Government, and to provide new Guards for their future security."

"I rest that petition on the Declaration of Independence," Adams concluded.

Henry Wise, leader of the opposition, recalled scornfully JQA's support for the payment to their American owners for slaves carried off by the British during the War of 1812, which had been one of the terms of the Treaty of Ghent. "That one should so have outlived his fame," he orated. "The gentleman is politically dead; dead as Burr— dead as Arnold."[10]

Theodore Weld helped by gathering the materials Adams needed for his defense. The old man, who had to withstand the daily tirades against him, was grateful. But the House never heard or saw anything but the clear hard tones of the former President's voice and his unflinching stance. The "fiery ordeal" seemed to give him a renewal of energy. At the end of the day, Weld reported, he was equal to reviewing the main points of the next day's argument and rehearsing his gestures and elocution. Adams was spared no recrimination. Some of them went back to his quarrel with the Federalists during the Jefferson administration. Threats of assassination that came in from the South only amused the former President. He reported one of them to the House humorously.

In truth, the bitter struggle rejuvenated the embattled Nestor. He went off to the House each day to face the abuse with great calm while Mrs. Adams grew more and more distraught, suffering fainting fits and illness. These manifestations of distress in his behalf did not stop Adams. The battle of wits between him and the Southern pair, Marshall and Wise, whetted his appetite for more. The newspapers printed columns full of the debate until Adams accused the *Intelligencer* of suppressing some parts of his speeches and falsifying others. The editors became angry and refused to report his speeches at all.

For a time it looked as if the altercation would have no end. At one point Adams said that it would take him three weeks more to conclude his defense. But abruptly on February 7, it ended. Adams entered the House and, as soon as he got the floor, stated that he was prepared to continue but willing to stop. A Virginia Whig, John Minor Botts, moved to lay the whole subject on the table forever and the proposal was carried 106 to 93. Moments later, the House voted to reject the Haverhill petition by a vote of 166 to 40.

The fact that Adams had won personal vindication was secondary to the fact that somehow public opinion was moving toward an acceptance of his principle that the presentation of petitions was a sacred constitutional right. Nevertheless it was a famous victory for the old warrior. Francis Pickens of South Carolina, a member of the opposition, admitted that his side had been thoroughly routed. "Well, that is the most extraordinary man on God's footstool," he said.

Victory came close upon vindication. On December 3, 1844, JQA read his proposal: "Resolved: That the twenty-fifth rule [gag rule] for conducting business in the House . . . is hereby rescinded." Despite the attempt to table it or delay it when the President's son brought in Tyler's annual message, the vote was taken. At last it was carried— 168 votes to 80 votes. It passed because the Northern Locofocos, angry that they had been forced to give up Van Buren and accept Polk as the Democratic presidential candidate, voted with the Northern Whigs against the Southern bloc. The eight-year fight was won and the scene set for further inroads against slavery.

Concurrent with the struggle over the "gag rule," John Quincy Adams was involved in the *Amistad* case, which absorbed much of his

time and all of his "good feeling." The mystery of the ghost ship that
had been sighted in the summer of 1839 along the Atlantic coast was
resolved when, on August 26, two sea captains at Sag Harbor, Long
Island, found four Blacks wrapped in blankets when they were hunting along the dunes. The Blacks, who did not speak English, led the
Americans by means of sign language to the top of a dune from
where they sighted the long, low black ship with tattered sails and no
flag. A United States Coast Guard vessel out of Gardiners Island
sighted the derelict at the same time, boarded it, and took the occu-
pants off as prisoners. There were two white men aboard who told a
story of piracy and murder, illegal slave trading and terror.

The Blacks had been imported from Africa by a Portuguese slaver
and unlawfully taken to Havana. Two Cubans bought them, obtained
false papers for them, and loaded them on the coastal steamer *Amistad*
to be carried to Puerto Principe for sale. When the *Amistad* was at
sea for four days, the slaves mutinied and killed the captain and the
cook. They were under the impression, owing to a grisly joke on the
part of the cook, that they were going to be killed and eaten. Cinque,
the leader of the slaves, spared two Cubans to sail the ship to Sierra
Leone, but instead the white men fooled the mutineers by reversing
the ship's direction at night.

At the trial, held on a ship anchored in the New London harbor,
the Cubans accused the Blacks of piracy and claimed them as their
property. The judge decided that the prisoners should be held in
the New Haven jail until they could be tried in Hartford in mid-
September.

The Van Buren administration was inclined to agree to Spain's
demands to give up the ship and the slaves, but American abolitionists and antislavery groups, rallied by Lewis Tappan, immediately
joined forces to raise money for the defense of the terrified Blacks.
The relief committee, aware that what was needed most was a pres-
tigious person who was nationally known to help their cause, decided
to solicit the aid of John Quincy Adams. They persuaded Ellis
Gray Loring, an old friend of Adams, to write to him asking his
opinion on the case. After reading the letter and struggling with his
New England conscience, JQA said, in substance, that even if the
Amistad Blacks had committed piracy and murder, they were entitled to a trial and to American justice. He also pointed out that the
unfortunates were victims of the African slave trade.

The case became a matter of curiosity, interest, and sympathy throughout the United States. Roger Baldwin, an attorney for the defendants, convinced the New Haven judge of the rights of his clients, declaring that they had been illegally enslaved by Spain and that they must be transported back to Africa and delivered home. President Van Buren was angry about the decision, because the secretary of state had already assured the Spanish minister that the captives would be returned to Cuba. Consequently, the case was appealed to a district court and when there, too, the original decision was upheld, it was appealed to the Supreme Court to be acted on in January 1841. Until then the Blacks were to be confined in the New Haven jail. The unfortunate prisoners became famous throughout the United States and were visited and gazed at by many sightseers. They were also subjected by their abolitionist friends to learning English and the Bible after a seaman was located who understood the Mendi language.

Inevitably, enthusiasm and interest in the curious captives died down and contributions for their legal defense ceased to come in. Many of the lawyers who had been active on the case withdrew when there were no longer any funds. With some reluctance, because the abolitionists resented Adam's conciliatory position on slavery, Loring and Lewis Tappan visited the former President at Quincy. They asked him to be Baldwin's assistant counsel when the *Amistad* case came before the Supreme Court. It was twenty years since he had argued a case in court, Adams protested, and besides, his obligation was to spend his time and effort in the House. His defenses toppled, however, when the abolitionists convinced him that the lives of the captives lay in his hands.[11]

Charles Francis Adams, later to become a "conscience" Whig and the vice-presidential candidate on the Free Soil ticket, disapproved of his father's capitulation, fearing that it would interfere with his own nomination to the Massachusetts House of Representatives. But John Quincy had given his word. The old man went to New Haven to work with Roger Baldwin on the arguments. He was then taken to see his clients—thirty-six men and two children. The former President was impressed with the "remarkable faces of Cinque and Grabow" but skeptical about the progress the Blacks had made in their education and conversion.

JQA's motion to dismiss the case against the captives was rejected because the Spanish minister was insisting harder than ever that the defendants must be delivered to Havana. So, with "a heavy heart, full of undigested thought" and fearful that his ability to sustain his cause was inadequate, Adams went to court. To his surprise, the case was delayed owing to Justice Story's absence from Washington. A further delay occurred when Adams's coachman, Jerry Leary, was killed in an accident.

Finally, on Washington's Birthday, the case was heard. Attorney General Gilpin and Roger Baldwin led off with arguments against and for the defendants while the former President agonized over his brief, which he kept rewriting. When the court adjourned, he went to the Library of Congress to study James Madison's statement in the Virginia Convention on slaves as persons and as property. He continued to work feverishly on his presentation in the clerk's room until the court met.

His moment at hand, Adams was profoundly disturbed when he looked around and saw the black-robed justices in front of him, the full courtroom, and the ladies in the gallery. However, as soon as he started to speak, Old Man Eloquent confessed, "my spirit did not sink within me." For four and a half hours, he argued "one fundamental principle—the ministration of justice." Without hesitation, he castigated the administration for bowing to the pressure of a foreign government and placing itself "on the side of injustice." The presentation was, as Justice Story wrote, "extraordinary . . . for its power and its bitter sarcasm."[12]

Feeling buoyed up and more confident after his first day in court, Adams returned the next day to find that Justice Philip Barbour had died suddenly and Chief Justice Taney had declared the court closed until March 1. Upon his return, Adams resumed his argument with another marathon speech of four hours that rested heavily on the right of habeas corpus. If the President turned over the *Amistad* captives to Spain, he argued, what might happen to the possible freedom of every American citizen? "Would it not have been by the tenure of executive discretion, caprice or tyranny—at the dictate of a foreign minister?"

Before closing, Adams indulged in an aside that stretched his prerogative as a former President but awed the audience. "As I cast my eyes along these seats of honor and of public trust, now occupied by you, they seek in vain for one of those honored and honorable persons whose indulgence listened then to my voice. Marshall—Cushing—Chase—Washington—Johnson—Livingston—Todd—Where are they? . . . Gone! Gone! All gone!"[13] The attorney general's closing statements pointedly avoided any reference to JQA's arguments and dealt only with Baldwin's presentation of the case. The chief justice announced that the decision would be delivered on March 9.

"The Captives are free!" Adams wrote to Tappan. The opinion was delivered by Justice Story, who affirmed the decision of the lower court. He declared the Blacks free and ordered that they be sent back by the United States to their African homes. To the ex-President, the verdict clearly indicated that the *Amistad* captives must be carried home at government expense and, perhaps, compensated for their eighteen months of false imprisonment. Adams asked Daniel Webster, the new President's secretary of state, to request passage to Africa for the Blacks, who had not been awarded ownership of the *Amistad*, their lawful prize of war, JQA felt, which would have carried them home or provided them with money to buy their own passage home. Webster, overwhelmed by the unexpected request, agreed to the proposal, promising to speak to the secretary of the navy about a ship. Meanwhile, the Africans were released from prison and sent to Farmington, Connecticut, to further their education and to work.

In November 1846, John Quincy Adams suffered a slight paralytic stroke that affected his speech and right side. After several months, frail but unwilling to give up public life, he resumed his seat in the House. He participated in debate only once, when he responded to a proposal for an appropriation of $50,000 to compensate the owners of the *Amistad* for their losses. In a weak, quavering voice, Adams spoke for the freedom of the *Amistad* captives and against the illegal Spanish claims. To pay would be to depreciate the decision of the United States Supreme Court and to rob the American people, he said. The issue was, of course, one between the proslave and antislave blocs, and until the abolition of slavery in the United States, the Spanish government revived the subject of reparations regularly.

Less than two months before John Quincy Adams died, the executive committee of the American and Foreign Antislavery Society presented him with a resolution that they had passed. It was to be delivered to him while he was in New York en route from Quincy to Washington, but the committee missed him. The resolution thanked him for "all that he has done in Congress and elsewhere on behalf of the antislavery cause." It wished him well "during the approaching session and while his valuable life shall be preserved."

JQA was, at the last, fully accepted as an important contributor to the antislavery cause.

William Howard Taft was always ambitious, industrious, and success-oriented, despite the contrary image that he presented of an amiable fat man. Just one place away from the top of his class at Yale, a member of Phi Beta Kappa, his first experience on the bench was in 1887, when he was thirty years old. Just two years later there were rumors that he was being considered for associate justice of the Supreme Court. "My chances of going to the moon and of donning a silk gown at the hands of President Harrison are about equal," he wrote to his father. But it was his self-confessed dream, freely admitted by him as early as the 1890s and ever after.

Taft's wish for the highest judicial seat in the land was satisfied finally in June 1921, although it had been a struggle to get there. With an enthusiasm that he failed to bring to the highest executive post, Taft set out to improve and reform the court. The greatest administrative problems facing the Supreme Court at that time were the backlog of work and the divisiveness in the court demonstrated by the many dissenting opinions that were handed down. In order to solve the excessive case load, it was necessary to get Congress to pass the Judges Bill, which would allow the Supreme Court to choose the cases that came before it on the basis of their importance to the nation as a whole and not to the individual litigant. In this way, problems that concerned constitutionality would receive primary attention. Taft used all his political know-how and his congressional contacts to ensure the passage of the bill. By the time he retired in 1930, after a decade of service, Chief Justice Taft could claim that the court was almost free of a backlog of cases.

Divisiveness and the passion for dissent were subjects that excited Taft's ire. He therefore felt free to make suggestions to the President whenever a vacancy occurred in his court. Pierce Butler was one of Taft's selections whom Harding appointed. The chief justice approved of Harlan Stone also, but regretted his support when the former attorney general turned out to be a liberal and, even worse, a chronic dissenter. His pet peeve on the court was Justice Brandeis, whom Taft never forgave for opposing him on the Ballinger case during his presidency. Brandeis's liberal views were less annoying to him than his propensity for "usually being against the court."

The cases that Taft sat on during his term of office covered many subjects and many aspects of the American constitutional system. He was generally conservative in his interpretation of the law but, having been President, was not always opposed to enlarging the powers of government. In the case of federal regulation of the railroads, he was willing to grant Congress almost unlimited power when the railroads were engaged in interstate commerce. If "the nation cannot exercise complete effective control over interstate commerce without incidental regulation of intrastate commerce, such incidental regulation is not an invasion of state authority," Taft wrote. In later cases, this position was extended to include the regulation of industries other than the railroad.

But one case does not make a liberal. In the Drexel Furniture Company of North Carolina case, Taft stated that the Congress cannot use its taxing power unconstitutionally even though its purpose was the humane one of stopping child labor. The law said that a company that employed children under the age provided for in the act would be taxed ten percent of its annual profit. The Drexel Furniture Company was accused of hiring a fourteen-year-old boy. In his decision, which he was able to persuade Brandeis and Holmes to accept, Taft said: "The good sought in unconstitutional legislation is an insidious feature because it leads citizens and legislators of good purpose to promote it without thought of the serious breach it will make in the ark of our convenant." Taft was not without guilt for this appearance of being against child labor, but he defended himself on the grounds that "we cannot strain the Constitution of the United States to meet the wishes of good people." It particularly annoyed him that Harvard President Emeritus Charles Eliot condemned the court, even though Taft pointed out that his "favorite," Brandeis, had agreed with the decision.[14]

Among the cases that concerned Chief Justice Taft the most was *Myers* v. *United States*, which touched upon presidential power. Taft worked on it for a year or more, researching into the history of American government. The case, Taft wrote, presented the question of whether, under the Constitution, the President has the exclusive power of removing executive officers of the United States whom he has appointed by and with the consent of the Senate. Myers had been appointed postmaster in Portland, Oregon, in 1917 for four years and then removed by order of the postmaster general acting under the President's direction in 1920.

In his lengthy decision, Taft rested his argument on three sources:

the debate in the first House of Representatives in 1789, President Jackson's message of protest to Congress in 1834 when Duane, his secretary of the treasury was removed, and, above all, the Tenure of Office Act. Without the absolute power of removal, the former President wrote, "it would make it impossible for the President in case of political or other difference with the Senate or Congress to take care that the laws be faithfully executed."[15] The decision invalidated both the Tenure of Office Act, which had been defied by Andrew Johnson and was used as the chief count against him when he was impeached by the hostile Radical Republican Congress, and a later 1876 law which denied the President the unrestricted power of removal of first-class postmasters. Since these appointments were prime sources of patronage for United States senators, who were usually given free rein by the President, this act also had political overtones. It was said of this opinion that it would rank as one of the chief justice's most important contributions to constitutional law. It also gave him the opportunity to vindicate a former president, Andrew Johnson. He therefore did not take kindly to the dissents of Justices McReynolds and Brandeis. The two dissenters, Taft asserted, were disloyal to the court and sacrificed all "to the gratification of their own publicity."[16]

The 22,000-word opinion of the chief justice handed down in October 1926 was almost equaled in verbosity by his opponents. Justice Holmes called Taft's arguments "spiders' webs inadequate to control the dominant facts." The office they were dealing with, Holmes said in his brief dissent, "owes its existence to Congress and the Congress may abolish it tomorrow. Congress gave the President the power to appoint to it and can take it away." Justice McReynolds, dissenter from the right, searched history also and found no authority there for the President to remove a duly appointed officer. In a separate dissent, Brandeis, from the left, also disputed Taft's historical analysis. It was contrary to the spirit of the Founding Fathers to give the President unlimited removal powers, because it interfered with the freedom of the individual, who then would be subject to "the arbitrary or capricious exercise of power," he said.[17]

Taft hated the lack of unanimity on the court, particularly in this case. Brandeis, he judged, was being consistent." He loves the kicker, and is therefore in sympathy with the power of the Senate to prevent the Executive from removing obnoxious persons because he always sympathized with obnoxious persons," Taft wrote.[18] The settlement of the case was delayed many times because McReynolds, "always inconsiderate," got his dissent in even later than Brandeis.

Taft's historical analysis was shaky, but the decision held until President Franklin D. Roosevelt tried in 1933 to remove Humphrey, a member of the Federal Trade Commission, basing his belief that the Federal Trade Commission Act which forbade it would be held unconstitutional based on the decision in the Myers case. Humphrey sued for his salary, and finally in 1935, the Supreme Court unanimously held for him. Thus the Myers decision was limited to purely executive officers.

Although disliking dissent, Taft was forced to take that position in the *Adkins* v. *Children's Hospital* case, which concerned a minimum wage law for women. The issue involved was whether the law deprived the individual, under the Fifth Amendment, from "the right to contract about his own affairs." Justice Sutherland, who realized he was on sensitive ground since his case involved the health and well-being of women, wrote that the Nineteenth Amendment changed "the contractual, political and civil status of women" so that now differences between the sexes were "almost, if not quite to the vanishing point," a point of view that today's woman's rights movement would endorse.

Taft answered Sutherland's argument, maintaining that the Nineteenth Amendment "did not change the physical strength or limitations of women." Legally speaking, he did not see how this situation differed from the decisions in earlier cases which upheld the right to limit the hours women could work. In "absolute freedom of contract the one term is as important as the other," he maintained. The case was damaging to the court, Samuel Gompers said, because in cases involving humanity, "the court ranges itself on the side of property and against humanity."

The most celebrated case of its era never reached the Supreme Court, and Taft had a hand in that. At 2:00 A.M. on August 22, 1927, barely twenty-four hours before Sacco and Vanzetti were to be executed, a telegram arrived at Murray Bay, Taft's summer home, from the lawyer of the condemned shoemaker and fish peddler, asking for a stay of execution until the case could be appealed to the Supreme Court. Taft would have had to leave Canada and cross the border to deliver the stay of execution, but he saw no reason to disagree with Associate Justice Holmes's denial of the request. He refused and added that no federal question was involved in the Massachusetts case.

After the two Italian immigrants, who died proclaiming their innocence and whom many believed innocent, were executed, the Canadian government thought it necessary to guard the chief justice's house lest he be attacked by angry radicals. Nothing occurred. Taft, however, had no sympathy for the cause. He wrote to President Lowell of Harvard that the movement to exonerate Sacco and Vanzetti "had been created by large contributions of female and male fools and had been circulated through all the communistic and criminal classes the world over." He defended his act by pointing out that the uproar over the case had been nothing but "perverse propaganda" and now was quiet, which proved that he had "pricked the bubble as it now proves to have been."[19] Taft's conservatism made many blind spots for him.

When Taft dreamed of being chief justice, he saw it as a retreat from the venality of the world where he would be able to deal out perfect justice instead of having to be manipulative and adjust to the intricacies of politics. But the court did not really provide that ivory tower. As chief justice, Taft sometimes had to deal with sensitive internal problems. For instance, it was his task to persuade the failing Justice McKenna, who was seventy-nine in August 1922, to retire. He did not resign until January 1925 and only after the chief justice was forced to tell him that he was being given only the simplest cases to handle.

The court was not untouched by politics despite the separation of powers provided for in the United States Constitution. Robert La Follette proposed an amendment to the Constitution which would give Congress the right to repass legislation declared unconstitutional by the Supreme Court and then incorporated it as part of his 1924 presidential campaign, adding to it a proposal for the popular election of all judges. Taft was furious at him. In 1923, Senator Borah proposed an amendment that provided that no congressional law could be invalidated except by the assent of seven justices.

These threats to the sanctity of the Supreme Court made Taft urge Coolidge's election, asserting that he alone could save the Republican party. Any Republican who favored the Wisconsin senator should be thrown off the ticket, he said. He would have liked to see Coolidge run again in 1928 but accepted Hoover. Taft was not a bigot about

Al Smith's Catholicism. "They are as loyal as any other denomination," he wrote. "So far as I know, and I have known a great deal about it, the Catholic Church has never affected detrimentally the Americanism and loyalty of its communicants in this country." He feared Al Smith's connection with Tammany Hall, not his religion. And in his case, as with any other presidential candidate, Taft's primary concern was whether he would respect the court and "not put anybody on it who will be a serious menace, if he has the opportunity."[20]

John Quincy Adams died with his boots on. He was overcome and slumped over his desk in the House of Representatives a moment after he cried no, loud and strong, to a resolution to thank certain military officers for their service in the Mexican War, which he opposed. The prostrated ex-President was carried to the Speaker's chamber, where he lay, attended by friends and physicians, until he died murmuring intelligibly, "This is the last of earth: I am content."

Chief Justice William Howard Taft missed such a fitting end. His obesity put a fearful strain on his heart. At one time he weighed 326 pounds and while in the White House gained weight due to constant frustration. Being happy as chief justice, he dieted down to 244 pounds, but the damage had already been done. All through the Supreme Court years, he had frequent attacks of one thing or another, which sometimes limited his activities. By the summer of 1929, he was quite ill and on February 5, 1930, sent his resignation to President Hoover. A trip to Cincinnati to attend the funeral of his beloved half brother, Charles Taft, almost killed him. In February he went to Asheville, North Carolina, to recover his health but he only got worse. He returned to Washington to die, a great hulk of bones. On March 8, 1930, he died.

In terms of self-satisfaction, these perfect careers meant a great deal to the two ex-Presidents, both of whom had suffered frustrating administrations. Adams, who lived before the advent of the imperial presidency, was able to make the transition to a lesser position in the government with little difficulty. In a sense, he played a dual role, for on certain ceremonial occasions he was invited to participate along with the President in office. It could be argued that being chief justice of the United States is but a rung lower than president and, in terms of permanency, perhaps a step up. Even Chief Justice Taft's official photograph displays his complacent contentment with the post.

An assessment of the value that the experience of the presidency brought to their second careers is not simple. The courage that JQA showed had been amply displayed before, when he had been in Congress and, contrary to his party, favored Jefferson's Embargo Act. His obstinate insistence on doing what he believed to be right was an integral part of his personality, but he might have felt even stronger, psychologically, after having been the nation's highest public servant. In the instance of Taft's position in *Myers* v. *United States*, his experience probably reenforced his sense of the need for full executive power to fire all appointees. On the other hand, he may have taken that position anyhow. Perhaps it is best simply to look at these two postpresidential careers as fortuitous developments that added to the interest and the productivity of Adams's and Taft's later years.

Literary Lives

Long before presidential libraries were built to be monuments to the twentieth-century imperial presidents and to house their voluminous papers, their more modest predecessors lightened their declining years with accounts of their lives and administrations. "Writing is almost the only dignified occupation a President can follow after leaving office," Ike's son wrote.

John Adams, whose post-presidential years lasted for a quarter of a century, set the style. Bowing to the urgings of his son, John Quincy, his constant New York correspondent, F. A. Van der Kemp, and the illustrious Dr. Benjamin Rush, Adams made several chaotic but valuable forays into autobiography. The first installment carried his readers, who were to be restricted to his own descendants ("not for the public"), through his ancestry and early years up to his entrance into Harvard College.

Always defensive, Adams gave as his "excuse" for embarking on the story of his life the wish his posterity might have "to see in my own handwriting a proof of the falsehood of that Mass of odious Abuse of my Character, with which News Papers, private Letters and public Pamphlets and Histories have been disgraced for thirty Years." This very brief section revealed that the eminent statesman had wanted to be a farmer and, from the age of ten, was "of an amorous disposition" and very fond of "the Society of females," but could assure his children that "no illegitimate Brother or Sister exists or ever existed." For this proof of virtue, the ex-President was grateful to his parents' teachings.[1]

After dropping the manuscript for two years, Adams resumed the project, although he feared that everyone would see it as nothing more than a "Hymn to Vanity" and, furthermore, working on it and reminding himself of his role in public affairs would so "inflame my passions" that it would "set me on fire and I should have Occasion for a Bucket of Water constantly by my side to put it out."[2]

Nevertheless, Adams resumed the narrative in 1804 and carried it through the Harvard years, the development of his law practice, and the early stages of the American Revolution, closing with the signing of the Declaration of Independence in 1776. A highlight of this section is Adams's account of the Boston Massacre and the trials that followed. In explanation of his part as the British Captain Preston's lawyer, he said that once he had been asked to undertake his defense, "I had no hesitation in answering that Council ought to be the very last thing that an accused Person should want in a free Country." But, he said, it was "the most exhausting and fatiguing" case he ever tried, particularly since it caused "popular Suspicions and prejudices" against him "that never wore off."[3]

"Travels and Negotiations," the title the ex-President chose for his years of negotiating for the new country, provides the charm of unfamiliarity for the reader. In this section the unsophisticated New Englander described his hazardous voyage to France in the company of his young son, John Quincy, and his first exposure to French culture. The "indecent" manners of the French women of rank could never be reconciled with a Republican government, Adams asserted. "We must therefore take great care not to import them into America," he added.[4]

This section gives an excellent picture of the life of Americans in France at this time and some candid sketches of some of them. Benjamin Franklin, at whose home in Passy Adams resided for a time, suffers from the Adams pen. Not only was the popular American's French ungrammatical and inaccurately pronounced, but he was more inclined to accept invitations than to attend to business. Before he came, Adams stated, there was no minute book, no letter book, no account book kept, or if there was, Silas Deane and Ben Franklin had concealed them. The business of the commission would never be done unless he did it, Adams concluded as time went on. Quarrels among the American colleagues delayed and impeded business further, and "the Life of Dr. Franklin was a scene of continual discipation [sic]."[5] Contemporary letters and diary entries give credence to the Adams account of the period, but it is his retrospective comments that add spice to the primary material.

This part of the autobiography ends abruptly in July 1778, and part three resumes over a year later, in September 1779, with Adams ready to leave for France once more as the only American peace commissioner to negotiate a treaty of peace and commerce with Great Britain. After an adventurous trip through Spain with his two young sons, Adams arrived in Paris to find that, as he had suspected earlier, France wished to keep the United States "embroiled with England as much and as long as possible, even after a peace." The French minister's first step to accomplish this purpose was, according to Adams, to intrigue with the American Congress to get Adams's sole commission annulled. The Comte de Vergennes was successful in achieving this end and Adams, agitated once again by the reminder of the Frenchman's treachery, broke off his autobiography and did not resume it.

Thomas Jefferson waited until the age of seventy-seven to begin his foray into the field of personal memoirs. Writing for his family, the third President worked on his brief account from January until July 1821, covering impressions of his life up to 1789. A large section of the manuscript is devoted to the French Revolution because of the "interest which the whole world must take in this Revolution," Jefferson said.[6]

In contrast to Adams's anecdotal, erratic style, Jefferson's short account of his early life is controlled and well organized. A sizable number of pages are devoted to deliberations over the Declaration of Independence, particularly to the rejection of the clause "reprobating the enslaving of the inhabitants of Africa." Jefferson explains that it was struck out "in compliance to South Carolina and Georgia, who never attempted to restrain the importation of slaves, and who, on the contrary, still wished to continue it." The Northerners, too, he believed, "felt a little tender" because, though they had few slaves, they had been "considerable carriers of them to others."[7]

Very little of his personal life is discussed in Jefferson's autobiography. Only by way of explaining his reason for accepting an appointment to go to Paris as a peace commissioner in November 1782 does he mention that two months earlier he had "lost the cherished companion of my life, in whose affections, unabated on both sides, I had lived the last ten years in unchequered happiness."

However, news that a provisional peace treaty had been signed by the commissioners already there canceled Jefferson's trip, and he did not go abroad until 1784, when his mission was to try to make treaties with European countries. The following year, he succeeded Dr. Franklin as minister to France.

The American Revolution "seems first to have awakened the thinking part of the French Nation in general, from the sleep of despotism in which they were sunk," Jefferson wrote. Also, the French officers who had been to America, mostly young men, came back with "new ideas and impressions." Therefore, Jefferson felt an interest greater than that of a mere spectator in the events of the French Revolution that he witnessed. His long section on that upheaval, written with hindsight but with feeling, conveys much of the atmosphere of the period. Jefferson places the blame for the execution of the king and for the reign of terror on Marie Antoinette. King Louis, he believed, would have accepted a constitution, but "he had a Queen of absolute sway over his weak mind" who was "proud, disdainful of restraint, independent at all obstacles to her will, eager to the pursuit of pleasure, and firm enough to hold to her desires, or perish in their wreck." Her gamboling and dissipation, he said, were a serious item in the bankruptcy of the treasury, and her opposition to reform led to the guillotine for her and her husband and to the "subsequent crimes and calamities which will forever stain the pages of modern history." Had there been no queen, there would have been no revolution, Jefferson believed. Because he had the confidence of the leading French patriots, particularly Lafayette, Jefferson was certain that he had accurate information on the events of the revolution. Also, since he had comfortable working relationships with the European diplomats stationed in France, he had information about the other side. Unfortunately, however, Jefferson was unable to witness the end of the revolution, because President Washington recalled him to serve as secretary of state in the new government and refused all appeals to postpone the return journey.[8]

The last pages of the autobiography are devoted to an account of Jefferson's visit to the dying Franklin, who gave into his keeping an autobiographical narrative of the 1775 negotiations between Franklin and the British ministry for the purpose of effecting a reconciliation between the American colonists and the mother country. After Franklin's death, Jefferson returned the manuscript to the seer's grandson and literary agent, William Temple Franklin, and then fretted about it for he feared that the episode had been suppressed. Although Jefferson had not seen the published collection of Franklin's works, he had been told that the document was not included. Perhaps Dr. Franklin had meant the papers "as a confidential deposit in my hands, and I had done wrong in parting from it," the aged ex-President worried. He need not have despaired; whether due to the efforts of William Temple Franklin or not, posterity has the account in Franklin's published papers. Abruptly, after a discussion of the Franklin episode, the autobiography stops with the statement "So far July 29, 1821."⁹

Monroe's son-in-law, John Hay, suggested that the former President work on his autobiography, and he did, but only reached the year 1805, when he was the American minister to England. The fragment is four hundred manuscript pages, written in the third person in Monroe's almost illegible handwriting. It is, nevertheless, well written in a formal, matter-of-fact style. Some passion does enter into it when Monroe deals with the frustrations of his first French mission, for which he was never properly paid and from which he was peremptorily recalled. One function of the autobiography was connected with this event, for at this time the ex-President was engaged in trying to collect these claims from Congress. He also hoped for some money from the sale of the finished manuscript to bolster his decaying property.

Though the autobiography has often been condemned by Monroe's biographers as a boring, pedestrian work, Stuart Gerry Brown's presentation of it in printed form has greatly enhanced its appeal. It is valuable and interesting because it describes the development of a Virginia planter into a practiced, practical diplomat. The last President to have been old enough to participate in the Revolution, Monroe was always an ardent republican and Francophile. Despite his stilted prose, the youthful Virginian's enthusiasm for the French revolutionaries who rejected their monarch comes through. On his second mission to France, Monroe was disappointed that republican fervor had given way to admiration for the first consul. When he learned that he was expected to be at Napoleon's coronation, he wrote that it did not accord with his principles or feelings to be present at such an event, but he understood that if he should leave France for Spain before the event, it might defeat the mission for which he had been sent overseas.

The book is modest. Monroe underplays his role in the American revolution and is circumspect about claiming major credit for the Louisiana Purchase. Partly this modesty is due to his wish to avoid upsetting the powerful Livingston family, whose support for his claims he might still need. Robert R. Livingston was the American minister to France when Monroe was named by Jefferson minister plenipotentiary for the purpose of participating in the negotiations. Nonetheless, if the book is read as a history of the growth and education in foreign affairs of the President who was responsible for the Monroe Doctrine, it can be regarded as an interesting and significant work.

Much more disappointing, because it is so sparing in personal detail and so verbose about matters that lack great interest, is Martin Van Buren's autobiography. Written when he was seventy-one years old and living in Italy, the work stops before his election to the presidency. The bulk of the book discusses New York politics and the Jackson administrations. Van Buren said that he did not continue the narrative through his own presidency because, like Jefferson, he grew tired of talking about himself.[10]

There are some interesting and original sections to relieve the tedium of the work. While visiting Jefferson, an octogenarian at the time, Van Buren noted a volume in his library labeled "Libels." Its contents consisted of abusive articles about him that he had cut out of newspapers. Van Buren showed it to Jefferson, who laughed and said that throughout his life he had been indifferent to "the groundless attacks to which public men were exposed." There is an enlightening chapter on the "Eaton malaria" that broke up Jackson's cabinet and led to Van Buren's resignation as secretary of state. The former President's ambivalence about the scandal is apparent throughout the narrative. When he resigned, Van Buren wrote, he believed that he had abandoned whatever chance he ever had of reaching the presidency.[11]

The autobiography was based on letters and records, because, as the former President explained, "however tenacious the memory and however honest the intention it is scarcely possible that the reflections of any man should be entirely uninfluenced by the chances and changes of the intermediate period." Though his statement is valid, his book's greatest shortcoming is that its author never allowed his memory to wander from his notes. His statements seem stilted and overconsidered. No hints come through about his administration, and apparently this is the way the ex-President wanted it. The rough notes found among his papers indicate that he never expected to continue the project.

The two volumes of Grant's personal memoirs, best-sellers in their day, are well-written and valuable accounts of his prepresidential life, particularly the campaigns he fought in during the Civil War. The story behind the writing of them is, perhaps, the most moving that can be told about any former president. The full story has been told earlier, but some further comments may be appropriate. In the preface to his memoir, Grant mentioned that he had written it under a sentence of death, which caused some critics to say that parts of the work were maudlin with self-pity. It does not seem so to this reader. On the contrary, it may be that knowledge of his fatal illness allowed the usually taciturn General to let his thoughts flow more freely. And, further, some of the more difficult and demanding sections, such as the chapter on the Wilderness campaign, had been completed before Grant became desperately ill.

On occasion, Grant let his politics creep into the books. Although he gained his military experience in the Mexican War, he opposed it as "one of the most unjust ever waged by a stronger against a weaker nation." It was reprehensible that the republic of the United States should follow the example of European monarchies "in not considering justice in their desire to acquire additional territory." The Civil War was an outgrowth of that war, Grant maintained, and thus it can be seen that "nations like individuals are punished for their transgressions."[12]

Grant's expressed aim was to write a truthful history. He pointed out that the Mexican War had been a breeding ground for future presidents. General Taylor was elected in 1848. General Scott ran in 1852 and was defeated by General Franklin Pierce. Grant remained silent, however, about the effect of the Civil War on his own career.

Much of the interest engendered by the memoirs is that Grant names names and makes judgments. After Shiloh and the subsequent capture of Corinth, he commented, a movable force of 80,000 men would have sufficed to hold all the territory acquired and would have set in motion "the accomplishment of any great campaign for the suppression of the rebellion." It was, of course, not done. He takes credit for inventing the idea of the Freedmen's Bureau when, in the campaign against Vicksburg, he used freedmen to pick the cotton in the abandoned plantations. The cotton was then sent to Northern factories and the freedmen paid twelve and a half cents a pound, but not directly. The money earned was put into a fund to feed, clothe, and house the freedmen and supply them with "many comforts they had never known before."[13]

Vicksburg, Grant judged, was a necessary victory. The country had been disheartened by the failure of the armies, and the last election had gone against those who supported the vigorous prosecution of the war. "The fate of the Confederacy was sealed when Vicksburg fell," Grant insisted, and ever after "the *morale* was with the supporters of the Union."[14]

It was not until March 1864 that General Grant first met President Lincoln, who told him that he never professed to be a military man and never wanted to interfere with his commanders, but their procrastination and the pressure from the people and Congress "which was always with him" forced him to issue his military orders. All he ever wanted, Lincoln said to his latest commanding general, was someone who would take the responsibility and call on him for assistance with government power. Grant admired Lincoln for many qualities, not the least of which was that he never heard him vengeful or abusive to an enemy. He was always generous and kindly toward the Southern people.[15]

Grant was most anxious to set himself up against Robert E. Lee. It irked him that officers who had been in the Army of the Potomac often said: "Well, Grant has never met Bobby Lee yet!" Many Union men and officers believed that the Confederate Army of Northern Virginia was superior to the Union Army of the Potomac. Grant did not share this opinion and wanted to prove it untrue. After the capture of Petersburg, Grant sent for Lincoln so that they might plan the next advance. He pointed out that it was imperative for the health of the country that the Eastern armies vanquish the enemy who had so long resisted. Lee and his army must be captured, Grant insisted, or else the West would always throw up to the East their failure to capture an army. Lincoln agreed and gave his consent to Grant's plans.[16]

Insisting upon honesty rather than romance, Grant revealed that the supposed meeting between him and Lee under the famous apple tree was a myth. It was General Babcock who had come upon Gen-

eral Lee sitting in an apple orchard on an embankment with his feet
in the road below and his back against a tree. Grant's description of
the surrender also clashed with legend. Lee had much dignity, the
Union General conceded, but he also had an impassive face, so it was
impossible to tell whether he felt inwardly glad that the end had
come or sad over the result but too reserved to show it. But "my
own feelings which had been quite jubilant on the receipt of his
letter [of surrender], were sad and depressed," Grant wrote. He did
not rejoice at the fall of a foe who had fought so long and suffered
so much, particularly since their cause had been "one of the worst
for which a people ever fought." As for the terms of the surrender,
Grant confessed that he wrote them on the spot and only when he
started to write did he know what was on his mind. The stories about
Lee surrendering his sword and Grant handing it back were "purest
romance," he said.[17]

The book has good narrative flow and is surprisingly readable.
Though the memoirs contain little humor, there are some touching
sections. Twelve hundred and thirty-nine pages long, it was completed in eleven months and in two years earned $450,000 from the
sale of 300,000 copies. Not long before his death, unable to talk because of the terrible pain in his throat, Grant, who did not live to
see his book published, wrote a note to his physician, Dr. Douglas.
"I said I had been adding to my book and to my coffin. I presume
every strain of the mind or body is one more nail in the coffin."[18]

In contrast to General Grant, Theodore Roosevelt, a facile and
prolific author, wrote his autobiography while still in vigorous health
and still politically viable. It appeared first serially in the *Outlook* in
February 1913, and later that year was published without changes as
a book. Nothing that Teddy Roosevelt wrote could be totally without interest, but his autobiography said little that was new or
startling. In his foreword, the author stated: "Naturally there are
chapters of my autobiography which cannot now be written."
Granted that limitation, the book still reads as exceedingly self-
serving and uncomfortably self-righteous. The Colonel admitted to
Henry Cabot Lodge that his hardest task was "to keep my temper
and not speak of certain people." He then lists the categories of his
hates: anti-imperialists, universal-peace-and-arbitration men, and the
editors of the *Evening Post*. In apology, perhaps, for his engagement
in some of the more extreme causes, TR added that "the various

admirable movements" in which he had been engaged developed among their members "a large lunatic fringe" and he had seen certain individuals "who in their revolt against sordid baseness go into utterly wild folly."[19]

The nonpolitical and nonpresidential chapters have an innocent Rooseveltian freshness, particularly when he talks about family life, Sagamore Hill, and the beauties of nature. But these matters were handled better in some of his other books, and some of the material is repetitive. The reader does get a brief though valuable glimpse of Roosevelt's boyhood. His poor health and poor eyesight caused him to develop a keen interest in natural history. At fourteen, he traveled with his family in Egypt and compiled an ornithology of the birds of Egypt, to which he added the birds of Germany after a later trip. The young man's first career choice was to be a natural scientist.

Politics, Roosevelt said, should never be an individual's only career. He bragged that he had several occupations to which he could turn, but despite his protestations, politics occupied most of his life from the time of his graduation from Harvard. When he was police commissioner of New York, Roosevelt, the patrician, learned something about the underprivileged and the exploited. His teacher was the muckraker Jacob Riis, "the man who was closest to me throughout my two years in the Police Department," he wrote. Visits to tenement houses while looking into a bill proposed by the Cigar Makers Union to prohibit the manufacture of cigars in these pestholes exposed the future President to "a useful experience." On one visit, during a hot New York summer, he witnessed the "gasping misery of the little children and of the worn out mothers." He was aroused to the need for reform and wanted to help the poor, the sick, the disadvantaged, and the victims of political corruption, but only those who were "worthy and deserving." In a tirade against prostitution, for instance, he recognized the economic ills that drove many girls to follow "the dreadful trade" but took the moral stand that he doubted that changing the economic system would eradicate the problem. A tinge of racism and ethnicism spoils much of TR's instinct for reform. On the subject of prostitution, he praises "certain races—the Irish conspicuously" for furnishing "relatively few inmates to houses of ill fame." He continues: "A girl who is lazy and hates hard work, a girl whose mind is rather feeble . . . or a girl who craves cheap finery and vapid pleasure, is always in danger."[20] This kind of moralizing mars the book. Even if we discount the tone as typical of its time, the autobiography is overwholesome.

Roosevelt wrote that he did not want to be vice-president and was never deceived by the machinations of Senator Platt and the other New York politicians. He had wanted to run for governor again, but when he saw that he could not have the nomination, he accepted the vice-presidency.

The presidential years are treated topically, with planned emphasis on the strengths of the Roosevelt administration. Of his foreign policy, Theodore Roosevelt said triumphantly: "Throughout the seven and a half years that I was President, I pursued without faltering one consistent foreign policy, a policy of genuine international good will and of consideration of the rights of others and at the same time of steady preparedness." The autobiography ends with curious abruptness. TR described the voyage of the American battle fleet around the world, which, he maintained, was "in my own judgment the most important service that I rendered to peace." It was so because it showed Americans and others that the Pacific was as much its own home waters as the Atlantic.[21]

The autobiography does not throw any new light on presidential decision-making or on the character of Theodore Roosevelt. Some of the omissions are startling, particularly the absence of William Howard Taft, his chosen successor. While composing the work, the former President asked for memoranda from many of his former associates to clarify the events of the administration and its policies, but the book emerged as a highly personal Rooseveltian opus.

Lawrence Abbott gave a plausible explanation for the book's reading like an improvisation. After the excitement of the Bull Moose campaign, TR's colleagues at the *Outlook* thought it would be best for all concerned if he avoided controversial political subjects for a time. When Abbott suggested "some chapters of autobiographical reminiscences," the ex-President responded that he did not want to write about himself and that Mrs. Roosevelt would not like it. Abbott persisted until Roosevelt consented to allow him to come to Oyster Bay, interview him with a stenographer, and then put the notes in shape. If he and Mrs. Roosevelt disliked the result, Abbott assured him, "we can kill it," but if it were acceptable, other interviews would follow.

Frank Harper, who acted as the stenographer, had accompanied

Roosevelt in the same capacity on his European trip. Abbott cautioned Harper to intrude himself as little as possible and to take down everything including interpolations and comments, whether coherent or not. The method worked effectively. Abbott sat down with the Colonel in his study and said, assuringly, that he did not want him to dictate but just to answer some questions that would spark stories from his early life. Abbott interested him at once by reminding him that he had often told him that he was a sickly boy and yet "from the time I first knew you, you have been an extraordinarily vigorous and athletic man. What kind of boyhood and education did you have that would have produced such a striking result out of such an inauspicious beginning?" Roosevelt's skill as a raconteur was immediately released. He talked in a fresh and easy manner until he suddenly became aware of Harper's presence. Immediately, he straightened up and his tone became formal and literary. Abbott waited patiently until he could slip in another question and revive the anecdotal style.[22]

Abbott took Harper's copious notes home, arranged them in sequence, cut and pasted, but did not add or change a sentence. He then submitted the result to TR to be used as chapter one of his book. The scheme worked more or less. Those chapters that used Abbott's technique achieved the goal of informality and have some interest; the others suffered from the faults of most presidential memoirs. They try too hard for justification.

In 1951, Herbert Hoover published a three-volume memoir starting with his early life and ending on the eve of World War II. Most of it, however, was not written at the time. The account of Hoover's childhood and professional career as an engineer was written intermittently during 1915–1916 when he was journeying back and forth through Europe for Belgian relief. While waiting for boats, trains, and officials, Hoover worked on these sections for his two sons, hoping that they would be inspired to become engineers also. The parts on World War I were written at intervals during 1920–1924 and were retained as written, without much change. The author said that he could have revised the volume with the benefit of twenty-five years' perspective but decided it had more value as a reflection of his views at that time.[23]

The first part of Volume Two, covering 1919–1921, was written in 1925–1926, but the part covering 1921–1933 Hoover composed after he left the presidency. The final volume, *The Great Depression*, was written for the most part right after he left office. Its very long section on the election of 1932 was necessary, Hoover explains, because "it was a turning point in American life—and possibly in that of the world." In defense of his handling of the depression, he wrote: "Throughout I have endeavored to treat persons and events with the restraint of a post mortem."[24]

The most unique part of the Hoover memoirs is the final section, called "The Aftermath." Other ex-presidents had strongly opposed their successors' policies but had never included their views in their personal histories. If Hoover has been regarded as a mild-tempered man, given to understatement, this furious outburst against New Deal "collectivism" belies that myth. The chapter headings alone express the utmost outrage: "Fascism Comes to Agriculture," "Fascism Comes to Business," "Fascism Comes to Labor—With Consequences," "Introduction to Socialism Through Electrical Power," etc. A rabid anticommunist, Hoover accused the New Deal of including in its train the whole gamut from old-line Democrats "to the traitors who call themselves liberals."

The recognition of Russia infuriated Hoover. It had been refused by Wilson, Harding, Coolidge, and him and by their respective secretaries of state because, as was pointed out during the Wilson administration, bolshevism depended on world revolution. If a neighbor is wicked, Hoover said, we do not necessarily attack him but we do not establish his respectability in the community by asking him home. The communist organizations and the communist-front organizations that had bored their way into "every vital organ in the country, including the government," were to blame. Major responsibility must also be assigned to the "communist infected C.I.O."

Most phases of the New Deal, from the NRA to the TVA, he criticizes as fascistic, collectivist, or just ineffective. Particular scorn is directed against FDR's court-packing plan. Its purpose, Hoover declares, was to subordinate the court to the personal power of the executive, which would revise the Constitution to mean what "he" (FDR) wants it to mean.

The tone of the book is dogmatic and too hysterical to be an effective critique of the New Deal. It also fails as an attempt to prove that the New Deal achieved nothing but a nine-year extension of the

Great Depression. It served mainly as fodder for the ultraconservatives and as ventilation for Hoover's righteous anger at being ignored by his successor.

Dwight D. Eisenhower called his account of his life up to the presidency *At Ease: Stories I Tell to Friends*, but it is, more accurately, an informal autobiography. In this book, Ike was not obliged to explain the European theater in World War II "in order to give a better picture of what was done in your [Ike's] theater and by your headquarters than any other, sometimes biased or prejudiced reports," reasoning that convinced him to write *Crusade in Europe*. He also did not have to justify and explain the eight years of the Eisenhower administration as he did in his two-volume history called *The White House Years*. Instead, this book is a ramble through the author's memories. It is sentimental, unsophisticated, warm, and genial. It provides glimpses of the man behind the familiar grin and explains his tremendous charisma. The style is informal, even intimate. If one did not like Ike before reading the book, it is hard to resist him after reading it.

One of the most important characters in *At Ease* is Abilene, Kansas, "a microcosm of rural life at that time." Ike was a natural, although impressive, product, and by speculating on the town, the reader becomes aware that Eisenhower was the last President to be born in the nineteenth century and to carry into the mid-twentieth some of its values, faults, and virtues.

Life in the pre-World War II professional army emerges vividly. New anecdotes about well-known figures add spice to the book. George Patton appears, and there are some sensitive pages about the tragedy of James Forrestal. More significant for Eisenhower's development, a story that he alone could tell, was the influence upon him of General Fox Conner, who had asked his good friend General Pershing to send Ike to Panama as his staff officer. Conner was a "tall, easygoing Mississippian" who "never put on airs of any kind." He made the Panamanian tour of duty "one of the most interesting and constructive of my life," Eisenhower said.

General Conner had an extraordinary library, especially in the area of military history, and started his aide on a course in military affairs by first lending him some historical novels, such as Conan Doyle's *The Exploits of Brigadier Gerard* and the American Winston Churchill's *The Crisis*. Having aroused his interest, Conner then introduced his pupil to the history and memoirs behind the fiction. Eisenhower read Grant's and Sherman's memoirs of the Civil War and, many times, Clausewitz's *On War*. The two men discussed and analyzed the books and, as a result, Ike developed a lifelong interest in the American Civil War.

Conner's taste in literature was not limited to military subjects. Ike was soon reading Shakespeare, Plato, Tacitus, Nietzsche, and others. "It is clear now that life with General Conner was a sort of graduate school in military affairs and the humanities," Eisenhower wrote. He was "the one more or less invisible figure to whom I owe an incalculable debt."[25]

In contrast to modern presidents, who detailed the histories of their administrations with the aid of careful researchers who were often former members of their staffs, James Buchanan struggled alone in the isolation of Wheatland composing his vindication of the last four months of his administration. "I have had no person to assist me in its preparation, make suggestions or even verify facts although they are mostly official," he complained. On the contrary, some of the ex-President's former associates were shy of, or even hostile to, the project. Stanton, for instance, now part of the Lincoln administration "deserted" it immediately, and Judge Jeremiah S. Black, who at first proposed writing the history of the Buchanan administration for $7,000, delayed the project and then decided not to do it. The problem was that Buchanan approved of Lincoln's action at Fort Sumter while Black opposed it as unconstitutional.[26]

Most of Buchanan's problems with his former friends were a result of changing loyalties. Two members of his Cabinet had gone over to the Confederacy, three were with the Republicans, and one was interested only in his business. But undeterred, although plagued with severe and recurring attacks of rheumatism, Buchanan finished the book in 1862. Its publication was delayed until 1866 lest the work seem to have as its intention the embarrassment of the Lincoln administration.[27]

Mr. Buchanan's Administration on the Eve of Rebellion places blame on Congress for persistently refusing to move against the seceded cotton states and thus stave off the rebellion. Buchanan hoped that when personal animosity against him had cooled, the record would be there to interpret his actions favorably. His defense is a judicious, well-documented, and clear presentation of his belief that the United States Constitution does not give the federal government the power to coerce a sovereign state but does provide the power to enforce laws against individuals in the states. The style of the book is heavy and ponderous, which does not invite the modern reader.

Although dismayed that his book had a very high price, Buchanan was pleased to note that several thousand copies sold at once and it seemed to be in demand. Consequently, he hired William B. Reed of Philadelphia to prepare a biography, expecting him to use notes taken by Mr. and Mrs. James Shunk, who had lived at Wheatland for six months gathering anecdotal material for such a work. The Shunks never passed on their material to Reed and Reed never finished the biography, so *On the Eve* has to stand as the sole contemporary Buchanan work.

More interesting to consider than the contents of the carefully researched, antiseptic volumes of White House memoirs turned out by mid-twentieth-century ex-presidents is the method used in their composition. No longer does the author take quill or pen in hand to start his laborious task. Instead, a team of experts surround the project with expertise, system, and all the modern research tools. At stake is not only the former President's future reputation but also a large advance from the publisher and the expectation of enormous sales.

In the Truman archives, there is a letter from two prominent historians listing the names of possible researchers who would be competent and were in sympathy with the former President's outlook. The Truman memoirs, which took two years to write, were developed initially from question-and-answer sessions between Truman and his Kansas City staff. Next there were intensive dictation sessions, which were then transcribed into typescript after being copiously annotated. Finally, Truman corrected the copy carefully in his own hand. After the process was completed, the facts were checked meticulously against files and figures. Truman said that he was particularly grateful to his wife for her line-by-line scrutiny of the work.[28]

Allan Nevins praised the Truman memoirs for their distinction, incisiveness, and shrewdness. "There was greatness in the man, and the flavor of the greatness comes over into his book," he wrote. There is also much in the work to appeal to the general public. Truman included engaging letters written to his mother and sister Mary on every subject, beginning with the first days of his new job. "Dear Mamma and Mary, Well I've been the President for nine days. And such a nine days no one ever went through before, I really believe." His chatty, modest tone never changed in all the many subsequent Mamma-Mary letters.[29]

One-third of Volume Two of the Truman memoirs is devoted to the Korean War, or "Mr. Truman's War," as its detractors called it. "Give 'em hell Harry" said that he considered the phrase a badge of honor but he knew very well that the war had cost him his job and needed the explanations and justifications that he expended on it. The MacArthur controversy was also given ample space. Truman saw the struggle between the President and the popular general as a vindication of the supremacy of civil power. Contemporary historians debate over whether Truman's White House years were "as lustrous as they were stormy," but the public and, curiously, the young, are now making a folk hero out of the feisty Missourian. "America needs you, Harry Truman," the musical group called Chicago Rock blared in 1975.

John Eisenhower presents a revealing account of the writing of his father's White House memoirs in his own autobiography, *Strictly Personal*. Ike accepted his son's offer to resign from the army to be his chief assistant in the project. The Monday after Kennedy's Friday inaugural, work was started on the books at Eisenhower's Gettysburg office while the ex-President and his wife traveled south to Augusta, Georgia, and then to California. From the outset, John Eisenhower realized that one man could not do all the research, so William B. Ewald, Jr., who had been a staff officer at the White House, joined the team along with Samuel S. Vaughan, a senior editor at Doubleday, who served as the company's representative.

Eisenhower was more dependent on written records for this book than he had been for *Crusade in Europe* and so was given rough drafts of almost every chapter to work with. He would cut and rewrite over and over again until he was satisfied. Readers of the memoirs can attest to John Eisenhower's judgment that "the best part of the Old Man's Memoirs were those he wrote himself." The rest is somewhat stilted and disappointing, far inferior to Ike's other books.[30]

Lyndon Johnson's book *The Vantage Point* suffered even more acutely from the team approach. His collaborators were former White House men who became the ex-President's associates at the University of Texas. Among them were Walt Rostow, Johnson's former special assistant for national security affairs; William J. Jordan, the White House spokesman for the peace talks; and former White House speech writers Harry Middleton and Robert Hardesty. "This is how I saw it from my vantage point," was Johnson's theme. Granted the hard-beset ex-President had a gargantuan task trying to explain the unpopular, divisive war that destroyed his brilliant political career; nonetheless, the argumentative tone of the book and its sometimes doubtful credibility marred it and also resulted in disappointingly small sales for such a work. For example, the Johnson quotes from the Pentagon Papers, which were, at the time, available to him but not to others, are at variance with the documentary evidence in the papers, which are now public property.[31]

The Johnson book also sparked speculation on the question of researching contemporary history and political affairs. Presidents, for instance, can leak classified material to the press or elsewhere when it suits them or they can save it for their memoirs. Truman quoted freely from secret CIA material in his memoirs and Eisenhower and Johnson also used similar sources. Thus it can be argued that the public is deprived of the truth at the time an event occurs, but is then told about it through such personal reminiscences, at a price.[32]

A unique work written by an ex-president is Herbert Hoover's *Ordeal of Woodrow Wilson*. It is the first and only account written by one President about another under whom he served. Hoover was Wilson's food administrator during World War I and was in Paris during the peace negotiations, so much of the material used in the book is from Hoover's own archives.

It is a very compassionate book and significant because Wilson's "ordeal" is seen through the eyes of Hoover after he has served as President and suffered his own ordeal of rejection and misunderstanding. The book presents a portrait of Wilson but also a portrait of Hoover. At the time, John Maynard Keynes said about the American food relief administrator that he was "the only man who emerged from the ordeal of Paris with an enhanced reputation." The English economist attributed this to Hoover's sense of reality, knowledge, magnanimity, and disinterestedness, which, if found in others, "would have given us the Good Peace."[33]

Wilson's decision to yield to the desires of his avaricious colleagues in order to save his League of Nations is almost justified in the book. These compromises, Hoover asserts, "sowed the whole earth with dragons' teeth," but the President believed that the league could then "redeem the world from these evils." Hoover cites Wilson's compromises on the Japanese demands, the dismemberment of Germany, the Rhineland, the Saar, the union of Germany and Austria, reparations, and mandates. The harshest judgment Hoover makes is on the last item. He blames Wilson for having too much confidence in General Smuts, a man who he should have realized had his own imperialist designs foremost in his mind. "It is my belief that the President, to put it bluntly, was just fooled. He was entirely under an illusion as to the ultimate effect of the mandates," Hoover said.[34]

Hoover's personal and compulsive fear of communism dominates much of his account. The Bolshevik Revolution in Russia in 1917 had so sensitized him to the problem that he places much of the blame for postwar suffering on the Communist uprisings, particularly in Eastern Europe and Germany. He is honest enough to admit, however, that part of his antagonism to a continued Allied blockade of Germany in order to force that country to sign the peace treaty was not entirely humanitarian. "My staff and I asked ourselves how many days of starvation the German Government could endure before it went over to communism or to military dictatorship."[35]

Never minimizing Wilson's accomplishments, Hoover was aware that the President mistook the politeness of his colleagues on the peace team for friendship. But he has only genuine sympathy for the harried, strained chief executive just over a major foreign war and seven months of negotiations in Paris, and further pushing his worn and weakened frame to urge acceptance of his treaty on his people. The enigma of Wilson's refusal to accept compromise on the league is simply explained. Wilson had accepted far more compromise at Paris than had been urged in the league reservations, Hoover admitted. But Hoover, who was a staunch defender of the league, explained that Wilson's illness had isolated him from the political currents of the moment and from the personal contacts that might have persuaded him to cooperate with the Senate. "While his mind may have been clear in the opinion of those around him, his lack of contact with the people and their leaders separated him from the reality of which sound compromises are made."[36]

Wilson's ultimate vindication, Hoover pointed out, was the establishment of the United Nations. The spirit of the great and martyred wartime President hovered over the world organization—except for one thing. Wilson would not have tolerated the admission of aggressive dictatorshops—Hoover's euphemism for the Communist countries. Wilson, said Hoover, saw the league as an association of "free nations."[37]

The book, which was the result of fourteen years of pouring over about 300,000 items relating to the period culled from over a half a million pieces, was very important to the aged ex-President. Many nights he read himself to sleep with the material because it represented to him not only an exercise in nostalgia but also an opportunity to correct some of the misrepresentations about Wilson that had been published, particularly those concerning his philosophy of life and his character. The Wilson crusade failed, Hoover explained to Harrison Salisbury in 1958, "but his life was a kind of Greek tragedy."[38] Since Hoover regarded Wilson as his guiding light, perhaps his defense of him gave him hope that some day he, too, would be defended and his policies reassessed by a willing, sympathetic champion.

Another work of unique interest, although not, strictly speaking, a book, is the Adams-Jefferson correspondence, particularly the letters written during their years of retirement. After a breach caused by a misunderstanding over political matters was healed in 1812, the aging seers corresponded regularly until their deaths, within hours of each other, on July 4, 1826, the fiftieth birthday of the United States. Most of the Adams-Jefferson letters discuss the authors' philosophies and so add significantly to American intellectual history. Contemporary political matters were ignored almost completely, but their own past experiences were rehashed good-humoredly, often at the expense of their fellow revolutionaries. The interests of the illustrious pair were divergent but complementary. Jefferson, whose absorption with natural history, art, architecture, agriculture, and education was expounded at length with many other distinguished correspondents, tried to stay within Adams's narrower concern— political philosophy, religion, and the classics—in their exchanges. They did share an unbounded love of books.

Though the aging process did not spare them completely, Adams and Jefferson were both fortunate in that their minds remained active until their deaths. Even in his ninetieth year, Adams was sharp, although he needed an amanuensis. The two men never met after their retirements, but their affection for each other seemed to grow with the proliferation of letters. A year or so before he died, Adams wrote to the Sage of Monticello: "Every line from you exhilarates my spirits and gives me a glow of pleasure." Jefferson, in his last letter to Adams, paid him a graceful tribute. Advising him that his grandson, Thomas Jefferson Randolph, would be in Boston, he asked that the second President receive him. "Like other young people, he wishes to be able, in the winter nights of old age, to recount to those around him what he has heard and learnt of the Heroic Age preceding his birth, and which of the Argonauts particularly he was in time to have seen."[39]

Diaries are in a class by themselves, because they are daily, spontaneous entries rather than attempts at recapturing or interpreting the past. Such indefatigable diarists as John Quincy Adams and Rutherford B. Hayes continued their jottings through their post-presidential years. The Adams *Diary* is priceless, of course, for its record of JQA's brilliant congressional career and for its many incisive, sometimes acid, comments on men and events. Its twelve volumes, edited by Charles Francis Adams, are incomplete, but eventually the Adams Papers Foundation will present it in its entirety.

The aura of the presidency is undisputedly suffused over these literary productions. No matter how poor and disappointing an ex-presidential work may be, it has an instant market. This will be as true of Richard Nixon's work in progress as it has been in the past. Most compelling, however, is that these presidential memoirs reflect their authors' universal concern for the way their administrations will be viewed by future generations. How will posterity grade them? The only further influence that a former president can have on that judgment is to try to enhance his reputation by conducting his own defense through his memoirs.

Epilogue: The Proper
Use of Ex-Presidents

Suggestions both humorous and serious have been made by many, including the former presidents themselves, about what should be done with them after the White House. Cleveland said that the suggestion of the editor of the Louisville *Courier-Journal* to "take them out and shoot them" was "worthy of attention." In somewhat the same vein, Taft advised a dose of chloroform to be followed by a funeral pyre. It would make a fitting end for someone who had held the highest office in the land and would "secure the country from the troublesome fear that the occupant could ever come back." It would also "fix his place in history, and enable the public to pass on to new men and new measures. I commend this method for consideration."[1]

The most frequent serious proposal has been to give former presidents a seat in the Senate. Taft derided this idea of William Jennings Bryan, saying it was because Bryan had been "a near President" several times that he felt qualified as an expert. There was too much discussion in the Senate already, Taft observed; there was no need to add "the lucubrations of ex-Presidents."[2] Earlier, Rutherford Hayes rejected the idea of life senatorships for other reasons. The Senate was already burdened with inequality because the small states had the same representation as the large, he wrote. The Senate, also, was becoming "the rich man's place" and to add life members to it would be "inconsistent with the principle of popular government." He pointed out that had this idea been in operation during the Civil

War, with Buchanan, Tyler, Fillmore, Pierce, and Van Buren members, New York would have had four senators and New Hampshire, Pennsylvania, and Virginia, three each. "Would it not cause discontent?" he asked.[3]

During the Kennedy administration, Senator Claiborne Pell asked the President to comment on a Senate bill which would make ex-presidents of the United States nonvoting senators-at-large with the privilege of speaking on the floor and of participating on committees. Diplomatically, Lawrence O'Brien answered that the President agreed with the objective "of ensuring that the nation receive maximum benefit from the experience and knowledge" of the ex-President but could not comment on legislation as "it could be construed as being a self-serving action on his part."[4]

Mike Mansfield proposed to Kennedy a somewhat different setup. Retired presidents would be made permanent members of a kind of consultative council of state which would meet and perform "such tasks as the incumbent President might request." Kennedy replied that he felt such a council would limit the individual freedom of former presidents and make them "more or less duty bound to the Administration that is in office." He also noted that the retirees lack the up-to-date information for sound judgment.[5] These and similar suggestions reflect the feelings of many that there is a certain wastefulness in throwing away all the know-how that a president acquires in his one or two terms in office.

The Founding Fathers did not worry about this problem. Benjamin Franklin reflected their thinking in one of his few utterances during the 1787 Constitutional Convention in Philadelphia. He said: "In free governments the rulers are the servants and the people their superiors and sovereigns. For the former, therefore, to return among the latter was not to degrade but to promote them." Ex-President Truman said that he kept these words in mind while in the White House and that "I've had it in mind ever since I got my—promotion."[6]

In considering the employment of ex-presidential talents, no rule of thumb can be applied. As long as the party system continues, an ex-president from a party other than the incumbent's is more useful as a gadfly than as an ex officio member of the administration who, out of courtesy, would be forced to rubber-stamp its decisions. In the Senate, with no specific constituency and no vote, he would be a tolerated anomaly. Any artificial position that would be created for the retired chief executive would upset the careful constitutional balance and cause awkwardness and, possibly, embarrassment to the elected President.

The imperial presidency, which can be criticized for separating and insulating the man in office from the people, should not be encouraged by elevating former presidents. The shadow of the presidency is enough for the ex-President to endure. He can adjust to it best if he is allowed to move comfortably and privately from "a life of utmost intellectual activity to one of most sluggish repose," as John Adams described it. Or, as Hayes wrote, no former President can escape completely the unfortunate influence on habits, disposition, and character of "the high place." He grows used to being "flattered and supported under all circumstances whether right or wrong, or wise or foolish. . . . Human nature can't stand this long."[7]

A former president usually has prestige with the public, and it is justifiable for the administration to use it but not to abuse it. John Adams's request of Washington that he help in matters military had credibility. Richard Nixon's "briefing" of Lyndon Johnson on the Vietnam War was understood by the Texan to be a bid for support and not a valid exposure to the truth. Hoover doubted Truman's sincerity when the President first sought his assistance, but in time it became apparent that the President was acting in good faith. The fact that a political motivation is always in the background, however, is a reality that an ex-president can accept if it is tempered with some real regard for his expertise.

The President in office has an obligation to treat the retired Presidents with respect and courtesy. FDR's behavior toward Hoover was shabby. Lincoln's paranoia about some of his predecessors was unbecoming. And the Truman-Eisenhower rift was undignified. Lyndon Johnson's fulsome behavior toward Truman bordered on exploitation, for his frequent visits to Independence were always well publicized. In this case it is hard to judge which facet of the Johnson character was dominant—his sentimentality, his desire to act with kindness to the former President so that he might look forward to the same treatment from his successors, or his profound political sense.

Exploitation of former presidents is not limited to the incumbent President and his administration. The political party can pressure him into service for fund raising or campaigning. Philanthropic, patriotic, and religious organizations of all kinds can also be a nuisance. Hoover, who was an ex-President even longer than John Adams, realized that the pitfalls are many. He wrote to Truman, his fellow member in the most exclusive club in the world: "I think we need an agreement that we will not allow promoters of causes to trap us into joint actions for their schemes without our having prior consultations."[8]

Once having held the top job in the United States, no ex-president can hope for obscurity. A sense of history drives them to protect and defend their administrations in statements and writings. This influences their actions and their behavior in retirement. According to John Adams, he and Jefferson were happy in their post-presidential years but George Washington was not. His uneasiness was activated by "the great changes" in the politics of the country, which might be for the better but he feared were for the worse.[9] From then to now, the President faced the inevitable truism that "the buck stops here." Hence the retired President has an awareness that no others can have of the awful isolation of the American presidency. It creates a bond even among former enemies. "There has never been a single man who filled that office who did not respect it when he left," Truman said. Hoover, who had no reason to admire Franklin Roosevelt, always shut people up when they started to tell improper Roosevelt stories. He did not want to hear disrespect for the presidency.[10]

For the people, an ex-president is a link with the past, a symbol of continuity, and an exercise in nostalgia. If he lives long enough, no matter how unpopular on leaving office, he acquires respect. The public is fickle in its bestowal of favors but also has a short memory for those it disliked. Retired chief executives become sages, nestors, beloved elder statesmen, or even folk heroes.

In the past, ex-presidents have chosen to write, to teach, to lecture, to run again for office, or to serve as special ambassadors, as chairmen of special committees, or as advisors. Some have preferred to retire to private life. The proper use of ex-presidents is to let them determine the disposition of their twilight years according to their own preferences and abilities.

NOTES

Preface: The Twilight Years

1. George E. Reedy, *The Twilight of the Presidency*, p. 22.
2. Harry J. Sievers, *Benjamin Harrison: Hoosier President*, p. 252.
3. Lyndon B. Johnson, *The Vantage Point*, p. 569.

PART I

Chapter 1. Warmaking

1. Alexander DeConde, *The Quasi-War*, p. 96.
2. George Washington, *Writings of Washington*, ed. J. C. Fitzpatrick, 35 vols., 35:19.
3. Ibid.
4. Ibid.
5. James Thomas Flexner, *George Washington: Anguish and Farewell*, pp. 353–54.
6. Broadus Mitchell, *Alexander Hamilton: The National Adventure*, p. 427.
7. Washington, *Writings*, 36:476–77.
8. Ibid.
9. John Adams, *The Works of John Adams*, ed. Charles Francis Adams, 10 vols., 10:22–24.
10. Page Smith, *John Adams*, 2 vols., 2:1109.
11. John Adams, *Works*, 10:105–6; John Adams to John Quincy Adams, February 20, 1815, Adams Papers Microfilm, no. 422; John Adams to John Quincy Adams, June 17, 1815, APM, no. 424.
12. Thomas Jefferson, *The Writings of Thomas Jefferson*, ed. A. A. Lipscomb and A. E. Berger, 20 vols., 13:92–94.
13. Ibid., pp. 144–49.
14. Ibid., pp. 232–36; 259–61.
15. Ibid., pp. 265–68.
16. Ibid., pp. 381–84.
17. Ibid., pp. 202–6.
18. Ibid., pp. 216–17.
19. Ibid., pp. 226–30.
20. Ibid., pp. 432–34.
21. Merrill D. Peterson, *Thomas Jefferson and the New Nation*, p. 935.
22. Marie B. Hecht, *John Quincy Adams*, pp. 620, 623.
23. Lyon G. Tyler, ed., *The Letters and Times of The Tylers*, 3 vols., 2:435; Robert Seager II, *And Tyler Too*, pp. 327–28.
24. Seager, *Tyler*, p. 328; Tyler, ed., *Letters*, 2:149–50.
25. Tyler, ed., *Letters*, 2:477–79.
26. Ibid., p. 375.
27. Millard Fillmore, *Papers of Millard Fillmore*, ed. F. H. Severance, 2 vols., 2:390–91.
28. Ibid., p. 61.
29. Tyler, ed., *Letters*, 2:577.
30. Robert G. Gunderson, *Old Gentlemen's Convention*, p. 13.

31. Tyler, ed., *Letters*, 2:596–98; Gunderson, *Old Gentlemen's Convention*, pp. 9–10.
32. Tyler, ed., *Letters*, 2:598–60.
33. Seager, *Tyler*, p. 456.
34. Tyler, ed., *Letters*, 2:616.
35. Ibid., p. 607.
36. Ibid., pp. 600, 642.
37. Roy F. Nichols, *Franklin Pierce*, pp. 515, 521–22, 517.
38. Ibid., pp. 516–17.
39. Ibid., p. 518.
40. Van Buren to Franklin Pierce, April 20, 1861, Van Buren Papers Microfilm, Library of Congress, no. 34.
41. Nichols, *Pierce*, pp. 519–20; Glyndon Van Deusen, *William Henry Seward*, p. 90.
42. Abraham Lincoln, *The Collected Works of Abraham Lincoln*, ed. Roy P. Basler, 8 vols., 4:505.
43. Julian Hawthorne, *The Memoirs of Julian Hawthorne*, p. 127; Mark Van Doren, *Nathaniel Hawthorne*, p. 257.
44. Nathaniel Hawthorne, *Our Old Home*, p. xi.
45. Philip S. Klein, *President James Buchanan*, p. 406.
46. James Buchanan, *The Works of James Buchanan*, ed. John Bassett Moore, 12 vols., 11:188–89.
47. Lincoln, *Works*, 4:422.
48. Buchanan, *Works*, 11:324.
49. Ibid., p. 240.
50. Ibid., pp. 268–69, 271.
51. Robert J. Rayback, *Millard Fillmore*, p. 425.
52. Fillmore, *Papers*, 2:62–63.
53. Rayback, *Fillmore*, p. 425.
54. Fillmore, *Papers*, 2:402–6.
55. Ibid., pp. 85–90.
56. Tyler, ed., *Letters*, 3:662.
57. Ibid., pp. 662–65.
58. Seager, *Tyler*, pp. 489–90.
59. Nichols, *Pierce*, pp. 525–26.
60. Ibid., p. 525.
61. Ibid., pp. 526–27.
62. Buchanan, *Works*, 11:384–86.
63. Grover Cleveland, *The Letters of Grover Cleveland*, ed. Allan Nevins, pp. 491–92.
64. Allan Nevins, *Grover Cleveland*, pp. 743–44.
65. Cleveland, *Letters*, p. 495.
66. George F. Parker, *Recollections of Grover Cleveland*, pp. 249–50.
67. Cleveland, *Letters*, pp. 513–14.
68. *New York World*, February 25, 1915; Henry F. Pringle, *The Life and Times of William Howard Taft*, 2 vols., 2:869–70.
69. Pringle, *Taft*, 2:472–75.
70. Theodore Roosevelt, *The Letters of Theodore Roosevelt*, ed. Elting E. Morison, 8 vols., 8:840–41.
71. Ibid., pp. 883–84, 922.
72. Ibid., pp. 867–68.
73. Ibid., pp. 1094–96, 1124–25, 1159–60.
74. Ibid., pp. 1161, 1163.
75. Pringle, *Taft*, 2:915.

76. William Manners, *TR and Will*, p. 314.

77. Ibid., p. 300.

78. *New York Times*, July 20, 1918.

79. Alice R. Longworth, *Crowded Hours*, p. 246; Roosevelt, *Letters*, 8:1201.

80. Alvin Johnson, *Pioneer's Progress*, p. 253.

81. Joseph L. Gardner, *Departing Glory*, p. 373.

82. Roosevelt, *Letters*, 8:1195.

83. Lawrence F. Abbott, *Impressions of Theodore Roosevelt*, p. 305.

84. Roosevelt, *Letters*, 8:1280.

85. Ibid., p. 1286.

86. Ibid., p. 1320.

87. Ibid., p. 1399.

88. William Allen White, *The Autobiography of William Allen White*, p. 551.

89. Cordell Hull, *The Memoirs of Cordell Hull*, 2 vols., 1:202.

90. *New York Times*, March 9, 1938; Eugene Lyons, *Herbert Hoover*, p. 357; James V. Compton, *The Swastika and the Eagle*, p. 16.

91. *New York Times*, October 23, 26, 27, 1946.

92. Joan Hoff Wilson, *Herbert Hoover*, pp. 245, 247.

93. Herbert Hoover, *An American Epic*, 4 vols., 4:20–21.

94. Herbert Hoover to Cordell Hull, December 20, 1940, Cordell Hull Papers, Herbert Hoover Library.

95. Herbert Hoover to Cordell Hull, March 5, 1941, Cordell Hull Papers, Herbert Hoover Library.

96. Cordell Hull to Herbert Hoover, March 14, 1941, Cordell Hull Papers, Herbert Hoover Library.

97. Herbert Hoover to Robert A. Taft, April 20, 1941, Robert A. Taft Papers, Herbert Hoover Library.

98. Hoover, *American Epic*, 4:56–57.

99. Ibid., pp. 62–64.

100. Cordell Hull to Herbert Hoover, June 28, 1941, Cordell Hull Papers, Herbert Hoover Library.

101. Herbert Hoover to Cordell Hull, June 3, 1941, Cordell Hull Papers, Herbert Hoover Library.

102. Hoover, *American Epic*, 4:72.

103. Herbert Hoover to Alfred Landon, November 1, 1941, Alfred Landon Papers, Herbert Hoover Library.

104. Herbert Hoover to Alfred Landon, November 29, 1941, Alfred Landon Papers, Herbert Hoover Library.

105. Herbert Hoover to Alfred Landon, September 4, 1942, Alfred Landon Papers, Herbert Hoover Library.

106. Herbert Hoover to Harry Truman, December 19, 1962, Harry Truman Papers, Herbert Hoover Library.

107. Herbert Hoover to Cordell Hull, April 3, 1944, Cordell Hull Papers, Herbert Hoover Library.

108. *Science Digest*, May 1971.

109. *New York Times*, May 2, 1970.

110. Richard Harwood and Haynes Johnson, *Lyndon*, p. 157.

111. *New York Times*, May 23, 1971.

112. Ibid., November 18, 1966.

113. *Kansas City Star*, May 19, 1967.

114. *New York Times*, August 6, 1968.

Chapter 2. Peacemaking

1. Jefferson, *Works*, 14:221–25.
2. Pringle, *Taft*, 2:737.
3. Ibid., pp. 929–30.
4. Roosevelt, *Letters*, 8:938–39.
5. Pringle, *Taft*, 2:931.
6. Roosevelt, *Letters*, 8:1140–42.
7. Pringle, *Taft*, 2:934.
8. Ibid., p. 937.
9. Ibid., p. 939.
10. Ibid.
11. Ray Stannard Baker, *Woodrow Wilson: Life and Letters*, 8 vols., 8:253.
12. Ibid., p. 377.
13. Colonel House, *The Intimate Papers of Colonel House*, ed. Charles Seymour, 4 vols., 4:225.
14. *New York Times*, December 17, 1918.
15. Thomas A. Bailey, *Woodrow Wilson and The Great Betrayal*, p. 266.
16. *New York Times*, March 28, 1919.
17. Bailey, *The Great Betrayal*, p. 266.
18. *New York Times*, August 28, 1920.
19. Herbert Hoover, *The Ordeal of Woodrow Wilson*, p. 298; Bailey, *Wilson and The Great Betrayal*, 325
20. Roosevelt, *Letters*, 8:1380–81; *New York Times*, October 10, 14, 1918; *Kansas City Star*, November 18, 1918.
21. Roosevelt, *Letters*, 8:1396–99.
22. Theodore Roosevelt, *Roosevelt in the Kansas City Star*, ed. Ralph Stout, pp. 292–95.
23. Herbert Hoover and Hugh Gibson, *The Problems of Lasting Peace*, p. ix; Herbert Hoover Library.
24. Herbert Hoover to Alfred Landon, February 18, 1945, Alfred Landon Papers, Herbert Hoover Library.
25. Memorandum, May 28, 1945, Herbert Hoover Library.
26. Hoover, *American Epic*, 4:124, 177.
27. Herbert Hoover to Harry Truman, April 21, 1946, Harry Truman Papers, Herbert Hoover Library.
28. Herbert Hoover to Harry Truman, January 19, 1947, Harry Truman Papers, Herbert Hoover Library; Hoover, *American Epic*, 4:226.
29. Herbert Hoover to Harry Truman, March 18, 1947, Harry Truman Papers, Herbert Hoover Library.
30. Lucius Clay to Herbert Hoover, April 7, 1947, Herbert Hoover Library.
31. Herbert Hoover to George C. Marshall, May 12, 1947, Herbert Hoover Library.
32. Wilson, *Hoover*, 255.

Chapter 3. Running Again

1. Samuel Hart to Martin Van Buren, June 28, 1841; A. Vanderpoll to Martin Van Buren, August 10, 1841; Henry Horn to Martin Van Buren, November 13, 1841; Van Buren to Henry Horn, November 26, 1841; John Law to Martin Van Buren, December 10, 1841, Martin Van Buren Presidential Papers Microfilm, Library of Congress, no. 22.

2. John Slidell to Martin Van Buren, March 10, 1842, Van Buren Papers Microfilm no. 22; *Natchez* (Miss.) *Daily Free Trader*, April 19, 1842.

3. Andrew Jackson, *Correspondence of Andrew Jackson*, ed. John Spencer Bassett, 6 vols., 6:177.

4. George Hopkins to Martin Van Buren, February 20, 1843; Benjamin Park to Silas Wright, May 10, 1843, Van Buren Papers Microfilm, no. 22.

5. Jackson, *Correspondence*, 6:276–77.

6. Amos Kendall to Martin Van Buren, April 19, 1844; Smith Van Buren to Martin Van Buren, April 23, 1844, Van Buren Papers Microfilm, no. 25.

7. Thomas Ritchie to Martin Van Buren, May 5, 1844, Van Buren Papers Microfilm, no. 25.

8. Jackson, *Correspondence*, 6:284, 285.

9. Ibid., pp. 289–91, 293–94.

10. John C. Rives to Martin Van Buren, Jr., May 20, 1844; Martin Van Buren to Benjamin Butler, May 20, 1844, Van Buren Papers Microfilm, no. 25.

11. Jackson, *Correspondence*, 6:296.

12. George Bancroft to Martin Van Buren, September 6, 1844, Van Buren Papers Microfilm, no. 26.

13. George W. Thompson to Martin Van Buren, December 23, 1846; Martin Van Buren to Samuel Waterby and others, June 20, 1848, Van Buren Papers Microfilm, no. 26.

14. Arthur Schlesinger, Jr., *The Age of Jackson*, pp. 464–65.

15. Charles Francis Adams to Martin Van Buren, July 16, 1848, Van Buren Papers Microfilm, no. 28.

16. Martin Duberman, *Charles Francis Adams*, p. 149.

17. Ibid., pp. 150–51.

18. James K. Polk, *Polk: The Diary of a President*, ed. Allan Nevins, p. 328.

19. Ibid., pp. 337–38.

20. Ibid., p. 352.

21. Fillmore, *Papers*, 1:428.

22. Ibid., pp. 435–36.

23. Rayback, *Fillmore*, p. 387.

24. Ibid., pp. 391–92.

25. Fillmore, *Papers*, 2:358–59.

26. Rayback, *Fillmore*, pp. 403–6; Fillmore, *Papers*, 2:10–11.

27. Fillmore, *Papers*, 2:16–17.

28. Rayback, *Fillmore*, pp. 406–7; Fillmore, *Papers*, 2:27–28.

29. Fillmore, *Papers*, 2:365–66.

30. Rayback, *Fillmore*, pp. 413–14.

31. Adam Badeau, *Grant in Peace*, p. 316.

32. Herbert S. Parmet and Marie B. Hecht, *Never Again: A President Runs for a Third Term*, p. 34.

33. William B. Hesseltine, *Ulysses S. Grant: Politician*, p. 434.

34. Badeau, *Grant in Peace*, p. 318.

35. J. T. Headley, *The Life and Travels of Grant*, p. 582.

36. Badeau, *Grant in Peace*, p. 321; Alfred R. Conkling, *The Life and Letters of Roscoe Conkling*, p. 587.

37. Badeau, *Grant in Peace*, p. 319.

38. Conkling, *Letters*, pp. 597–600.

39. Ibid., pp. 602–3; opposite, 600–601.

40. Henry L. Stoddard, *As I Knew Them*, pp. 109–110.

41. Conkling, *Letters*, p. 603.
42. Ibid., p. 608.
43. Ibid.
44. Stoddard, *As I Knew Them*, pp. 109–10.
45. Nevins, *Cleveland*, p. 448.
46. Cleveland, *Letters*, pp. 212–13.
47. Ibid., p. 219.
48. Parker, *Cleveland Recollections*, p. 128.
49. Cleveland, *Letters*, p. 235.
50. Ibid., pp. 221–22.
51. Nevins, *Cleveland*, p. 466.
52. Cleveland, *Letters*, p. 245.
53. Parker, *Cleveland Recollections*, p. 151.
54. Cleveland, *Letters*, p. 248.
55. Parker, *Cleveland Recollections*, p. 162.
56. Horace S. Merrill, *Bourbon Leader: Grover Cleveland and the Democratic Party*, p. 157.
57. Nevins, *Cleveland*, pp. 497–98.
58. Cleveland, *Letters*, pp. 295–96.
59. Ibid., pp. 302, 310.
60. Parker, *Cleveland Recollections*, pp. 169–71.
61. Ibid., p. 172.
62. Nevins, *Cleveland*, p. 508.
63. Roosevelt, *Letters*, 7:99.
64. Gardner, *Departing Glory*, pp. 188–91.
65. George E. Mowry, *Theodore Roosevelt and the Progressive Movement*, p. 144.
66. Roosevelt, *Letters*, 7:122.
67. Mowry, *TR and Progressive Movement*, p. 148.
68. Roosevelt, *Letters*, 7:147.
69. Ibid., p. 148.
70. Ibid., p. 159.
71. Ibid., p. 162.
72. Ibid., pp. 286–87.
73. Ibid., p. 215.
74. Ibid., p. 273.
75. Ibid., pp. 475, 479.
76. Henry Adams, *Letters of Henry Adams*, ed. W. C. Ford, 2 vols., 2:578.
77. Ibid., p. 587.
78. Gardner, *Departing Glory*, p. 234.
79. Abbott, *Roosevelt Impressions*, p. 84.
80. Longworth, *Crowded Hours*, p. 203.
81. *New York Times*, June 20, 1912; Henry F. Pringle, *Theodore Roosevelt*, pp. 564–65.
82. White, *Autobiography*, p. 487.
83. Henry Adams, *Letters*, 2:602.
84. Roosevelt, *Letters*, 7:583.
85. Gardner, *Departing Glory*, p. 270.
86. Roosevelt, *Letters*, 7:632.
87. Corinne Roosevelt Robinson, *My Brother Theodore Roosevelt*, p. 274.
88. Longworth, *Crowded Hours*, p. 219.

89. Mowry, *TR and Progressive Movement*, p. 278; Longworth, *Crowded Hours*, p. 121.
90. Richard W. Leopold, *Elihu Root*, p. 88.
91. Mowry, *TR and Progressive Movement*, p. 254.
92. Parmet and Hecht, *Never Again*, p. 5.
93. Roosevelt, *Letters*, 7:481, 498.
94. Ibid., p. 641.

Chapter 4. Partisan Politics

1. *New Yorker*, February 10, 1975; *Newsweek*, May 19, 1975.
2. Flexner, *GW: Anguish and Farewell*, pp. 429–31.
3. Martin Van Buren, *The Autobiography of Martin Van Buren*, Annual Report of the American Historical Association, 1918, p. 178; Leonard Baker, *John Marshall*, pp. 298, 314.
4. Smith, *John Adams*, 2:1079–80.
5. Monroe, *Writings*, 3:149–50; Harry Ammon, *James Monroe*, pp. 558–60.
6. Tyler, *Letters*, 2:551–52; Seager, *Tyler*, p. 436.
7. Fillmore, *Papers*, 2:431–35.
8. Buchanan, *Works*, 11:371–72, 377–78.
9. James R. Brewer to Andrew Johnson, October 22, 1870, Andrew Johnson Presidential Papers Microfilm, no. 37.
10. *Atchison* (Kansas) *Champion*, December 1872.
11. Jonathan McCormack to Andrew Johnson, April 20, 1874; L. J. Der Pose to Andrew Johnson, May 26, 1874, Andrew Johnson Papers Microfilm, no. 38.
12. Lloyd Paul Stryker, *Andrew Johnson*, pp. 809–10.
13. Ibid., p. 817.
14. J. Moody to Andrew Johnson, Andrew Johnson Papers Microfilm, no. 39.
15. Rutherford B. Hayes, *Diary and Letters of Rutherford Burchard Hayes*, ed. C. R. Williams, 4:113, 382.
16. Ibid., pp. 393–94.
17. Sievers, *Harrison*, 3:260, 261.
18. Cleveland, *Letters*, pp. 473, 506.
19. Ibid., pp. 532, 533.
20. Ibid., pp. 538, 541.
21. Parker, *Cleveland Recollections*, p. 207; Cleveland, *Letters*, p. 582; Eugene Roseboom, *A History of Presidential Elections*, p. 339.
22. Parker, *Cleveland Recollections*, pp. 219, 221.
23. Stoddard, *As I Knew Them*, p. 447.
24. White, *Autobiography*, pp. 525.
25. Roosevelt, *Letters*, 8:1062.
26. Henry Adams, *Letters*, 2:627.
27. Baker, *Wilson*, 6:246; White, *Autobiography*, p. 523.
28. Baker, *Wilson*, 6:295; Roosevelt, *Letters*, 8:1124.
29. *New York Times*, November 8, 1916.
30. Roosevelt, *Letters*, 8:1123, 1124, 1137.
31. Bailey, *Great Betrayal*, pp. 345–48.
32. Hull, *Memoirs*, 1:119, 120.
33. Ibid., p. 117; Gene Smith, *When the Cheering Stopped*, p. 234.
34. Herbert Hoover to William Allen White, June 22, 1936, William Allen White Papers, Herbert Hoover Library.

35. John D. M. Hamilton to Herbert Hoover, June 16, 1936; Herbert Hoover to John D. M. Hamilton, June 24, 1936, John D. M. Hamilton Papers, Herbert Hoover Library.

36. Transcript of Telephone Conversation between Herbert Hoover and Alfred Landon, September 2, 1936; Herbert Hoover to Alfred Landon, September 2, 1936, Alfred Landon Papers, Herbert Hoover Library.

37. Letter to John D. M. Hamilton, November 4, 1936, John D. M. Hamilton Papers, Herbert Hoover Library.

38. Parmet and Hecht, *Never Again*, p. 70; *Chicago Daily News*, November 16, 1939.

39. Parmet and Hecht, *Never Again*, p. 124.

40. Ibid., p. 132.

41. Ibid., p. 137.

42. Judge Charles W. Fisher, Oral History, July 31, 1971, Herbert Hoover Library.

43. Herbert Brownell, Jr., Oral History, March 29, 1969, Herbert Hoover Library.

44. Ward Bannister to Herbert Hoover, September 6, 1949, Ward Bannister Papers, Herbert Hoover Library.

45. Press release, July 9, 1952; Telegram, Herbert Hoover to Dwight D. Eisenhower, October 8, 1952; Herbert Hoover to Dwight D. Eisenhower, November 17, 1952, Dwight D. Eisenhower Papers, Herbert Hoover Library.

46. Dwight D. Eisenhower to Herbert Hoover, July 2, 1956, Dwight D. Eisenhower Papers, Herbert Hoover Library.

47. Ellen Brumback, Oral History, June 5, 1967, Herbert Hoover Library.

48. Ibid.

49. Herbert Hoover to Barry Goldwater, July 16, 1964, Barry Goldwater Papers, Herbert Hoover Library.

50. Harry Truman to Robert G. Nixon, INS Staff Correspondent, n.d., n.t., Harry S. Truman Library.

51. *New York Times*, June 18, 1953; Paul G. Welles to Charles S. Murphy, June 26, 1953, Harry S. Truman Library.

52. Joseph P. Lash, *Eleanor: The Years Alone*, pp. 255–56.

53. Theodore C. Sorenson, *Kennedy*, p. 82.

54. Truman address, April 17, 1968, Harry S. Truman Library.

55. *Pittsburgh Post-Gazette*, October 9, 1956.

56. Calvin W. Rawlings to Paul M. Butler, October 26, 1956; Papers of Charles S. Murphy, Harry S. Truman Library.

57. Herbert S. Parmet, *The Democratic Umbrella*, manuscript; Leon Keyserling to Herbert S. Parmet, February 19, 1975, private papers.

58. Sorenson, *Kennedy*, pp. 152–53; Theodore H. White, *The Making of the President, 1960*, pp. 152–53.

59. White, *Making of the President, 1960*, pp. 152–53.

60. *Independence* (Missouri) *Pictorial Shopper*, August 25, 1960.

61. Merle Miller, *Plain Speaking*, p. 178.

62. *Washington Star*, October 13, 1960; *Kansas City Times*, October 13, 1960; Sorenson, *Kennedy*, p. 203.

63. *Washington Star*, October 13, 1960.

64. Miller, *Plain Speaking*, p. 187.

65. *New York Times*, May 9, 12, 1961.

66. Ibid., October 15, 1961.

67. Ibid., October 16, 1961.

68. Ibid., December 29, 1963.

69. Theodore H. White, *The Making of the President, 1964*, p. 153.

70. Ibid., pp. 346–47.
71. *New York Times*, December 23, 28, 1967.
72. Ibid., July 19, 1968.
73. Gary Wills, *Nixon Agonistes*, p. 46; *New York Times*, November 7, 1968.
74. Leo Janos, "Last Days of the President," *Atlantic Monthly* (232:35–41, July 1973), p. 40.
75. *New York Times*, August 17, 1972.

Chapter 5. Tools of the Incumbents

1. Ammon, *Monroe*, p. 280.
2. Jefferson, *Writings*, 12:330–33.
3. Armin Rappaport, ed., *The Monroe Doctrine*, p. 59.
4. Ibid.
5. Ibid., p. 61.
6. Hecht, *John Quincy Adams*, p. 357; Madison, *Writings*, 9:172.
7. Ralph Ketcham, *James Madison*, pp. 643–44.
8. Madison, *Writings*, 9:481–82, 480–81, 463–64.
9. Ibid., pp. 573, 491.
10. Tyler, *Letters*, 2:285–86.
11. Polk, *Diary*, p. 97.
12. James K. Polk to Martin Van Buren, January 4, 1845, Van Buren Papers, no. 26.
13. Martin Van Buren to James K. Polk, January 18, 1845, Van Buren Papers, no. 26.
14. James K. Polk to Martin Van Buren, February 22, 1845, Van Buren Papers, no. 26.
15. Martin Van Buren to James K. Polk, February 27, 1845; Mrs. Butler to Martin Van Buren, February 27, 1845; Martin Van Buren to James K. Polk, March 1, 1845, Van Buren Papers, no. 26.
16. Polk, *Diary*, p. 247.
17. Badeau, *Grant in Peace*, p. 330.
18. George Frederick Howe, *Chester A. Arthur*, p. 270.
19. Badeau, *Grant in Peace*, p. 397.
20. Cleveland, *Letters*, p. 560.
21. Theodore Roosevelt, *An Autobiography*, pp. 488–89.
22. Roosevelt, *Letters*, 3:503.
23. Cleveland, *Letters*, pp. 574–75.
24. Archie Butt, *Taft and Roosevelt*, 2:439, 442.
25. Francis Russell, *The Shadow of Blooming Grove*, p. 429.
26. Pringle, *Taft*, 2:956–57.
27. Ibid., p. 957.
28. Miller, *Plain Speaking*, p. 220.
29. Harry S. Truman, *Mr. Citizen*, p. 117.
30. Herbert Hoover to Harry S. Truman, June 19, 1949, Harry S. Truman Papers, Herbert Hoover Library.
31. Lyons, *Hoover*, p. 402.
32. Ibid.
33. Brownell Oral History, Herbert Hoover Library.
34. Ibid.
35. Dr. Theodore G. Klumpp, Oral History, Herbert Hoover Library.
36. Dwight D. Eisenhower to Herbert Hoover, October 15, 1956, Dwight D. Eisenhower Papers, Herbert Hoover Library.
37. John F. Kennedy to Herbert Hoover, August 9, 1961, John F. Kennedy Library.

38. Herbert Hoover to Lyndon Johnson, April 27, 1964, Lyndon Johnson Papers, Herbert Hoover Library.
39. Truman, *Mr. Citizen*, p. 18.
40. Ibid., pp. 19–20.
41. Miller, *Plain Speaking*, p. 343.
42. *New York Times*, February 7, 1961; July 15, 1958.
43. Richard M. Nixon, *Six Crises*, pp. 404–5.
44. Sorenson, *Kennedy*, pp. 231, 281.
45. Wire, Herbert Hoover to John F. Kennedy, January 19, 1961, John F. Kennedy Papers, Herbert Hoover Library.
46. *New York Times*, March 25, 1961.
47. John F. Kennedy to Herbert Hoover, March 2, 1961, John F. Kennedy Papers, Herbert Hoover Library.
48. *New York Times*, April 23, 1961.
49. Herbert Hoover to John F. Kennedy, April 28, 1961, John F. Kennedy Papers, Herbert Hoover Library; John F. Kennedy to Herbert Hoover, May 8, 1961, John F. Kennedy Library.
50. *New York Times*, May 2, 1961; Arthur M. Schlesinger, Jr., *A Thousand Days*, p. 292.
51. John F. Kennedy to Dwight D. Eisenhower, May 17, 1962, John F. Kennedy Library.
52. Herbert Hoover to Harry S. Truman, May 5, 1961, Harry S. Truman Library.
53. Memo to Kennedy, December 28, 1962, John F. Kennedy Library.
54. John F. Kennedy to Dwight D. Eisenhower, July 16, 1961; Telegram from Eisenhower through Colonel Robert Schulz to John F. Kennedy, John F. Kennedy Library.
55. John F. Kennedy to Dwight D. Eisenhower, December 9, 1961, John F. Kennedy Library.
56. Herbert Hoover to John F. Kennedy, February 3, 1962, John F. Kennedy Papers, Herbert Hoover Library.
57. Dwight D. Eisenhower to Charles P. Taft, Telegram, John F. Kennedy Library.
58. *New York Times*, September 11, 1962.
59. Miller, *Plain Speaking*, p. 343.
60. *New York Times*, August 27, 1963.
61. Ibid., August 7, 1962.
62. John F. Kennedy to Harry S. Truman, May 31, 1963, John F. Kennedy Library; Miller, *Plain Speaking*, p. 409.
63. Johnson, *The Vantage Point*, p. 31.
64. Ibid., p. 32; *New York Times*, December 25, 1963.
65. *New York Times*, December 28, 1966.
66. *Independence* (Missouri) *Examiner*, January 20, 1966.
67. Janos, "Last Days," p. 38.
68. *New York Times*, August 28, 1969.
69. Janos, "Last Days," p. 38.
70. *Newsweek*, May 21, 1973.

PART II

Chapter 6. Making Ends Meet

1. Harry S. Truman to Sam Rayburn, August 13, 1957, Sam Rayburn Library, Bonham, Texas.

2. Charles Murphy to Lyndon Johnson, February 7, 1957, Charles S. Murphy Papers, Harry S. Truman Library.

3. Excerpt from Congressional Record enclosed with Letter, Lyndon Johnson to Charles Murphy, February 19, 1957, Charles S. Murphy Papers, Harry S. Truman Library.

4. *Baltimore Sun*, February 8, 1957; *Washington Post*, February 9, 1957.

5. Washington, *Writings*, 35:429.

6. Sarah N. Randolph, *The Domestic Life of Thomas Jefferson*, p. 288.

7. Margaret Bayard Smith, *The First Forty Years of Washington Society*, p. 75.

8. Fawn M. Brodie, *Thomas Jefferson*, p. 430.

9. Jefferson, *Writings*, 14:190–94.

10. *The Adams-Jefferson Letters*, ed. Lester J. Cappon, p. 441.

11. Ibid., p. 443.

12. Peterson, *Jefferson*, p. 457.

13. Randolph, *Domestic Life*, p. 352; Thomas Jefferson, "Thoughts on Lotteries" in Saul Padover, *The Complete Jefferson*, pp. 1289–97.

14. Randolph, *Domestic Life*, p. 354.

15. Ibid., p. 356.

16. John Quincy Adams, *Memoirs*, 7:118.

17. Madison, *Writings*, 9:243–46.

18. Ketcham, *Madison*, pp. 613–14; Smith, *First Forty Years*, p. 233.

19. Madison, *Writings*, 9:221.

20. Monroe, *Writings*, 7:51–53; Ammon, *Monroe*, p. 554.

21. Ammon, *Monroe*, pp. 554–56.

22. Madison, *Writings*, 9:457–59.

23. John Quincy Adams, *Diary*, pp. 419–20.

24. John Spencer Bassett, *The Life of Andrew Jackson*, p. 744.

25. Marquis James, *The Life of Andrew Jackson*, p. 732.

26. Jackson, *Correspondence*, 6:41.

27. Ibid., pp. 70, 71.

28. Ibid., p. 146.

29. Ibid., p. 186; James, *Jackson*, pp. 754, 760.

30. James, *Jackson*, pp. 778, 891.

31. Randolph, *Domestic Life*, p. 353.

32. John Adams to John Quincy Adams, July 3, 1816, Adams Papers Microfilm, no. 432.

33. Holmes Alexander, *The American Talleyrand*, p. 389.

34. Rayback, *Fillmore*, p. 385.

35. Hesseltine, *Grant*, pp. 56–57.

36. Badeau, *Grant in Peace*, p. 429.

37. Mark Twain, *Mark Twain's Autobiography*, ed. Albert Bigelow Paine, pp. 238–41.

38. Mark Twain, *Mark Twain's Letters*, ed. Albert Bigelow Paine, 2:464.

39. Howe, *Arthur*, pp. 252–53.

40. Hesseltine, *Grant*, p. 451.

41. H. J. Eckenrode, *Rutherford B. Hayes: Statesman of Reunion*, p. 328.

42. Hayes, *Diary*, 4:640–41, 581–82.

43. Ibid., pp. 19, 22–23.

44. Nevins, *Cleveland*, p. 761.

45. Parker, *Cleveland Recollections*, p. 302.

46. Nevins, *Cleveland*, p. 761.

47. Sievers, *Harrison*, 3:254–56.

48. Hermann Hagedorn, *A Guide to Sagamore Hill*, p. 33.
49. Hermann Hagedorn, *The Roosevelt Family of Sagamore Hill*, p. 237.
50. *Roosevelt in the Kansas City Star*, pp. xxxviii, xi–xii.
51. Roosevelt, *Letters*, 8:1230.
52. Pringle, *Taft*, 2:856.
53. Ibid., pp. 856–57.
54. Edith Bolling Wilson, *My Memoir*, p. 327; Smith, *When the Cheering Stopped*, p. 208.
55. Donald R. McCoy, *Calvin Coolidge: The Quiet President*, p. 398; *New York Times*, May 25, 1933.
56. *New York Times*, May 25, 1933.
57. Pringle, *Taft*, 2:847–48.
58. *New York Times*, January 30, 1964.
59. Janos, "Last Days," p. 40.
60. *Newsweek*, November 11, 1974.
61. *New York Times*, August 30, 1974.
62. *Newsday*, January 16, 1975.
63. *Time*, August 11, 1975.

Chapter 7. Ex-Monarchs Abroad

1. Fillmore, *Papers*, 2:354.
2. Ibid.
3. Ibid., p. 487.
4. Glyndon Van Deusen, *Horace Greeley*, p. 197.
5. Fillmore, *Papers*, 2:304–7.
6. Ibid., p. 114.
7. Ibid., p. 357.
8. George Bancroft to Martin Van Buren, May 5, 1845; Martin Van Buren to George Bancroft, May 12, 1845, Van Buren Papers Microfilm, nos. 26, 27.
9. *New York Times*, January 7, 1853.
10. Newton Arvin, ed., *Heart of Hawthorne's Journals*, (Boston: 1929), pp. 319–22.
11. Lloyd Morris, *The Rebellious Puritan: Portrait of Mr. Hawthorne*, pp. 323, 334.
12. Ibid., p. 324.
13. Badeau, *Grant in Peace*, p. 297.
14. Headley, *Travels of Grant*, p. 13.
15. Badeau, *Grant in Peace*, pp. 273, 279.
16. Julia Dent Grant, *The Personal Memoirs of Julia Dent Grant*, ed. John Y. Simon, p. 207.
17. Headley, *Travels of Grant*, pp. 270–71.
18. Ibid., p. 362.
19. Ibid., p. 224.
20. Ibid., pp. 229–30.
21. Martin Duberman, *James Russell Lowell*, (Boston: 1966), p. 293.
22. Headley, *Travels of Grant*, p. 372.
23. Ibid., p. 390.
24. Ibid., p. 436.
25. Ibid., p. 464.
26. Julia Grant, *Memoirs*, p. 297; Headley, *Travels of Grant*, p. 494.
27. Badeau, *Grant in Peace*, p. 319.
28. Ibid., p. 518.

29. Roosevelt, *Letters*, 8:3–4.
30. Ibid.
31. Theodore Roosevelt, *African Game Trails*, p. 246.
32. Ibid., p. 178.
33. Roosevelt, *Letters*, 8:19.
34. Roosevelt, *African Game Trails*, p. 566.
35. Abbott, *TR Impressions*, p. 295.
36. Ibid., pp. 229–30.
37. Roosevelt, *Letters*, 8:61.
38. Ibid., p. 357.
39. Ibid., pp. 66, 358.
40. Abbott, *TR Impressions*, p. 219; Roosevelt, *Letters*, 8:69, 83.
41. Butt, *Taft and Roosevelt*, 2:319, 322.
42. Abbott, *TR Impressions*, p. 221; Roosevelt, *Letters*, 7:348.
43. Roosevelt, *Letters*, 7:350; Butt, *Taft and Roosevelt*, 1:424.
44. Roosevelt, *Letters*, 7:383.
45. Butt, *Taft and Roosevelt*, 1:421, 422, 423.
46. Roosevelt, *Letters*, 7:409–13.
47. Abbott, *TR Impressions*, pp. 149–52.
48. Roosevelt, *Letters*, 7:756–57.
49. Theodore Roosevelt, *Through the Brazilian Wilderness*, p. 187.
50. Ibid., p. 248.
51. Ibid., p. 277.
52. Ibid., p. 315.
53. Ibid., p. 328.
54. Roosevelt, *Letters*, 7:760, 761.
55. Ibid., p. 772.
56. *New York Times*, May 12, 13, 1956.
57. President and Mrs. Truman's European Trip, 1956, Papers of David D. Lloyd, Harry S. Truman Library; *New York Times*, May 17, 1956.
58. Dwight D. Eisenhower, *Crusade in Europe*, pp. 212–13.
59. *New York Times*, May 25, 1956.
60. Ibid., June 3, 1956.
61. Ibid., June 15, 1956.
62. Ibid., June 21, 1956.
63. Ibid., June 25, 1956.
64. Ibid., July 2, 1958.
65. Ibid., August 3, 1956.

Chapter 8. The Perfect Careers

1. John Quincy Adams, *Memoirs*, 4:203.
2. Hecht, *John Quincy Adams*, p. 504.
3. John Quincy Adams, *Diary*, 10:49.
4. Register of Debates XII: Part III: 3758–78; May 18, 19, 1836.
5. Hecht, *John Quincy Adams*, p. 550; John Quincy Adams, *Memoirs*, 9:365.
6. Hecht, *John Quincy Adams*, p. 563.
7. Congressional Globe, VII: 218.
8. Theodore Weld, Angelina Grimke Weld and Sarah Grimke, *Letters of Theodore Weld, Angelina Grimke Weld and Sarah Grimke, 1822–1844*, ed. Barnes and Dumond, p. 890.

9. John Quincy Adams, *Memoirs*, 11:711.
10. Hecht, *John Quincy Adams*, p. 592.
11. Theodore Weld, *Letters*, pp. 905–6.
12. John Quincy Adams, *Memoirs*, 10:431; Charles Warren, *The Supreme Court in United States History*, 2:76.
13. Hecht, *John Quincy Adams*, p. 582.
14. Henry Steele Commager, ed., *Documents of American History*, p. 153; Pringle, *Taft*, 2:1014.
15. Commager, *Documents*, pp. 153, 207.
16. Ibid., p. 207.
17. Max Lerner, *The Mind and Faith of Justice Holmes*, p. 288; Pringle, *Taft*, 2:1023–27.
18. Pringle, *Taft*, 2:1024.
19. Ibid., pp. 1047–48.
20. Ibid., p. 1064.

Chapter 9. Literary Lives

1. John Adams, *Autobiography*, 3:253, 261.
2. Ibid., 1:lxiv.
3. Ibid., 3:293–94.
4. Ibid., 4:37.
5. Ibid., p. 118.
6. *Complete Jefferson*, p. 1191.
7. Ibid., p. 1132.
8. Ibid., p. 1188.
9. Benjamin Franklin, *Benjamin Franklin's Autobiographical Writings*, ed. Carl Van Doren, pp. 347–99; *Complete Jefferson*, p. 1194.
10. Van Buren, *Autobiography*, p. 177.
11. Ibid., pp. 185, 446.
12. Ulysses S. Grant, *Personal Memoirs of U.S. Grant*, 1:53, 56.
13. Ibid., pp. 383, 424–26.
14. Ibid., p. 543.
15. Ibid., 2:222, 422–23.
16. Ibid., p. 460.
17. Ibid., pp. 488–92.
18. Horace Green, *General Grant's Last Stand*, p. 306.
19. Roosevelt, *Letters*, 7:710.
20. Roosevelt, *Autobiography*, p. 203.
21. Ibid., p. 553.
22. Abbott, *TR Impressions*, pp. 175–77.
23. Herbert Hoover, *The Memoirs of Herbert Hoover*, 1:v–vi.
24. Ibid., 3:v.
25. Dwight D. Eisenhower, *At Ease*, pp. 185, 187.
26. Buchanan, *Works*, 11:361–62.
27. Klein, *Buchanan*, p. 418.
28. Charles S. Murphy to David D. Lloyd, July 12, 1953, Charles S. Murphy Papers, Harry S. Truman Library; *New York Times*, September 4, 1955.
29. *New York Times*, November 6, 1955; Harry S. Truman, *Memoirs: Year of Decisions*, p. 74.
30. All of this material from John Eisenhower's autobiography *Strictly Personal*.

31. *New York Times*, October 17, 1971.
32. Ibid., November 18, 1971.
33. Hoover, *Ordeal of Woodrow Wilson*, p. 335.
34. Ibid., pp. 207, 228.
35. Ibid., p. 236.
36. Ibid., p. 293.
37. Ibid., p. 302.
38. *New York Times*, April 27, 1958.
39. *Adams-Jefferson Letters*, pp. 609, 614.

Epilogue: The Proper Use of Ex-Presidents

1. Cleveland, *Letters*, pp. 203–4; Pringle, *Taft*, 2:845–46.
2. Pringle, *Taft*, 2:845–46.
3. Williams, *Hayes*, 2:336.
4. Laurence O'Brien to Claiborne Pell, May 25, 1963, John F. Kennedy Library.
5. John F. Kennedy to Mike Mansfield, April 12, 1962, John F. Kennedy Library.
6. Carl Van Doren, *Benjamin Franklin*, p. 752; Miller, *Plain Speaking*, pp. 431–32.
7. Charles Francis Adams, *Life of John Adams*, 2:359; Hayes, *Diary*, 4:450.
8. Herbert Hoover to Harry S. Truman, March 27, 1960, Harry S. Truman Papers, Herbert Hoover Library.
9. John Adams, *Works*, 10:17.
10. Miller, *Plain Speaking*, p. 4; Don K. Price, Oral History, July 20, 1970, Herbert Hoover Library.

BIBLIOGRAPHY

MANUSCRIPT SOURCES

Adams Family Papers, Massachusetts Historical Society (Microfilm edition
    at Columbia University)
Herbert Hoover Library
    Post Presidential File
John F. Kennedy Library
Harry S. Truman Library
        Charles S. Murphy Papers
        David D. Lloyd Papers
James Monroe Papers, New York Public Library
Presidential Papers, Library of Congress Microfilm
        Van Buren Papers
        Andrew Johnson Papers
        Ulysses S. Grant Papers

NEWSPAPERS

New York *World*
New York *Times*
Kansas City *Star*
Natchez, Mississippi, *Daily Free Trader*
Atchison, Kansas, *Champion*
Chicago *Daily News*
Washington *Star*
Kansas City *Times*
Independence, Missouri, *Pictorial Shopper*
Washington *Post*

PRINTED PRIMARY SOURCES

The Letters of Henry Adams. W. C. Ford, ed. 2 vols. London, Constable, 1930.
The Works of John Adams. Charles Francis Adams, ed. 10 vols. Boston, Little
    Brown and Company, 1856.
Diary and Autobiography of John Adams. L. H. Butterfield, ed. 4 vols. New
    York, Atheneum, 1964.
The Adams-Jefferson Letters. Lester Cappon, ed. New York, Simon and
    Schuster, 1971.
The Diary of John Quincy Adams, 1794–1845. Allan Nevins, ed. New York,
    Longman, Green and Co., 1928.
*Memoirs of John Quincy Adams Comprising Portions of His Diary from
    1795–1848.* Charles Francis Adams, ed. 12 vols. Philadelphia, Lippincott,
    1874.
The Works of James Buchanan. John Bassett Moore, ed. 12 vols. Philadelphia,
    1908–1911.

The Letters of Grover Cleveland. Allan Nevins, ed. Boston, Houghton, Mifflin Co., 1933.

Documents of American History. Henry Steele Commager, ed. New York, Appleton-Century-Crofts, 1963.

Eisenhower, Dwight D. *At Ease.* Garden City, New York, Doubleday, 1967.

———. *Crusade in Europe.* Garden City, New York, Doubleday, 1948.

Eisenhower, John D. *Strictly Personal.* Garden City, New York, Doubleday, 1974.

The Fillmore Papers. F. H. Severance, ed. 2 vols. Buffalo, New York, Buffalo Historical Society, 1907.

Benjamin Franklin's Autobiographical Writings. Carl Van Doren, ed. New York, The Viking Press, 1945.

The Personal Memoirs of Julia Dent Grant. John Y. Simon, ed. New York, G. P. Putnam's Sons, 1975.

Grant, Ulysses S. *General Grant's Letters to a Friend, 1861–1880.* New York, 1897.

———. *Personal Memoirs of U.S. Grant.* New York, Charles L. Webster & Co., 1885.

Harrison, Benjamin. *This Country of Ours.* New York, Scribner, 1922.

The Memoirs of Julian Hawthorne. New York, Macmillan, 1938.

Hawthorne, Nathaniel. *Our Old Home.* Boston, Ticunor and Fields, 1863.

Diary and Letters of Rutherford B. Hayes. C. R. Williams, ed. 4 vols. Columbus, Ohio, 1925.

Hoover, Herbert. *The Memoirs of Herbert Hoover.* 3 vols. New York, Macmillan, 1951–52.

———. *An American Epic.* 4 vols. Chicago, Henry Regnery Company, 1964.

The Intimate Papers of Colonel House. Charles Seymour, ed. 4 vols. Boston, Houghton Mifflin Company, 1928.

The Memoirs of Cordell Hull. 2 vols. New York, Macmillan, 1948.

The Correspondence of Andrew Jackson. John Spencer Bassett, ed. 6 vols. Washington, D.C., Carnegie Institution of Washington, 1933.

The Complete Jefferson. Saul Padover, ed. New York, 1943.

The Writings of Thomas Jefferson. A. A. Lipscomb and A. E. Bergh, eds. 20 vols. Washington, D.C., 1903.

Johnson, Alvin. *Pioneer's Progress.* New York, The Viking Press, 1952.

Johnson, Lyndon B. *The Vantage Point.* New York, Holt Rinehart and Winston, 1971.

The Collected Works of Abraham Lincoln. Roy P. Basler, ed. 8 vols. New Brunswick, New Jersey, Rutgers University Press, 1953.

Longworth, Alice R. *Crowded Hours.* New York, Charles Scribner's Sons, 1933.

The Writings of James Madison. Gaillard Hunt, ed. 9 vols. New York, G. P. Putnam's Sons, 1906.

The Autobiography of James Monroe. Stuart Gerry Brown, ed. Syracuse, New York, Syracuse University Press, 1959.

The Writings of James Monroe. Stanislaus M. Hamilton, ed. 7 vols. New York, G. P. Putnam's Sons, 1898–1903.

Polk: The Diary of a President, 1845–1849. Allan Nevins, ed. New York, Longman, Green and Co., 1929.

Roosevelt in the Kansas City Star. Ralph Stout, ed. Boston, Houghton Mifflin Company, 1921.

Roosevelt, Theodore. *African Game Trails.* New York, Charles Scribner's Sons, 1926.

———. *An Autobiography.* New York, Macmillan, 1916.

———. *Through the Brazilian Wilderness.* New York, Charles Scribner's Sons, 1926.

The Letters of Theodore Roosevelt. Elting E. Morison, ed. 8 vols. Cambridge, Massachusetts, Harvard University Press, 1954.

Taft and Roosevelt; The Intimate Letters of Archie Butt, Military Aide. 2 vols. Garden City, New York, Doubleday, 1930.

Truman, Harry S. *Memoirs.* 2 vols. Garden City, New York, Doubleday, 1955.

———. *Mr. Citizen.* New York, Bernard Geis Associates, 1960.

The Autobiography of Mark Twain. Charles Neider, ed. New York, Harper & Brothers, 1959.

Mark Twain's Letters. Albert Bigelow Paine, ed. 2 vols. New York, Harper & Brothers, 1917.

The Letters and Times of the Tylers. Lyon G. Tyler, ed. 3 vols. Richmond, Virginia, Whillet & Shepperson, 1884.

The Autobiography of Martin Van Buren. Annual Report of the American Historical Association for the year 1918 (Vol. 11). Washington, Government Printing Office, 1920.

The Writings of Washington. J. C. Fitzpatrick, ed. 39 vols. Washington, D.C., George Washington Bicentennial Commission, Houghton Mifflin and Company, 1931–1944.

Weed, Thurlow. *Autobiography.* Harriet A. Weed, ed. Boston, Houghton Mifflin and Company, 1884.

The Letters of Theodore Weld, Angelina Grimké Weld and Sarah Grimké. Gilbert H. Barnes and Dwight L. Dumond, eds. Gloucester, Massachusetts, Peter Smith, 1963.

The Autobiography of William Allen White. New York, Macmillan, 1946.

Wilson, Edith Bolling. *My Memoir.* Indianapolis, Bobbs-Merrill, 1938.

SELECTED BOOKS

Abbott, Lawrence F. *Impressions of Theodore Roosevelt.* Garden City, New York, Doubleday, Page and Company, 1920.

Adams, Charles Francis. *Life of John Adams.* Boston, 1850.

Alexander, Holmes. *The American Talleyrand.* New York, 1935.

Ammon, Harry. *James Monroe: The Quest for National Identity.* New York, McGraw-Hill Book Company, 1971.

Badeau, Adam. *Grant in Peace.* Hartford, Connecticut, S. S. Scranton & Company, 1887.

Bailey, Thomas A. *Woodrow Wilson and the Great Betrayal.* New York, Macmillan, 1945.

Baker, Leonard. *John Marshall*. New York, Macmillan, 1974.

Baker, Ray Stannard. *Woodrow Wilson: Life and Letters*. 8 vols. Garden City, New York, 1937.

Bassett, John Spencer. *The Life of Andrew Jackson*. New York, Macmillan, 1928.

Brodie, Fawn M. *Thomas Jefferson*. New York, W. W. Norton & Co., 1974.

Compton, James V. *The Swastika and the Eagle*. Boston, Houghton Mifflin Company, 1967.

Conkling, Alfred R. *The Life and Letters of Roscoe Conkling*. New York, Charles L. Webster & Company, 1889.

DeConde, Alexander. *The Quasi-War: The Politics and Diplomacy of the Undeclared War with France 1797–1801*. New York, Charles Scribner's Sons, 1966.

Duberman, Martin. *Charles Francis Adams: 1807–1886*. Boston, Houghton Mifflin Company, 1961.

———. *James Russell Lowell*. Boston, Houghton Mifflin Company, 1966.

Eckenrode, H. J. *Rutherford B. Hayes: Statesman of Reunion*. New York, Frederick Ungar Publishing Company, 1930.

Flexner, James Thomas. *George Washington: Anguish and Farewell*. Boston, Little, Brown and Company, 1969.

Gardner, Joseph L. *Departing Glory: Theodore Roosevelt as Ex-President*. New York, Charles Scribner's Sons, 1973.

Green, Horace. *General Grant's Last Stand*. New York, Charles Scribner's Sons, 1936.

Gunderson, Robert G. *Old Gentlemen's Convention: The Washington Peace Conference of 1861*. Madison, Wisconsin, 1961.

Hagedorn, Hermann. *A Guide to Sagamore Hill*. New York, Theodore Roosevelt Association, 1953.

———. *The Roosevelt Family of Sagamore Hill*. New York, Macmillan, 1954.

Harwood, Richard and Johnson, Haynes. *Lyndon*. New York, Praeger Publishers, 1973.

Headley, J. T. *The Life and Travels of Grant*. Philadelphia, Hubbard Bros., 1879.

Hecht, Marie B. *John Quincy Adams: A Personal History of an Independent Man*. New York, Macmillan, 1972.

Hesseltine, William B. *Ulysses S. Grant: Politician*. New York, Frederick Ungar Publishing Company, 1935.

Hoover, Herbert. *The Ordeal of Woodrow Wilson*. New York, McGraw-Hill Book Company, 1958.

Hoover, Herbert and Gibson, Hugh. *The Problem of Lasting Peace*. Garden City, New York, Doubleday, 1942.

Howe, George Frederick. *Chester A. Arthur*. New York, Frederick Ungar Publishing Company, 1935.

James, Marquis. *The Life of Andrew Jackson*. Indianapolis, The Bobbs-Merrill Company, 1938.

Janos, Leo. "The Last Days of the President," *Atlantic Monthly*, July 1973.

Ketcham, Ralph. *James Madison*. New York, Macmillan, 1971.

Klein, Philip S. *President James Buchanan.* University Park, Pennsylvania, The Pennsylvania State University Press, 1962.

Kurtz, Stanley. *The Presidency of John Adams.* Philadelphia, University of Pennsylvania Press, 1957.

Lash, Joseph P. *Eleanor: The Years Alone.* New York, W. W. Norton and Company, 1972.

Leopold, Richard W. *Elihu Root.* Boston, Little, Brown and Company, 1954.

Lerner, Max. *The Mind and Faith of Justice Holmes.* Boston, Little, Brown and Company, 1943.

Lyons, Eugene. *Herbert Hoover: A Biography.* Garden City, New York, Doubleday, 1964.

McCoy, Donald R. *Calvin Coolidge: The Quiet President.* New York, Macmillan, 1967.

Manners, William. *TR and Will.* New York, Harcourt, Brace & World, 1969.

Marx, Rudolph. *The Health of the Presidents.* New York, G. P. Putnam's Sons, 1960.

Merrill, Horace S. *Bourbon Leader: Grover Cleveland and the Democratic Party.* Boston, 1957.

Miller, Merle. *Plain Speaking.* New York, G. P. Putnam's Sons, 1973.

Mitchell, Broadus, *Alexander Hamilton: The National Adventure: 1788–1804.* New York, Macmillan, 1962.

Morris, Lloyd. *The Rebellious Puritan: Portrait of Mr. Hawthorne.* New York, Harcourt, Brace and Company, 1927.

Mowry, George E. *Theodore Roosevelt and the Progressive Movement.* Madison, Wisconsin, The University of Wisconsin Press, 1947.

Nevins, Allan. *Grover Cleveland.* New York, Dodd, Mead & Company, 1958.

Nichols, Roy F. *Franklin Pierce.* Philadelphia, University of Pennsylvania Press, 1931.

Nixon, Richard M. *Six Crises.* Garden City, New York, Doubleday, 1962.

Parker, George F. *Recollections of Grover Cleveland.* New York, The Century Co., 1909.

Parmet, Herbert S. *Eisenhower and the American Crusades.* New York, Macmillan, 1972.

Parmet, Herbert S. and Hecht, Marie B. *Never Again: A President Runs for a Third Term.* New York, Macmillan, 1968.

Peterson, Merrill D. *Thomas Jefferson and the New Nation.* New York, Oxford University Press, 1970.

Pringle, Henry F. *The Life and Times of William Howard Taft.* 2 vols. New York, Farrar & Rinehart, 1939.

———. *Theodore Roosevelt: A Biography.* New York, Harcourt, Brace and Company, 1931.

Randolph, Sarah N. *The Domestic Life of Thomas Jefferson.* Cambridge, Massachusetts, University Press, 1939.

Rappaport, Armin, ed. *The Monroe Doctrine.* New York, Holt, Rinehart and Winston, 1966.

Rayback, Robert J. *Millard Fillmore.* Buffalo, New York, 1959.

Reedy, George E. *The Twilight of the Presidency*. New York, New American Library, 1970.

Robinson, Corinne Roosevelt. *My Brother Theodore Roosevelt*. New York, Charles Scribner's Sons, 1921.

Roseboom, Eugene. *A History of Presidential Elections*. New York, Macmillan, 1970.

Russell, Francis. *The Shadow of Blooming Grove*. New York, McGraw-Hill Book Company, 1968.

Schlesinger, Arthur M., Jr. *The Age of Jackson*. Boston, Little, Brown and Company, 1946.

———. *A Thousand Days*. Boston, Houghton Mifflin Company, 1965.

Seager, Robert. *And Tyler Too: A Biography of John and Julia Tyler*. New York, McGraw-Hill Book Company, 1963.

Sievers, Harry J. *Benjamin Harrison: Hoosier President*. 3 vols. Chicago, Henry Regnery Co., 1968.

Smith, Gene. *When The Cheering Stopped*. New York, William Morrow and Company, 1964.

Smith, Margaret Bayard. *The First Forty Years of Washington Society*. New York, Frederick Ungar Publishing Co., 1965.

Smith, Page. *John Adams*. 2 vols. Garden City, New York, Doubleday, 1962.

Sorenson, Theodore C. *Kennedy*. New York, Harper & Row, 1965.

Stoddard, Henry L. *As I Knew Them: Presidents and Politics from Grant to Coolidge*. New York, Harper & Brothers, 1927.

Stryker, Lloyd Paul. *Andrew Johnson*. New York, Macmillan, 1929.

Van Deusen, Glyndon. *Horace Greeley*. New York, Hill and Wang, 1964.

———. *William Henry Seward*. New York, Oxford University Press, 1967.

Van Doren, Carl. *Benjamin Franklin*. New York, The Viking Press, 1938.

Van Doren, Mark. *Nathaniel Hawthorne*. New York, Viking, 1957.

Warren, Charles. *The Supreme Court in United States History*. 2 vols. Boston, Little, Brown and Company, 1926.

White, Theodore H. *The Making of the President, 1960*. New York, Atheneum, 1961.

———. *The Making of the President, 1964*. New York, Antheneum, 1965.

Williams, Charles R. *Life of Rutherford B. Hayes*. Boston, Houghton Mifflin, 1914.

Wills, Gary. *Nixon Agonistes*. New York, New American Library, 1969.

Wilson, Joan Hoff. *Herbert Hoover*. Boston, Little, Brown and Company, 1975.

Young, John Russell. *Around the World with Grant*. New York, 1879.

Index

Index

Abbott, Lawrence F., 38, 250, 299–300
Acheson, Dean, 144, 145, 169
Adams, Charles Francis, 75, 76, 77, 192,
    202, 219, 271, 279, 309
Adams, George Washington, 271
Adams, Henry, 7, 102, 103, 109, 131
Adams, John, 194
  autobiographical writings, 289–91
  bibliophile, 191, 201
  embassy to French Directory, 117, 118
  friendship with Jefferson, 192, 308–309
  Ghent treaty negotiations influence, 7,
    53
  military-political maneuverings for
    expected war with France, 3, 4, 5–6,
    154
  party/power politics attitude, 118
  self-view during retirement, 312, 313
  War of 1812 support, 6
Adams, John Quincy, 289, 290
  Amistad case role, 277–81
  congressional career, post-presidential,
    141, 271–82, 287–88
  death, 76
  Diary, 197, 270, 309
  election campaign (1824), 70, 118, 119,
    271
  financial situation, retirement, 201–202
  Ghent treaty negotiations, 6–7, 53
  Mexican War opposition, 11
  Monroe Doctrine position, 156
  Monticello lottery sale role, 192, 193
  Panama Congress (1826), 195
Adams, Louisa, 271, 277
Adams, Passy, 290
Adams, Sherman, 174, 266
Adams-Onis Treaty, 270
Addams, Jane, 108
Adenauer, Konrad, 67, 268
Adkins v. Children's Hospital, 285
African Game Trails (T. Roosevelt), 216
Agassiz, Louis, 22
Agnew, Spiro T., 183
Akeley, Mr. and Mrs. Carl, 248
Alabama Claims, 235
Albert, Prince, 23
Alcott, Bronson, 22
Alexander, Eleanor, 257
Alfonso XIII, King of Spain, 238, 255
Alien and Sedition Acts, 157
Allan, Charles B., 79
Allen, Robert S., 135
Allison, William B., 125
American Red Cross, 43
Amistad case, 277–78
Amos, James, 40
Anderson, E. Ellery, 91
Anderson, Major, 22, 24
Anderson, Robert, 181
Arnold, Benedict, 276
Arthur, Chester A., 88, 161–63, 209
Asquith, Mr. (British official), 256

Association of Presidents of Life Insurance Companies, 214
Astor, John Jacob, 10, 161
At Ease: Stories I Tell to Friends (D. D. Eisenhower), 302
Atlee, Clement, 266

Babcock, General, 296
Badeau, Adam, 83, 85, 86, 89, 160–61, 204, 205, 206, 208, 210, 232, 233, 234, 235, 244
Baker, Newton D., 36, 37, 219
Baker, Ray Stannard, 40, 100, 131
Baldwin, Roger, 279, 280, 281
Ballinger case, 282
Bancroft, George, 73, 159, 160, 229
Bannister, Ward, 139
Barbour, James, 73, 192
Barbour, Justice Philip, 280
Bass, Governor, 100
Bass, John F., 34
Battle of New Orleans, 10, 198
Baudouin, King of Belgium, 265
Bay of Pigs, 176–77
Beaconsfield, Lord, 232
Beale, Edward F., 162
Beard, Charles, 67
Beneridge, Albert J., 103, 107, 108
Benton, Thomas Hart, 11
Bentsen, Lloyd M., 151
Berlin, Richard, 187
Biddle, Nicholas, 194
Bismarck, Otto von, 237–38
Bissell (Cleveland friend), 94
Black, Jeremiah S., 303
Blaine, James F., 86, 88, 89, 124, 160
Blair and Rives, 200, 201
Blanchard, Paul, 145
Borah, William E., 59, 107, 166, 286
Borrow, George, 247
Boston Massacre, 290
Botts, John Minor, 277
Bourne, Senator, 107
Boutros Pasha, 256
Bowles, Chester, 144
Boyce, Alice, 181
Bradley, Gen. Omar, 221
Brandegee, Frank B., 58, 87
Brandeis, Louis D., 33, 166, 282, 284–85
Brice, Senator, 93
Briggs, Alderman, 81
Bright, John, 277

Brooks, Peter Chardon, 202
Brown, A. V., 158
Brown, John, 97
Brown, Stuart Gerry, 293
Brownell, Herbert, 139, 170
Browning, Elizabeth Barrett, 247
Brumback Ellen, 140
Bryan, William Jennings, 33, 60, 125, 126, 127, 128
Bryant, Mayor, 85
Bryant, William Cullen, 123
Buchanan, James, 230, 311
    Civil War scapegoat, 22–23
    discredited, 23–24, 117, 120
    election, 77, 82, 83
    Lincoln policy opposition, 29–30
    memoirs, 303–304
    secession, do-nothing role, 14, 15–16, 18, 19
    Secretary of State, 33
Bull Moose Convention, 107
Bunyan, John, 247
Burr, Aaron, 6, 276
Burrows, Silas, 197
Busby, Horace, 184
Butler, Benjamin, 71, 73, 74, 75, 159
Butler, Mrs. Benjamin, 159
Butler, J. G., 58
Butler, Nicholas Murray, 55
Butler, Pierce, 282
Butt, Archie, 245, 246, 252, 254
Byrd, Colonel, 191

Cabell, J. C., 191, 192
Cajazeira, Dr., 259, 260
Calhoun, John, 11, 71
Cambreleng, Churchill C., 74, 159
Cameron, Don, 84, 122
Cameron, Simon, 21
Campbell, Sir Gerald, 44–45
Campbell, John A., 14
Canning, George, 155, 156
Cannon, Joe, 209
Carnegie, Andrew, 55, 220, 253
Carow, Emily, 251
Cash, Lewis, 73, 74, 76, 77
Castle, William, 41
Castlereagh, Lord, 8
Castro, Fidel, 176, 179–80
Chaffee (Grant in-law), 205
Chandler, William, 162

Chapman, Frank, 258
Charles L. Webster Company, 208
Chase, Salmon P., 75
Cherrie, George K., 258, 259–60, 262
Chesapeake, U.S.S., 7
Chicago Rock, 305
China, 240–42, 244
Choate, Joseph, 164
Chulahlongkorn, King of Siam, 240
Churchill, Winston, 302
Churchill, Sir Winston, 43, 173, 178, 266, 268
Cinque (slave leader), 278, 279
Civil War, 13–30, 295–97
Clay, Henry, 70, 72, 78, 271
Clay, Lucius D., 66, 67
Clemenceau, Georges, 36
Clemens, Samuel (Mark Twain), 207–208, 210, 236, 247
Cleveland, Grover, 165, 209, 211
    attitude toward ex-presidents, 310
    coal strike solution, T. Roosevelt and, 163–64
    party power, 126, 127
    Philippines intervention opposition, 31
    retirement activities and finances, 212–14
    second term, 89–96, 115, 116, 124
    Spanish-American War opposition, 30–31
Cleveland, Mrs. Grover, 89, 94
Clifford, Clark, 144
Cochran, Bourke, 94
Colby, Bainbridge, 56, 57, 130, 131, 217, 218
Coleridge, Samuel Taylor, 262
Conkling, Roscoe, 83, 84, 85–87, 88, 89, 122, 160, 161
Connally, John, 152
Conner, Gen. Fox, 302–303
Coolidge, Calvin, 286, 301
    retirement activities and finances, 219–20
Cooper, James Fenimore, 247
Cox, James N., 60, 133
Cramer, M. J., 161
Crane, Murray, 164
Creager, R. B., 137
Creel, George, 33
Crisis, The (Winston Churchill), 302
Cromer, Lord, 256
Cronkite, Walter, 222

Crusade in Europe (D. D. Eisenhower), 265, 302, 305
Cummins, Senator, 107
Cunninghame, R. J., 245, 248
Cushing, Caleb, 15, 119

Daley, Richard J., 151
Danielson, Jack, 198
Davis, Garrett, 23
Davis, Jefferson, 20, 25, 27, 29, 209
Davis, Richard Harding, 112
Dawes, Secretary of the Treasury, 165
Dawson, Francis W., 247
Day, William R., 167
Deane, Silas, 290
DeGaulle, Charles, 266, 268
Depew, Chauncey, 31
Derby, Lord, 232
Dewey, Thomas E., 137, 138, 139
Diary (John Quincy Adams), 270, 309
Diary (Polk), 160
Dickens, Charles, 247
Dirksen, Everett, 141
Dix (Republican presidential candidate), 99
Dixon, James M., 101
Dodge, William, 18
Doheny, E. L., 218
Donelson, Andrew, 73
Dougherty, H. M., 165, 166, 167
Douglas, Dr. (Grant physician), 297
Drinker, Henry Sturgis, 55
Dulles, John Foster, 67

Eden, Sir Anthony, 266
Edmunds, George F., 86, 88
Edward VII, King of England, 254, 264
Eisenhower, Barbara Anne, 267
Eisenhower, David, 267
Eisenhower, Dwight D., 167, 222
    autobiographical writings, 302–303
    election campaign (1952), 139–40, 143
    European tour (1962), 267–68
    Gettysburg farm, retirement and finances, 220–21
    Hoover Commission and, 167, 169–71, 174
    JFK and, 175, 176–80
    LBJ and, 51, 68, 181, 182
    Nixon and, 140, 174, 182
    party power role, 147, 148–51

Truman rift, 172–74, 264, 265, 312
Vietnam War role, 50–52
Eisenhower, John, 51, 173, 220, 289, 305
Eisenhower, Mamie, 150, 267, 268
Eisenhower, Milton, 149
Eliot, Charles, 283
Elizabeth II, Queen of England, 268
Emancipation Proclamation, 22
Embargo Act (1807), 7, 190, 288
Emerson, Ralph Waldo, 21, 22, 247
Equitable Life Assurance Company, 213, 214
Essex Junto, 6
Ewald, William B., Jr., 305

Fabri, Madame, 85
Fairbanks, Charles, 129
Ferdinand I, King of Bulgaria, 254
Fillmore, Mary Abigail, 78, 79, 226
Fillmore, Millard, 311
  Civil War opposition, 24–26, 30
  European tour (1855), 226–29, 232
  Know-Nothing candidate, 77–83, 115–116, 226
  law practice, 203
  political role, post-presidential, 120
  Secession mediator, 14–15
Finland, 48
Finletter, Thomas, 143
Fish, Hamilton, 161
Fish, James D., 210
Fish, Nicholas, 161
Fisher, C. W., 139
Flagg, Azariah C., 159
Flinn, William, 101, 103
Floyd, John B., 24
Fogazzaro, Antonio, 251
Foote, Thomas M., 228
Forbes, Charles R., 165
Ford, Gerald, 222, 273, 274
Forrestal, James, 168, 302
Fourteen Points, 36
France, 3, 4, 5, 290
Franklin, Benjamin, 194, 290, 292–93, 311
Franklin, William Temple, 292–93
Freedman's Bureau, 296
Frelinghuysen, F. T., 122, 161, 162
Frémont, John, 82
French Revolution, 292
Frye, Senator, 88
Fulbright, William, 180

Galbraith, John Kenneth, 49
Gardiner (Tyler in-law), 27
Gardner, Gilson, 100
Garfield, James A.
  party political role, 87, 88, 89, 124, 160–61
Gates, Seth M., 274
George V, King of England, 254
Ghent, Treaty of (1814), 7, 53–54, 276
Gibbon, Edward, 259
Gibbons, Cardinal, 99, 252
Gibson, Hugh, 63
Giddings, Joshua, 75, 275
Gilder, Richard W., 95, 213
Gilpin, Attorney General, 280
Glascock, Governor, 100
Godkin, William, 96
Goldwater, Barry M., 117, 141, 147, 148, 149
Gompers, Samuel, 285
Goodman, M. B., 21
Goodpaster, General, 181
Göring, Hermann, 42
Gorman, Arthur P., 93
Gouverneur, Maria, 196
Gouverneur, Samuel, 193, 196, 197
Grabow (slave leader), 279
Grant, Col. Frederick, 208, 238
Grant, Jesse, 232, 234
Grant, Nellie, 210
Grant, Ulysses (son), 204, 205, 232
Grant, Ulysses S., 121, 122, 123, 124, 303
  Civil War accounts, 295–97
  Samuel Clemens and, 207–208
  commission restored by Congress, 209–10, 220
  impoverishment and ruin, 204–11, 225
  literary output, 205, 206, 207–11, 295
  party power, 160–63
  third term sought, 83–89, 114, 115, 161
  throat cancer, 206, 207, 208, 210
  world tour (1877), 231–44, 263, 268
Grant, Mrs. Ulysses S., 83, 84, 204, 205, 206, 207, 208, 234, 236, 238, 239, 242, 243
Grant Relief Bill, 209
Grant and Ward, 204, 210
Gray, Francis C., 191
Gray, George, 127
Gray, Gordon, 181
Grayson, Dr. (Wilson physician), 218

"Great Complaint against the Tariff, The" (Madison), 157
Great Depression, The (H. Hoover), 301
Greeley, Horace, 16, 79, 227–28
Gregory, Attorney General, 58
Grey, Sir Edward, 256, 257
Guizot, François P. G., 229
Gut, Camille, 45
Guthrie, James, 120

Haakon, King of Norway, 253
Hadley, Governor, 100, 107
Hague Convention, 127
Hale, John P., 76
Halperin, Morton H., 222
Halpin, Maria, 92
Hambro, Dr. Carl J., 45
Hamilton, Alexander, 3, 4, 5, 6
Hamilton, John D. M., 135, 136, 137
Hampton, General, 155
Hanna, Mark, 125, 126
Hardesty, Robert, 306
Harding, Warren G., 301
  election, Taft and, 132, 133, 165–67
  League of Nations, party politics and, 60, 61, 63
  Supreme Court appointments, 165–67, 283
Harding, Mrs. Warren G., 165
Harper, Frank, 258, 299–300
Harriman, Averell, 141, 142
Harrison, Benjamin, 90
  activities and life style, retirement, 214–15
  election (1888), 116, 124
  election loss (1892), 96
  Grant supporter, 87
  Hague Convention delegate, 127
  party power, 125, 126
  Spanish-American War support, 30
  Supreme Court appointment, 282
Harrison, Mrs. Benjamin, 94
Harrison, Maj. Russell, 30
Harrison, William Henry, 69
Harrity, William F., 95
Harte, Bret, 247
Harum, David, 220
Haven, Solomon H., 79, 80
Hawthorne, Julian, 21, 203, 230
Hawthorne, Nathaniel, 21, 22, 230–31
Hawthorne, Sophia, 231

Hawthorne, Una, 230, 231
Hay, Eliza Monroe, 196
Hay, George, 196
Hay, John, 293
Hayes, Rutherford B., 232, 310
  activities and life style, retirement, 211–12
  diary, 309
  election (1876), 84
  party role, 124
  Porter exoneration, 209
  presidency attitudes, 312
Hearst, William Randolph, 31
Heller, Edward, 245
Hill, David B., 90, 92, 93, 94, 116
Hill, David Jayne, 250
Hilles, Charles, 165
Hitchcock, Gilbert M., 59
Hitler, Adolf, 41–42, 46, 47
Hoar, George, 87
Holmes, Oliver Wendell, 166, 247, 283, 286
Holt, Joseph, 22, 23, 24
Hoover, Herbert
  Finland supporter, 48
  food relief, WW I and II programs, 32, 36, 38, 43–47, 64–68
  Hitler visit, 41–42
  incumbent's use and consideration of, 167–79, 181–82, 312
  memoirs, 300–302
  party power role, 135–41
  peace plans, 63
  presidency attitudes, 313
  Taft and, 286, 287
  unpopularity, 40–41, 117
  Wilson biography, 306–308
  World War II, FDR supporter, 47–48
Hoover Commission, 168–72
Hopkins, Dr., 21
House, Colonel, 58, 131
Houston, Sam, 71, 158
Hudson, Charles, 11
Hughes, Charles Evans, 129, 130, 131, 132, 165, 166
Hull, Cordell, 41, 43–44, 46, 134, 135
Humphrey, Hubert, 146, 285

Independent Treasury Bill, 198
Irvin, Governor, 85
Irving, Washington, 78

Irwin, Wallace, 215
Ives, Dr., 24

Jackson, Andrew, 202, 284, 294
  Battle of New Orleans, 10
  financial difficulties, 197–201
  health, 70, 134
  New Orleans fine refund claim, 198, 199, 200
  nullification controversy, 157
  party power role, 118, 119, 195
  second term, 196
  Texas annexation role, 71, 72, 158
Jackson, Andrew, Jr., 198, 199, 200–201
Jackson, Harry M., 145
Jackson, Sarah, 201
Jefferson, Charles, 94
Jefferson, Joseph, 94, 213
Jefferson, Thomas, 118, 202, 229, 276, 294, 313
  Adams-, correspondence, 308–309
  autobiographical writings, 291–93
  bankruptcy and estate sale, 191–93
  Chesapeake defense plans, 8–10
  debts, 189–90, 194
  library sale to Congress, 190–91, 225
  Madison mentor, 154–55, 157
  Monroe Doctrine consultation, 155–57
  Monticello estate, 189
  Thoughts on Lotteries, 201
  War of 1812 role, 6, 7–11, 33, 53–54, 288
Jenner, Senator, 173
Jewett, Elam R., 228
Johnson, Alvin, 36
Johnson, Andrew, 30, 280
  impeachment, 117, 122, 284
  Senate campaign and election, 121–23
Johnson, Governor, 100
Johnson, John A., 128
Johnson, Lady Bird, 51, 183, 221
Johnson, Lyndon B.
  Eisenhower and, 51, 182
  election, 149
  ex-presidents and, consideration and use of, 181–83
  Hoover and, 172, 181–82
  Nixon and, 182–84, 312
  party political power, 151–52
  Presidential Retirement Bill support, 187–88
  retirement, 221–22

Senate leadership, 143, 144
transition expenses, 223
Truman and, 51, 147, 177, 182
Vantage Point, The, 49, 305–306
Vietnam War and, 49–51, 68, 117
Johnston, Albert Sidney, 209
Jordan, William J., 306
Jusserand, Jean Jules, 34

Karger, Gus, 166, 167
Kearns, Doris, 49
Keats, John, 247, 257
Kefauver, Estes, 142
Kemble, Fanny, 235
Kendall, Amos, 72
Kennedy, Jackie, 175
Kennedy, John F., 305
  Eisenhower and, 147, 221
  ex-presidents and, consideration and use of, 174–81, 311
  Hoover and, 171–72
  Nixon-, debates, 140
  Truman and, 142, 144–45, 146
Kennedy, Joseph P., 146, 169, 171, 174, 180
Kentucky Resolutions, 157
Keynes, John Maynard, 306
Keyserling, Leon, 144
King, Preston, 74, 75
Kipling, Rudyard, 109
Kirkwood, Irwin, 216
Kissinger, Henry, 183
Kitchner, Lord Horatio H., 256
Knights of the Golden Circle, 20
Knox, Henry, 5
Korff, Rabbi Baruch, 224
Kosciusko, Gen. Thaddeus, 8
Kosmos (Baron Von Humboldt), 228
Kung, Prince, 240–42

Lafayette, Marquis de, 194, 292
La Follette, Robert, 98, 100, 101, 104, 106, 107, 129, 286
Lake, Anthony, 222
Lamar, L. Q. L., 93
Landon, Alfred, 47, 63, 135, 136
Lane, Harriet, 23
Lansing, Robert, 32
Lazar, Irving, 224
League to Enforce Peace, 54–55, 56
League of Nations, 57–62, 63
Leary, Jerry, 280
Leavitt, Joshua, 75, 76

Lee, Arthur Hamilton, 34, 39, 61, 99, 129
Lee, Henry, 27
Lee, Gen. Robert E., 27, 209, 296–97
Lees, Arthur, 254, 263
Leishman, Ambassador, 250
Leopold, King of Belgium, 234
Leschene, M., 228
Leslie, Charles, 227
Lewis, Dean, 109
Lewis, William Draper, 105
Library of Congress, 191
Lincoln, Abraham, 20, 24, 240, 303
    Civil War policies, 21–22
    election (1860), 13, 77, 119
    election (1864), 96, 120
    Fillmore and, 14
    funeral, 29
    in Grant memoirs, 296
    Pierce loyalty and, 19, 21
    secession position, 17–18, 26
    Tyler and, 28
Lindbergh, Anne, 41
Lindbergh, Charles, 41, 137
Linn, Louis, 200
Linton, Justice, 167
Livingston, Robert R., 294
Livingstone, Dr. David, 236
Lodge, Henry Cabot, 32, 38, 58, 59, 60,
    97, 102, 112, 130, 131, 148, 251, 258,
    297
Logan, John A., 84, 122
Longfellow, Henry Wadsworth, 22, 247
Longworth, Alice Roosevelt, 36, 60, 101,
    106, 110, 112, 113, 215
Longworth, Nicholas, 97, 102
Lorimer, William, 98
Loring, Alden, 245
Loring, Ellis Gray, 278, 279
Louis XVI, King of France, 292
Louisiana Purchase, 294
Lowell, A. Lawrence, 57, 286
Lowell, James Russell, 22, 90, 162, 238
Lundy, Benjamin, 273
Lyon, Lord, 23
Lyra, Lieutenant, 259, 260, 262

McAdoo, William Gibbs, 219
MacArthur, Gen. Douglas, 139, 221, 305
McCarthy, Joseph, 173
McClellan, General, 120
McComber, Charles, 80
McCormick, Medill, 101

McCoy, Donald, 220
McFarland, Henry, 21
McFowle, Bishop James, 251
McGovern, Francis E., 106
McGovern, George, 151, 152
McHenry, James, 4, 5
McIntosh, Caroline C., 203
McKenna, Justice, 286
McKinley, William
    assassination, 111, 112
    election (1896), 125, 126
    election (1900), 127
    presidency view, 31
    Spanish-American War policy, 30
McLean, John, 75
MacMahon, President, 235
MacNeil, Neil, 170
MacNider, Hanford, 137
McReynolds, Justice, 284–85
Madison, Dolley, 194, 195
Madison, James
    Jefferson friendship, 154, 192
    Monroe and, 155–57, 196
    Montpelier estate and debts, 193–95
    party politics, neutrality in, 119
    tariff nullification position, 157–58
    Virginia Convention statement on
        slaves, 280
    War of 1812 and, 6–9, 11, 33, 53–54
Mansfield, Mike, 311
Marcy, William L., 159, 160
Marie Antoinette, 292
Markham, Sir Clement Robert, 263
Marshall, Gen George C., 67, 143, 173
Marshall, John, 118, 280
Marshall, Thomas, 276, 277
Marshall, Verne, 137
Martin, Elbert, 111
Martin, Joe, 137, 138
Mason, James, 25
Maud, Queen of Norway, 253
Maude, General, 37
Maxwell, Hugh, 226
Mearns, Lt. Col. Edgar A., 245
Memoirs (Hull), 41
Memoirs (Ulysses S. Grant), 207, 208–11
Merritt, Dudley, 160, 161
Metternich, 229
Mexican War, 11–13, 160, 295
Middleton, Harry, 306
Miller, Herbert, 222
Miller, Leo, 258

Miller, Merle, 145
Miller, W. D., 71
Milligan, Joseph, 190
Milton, John, 247, 257
Missouri Compromise, 76
*Mr. Buchanan's Administration on the
Eve of Rebellion* (James Buchanan),
303
Moley, Raymond, 41
Molotov, V. M., 265
Monroe, James, 28
autobiography, 293–94
death, 197
debts and claims case against U.S., 193,
195–97
election (1808), 155
party politics role, 118–19
personal tragedies, 196
retirement, 225
Secretary of State, 8, 9
Monroe Doctrine, 59, 63, 155–57, 271
Monticello, 189, 192–93
Montpelier, 193–94
Moody, Justice, 164
Mooney, John, 220
Moos, Malcolm, 149
Morgan, J. P., 163, 219
Morgan, John T., 30
Morgenthau, Henry, 44
Morpeth, Lord, 275
Morsund, Judge A. W., 221
Morton, Levi, 31, 125
Moss, John E., 223
Mount Vernon, 188–89
Müller, Gen. Lauro, 257, 263
Munsey, Frank, 103
Murphy (Tammany Hall), 98
Murphy, Charles J., 187
Myers v. United States, 283–85, 288

Napoleon Bonaparte, 7, 11, 229, 293
Napoleon III (Louis Bonaparte), 227
National Committee on Food for the
Small Democracies, 43
National Socialists, 41, 42
National War Labor Board, 34–35
Nevins, Allan, 91, 127, 304
New, Harry S., 165
Newberry, Truman H., 101
New Deal, 301–302
Nicholas II, Czar, 252
Nixon, Richard M., 49

Democrats for, 152
Eisenhower and, 147, 150, 151, 182–83
financial situation and exile, 222–25
JFK and, 140, 174–75
LBJ and, 183–84, 312
memoirs, 224, 309
party politics role, 117
phlebitis, 222–23
Truman and, 145, 146, 267
Vietnam War demonstration, 50
Norris, George W., 166

O'Brian, Lawrence, 151, 311
O'Connell, Archbishop, 251
O'Laughlin, John C., 101
Olney, Richard, 128
Ordeal of Woodrow Wilson (H.
Hoover), 306–308
Order of the Star-Spangled Banner, 79
Orders in Council (Great Britain), 7, 8,
9
Osborn, Governor, 100
Oscar, King, 238

Page, Walter Hines, 56
Paine, Thomas, 196
Panama Congress (1826), 195
Park, Benjamin, 71
Parker, Alton B., 128
Parker, George F., 90, 91, 127, 212–13
Parker, John M., 130
Patterson, Robert, 66
Patton, Gen. George S., 302
Peabody, George, 227
Pearson, Drew, 135, 221
Peel, Sir Robert, 227
Pell, Claiborne, 311
Pendleton, George H., 120
Penrose, Boies, 132
Pentagon Papers, 306
Perkins, George W., 103, 109, 115, 130
Perkins, Governor, 85
Pershing, Gen. John J., 37, 43, 302
Phillips, Cabell, 148
Pichon, Stephen, 254, 255–56
Pickens, Francis, 277
Pickering, Timothy, 3
Pierce, Benny, 229–30
Pierce, Franklin, 77, 158, 311
Civil War opposition, 19–20, 28–29
European trip, 230–31
Hawthorne and, 230–31

loyalty smear campaign, 20–22, 29, 30
Mexican War general, 295
party politics role, 119–20
retirement life style, 203
secessionist, 13–14
son's death, 229–30
wife's illness, 229–31
Pierce, Mrs. Franklin, 229–30, 231
Pierrepont, Edwards, 232, 234, 268
Pinchot, Gifford, 101, 109
Pinckney, Charles Cotesworth, 5, 195, 272
Pius X, Pope, 250, 251
Planché, Maj. Jean B., 199
Platt, Senator, 299
Plumer, William, 6
Plunkett, Horace, 110
Poe, Edgar Allan, 247
Polish Relief Commission, 43
Polk, James K.
dark horse candidate, 71, 72, 73, 158
Free Soil criticism, 76–77
Mexican War declaration, 11
Van Buren and, 158–60, 229
Porter, General, 209
Potsdam Agreement, 67
Pratt, Admiral, 43
Presidential Retirement Act, 187–88, 220
Preston, Captain, 290

Quincy, Josiah, 95

Randall, Samuel J., 209
Randolph, Col. Jefferson, 189
Randolph, John, 189
Randolph, Martha Jefferson, 189, 193
Randolph, Thomas Jefferson, 191, 309
Rayburn, Sam, 143, 144, 187
Reciprocity Treaty, 162
Reed, William B., 304
Reed, Senator, 133, 166
Rice, Cecil A. Spring, 245
Richardson, Richard Joseph, 271
Riis, Jacob, 298
Ringgold, Tench, 195, 197
Ritchie, Thomas, 72
Rives, John, 73
Rives, William Cabell, 196
Robertson, Judge, 15, 16
Robertson, William A., 160
Robinson, Corinne, 112
Rockefeller, Nelson, 147, 148
Rogge, O. John, 42

Romero, Matias, 183, 205
Romney, George, 148
Rondon, Col. Candido M. da S., 257–59, 261, 262
Roosevelt, Alice Hathaway Lee, 215
Roosevelt, Archibald, 37, 38, 39, 40, 217
Roosevelt, Bamie, 35, 39
Roosevelt, Corinne, 246
Roosevelt, Edith Kermit, 215, 245, 246, 250, 251, 258
Roosevelt, Eleanor, 142
Roosevelt, Ethel, 250
Roosevelt, Franklin D., 136, 142, 145, 183
Hoover and, 41, 42, 48, 63, 68, 137, 140, 168, 301, 312, 313
Humphrey FTC removal, 285
Roosevelt, Col. J., 111
Roosevelt, Kermit, 37, 245, 248, 249, 250, 258, 260, 262
Roosevelt, Quentin, 37, 38, 39–40, 217
Roosevelt, Theodore
armistice position, 55, 61, 62
assassination attempt, 111
autobiography, 297–300
coal strike and, 163–64
death, 40
free-silver position, 127
literary production, 216–17
party politics, 129–32
retirement life style and activities, 215–17
second term race, 69, 96–115
W. H. Taft rapprochement, 35, 245
travels, 244–63
World War I militancy, 37–40
Roosevelt, Theodore, Jr., 37, 40, 166, 217, 257
Root, Elihu, 57, 60, 98, 106, 107, 113, 129, 131, 164, 165
Rosenman, Judge and Mrs. Samuel, 266
Rostow, Walt, 305
Rush, Dr. Benjamin, 289
Rush, Richard, 155, 156
Russell, Governor, 94

Sacco and Vanzetti, 285–86
Saint, The (Antonio Fogazzaro), 251
Salinger, Pierre, 178
Salisbury, Harrison, 308
Sampson, Arthur F., 223
Sartoris, Algernon, 235
Schrank, John F., 111

Schulz, Col. Robert, 220
Schurz, Carl, 123
Scott, General, 295
Scott, Sir Walter, 247
Scranton, Mary, 148
Scranton, William, 148, 149
Secret Service, 225
Seddon, James A., 18
Seward, Clarence, 208
Seward, William H., 20, 22, 24, 25
Seymour, Horatio, 120
Sheehan, W. P., 94
Shelley, Percy Bysse, 247, 257
Sheridan, Gen. Philip, 123, 237
Sherman, John, 86, 87, 88, 122, 124
Sherman, Lawrence, 129
Sherman, Gen. William Tecumseh, 233, 303
Shields, Senator, 133
Shriver, Sargent, 151, 152
Shunk, Mr. and Mrs. James, 304
Sikorski, General, 45–46
Sinclair, Harry F., 218
Slidell, John, 25, 70
Smith, Al, 287
Smith, James, 128
Smith, Jerry, 89
Smith, Margaret, 194
Smith, Martha Bayard, 189
Smith, Samuel H., 190
Smuts, Gen. Jan C., 307
Snyder, Murray, 264
Sorenson, Theodore, 145
Spangler, Harrison P., 137
Spanish-American War, 30–31
Spencer, Herbert, 247
Spingarn, Dr. Sylvia, 49
Sprigg (abolitionist), 274
Stanley, Henry M., 236
Stanton, Edwin, 23, 74
Stetson, Francis L., 95
Stevenson, Adlai E., 93, 94, 95, 141, 142, 145
Stillman, James, 127
Stimson, Henry L., 98, 102
Stoddard, Henry P., 87, 107, 129
Stone, Harlan, 282
Story, Justice, 280
Stout, Ralph, 216
Stover, Mary, 123
Straus, Nathan, 127
Straus, Oscar, 35, 108, 127

Strictly Personal (John Eisenhower), 305
Stubbs, Governor, 100
Sumner, Charles, 28
Sutherland, Justice, 166, 167, 285
Symington, Stuart, 142, 145

Taft, Charles, 35, 287
Taft, Eleanor, 35
Taft, Robert, 36, 48, 63, 137, 138, 139
Taft, William Howard, 140, 211, 229
  Carnegie pension refusal, 220
  ex-presidents, attitude toward, 310
  party politics role, 129, 131, 132
  peace league proposals, 54–63, 68
  retirement and financial situation, 217
  second term race, 97–106, 110, 112, 113, 116
  Supreme Court role, 165–67, 270, 282–88
  TR and, 35, 40, 245, 254
  Vatican altercation, 251–52
  World War I attitudes, 32–33
Taney, Chief Justice, 280
Tappan, Lewis, 279, 281
Tarbell, Ida, 40
Tarleton, Leslie, 245
Taylor, Bayard, 238
Taylor, Zachary, 76, 77, 160, 295
Thackeray, William Makepeace, 247
Thayer, William Roscoe, 263
Thiers, Ambassador, 45
This Country of Ours (B. Harrison), 215
Ticknor, George, 191
Tilden, Samuel J., 74
Timon, Bishop, 82
Todd, Payne, 194, 280
"Travels and Negotiations" (John Adams), 290
Trent Affair, 25
Trevelyan, Sir George, 112
Trist, Nicholas, 157, 158
Truman, Bess, 146, 182, 304–305
Truman, Harry S., 48, 152, 222, 306
  Eisenhower and, 172–74
  European tour, 263–67
  ex-presidency, attitudes toward, 311, 313
  Hoover food relief program enlistment, 64–68, 167–69, 172, 178, 312
  LBJ and, 51, 182
  memoirs, 304–305
  Nixon and, 143, 145

party power and activities, post-
  presidential, 141–47
retirement plans, 187
Eleanor Roosevelt and, 142
Tumulty, Joe, 133
Twain, Mark (Samuel Clemens), 207–208,
  210, 236, 247
Tyler, John, 69, 200, 277, 311
  Confederacy leadership role, 26–28, 30
  death, 28
  Mexican War support, 11–12
  party power, 119
  secession mediation role, 13, 15–19
  Texas annexation support, 70, 158
  Wilmot Proviso opposition, 12–13
Tyler, John, Jr., 12
Tyler, Julia, 16, 17, 26, 28, 119
Tyler, Robert, 12, 27

United Nations, 63

Val, Merry de, 250, 251
Valkenburg, Van, 99
Van Buren, John, 74, 75, 76, 229
Van Buren, Martin, 198, 311
  Amistad case position, 278–79
  autobiography, 227, 294–95
  Civil War positions, 20, 30
  European tour, Fillmore meetings
    during, 227, 228, 229, 232, 268
  Polk Cabinet, advice on, 158–60
  retirement attitude and activities,
    202–203
  secession mediator, 14
  second term candidacy, 69–77, 115, 277
  Wilmot Proviso support, 12
Van Buren, Martin (son), 227
Van Buren, Smith, 72
Vandenberg, 137
Vanderbilt, William A., 205, 206, 207
Vanderkemp, F. A., 289
Vantage Point, The (LBJ), 49, 181, 305
Vatican, 228, 250–52, 264
Vaughan, Samuel S., 305
Vergennes, Comte de, 291
Versailles Treaty, 60
Victor Emmanuel III, King of Italy, 246,
  252–53
Victoria, Queen of England, 23, 203, 227,
  233, 234
Vietnam War, 49–52, 68
Vilas, W. F., 95

Virginia Resolution, 157
von Humboldt, Baron, 228–29
von Ribbentrop, General Joachim, 42

Wagner, Richard, 235
Walker, Robert J., 158, 160
Walker, Thomas, 275
Walsh, Frank P., 34
Wanamaker, John, 214
War of 1812, 6–7, 8–11, 190, 276
Ward, Ferdinand, 204
Ward, William S., 103
Washbourne, Elihu B., 88
Washington, George, 178, 194, 240, 280
  commission, expected war with France
    (1798) and, 3–6, 154, 312
  ex-presidency, attitude toward, 312
  Federalist party role, post-presidential,
    117–18
  Jefferson and, 192, 292
  Mount Vernon estate costs, 188–89
Watergate, 117, 184
Weaver, James, 96
Webb, Samuel C., 273
Webster, Daniel, 75, 123, 281
Weed, Smith W., 93
Weed, Thurlow, 24, 86
Weeks, John W., 129
Weld, Theodore, 273, 275, 276
West, Andrew F., 213
Westmoreland, Gen. William C., 183
White, Edward D., 165, 166, 167
White, Theodore, 148
White, William Allen, 40, 103, 109, 130,
  131, 258
White House Years, The (D. D.
  Eisenhower), 302
Whitney, Flora, 39, 40
Whitney, William C., 91, 93, 94, 95
Whittier, John Greenleaf, 22
Wilhelm, Kaiser, 246, 250, 253–54, 255
Wilhelmina, Queen of Holland, 253
Wilkes, Capt. Charles, 25
Wilkinson, General, 155
Willard, Belle, 258
Williams, Lewis, 196
Willkie, Wendell L., 137, 138
Wilmot, David, 12, 76
Wilmot Proviso, 12–13
Wilson, General, 163
Wilson, Henry, 122
Wilson, William L., 95

Wilson, Woodrow, 48, 68, 101, 128, 217, 301
  health, 134–35
  party politics role, 133, 134
  peace programs, 55–62
  retirement law practice, 217–19
  second term campaign, 107–13, 129, 131
  World War I policies, TR criticism of, 32–40
Wilson, Mrs. Woodrow, 133, 135
Windom, William, 88

Wise, Henry A., 119, 274, 276, 277
Wood, Charles, 206
World War I, 32–40, 47
World War II, 42–48
Wright, Silas, 71, 73, 159

Yarborough, Ralph, 151
Young, John Russell, 232

Ziegler, Ronald, 223
Zahm, Fr. John A., 258